Five Old Men of Yellowstone

Five Old Men
OF YELLOWSTONE

THE RISE OF INTERPRETATION IN THE FIRST NATIONAL PARK

STEPHEN G. BIDDULPH

THE UNIVERSITY OF UTAH PRESS | *Salt Lake City*

The Defiance House Man colophon is a registered trademark
of the University of Utah Press. It is based on a four-foot-tall
Ancient Puebloan pictograph (late PIII) near Glen Canyon, Utah.

17 16 15 14 13   1 2 3 4 5

LIBRARY OF CONGRESS CATALOGING-IN-PUBLICATION DATA
Biddulph, Stephen G., 1945–
  Five old men of Yellowstone : the rise of interpretation in the first
    national park / Stephen G. Biddulph.
      pages cm
  Includes bibliographical references and index.

  ISBN 978-1-60781-257-9 (cloth : alk. paper)
  ISBN 978-1-60781-246-3 (pbk. : alk. paper)
  ISBN 978-1-60781-247-0 (ebook)

  1. Yellowstone National Park—History. 2. Yellowstone National Park—Biography.
  3. National parks and reserves—Interpretive programs—Yellowstone National Park—
  History. 4. Park rangers—Yellowstone National Park—Biography. 5. Biddulph, Lowell,
  1906-1985. 6. Replogle, Wayne F. 7. Lystrup, Herbert T. 8. Marler, George D. 9. Beal,
  Merrill D., 1898-1990. I. Title.
  F722.B47 2013
  978.7'52—dc23

                                                                    2013006723

Frontispiece: Entrance to Yellowstone National Park, Wyoming.
(Photo provided by the author)

Printed and bound by Sheridan Books, Inc., Ann Arbor, Michigan.

To

RUTH, BETTY, MARIAN, LAURA, BESSY, AND REBECCA

Contents

Maps

Acknowledgments

Failure to recognize those who helped make this historical publication possible would be remiss on my part. First, I am deeply indebted to the Old Men who left a record of their service and passion for Yellowstone National Park (YNP). Wives (now all deceased) and family members of the Old Men provided important material support through letters and photos. My own siblings have also helped and provided encouragement. Howard Biddulph helped with initial research, and Susan (Biddulph) Sheffield read the manuscript and offered important suggestions on content. My wife, Elaine, has faithfully encouraged me and patiently tolerated my long obsession with this project.

Beyond family, Lee Whittlesey, Yellowstone National Park historian and archivist, has been a constant source of information and encouragement. Colleen Curry, Yellowstone's museum curator, and library staff of the Yellowstone Heritage and Research Center have assisted with photos and information without which the history would be incomplete.

I express appreciation to Peter DeLafosse and John R. Alley, acquisitions editors, and the staff of the University of Utah Press for their interest and support in making possible the publication of this history of the interpretive era of Yellowstone National Park. Lastly, I am indebted to Annette Wenda for her careful editing of the manuscript prior to publication.

Introduction

Soon after my father's death in the spring of 1985, I discovered among his personal and professional papers two photographs that ultimately proved the genesis of this work. The first was a faded black-and-white snapshot of him standing in front of the log Canyon ranger station in Yellowstone National Park. Complete with chaparajos, white shirt, cowboy hat, and neckerchief, he was a twenty-two-year-old buckaroo. The photo was labeled in my mother's handwriting: "Lowell's first summer at Canyon, 1928."

By 1960, when I was fifteen, my father already seemed old to me. His dark, wavy hair had disappeared, and the back and sides were silver, inspiring my grandmother to dub him "the bald eagle" of our family.[1] Still lithe and slender, he could hike to the tops of the highest peaks in Yellowstone, but he had lost the impulsiveness of youth to age and wisdom. He was at ease in nature but keenly observant, and he passed through the forests and meadows with an easy, rhythmic gait.

He knew intimately the flora and fauna of Yellowstone. He talked to the birds as he walked through the forests, chipping back to chickadees and juncos, cawing to ravens and crows, and hooting at owls. He knew the trees and plants of the forest by common and scientific name. Each of them he introduced to us children, including gnarled masses of "witches'-broom" in pine boughs and fluorescent green and black lichen dripping from lodgepole limbs. The stringy black lichen he called "old-man's beard," and we children attached pieces of it to our chins and upper lips with spit and pretended to be old men of the forest.

My father was both an ardent student and a teacher of nature. He knew where to find forest feasts of huckleberry, strawberry, raspberry, serviceberry,

Lowell Biddulph, first year as temporary ranger, 1928. (Photo provided by L. G. Biddulph)

chokecherry, and pine nuts. He showed us where to safely drink from mountain streams. He knew the geology of Yellowstone, and on mountain peaks he told us about the origin of the rocks and of ancient glaciers that once covered Yellowstone. He explained how the mountains and plateaus of Yellowstone were formed and how trees became petrified. Being with him in nature was an education, and I sensed in him a fullness of joy when there.

The second inspiring photo that I discovered was an eight-by-ten-inch black-and-white glossy of my father and four other ranger naturalists taken by the National Park Service (NPS) on August 7, 1960, at Old Faithful. I was personally acquainted with each of the men in the photograph from our summers spent in Yellowstone. Besides my father, Lowell Biddulph, there was Wayne F. Replogle from Coldwater, Kansas, known as "Rep"; Herbert T. Lystrup from Eau Claire, Wisconsin, known as "Bud"; George D. Marler from Thornton, Idaho, whom we knew simply as George; and Merrill D. Beal from Pocatello, Idaho, who often went by "Sam."

A copy of a Yellowstone National Park press release titled "The Five Old Men of Yellowstone" was paper-clipped to the photo. Typed on onion-skin paper, crinkled and yellowed with age, the release provided a one-paragraph summary of each man's service in Yellowstone National Park, noting that "at the end of the 1960 season, these five men had rendered 139 seasons of cumulative service to the park service."[2] The men's service to Yellowstone did not end the season the photo was taken, but continued on into the late 1960s

Five Old Men of Yellowstone. Picture taken at Old Faithful on August 7, 1960, celebrating 139 seasons of service to the park. (Courtesy of the National Park Service, Yellowstone National Park, YELL 115010)

and early '70s, in one case until 1977. When the last man finished active duty in Yellowstone, literally hauled out by hearse, the Five Old Men had spanned nearly a half century of service, totaling 180 seasons. I marveled at the sum of experience accumulated by these men during their extraordinary service to the park, and I lamented that their story of Yellowstone had not been told, for their period of service was truly a significant one in the park.

During their service, Yellowstone evolved as a true international attraction, with annual visitors increasing by 866 percent: from 231,000 in 1928 to more than 2 million in 1965. These men played leading roles in promoting that growth. They helped assemble information about the park's natural resources, which was standardized into usable interpretive data. One of these men, Merrill D. Beal, was on the cutting edge of the development of the park's human history. During this period, education and inspiration supplanted pleasure and recreation as national park core values. The science of ecology influenced park management policies that evolved out of long-held attitudes of human protection and artificial propagation to conservation-minded principles.

Interpretation was an outgrowth of these principles of education and conservation[3] and rose to a high-water mark during this time. An Interpretive Division was formally created, and interpretive services developed that included nature walks, cone talks, campfire programs, auto caravans, and game stalks. The Five Old Men and others helped develop and lead the programs within all three districts of Yellowstone. They grew old in service to the Grand Old Park and retired when interpretation and enlightenment were superseded by mass information, technology, and specialized research.

To put their time of service into historical perspective, Yellowstone National Park was only fifty-six years old when the first of these five men began service in the summer of 1928. Only fifty years had passed since the Nez Perce Indian War and their flight through the park. The US Cavalry had abandoned Fort Yellowstone only ten years earlier, and the spread-eagle men[4] were still the leadership corps in Yellowstone. The automobile had replaced the horse and stagecoach only thirteen years earlier (1915), and the establishment of the Ranger Naturalist Division was still ten years out.

The Yellowstone of the Five Old Men is gone. In 1990 Merrill Beal, the last of these five men, died, leaving no one to tell their story except someone from the second generation. And so, as the son of one of these men and one who knew all of them to some extent, I make the attempt. I am not a historian by training, only by passion, and my objective in writing this history is only to tell their story of the Grand Old Park as they knew it and to provide a rare insight into an era now lost to time.

Resources have come from official documents and personal memorabilia and histories archived in the Yellowstone National Park Heritage and Research Center in Gardiner, Montana; Brigham Young University and Idaho State University Special Collections; the University of Wyoming's American Heritage Center; and the Western History Collection at the University of Denver. Where practical and interesting, I have used direct quotes from the men's journals and personal histories. Otherwise, I have narrated their experiences based on documented evidence. As much as possible, I have allowed the Old Men to tell their own story of Yellowstone.

Throughout the book, I refer to the five men collectively as the "Five Old Men" or "Old Men," realizing that the term *old* is relative and was not accurately bestowed upon them until toward the end of their service. Nevertheless, it provides an interesting title for the book and historical accuracy to the nickname given to these five men by the National Park Service.

PART ONE

Hello, Yellowstone!

I went to the woods because I wished to live deliberately, to front only the essential facts of life, and see if I could not learn what it had to teach, and not, when I came to die, discover that I had not lived. I did not wish to live what was not life, living is so dear. I wanted to live deep and suck out all the marrow of life. If it were sublime, to know it by experience, and be able to give a true account of it in my next excursion.

—Henry David Thoreau, *Walden*

Chapter 1

The Wisdom of Nature

A PRAYER FOR WISDOM

The European incursion into what is now the United States of America brought a collision of cultural and religious ideologies. The European mind-set was one of subjugation, ownership, and development driven by personal wealth; the Native American, with few exceptions, was one of reverence for Mother Earth. Ironically, both ideologies had at their wellspring the belief that the earth was a divine creation given by a benevolent Father or Great Spirit.

The prototypical Native American belief was that the earth and all living creatures possessed a spiritual element. Their subsistence relied strictly on the earth's natural bounty, and they lived "with a perfect lightness, without injury or alteration."[1] By contrast, the immigrant walked heavily, drawing from his Bible the mandate to subdue the earth and exercise dominion over it. He raped the land, scarring and stripping its natural resources almost without constraint.

Industrialization was a consuming mind-set that pushed ever westward; one focused on progress that typically expressed itself in unmitigated pollution, consumption, and waste of natural resources. There was little room in the immigrant's progressive religion for the Native American's belief system or way of life. Thus, the Native American was subdued like the land and subjected to either change or annihilation. The following prayer offered by Chief Jasper Saunkeah of the Kiowa Tribe is one of pleading for the wisdom of nature:

Hear us, Oh Great Spirit in the sky: Our people are a very old people. We lived in this land thousands of moons before the White Man came. His way of life differed from ours and for many seasons there was bitter strife between us. Now, there is peace, but the heart of the Red Man is sad for the White Man has destroyed many of nature's most bountiful gifts and has forgotten that all things come from Mother Earth and go back to her.

Our sons lived like their fathers and grandfathers. . . . We lived simply and near to the earth. In the voices of the earth and the running waters and the wind in the sky we heard the sayings of the Great Spirit who made all things and gave them to us. We lived happily in a land where grass and trees never failed for thousands of moons and where meat and skins were plentiful.

Sad were our hearts when the White Man made great wounds in the earth in his haste to take riches from the soils of our fathers. We were sad, for with the wisdom of a thousand moons we knew that when the water runs red or brown our land is losing its strength and our grass and trees wither. We know that in a few short years that work of nature for thousands of years would be no more.

Oh Great Spirit, bring to our White brothers and us all the wisdom of nature and the knowledge that if her laws are obeyed, this land will again flourish and grasses and trees grow as before. Guide those who through their councils seek to spread the wisdom of their leaders to all people. Heal the raw wounds in the earth and restore our clear and beautiful streams. Bring again the sparkling waters from our springs and restore to our soil the richness, which strengthens men's bodies and make them wise in their councils. Bring to all the knowledge that great cities live only through the bounty of the good earth beyond their paved streets and towers of stone and steel. Amen.[2]

THE NATIONAL PARK IDEA

The establishment of Yellowstone National Park on March 1, 1872, came as an outgrowth of what has been called the "National Park Idea,"[3] the superego of the industrial era with its seething cities, factories, industries, and mechanical inventions. Although other preserves were established prior to Yellowstone National Park (Yosemite, for example), it was the first of the earth's unique tapestries to be set aside as a true national park. Such preserves were the result, at least partially, of the influence of wilderness prophets like Henry David Thoreau, John Muir, and John Burroughs, who cried passionately in the wilderness for industrialized man to return to nature. For such men, wilderness sanctuaries were places of worship for the spiritual renewal of the soul.[4]

Yellowstone proved to be one of the notable experiments of man's struggle to harmonize his rather voracious presence with nature's rhythm. The management of this first national park by the white man began with instincts and ideologies similar to that with which he subdued the wilderness and the children of nature who revered Mother Earth. Indeed, the creation of Yellowstone National Park rather quickly necessitated its rescue from its creators, who, with noble intentions but little forethought as to its purpose and no prior experience in administering a national park, found themselves lacking in foresight and knowledge.

The park's genesis foreshadowed problems. It was not given meaningful identity upon creation, designated only as "a certain tract of land lying near the head-waters of the Yellowstone River."[5] Its original purpose was equally nebulous, broadly described as "a pleasuring ground for the benefit and enjoyment of the people."[6] This inauspicious beginning left Yellowstone Park for nearly two decades without adequate funds, staff, or laws, and little leadership, other than a few zealous souls who with varying degrees of success tried to attract the attention of the government to its cause. In the absence of meaningful management, the park was victimized by profiteers, entrepreneurs, railroad tycoons, and poachers harboring selfish or profit motives, exactly the antithesis of those that purportedly inspired its original preservation.[7]

The newly created park was just over 2 million acres (3,312.5 square miles). This seemingly large area proved to be but a small fraction of a much larger ecosystem of interrelated mountain ranges, high plateaus, rivers, and lower valleys. Arbitrary park boundaries did not lend themselves to the migratory habits of big game animals that frequented its high plateaus during the summer months and wintered in the lower surrounding valleys. The original creation failed to take sufficiently into account the impact of the inevitable civilian population that would encompass the park or the raging conflicts that eventually arose between ranchers and the park's wild denizens, many of which instinctively wintered outside of Yellowstone's high plateaus.[8]

Within mere decades after its creation, an expansion of Yellowstone's boundaries became necessary in order to preserve more of the ecosystem. In the 1920s and '30s, Yellowstone's boundaries underwent at least six adjustments, adding an additional 56,027.66 acres. Its present area of 3,472 square miles

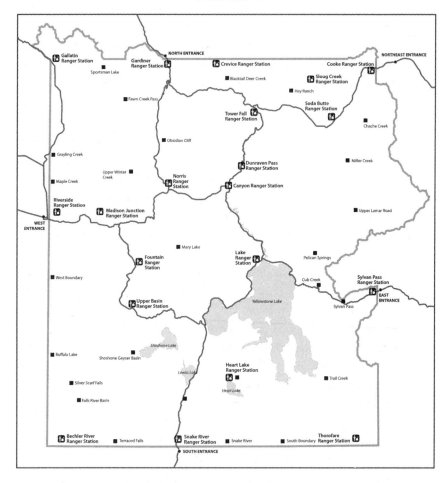

Map 1. The 1930 U.S. Geological Survey map of Yellowstone Park shows ranger stations and snowshoe patrol cabins extant at that time. Ranger stations are marked by large symbols and snowshoe patrol cabins with a smaller black square. (Adapted by Stephen G. Biddulph from the U.S. Geological Survey Topographical Map of Yellowstone Park 1930.)

(approximately 2,221,766 acres)[9] occupies the northwest corner of Wyoming, including slivers of land in the states of Montana and Idaho. Additional congressional acts formed national forests—Beartooth, Absaroka, Gallatin, Shoshone, Madison, Bridger, and Teton—that buffer this Wonderland from civilian encroachment.[10]

About the time that Yellowstone Park was created by an act of Congress, a wanton slaughter of elk, deer, bison, antelope, and bighorn sheep spread rampant across the West.[11] White hunters slaughtered thousands of big game animals across the Great Plains and throughout the Rocky Mountains, including Yellowstone Park. Big game disappeared in the park in the early 1880s at such an alarming rate that tourists complained to Superintendent Philetus W. Norris that they saw no animals at all during their stagecoach tours.[12]

Hunting in Yellowstone National Park was eventually prohibited in 1883 by order of Henry Teller, the secretary of the interior. American bison were slaughtered so dangerously close to extinction during this time that Yellowstone hosted perhaps the last remaining wild herd of buffalo in the United States.[13] The fortuitous augmentation of breeding bulls and cows brought to the park from two domestic herds, and the careful attention provided by rangers in feeding, inoculating, and protecting the animals, allowed the bison in the park to regenerate.[14]

Protection necessarily became the primary focus in the park for several decades following the neglect by the federal government and the slaughter of its big game. In 1880 Superintendent Norris hired a Pennsylvania-born, former Civil War soldier and mountain man named Harry S. Yount as a gamekeeper to watch over a modest-size herd of ungulates in the broad Lamar Valley of northeastern Yellowstone.[15] "Rocky Mountain Harry," as he was called, lived year-round in a cabin at the confluence of the Lamar River and Soda Butte Creek from which he tried single-handedly to protect game throughout the park.

Within less than a year, Yount was convinced that the job was more than one man could do, and he recommended the formation of a group of rangers for the task. Upon his resignation in 1881, he was replaced by a small police force of men called assistant superintendents, which proved equally inadequate. Finally, in 1886, the US Army was assigned to protect the park.[16] Between 1886 and 1901, the army constructed sixteen "soldier stations" at key locations around the park that housed contingents of soldiers assigned to catch poachers.[17]

Animal poaching was but one human threat to Yellowstone. An equal or even greater peril came from tourism. Yellowstone's extraordinary wonders unleashed a surge of tourists hungry to experience this priceless wonderland that lay vulnerable without protective regulations or means of enforcement. For a time, the only thing protecting Yellowstone from utter devastation was its inaccessibility to the public. That changed rather quickly with the railroad that brought the wealthy to Yellowstone's very borders. Industrialists and concessionaires wasted no time in accommodating the public's demand for plea-

suring in the park. Certainly, the objective of these business concerns was
never to overtly harm Yellowstone's naturalness. But they did not come lightly
or thoughtfully into Yellowstone, as had Native Americans for hundreds of
years. Rather, they came by steam engine and noisy coaches. They built roads
and bridges; constructed huge hotels, lodges, and cabins; and brought with
them all the human paraphernalia necessary for "luxury in the wilderness."[18]

THE ESTABLISHMENT OF THE NATIONAL PARK SERVICE

The army waged war against human and natural predators in Yellowstone for more than three decades. By 1916 an additional fourteen national
parks and twenty-one national monuments had been created throughout
the nation and were being poorly managed by the army or government
appointees. Stephen Tyng Mather, a man of means and influence in the
United States, recognized the need for better park management and was
instrumental in gaining congressional authorization to create a National
Park Bureau within the Department of the Interior.[19] President Wood-
row Wilson signed the bureau into existence on August 25, 1916, and
appointed Mather as the first director of the National Park Service, with
Horace Albright serving as assistant director. However, it was not until
July 1, 1918, that Congress allocated funds sufficient to recruit a corps of
forest rangers to replace the army in Yellowstone. Thirty-eight years after
Harry Yount's proposal for a ranger force, it became a reality. This corps of
forest rangers, many of whom had previously been army scouts in the park,
became known as the "spread-eagle men."[20]

The new Park Service was faced with the paradox of how to promote
Yellowstone's popularity without losing its primeval nature. On the one hand,
popularizing Yellowstone by showcasing its wonders was a strong motivation.
On the other hand, managing its natural resources and protecting them from
human destruction were essential tasks if Yellowstone was to survive.

Despite the urge to promote tourism, the determination of park managers
to protect Yellowstone's natural resources was devout. The problem was not
one of will as much as of mind. Ecological principles that are common
knowledge today were not developed, nor had they found their way into
park management philosophy in these early days.[21] Although the term *ecology*
(the study of relationships between living organisms and their natural environment) was coined by the German scientist Ernst Haeckel by 1866, relationships between living things in nature and their interconnectedness were
not fully appreciated. Management of nature was seen by early park managers

Five Old Men at Stephen Mather Memorial, Madison Junction, 1949. (Photo by
D. Condon; courtesy of the National Park Service, Yellowstone National Park,
YELL 19888-2)

more in monotone than Technicolor, as events rather than relationships, as
independent rather than interdependent. Insufficient consideration was given
to the consequence one action would have upon present and future conditions. Management of elk herds and that of the black-spotted (cutthroat)
trout are two examples.

Steps were taken early on by park management to artificially manage
game animals and fish in Yellowstone. Predators believed to pose a threat to
elk and buffalo were nearly or completely exterminated from Yellowstone
during the 1920s and early '30s. These included the mountain lion (cougar),
wolves, and coyotes. Having removed predators and under government protection, Yellowstone's indigenous elk and buffalo herds grew large and stable.
By the 1960s, studies raised fears that the northern elk herd in Yellowstone
was overgrazing and threatening soil erosion, as noted in a statement by park
managers in 1963: "Mistakes in management of plant cover can be rectified in
a man's life span....Centuries are required for replacement of top soil."[22] The

findings of these earlier studies were refuted by later studies that suggested no evidence in the reduction of sagebrush grasslands and root biomass, prime determinants of soil erosion. However, there remained evidence of heavy stripping of shrubby vegetation, aspen, and willows by as many as twenty thousand animals that foraged in the northern part of Yellowstone.

Park management discontinued the killing of predators in the 1930s, realizing the importance of these natural regulatory forces in keeping herds manageable. By the mid-1990s, the gray wolf was reintroduced to Yellowstone. The never-ending controversy between park officials and conservation and hunting groups over how to manage Yellowstone's wildlife suggests that nature is equipped to manage itself and that man's role is to learn to harmonize with its rhythms.

The black-spotted (cutthroat) trout was another learning object in Yellowstone ecology. At the time Yellowstone was created as a national park, almost half of its waters were barren of fish. Most alpine lakes and rivers above major waterfalls had no fish at all. Only thirteen species of fish are native to Yellowstone waters, and the black-spotted trout, the only species of fish native to the Yellowstone plateau, became a huge attraction for tourists who cultivated a passion for fishing and a taste for trout.[23]

Human tampering with nature's balance caused problems early on. Trout dinners became a delicacy at park hotels, precipitating a harvesting of trout from Yellowstone Lake that far outstripped the species' natural capacity to reproduce. Limits on daily catches were at first unrestricted and then remained too liberal. Lowell Biddulph remembered when there was no limit on the number of fish a person could keep. On Broad Creek during 1930, he caught twenty trout on as many casts. Fishing in key spawning areas for the black-spotted trout—notably the outlet of Yellowstone Lake at Fishing Bridge—dramatically diminished the trout's ability to reproduce.

Characteristic of man's earlier ignorance, he failed to see himself as the problem and pointed accusing fingers at Yellowstone's wild denizens. Similar to predators of the ungulates, people wrongfully targeted the otter, mink, muskrats, and white pelicans as the cause of demise of the trout. Efforts were made by US Fish and Game personnel to eliminate or reduce the predator's numbers, even going as far as to destroy some of the nests and young of the pelican at its primal nesting site on the Molly Islands in the southeastern arm of Yellowstone Lake. When it was realized that man, not nature, was the culprit, these innocent, maligned creatures were pardoned and other solutions were sought.

At first, park managers remained committed to sustaining the human demand for fish, and they sought artificial means to sustain it. As early as 1889, the Bureau of Fisheries began to artificially propagate the black-spotted trout on Yellowstone Lake using egg-collection stations to trap and milk the trout of eggs and fish hatcheries to spawn and grow the fingerlings.

Hybrid and exotic game fish, such as brown trout, rainbow trout, brook trout, and lake trout, were introduced to attempt to improve upon paradise. This has been helpful in some cases but harmful in others. Waterfalls and other natural barriers in Yellowstone waterways that protected the black-spotted trout from more aggressive fish populations were breached, threatening that fish population. The presence of lake trout in Yellowstone Lake, for instance, is a current-day threat to cutthroat trout.

Eventually, a more natural wildlife resource-management policy was envisioned thanks to scientific field research. Fish hatcheries were closed in Yellowstone by 1958 and daily catch limits enforced that were naturally sustainable by fish populations. Key spawning areas were restricted or designated as catch-and-release only, and fishing from Fishing Bridge was discontinued altogether.

THE INFLUENCE OF SCIENCE AND CONSERVATION

In the beginning decades of the twentieth century, two powerful but divergent forces of science and conservation formed a peculiar alliance in influencing values for Yellowstone Park, albeit for somewhat differing motives. For scientists, Yellowstone was a research laboratory; for conservationists, it was a cathedral for worship. Both lobbied for the park to be kept natural and pristine.

Scientists recognized Yellowstone Park to be one of the last frontiers of a dwindling wilderness, and its unique natural resources presented unmatched opportunities for scientific research. The loss of Yellowstone to a commercialized playground would be incalculable and the demise of a truly remarkable and unique natural laboratory.

Yellowstone was a sanctuary to the conservationist, its natural wonders a medium to enlighten both the spirit and the intellect of man, a deepening of awareness and appreciation for creation. The metamorphosis was to come through exposure to natural scenes of grandeur. A spiritual awakening or revelation, if you will, to the beauty of undefiled nature would theoretically counter the erosive effects of industrialization and urban liberalism.[24] Conservationists worked through national conservation groups, such as the

Campfire Club of America, Sierra Club, American Game Protective Association, National Audubon Society, and Izaak Walton League, to keep the park a pristine wilderness unsullied by human contamination.

Stephen Mather and Horace Albright, the new directors of the National Park Service, formed an advisory committee composed of a conglomerate of ecologists, scientists, conservationists, and bureau people to propose policies pertaining to the use of national parks.[25] Thus, the footings were established upon which the foundation of Yellowstone's educational program would be laid in future years.

Chapter 2

Foundations of Interpretation

EDUCATION BECOMES A NATIONAL PARK VALUE

The first intimation of education as a national park purpose came in the form of a letter written in May 1918 by the secretary of the interior, Franklin K. Lane, to Stephen Mather, the director of the newly organized National Park Service: "The educational, as well as the recreational, use of the national parks should be encouraged in every practicable way.... Museums containing specimens of wild flowers, shrubs, and trees and mounted animals, birds, and fish native to the parks, and other exhibits of this character, will be established as authorized."[1]

This early vision of national parks serving as a forum for education was not shared by most citizens or members of Congress, who were focused more on recreation and pleasure than learning. The infusion of educational values into the National Park Service ultimately did not come without help from outside sources. In 1918 Charles Wolcott, secretary of the Smithsonian Institution, helped organize the National Park Education Committee, which spawned the National Park Association in 1919. The association's purpose was to promote interpretation of natural sciences so richly illustrated in the national parks and to encourage the study of park history and traditions. The American Association of Museums was also influential, as will be seen later.

In spite of earlier precedents, Yosemite and Yellowstone were the first national parks to simultaneously develop substantial educational programs that other national parks would later emulate. These education programs provided for the collection of information about natural science through field observations and reporting (see chapter 11), the construction of museums to display indigenous flora and fauna (see chapter 14), and the development of educational programs, such as campfire lectures, nature walks and other guided tours, game stalks, and auto caravans (see chapter 15).

On June 19, 1919, Stephen Tyng Mather appointed his assistant, Horace Albright, to be Yellowstone's first superintendent under the National Park Service. Albright, in turn, appointed Milton P. Skinner to be the first park naturalist and assigned him to inaugurate an educational program. Skinner began collecting and publishing information about Yellowstone's natural resources, which were called *Yellowstone Letters,* and established a small museum at Mammoth to display various objects of nature. Upon Skinner's resignation in 1924, Edmund J. Sawyer assumed the position and began to expand and strengthen the educational program. He assembled and published field reports from rangers and other employees about many aspects of Yellowstone's natural resources and history, and the name of *Yellowstone Letters* was changed to *Yellowstone Nature Notes.*[2] These rich but homey publications enjoyed nearly forty years of success and formed the basis for a meaningful interpretation program. With the aid of Jack Ellis Haynes, the son of Frank J. Haynes, an influential concessionaire and photographer in Yellowstone, Sawyer continued to build upon the small museum begun by Skinner.

In 1925 Herman Work, the secretary of the interior, announced education as a primary objective of the National Park Service, equal to recreation. Dorr G. Yeager was transferred from Yosemite in 1928 to help develop Yellowstone's educational programs that ultimately became the foundation for the establishment of the Naturalist Division ten years later, under Dr. C. Max Bauer.

The same year that Yeager came to the park, funds were committed and plans laid for the construction of four trailside museums at key locations in Yellowstone made possible by a grant of $118,000 from the Laura Spelman Rockefeller Memorial.[3] The core of education and interpretation in Yellowstone for more than three decades, these trailside museums became libraries of nature filled with specimens of the natural environment and human history of the park.

THE NINETY-DAY WONDER

To adequately meet the needs of this new educational program, park administrators began recruiting college-educated personnel as permanent and seasonal park rangers and ranger naturalists. In 1929 the National Park Service

Left to right: Ranger naturalists Thompson, Biddulph, and Potter in front of Fishing Bridge Museum, ca. 1938. (Photo by D. Condon; courtesy of the National Park Service, Yellowstone National Park, YELL 42695)

established a Field Division of Education at Berkeley, California, with the primary purpose to hire and train park ranger naturalists.

It is interesting to note that four of the Five Old Men began service in Yellowstone at this time. None was trained through the National Park system, but they were all college graduates with degrees in natural science. Lowell Biddulph began as a temporary ranger in 1928 and Wayne Replogle in 1930. Herbert Lystrup began work the summer of 1929 as a ranger naturalist and George Marler in 1931. Merrill D. Beal began as a ranger naturalist in 1939 with the advent of the Naturalist Division.

Many of the rangers received their education at Colorado Agriculture and Mechanical College in Fort Collins, Colorado, which was renamed Colorado State University in the 1950s. These rangers graduated with degrees in forestry, range management, and other natural sciences, and they began to open the park to ecological theories of wildlife management. This suffusion of educated rangers and ranger naturalists was not lost on the spread-eagle men, most of whom had little or no formal college training. Harry Trischman, a former army scout and well-regarded district supervisor in Yellowstone, coined "ranger factory" as a term for Colorado A&M that remained for some time in park parlance.[4]

The position of park ranger was glamorized during the 1920s to such a point that young men applying for summer jobs had a distorted concept of a ranger's work. Roger Toll,[5] the park superintendent, was forced to caution all applicants that employment in Yellowstone was not designed to be a "pleasant summer's vacation amid the beauties and wonders of Yellowstone Park," but required special skills and qualities and demanded long hours and continual public service with moderate to low pay. Park historian Aubrey Haines noted, "Despite careful screening of applicants, enough misfits turned up every season to keep the expression 'ninety-day wonder' alive."[6] The nickname *ninety-day wonder* was born during this era and continued, like other euphemisms, for decades.

Herbert Lystrup, one of these ninety-day wonders, gave a somewhat different interpretation of the nickname:

> How appropriate that name is.... These men are "wonders" in our greatest national park. The men chosen possess sterling qualities. They are first of all lovers of nature and the great out-of-doors. They are possessed of radiating personalities able to cope with varying situations. Service to others is an outstanding trait imbued in their make-up. A thorough college education in sciences such as geology, botany, zoology ... is required. These men, though they are college men, are trained to be able to explain all the natural phenomena in simple terms which can readily and easily be understood by all who visit the Park. The name "The Ninety Day Wonder" is not a misnomer.[7]

Nevertheless, many first-year employees were disappointed in their work experience or simply could not measure up to the challenge. They voluntarily or otherwise did not return for another season, whereas the joy and fulfillment felt by the Five Old Men brought them back to the park for nearly a half century.

EARLY DEVELOPMENT OF EDUCATION

Throughout Yellowstone's history, various terms have been used to represent its evolving purpose in the mind of directors. Some have divided these terms conveniently into: *information* (1919), *education* (1925), *naturalist* (1932), and *interpretation* (1940).

With the advent of education as a purpose, a program of gathering and presenting information about Yellowstone's natural sciences was implemented by Horace Albright. Facts and information were gathered through study and observation, and this information was presented in a rather sterile manner.

By the mid-1920s, Yosemite and Yellowstone were developing substantive educational programs. One of the objectives of education was to make more responsible stewards of visitors to the park by teaching them about these wonders through specific learning programs. In a way, Yellowstone became both a classroom and a lab taught by those with some knowledge in a particular science.

As principles of ecology began to infiltrate the park management philosophy, a Naturalist Division and later an Interpretive Division was established. Programs moved away from rigorous education and the dispensing of information and embraced an interpretive function. Admittedly, interpretation includes elements of both education and information. However, interpretation has a deeper quality that allows revelation of both tangible and intangible qualities. Freeman Tilden, who wrote several important books about the purpose of national parks, viewed interpretation as "a voyage of discovery into the field of human emotions and intellectual growth." His motto, "through interpretation, understanding; through understanding, appreciation; through appreciation, protection," suggests the foundation for the true purpose behind the interpretive and education programs in the national parks."[8] Much of the purpose for interpretation was not merely to educate tourists but to inspire them with a sense of the grandeur of nature. The fact that a person might gain increased understanding of the science and nature of these wonders in the process was an added bonus.

The development of the interpretive program posed the challenge of finding and retaining personnel with the qualifications to adequately interpret Yellowstone's unique phenomena and do it in a manner pleasing to the public. The average visitor to Yellowstone at this time was not as informed as that of today, and neither were they of a mind-set to learn a great deal.

Yellowstone was a curiosity and intrigue, a place of pleasure and recreation. Thus, early interpreters needed a unique mix of knowledge and showmanship to hold the tourists' attention during campfire programs and other interpretive efforts. This was not easy to find in employees. Those steeped in scientific study tended to be the proverbial intellectual recluse that failed miserably at communicating inspiration to others. But the showman was often shallow and lacking in scientific knowledge.

Ranger naturalists of this time period were caught between the proverbial rock and a hard place. On the one hand, their training in natural science did not guarantee them a place of respect within the true scientific community. True field scientists discounted the ranger naturalist's scientific methods and knowledge. On the other hand, their education in natural science was looked down upon by the true rangers as lacking in the "he-men" qualities espoused by Harry Yount. Not uncommonly, rangers referred to them as "nature fakers" and "posy pickers."[9]

The Five Old Men were somewhat anomalies to this rule, although not entirely. Of the five, only George Marler was actually able to transcend the scientific barrier and be accepted as a true scientist because of his nationally recognized research in hydrothermal science. But he often felt snubbed by the he-men rangers and his work relegated as unimportant. Nevertheless, he was made a permanent park naturalist in about 1957, which carried some respectability and gave him permanent status.

Lowell Biddulph and Wayne Replogle earned their stripes as temporary rangers before becoming ranger naturalists and were frequently engaged in "he-man" activities, such as firefighting. Merrill Beal became a respected park historian through his research and publications in Yellowstone history. Herbert Lystrup was the longest-tenured interpreter in Yellowstone at retirement, commencing in 1929, and was appreciated and respected among both rangers and ranger naturalists. He seemed to find little or none of the posy-picking prejudice among the permanent men, or else he had a blind eye to it: "I was considerably impressed with the courtesy and helpfulness of the permanent men and the old temporary rangers. They introduced us around constantly, and put us at ease by telling us that the beginning was always confusing, but that all would ultimately work out."[10]

Despite the barriers, scientists and naturalists were allies in Yellowstone, because scientific research and interpretation were viewed as mutually supportive. Yellowstone was a vast, living laboratory for both scientist and naturalist to be used for study as well as interpretation. Scientists from respected universities and institutions of research found willing support in ranger naturalists who shared similar interests. Biddulph's field studies of Yellowstone geology, Lystrup's interests in biology, Beal's in history, and Replogle's in Indian lore brought them into frequent contact with researchers.

Scientists outside of Yellowstone used their influence with key people in the National Park Service to promote a naturalist's studies within the park.

Harvard professor of geology L. C. Graton's support of George Marler's winter research in 1952–53 with geysers and hot springs at Old Faithful is exemplary of this relationship between science and interpretation in Yellowstone.

YELLOWSTONE'S INTERPRETIVE CURRICULUM

The achievement of a collection of educational materials for Yellowstone's fledgling interpretive program was a labor-intensive process of observation, research, and publication. In truth, the process begun by ranger naturalists and later by scientists has never stopped and probably never will as long as there is something new to learn about Yellowstone.

In addition to information, ranger naturalists needed standardized policies and procedures to guide them in their interpretations. The first standardized guidelines for ranger naturalists came in the form of a *Ranger Naturalist's Manual,* prepared in 1926. This manual proved useful enough that it continued in more liberal revisions until 1945, but was mostly a hodgepodge of essays and information without much connectivity. The manual was not revised again until 1963 and became so obsolete in the intervening time that it became nearly useless.[11]

By the summer of 1930, Dorr Yeager and his Naturalist Division staff accomplished some major objectives in laying the foundation for an education-interpretation program. An administrative plan and *Manual of Instructions* (a fifty-five-page document) was published and distributed to all park employees, outlining policies, procedures, and organization. Additionally, a one-hundred-page *Employees Information Manual* was published, listing all points of interest in Yellowstone and a brief history of each. This was broken down into pamphlet form for each location in the park, and each naturalist received a copy of the pamphlet relative to his or her assignment. Also, twelve hundred information cards were distributed containing the names of major features in Yellowstone. Sawyer prepared a series of hand-painted "lantern slides" for use by ranger naturalists in their nightly campfire talks.[12] These first talks were held in ranger stations that often had a community room adorned with antlers, horns, animal skulls, and other paraphernalia. Later, these campfire talks were held at amphitheaters associated with the trailside museums.

Another impressive accomplishment by Yeager's educational team was the publishing of a two-hundred-page document titled *Yellowstone Information Manual: Volume I, Fauna.* Every known mammal and fifty different species of birds were included for distribution to employees for the 1930 season.[13] Additionally, 540 copies of *Nature Notes* were distributed and memoranda published to augment the standardized information in the manual. Of interest

Early community rooms were attached to a ranger station before museums and amphitheaters were built. (Courtesy of the National Park Service, Yellowstone National Park, YELL 15713)

is that in 1939, the estimates of big game animals in the park included (comparative estimates for 2011 made by game managers are shown in parentheses): 800 (5,000) antelope, 250 (500) bighorn sheep, 450 (500-600) black bears, 270 (600) grizzlies, 850 (4,000 summer only) buffalo, 1,000 (no count) deer, 14,300 (31,000 summer only) elk, and 700 (fewer than 1,000) moose. Rangers and naturalists were required to use the above figures in answering questions and in lecturing on large animals.[14]

With a standardized body of information about Yellowstone and a continuing means of collecting and reporting field observations, the park was poised to move forward with a reasonably adequate interpretive program. What remained was to assemble a qualified faculty of interpreters who could adequately and consistently guide student visitors through a short course in Yellowstone.

Army soldiers, porters, and early stage drivers had provided what could only be loosely described as the first interpretive efforts in Yellowstone. Such efforts were, in the words of Aubrey Haines, "seldom adequate. The soldiers lacked reliable information and the guides tended to develop a repertoire of stories to inspire generous tipping not all that far removed from Bridger."[15] Jim Bridger knew Yellowstone well but was known for his exaggerated stories. Hiram Chittenden said of him: "He was the greatest romancer of the West in his time, and his reckless exaggerations won for him a reputation which he could not shake off when he wanted to ... and were set down as the harmless vaporings of a mind to which truth had long been a stranger."[16]

Stage drivers became well known for tall tales that they provided unsolicited to tourists. Men such as Geyser Bob (John Edgar) told Paul Bunyan–like tales of falling into Old Faithful Geyser and emerging at Beehive Geyser across the Firehole River.

The appointment of Dr. C. Max Bauer as chief park naturalist positioned Yellowstone on the threshold of achieving the educational goals outlined by the National Park Service.[17] The Naturalist Division was created in 1938, thereby formalizing the interpretive program into an organized structure. By 1939 Bauer had assembled a core of ranger naturalists—among them the Five Old Men—that he would mold into an interpretive staff and upon whom he would put his stamp of excellence. The park was poised for unprecedented growth.

Chapter 3

Five Old Men of Yellowstone

The interpretive staff for 1939 was composed of four permanent and twenty seasonal naturalists, all men.[1] Although the 1939 Yellowstone roster contained no female interpreters, women had served in the National Park Service since its beginning in 1918. Claire Hodges served at Yosemite and Helene Wilson at Mount Rainier.

In Yellowstone, Superintendent Horace Albright recognized the value of qualified women serving as naturalists. The first to be hired was Isabel Basset (Wasson), a graduate of Wellesley College and Columbia University, who served in 1920 as an interpreter and guide in the geyser basins. Marguerite Lindsley (Arnold) was hired in 1925 as the first permanent naturalist in Yellowstone. Peg, as she was known, was the daughter of the assistant superintendent, Chester Lindsley, and married Ben Arnold, who served as a district ranger in the 1930s. Frieda Nelson was also hired in 1925 as a temporary naturalist, followed by Francis Pound (Wright) in 1926, and Herma Albertson (Baggley) in 1929. Herma married George Baggley, who served as chief ranger in Yellowstone from 1929 to 1935.

All five of the Old Men were on staff for the summer season of 1939. The permanent interpretive staff of 1939 included:

- C. Max Bauer: park naturalist. BS, University of Chicago, 1908. Major, geology. Minor, natural history. PhD, University of Colorado, 1932. Five years with the US Geological Survey, fifteen years in commercial geology, and six years teaching geology and natural science. Came to Yellowstone the spring of 1932.

- William E. Kearns: assistant park naturalist. BA, Colorado State College of Education, 1924. Major, education. Minor, biology. Three summers of graduate work at the University of Colorado. National Park Service Fellowship at Yale University, 1938. Ranger naturalist in Rocky Mountain National Park, 1932–33. Came to Yellowstone in 1934 as a junior park naturalist, promoted to assistant park naturalist in 1936.
- Francis E. Oberhansley: assistant park naturalist. BS, Utah State Agricultural College, 1924. Major, agronomy. Minors, biology and geology. Graduate work, Utah State Agricultural College, 1924. Senior ranger naturalist, Yellowstone, 1931–34. Park ranger, 1935. District ranger, 1936. Junior park naturalist, 1936–37. Assistant park naturalist, 1938.
- LeRoy Van Cott: Clerk-stenographer, Salt Lake City, Utah. BA, Brigham Young University (BYU), 1935. Major, business administration. Minor, music. Two years with the Forest Service, Department of Agriculture. Assistant clerk at Yellowstone Park for nine months.

The temporary (seasonal) ranger naturalists are listed in alphabetical order. The emphasis on education and teaching is obvious in their résumés:

- Bernard Bates: Manhattan Beach, California. AB, Stanford University, 1932. Major, geology. Minor, law. One year graduate work at Stanford University. Temporary ranger with Sequoia National Park, 1934–37. Ranger naturalist, first season.
- Harry L. Bauer: Santa Monica, California. BS, University of Illinois, 1919. Major, botany. Minor, zoology. MA, University of Colorado, 1922. PhD, University of Southern California, 1934. Teacher of science, Santa Monica Junior College. Ranger naturalist, Yellowstone, 1938.
- Samuel [B]eal: Rexburg, Idaho. BA, University of Utah, 1922. Major, western history. Minor, education. Graduate work, University of Utah and University of California, summers 1924, 1925, 1932, and 1934. Ranger naturalist, first season.
- Lowell Biddulph: Rexburg, Idaho. BA, Brigham Young University, 1928. Major, physical education. Minor, zoology. MA, University of Michigan, 1938. Dean of men, Ricks College. Temporary ranger, Yellowstone, 1928–30. Ranger naturalist, Yellowstone, 1938.

- Frederick W. Bieberdorf: Northfield, Minnesota. BS, A&M College, Oklahoma, 1926. Major, plant morphology. Minors, dendrology and ecology. MS, Iowa State College, 1927. PhD, Iowa State College, 1933. Professor of botany, St. Olaf College. Ranger naturalist, first season.
- F. Howard Brady: Sheridan, Wyoming. BA, University of Iowa, 1929. Major, geology. Minor, zoology. MS, University of Iowa, 1930. Two more years of graduate work, University of Iowa, 1931–32. High school science teacher, Sheridan. Ranger naturalist, Rocky Mountain National Park, 1935. Ranger naturalist, Grand Canyon National Park, 1936–37. Ranger naturalist, Yellowstone, 1938.
- Joseph Catmull: Salt Lake City, Utah. BS, University of Utah, 1929. Major, speech. Minor, natural science. Graduate study, University of Utah and University of Idaho, summers 1932–33. Teacher of speech, University of Utah. Ranger naturalist, Yellowstone, 1937–38.
- Irwin B. Douglass: Havre, Montana. BS, Monmouth College, 1926. Major, chemistry. Minor, bacteriology. PhD, University of Kansas, 1932 (?). Yosemite Field School of Natural History, 1935. Professor of chemistry, Northern Montana College. Ranger naturalist, Yellowstone, 1936–38.
- Phillip F. Fix: Boulder, Colorado. BS, Indiana University, 1929. Major, geology. MA, Indiana University, 1931. Graduate work, University of Colorado, 1937–39. Fellowship in geology, University of Colorado. Ranger naturalist, Yellowstone, 1934–38.
- William H. Headlee: Lafayette, Indiana. AB, Earham College, 1929. Major, bacteriology. Minor, parasitology. MS, University of Illinois, 1933. PhD, University of Louisiana, 1936. Assistant professor of biology, Purdue University. Ranger naturalist, first season.
- Herbert T. Lystrup: Eau Claire, Wisconsin. BS, University of Minnesota, 1926. Major, forestry. High school science teacher, Wisconsin. Ranger naturalist, Yellowstone, 1929–38.
- George Marler: Thornton, Idaho. BS, Brigham Young University, 1927. Major, zoology. Minor, geology. Graduate work and fellowship, Brigham Young University, 1932. Assay office in winter. Ranger naturalist, Yellowstone, 1931–32, 1937–38.
- Neil A. Miner: Mount Vernon, Iowa. BA, Syracuse University, 1932. Major, geology. Minor, zoology. MA, Syracuse University, 1934. PhD, University of Iowa, 1937. Professor of geology, Cornell College. Ranger naturalist, Yellowstone, 1935–38.

- Arthur Nash: Minneapolis, Minnesota. BA, Augsburg College, 1922. Major, botany. Minor, biology. PhD, University of Minnesota, 1938. Professor of biological sciences, Augsburg College. Ranger naturalist, Yellowstone, 1931–38.
- Wayne F. Replogle: Elgin, Illinois. BA, College of Emporia, 1926. Major, physical education. Minor, general science. Director of athletics. Temporary ranger, Yellowstone, 1930–35. Ranger naturalist, Yellowstone, 1936–38.
- Milton L. Royer: Columbia Station, Ohio. BA, Hiram College, 1921. Major, ecology. Minor, education. MA, Columbia University, 1924. Ranger naturalist, Yellowstone, 1938.
- John A. Thompson: Livingston, Montana. BS, Montana State College, 1930. Major, physical education. Minor, biology. Coach and science teacher, Park County High School. Ranger naturalist, Yellowstone, 1937–38.
- Harry Truman: Havre, Montana. BA, Ohio Wesleyan University, 1923. Major, botany. Minors, biology and chemistry. MA, Western Reserve University, 1929. PhD, University of Wisconsin, 1933. Professor of botany, Northern Montana College. Ranger naturalist, first season.
- Randell D. Watkins: Kearney, Nebraska. BS, North Texas State Teachers' College, 1929. Major, physical education. Minor, biology. University of Southern California, summer school, 1930–34. MA, University of Southern California, 1934. Athletic coach, State Teachers' College, Kearney, Nebraska. Ranger naturalist, Yellowstone, 1937–38.
- Harry Woodward: Hot Springs, South Dakota. AB, Dakota Wesleyan University, 1916. Major, education. Minor, biology. MA, Leland Stanford Junior University, 1929. Superintendent of city schools, Hot Springs, South Dakota. Ranger naturalist, Yellowstone, 1932, 1935–38.[2]

Of the twenty-four men on staff for the 1939 season, all were college educated: seven doctoral degrees, seven master degrees, and ten bachelor degrees. Seventeen of the twenty-four men were educators by profession: four in high school and thirteen at colleges or universities. Of course, the permanent men spent most of their career in the National Park Service, but none of the temporary men listed on the 1939 roster served Yellowstone with the steadiness of the Five Old Men. It is time now to introduce these Five Old Men. Dates of service in Yellowstone are shown in parentheses after their names.

Lowell G. Biddulph in front of the
Fishing Bridge Museum, ca. 1938.
(Courtesy of the National Park Service,
Yellowstone National Park, YELL 42689)

LOWELL GEORGE BIDDULPH (1928–68)

Lowell G. Biddulph was born in 1906 in Hooper, Utah. The second son of
seven, he was raised in Provo, Utah, and graduated from Brigham Young
University in 1928. His passion for nature, athletics, and mountain climbing was developed early in life through the influence of his father, Samuel, and a university mentor named Eugene L. Roberts.[3] Utah Valley is
shadowed on the north by the 11,752-foot Mount Timpanogos and in the
south by Mount Nebo, rising 11,929 feet above sea level. By the time Biddulph was eighteen, he had climbed Mount Timpanogos twenty-one times,
several occasions on moonlight hikes. As a college student, Biddulph was
commissioned by Roberts to lead the famous "Timp Hike" because of his
knowledge of the mountain.[4] This opportunity to lead these hikes gave
Biddulph valuable experience in leading future nature walks and hikes in
Yellowstone and imbedded in him a passion for hiking.

Biddulph's father was a high school math teacher, and all of his seven
sons were college educated. As an undergraduate at Brigham Young University, Biddulph majored in geology and physical education, minored in zoology, and lettered in three sports: basketball, football, and track.

Biddulph made his first trip to Yellowstone Park while still in his youth and was deeply intrigued by that region. Upon graduation from BYU, he accepted a teaching and coaching position at Madison High School in Rexburg, Idaho, beginning in the fall of 1928. Rexburg was a small farming community in the upper Snake River valley, about ninety miles south of Yellowstone and seventy miles west of the Grand Tetons. In Biddulph's words, he chose Rexburg because "it placed me within ninety miles of Yellowstone and Teton Parks, which fascinated me and put me close to my summer employment."[5]

Biddulph served in Yellowstone for thirty-three summers between 1928 and 1968. Three years were spent as a temporary ranger (1928–30) and thirty seasons (1938–68) as a ranger naturalist. He married Ruth Hobson in May 1931. In 1932 a daughter was born with a congenital heart defect that prevented their return to the park for five years. Biddulph spent those years teaching, coaching, and gaining additional education. Biddulph's daughter died of her condition in 1937, and the following summer (1938) he and his wife, Ruth, and a son returned to Yellowstone to heal and work in the newly organized Naturalist Division under Dr. C. Max Bauer.

The following year, Biddulph was offered the positions of head coach and dean of men at Ricks College (now Brigham Young University–Idaho) in Rexburg. He later obtained a doctor of education degree from the University of Utah and was appointed dean of students and head of the Athletic Department at Ricks College. He started the Geology Department there and taught physical fitness, fly tying, and hiking classes in addition to his administrative duties. Biddulph was active in church and community affairs in the upper Snake River valley, serving on the city council, as district commissioner for scouting, and as health chairman of Madison County. He was instrumental in developing a summer recreation program to promote fitness for Rexburg's youth.

The Biddulphs had five living children who spent each summer in the park. A vast majority of the thirty seasons that Biddulph served as a ranger naturalist were spent at Fishing Bridge, where he was the senior naturalist in charge of interpretation. During the years of World War II, Biddulph served at Old Faithful, Mammoth Hot Springs, and the South Entrance. For eight years he served as acting district naturalist and assistant district naturalist for the South District. He spent a great deal of time traveling the backcountry and taking photographs of the flora, fauna, and vistas of the park seldom before seen or photographed. Biddulph laid out several hiking trails in the

South District around Yellowstone Lake that are today enjoyed by many visitors who choose to get off the highways and into the backwoods.

He retired from the National Park Service after the 1968 season, from his administrative assignments at Ricks College in 1972, and from teaching in 1973.

HERBERT TSCHERNING LYSTRUP (1929–67)

In 1928 Jack Ellis Haynes, the son of Frank Jay Haynes, a famous photographer, artist, and concessionaire in Yellowstone Park, had a young college graduate named Herbert Lystrup working for him as a shipping clerk in his store at Selbe Street in St. Paul, Minnesota. It was this connection that landed Lystrup a summer job in 1929 working as a naturalist in Yellowstone Park. Lystrup had a degree in forestry, earned from the University of Minnesota, and had work experience with the US Forest Service in Arkansas and Idaho. Lystrup explained how he became a ranger naturalist:

> While employed there [Haynes Picture Store] I read several books published by Haynes. Among these was one titled "Trees and Flowers of Yellowstone National Park." I found several taxonomic errors. Mr. Jack Ellis Haynes had been informed by his St. Paul manager [Fred M. Hayes] of the errors. When I met Mr. Haynes late that season, he wanted to know why I questioned the genus and species of several plants. He wanted to know what botany, ecology, and taxonomy training I had. I suggested that I would gladly go to the University of Minnesota and seek confirmation of my findings. When the errors were confirmed, Mr. Haynes suggested that I apply for summer (seasonal) work as a ranger naturalist in Yellowstone National Park. Mr. Haynes was vitally interested in the Interpretive Division of the ranger service and I feel certain that his recommendation was instrumental in my being selected in 1929.[6]

In 1929, Lystrup was given a temporary appointment as a ranger naturalist in Yellowstone. That same fall, he was hired as a teacher of biology at Memorial High School in Eau Claire, Wisconsin. He held both positions for thirty-eight years.

Lystrup was one of the early seasonal naturalists in Yellowstone. He developed the first interpretive programs at Fishing Bridge. Although he spent a vast majority of his thirty-eight seasons at Old Faithful, he filled assignments

Herbert T. Lystrup in front of the Old Faithful Museum, ca. 1930. (Photo by D. Condon; courtesy of the National Park Service, Yellowstone National Park, YELL 19866)

at many locations throughout Yellowstone, including Madison Junction, Fishing Bridge, Canyon, Tower Fall, and West Entrance.

In 1932 he married Elizabeth Pontliana, whom he met and courted while she worked as a clerk at Hamilton Stores in the Upper Geyser Basin. Elizabeth worked at Hamilton Stores throughout their thirty-eight years of service in the park. The Lystrups had two children, Liz and Herbert (Tiff), who spent their summers in Yellowstone.

Lystrup served several years as a senior naturalist at Old Faithful and acting district naturalist and assistant district naturalist in the West District of Yellowstone for seven years. Lystrup's forte was interpretation and teaching people about nature. He was a fine observer and interpreter, but also a romanticist. He viewed surrounding nature with a keen, observant eye and enjoyed interpreting what he saw to others, hoping that nature would inspire and enlighten them to an appreciation similar to his own. He saw everything: the large and the nearly invisible, the brilliant and the mundane, the obvious and the obscure, the simple and the complex. His writings in *Nature Notes* and other publications reflect a man who found exhilaration and spiritual meaning in almost everything around him. He was at his best when standing in front of tourists, either by a campfire or along a forest trail, pointing out some tidbit of information or unique aspect of Yellowstone. His approach to teaching was with humor, friendliness, and down-to-earth observations.

Lystrup retired from both teaching and park service in the fall of 1967, not because of lack of interest, but due to deteriorating health. He remained vitally interested in Yellowstone and maintained a summer residence at West Yellowstone until his death in 1977. He wrote his first book, *The Ninety-Day Wonder: A Diary of a Ranger Naturalist in Yellowstone National Park, Wyoming,* in 1938 about the life of a seasonal ranger naturalist. Lystrup wrote two other books in 1969 after his retirement: *Shavings Off the Stick: True Stories of Yellowstone Park Told by a Veteran Ranger* and *Hamilton's Guide to Yellowstone National Park.* The latter book was a sequel to the famous guidebook on Yellowstone *Haynes Guide,* published by none other than his old mentor and champion, Jack Ellis Haynes.[7]

WAYNE FORDYCE REPLOGLE (1930–77)

Wayne F. Replogle grew up on ranches in southern Colorado and Coldwater, Kansas. His boyhood on the Great Plains and the men who influenced him, such as Kit Carson's grandson,[8] resulted in a lifelong infatuation with the Old West and the Plains Indians, all of which played a defining role in his contributions to Yellowstone.

Replogle was a versatile athlete at the College of Emporia in Kansas during the 1920s, participating in football, basketball, and several track and field events. He later became a high school coach and athletic director in Wyoming, Kentucky, and Illinois. While coaching football in Kentucky, he heard about a job working as a ranger in Yellowstone National Park and applied for summer work. Replogle noted in his memoirs:

> In 1929, I wrote a letter to the National Park Service requesting information pertaining to summer employment. I received the blanks back and I filled them out and sent them in, and many months later after I had forgotten I had filled them out there came a letter from the Department of Interior saying that I had been placed on call if so-and-so didn't take the job. Well, I finished my work in early May and I went to Washington DC to see a brother and then I drove back to Kansas where I was going to spend the summer. All these three weeks a telegram had been chasing me to report to Yellowstone and so I jumped into my automobile and...I drove night and day to get to Yellowstone.[9]

Wayne F. Replogle at Mammoth Hot Springs, ca. 1950. (Photo by D. Condon; courtesy of the National Park Service, Yellowstone National Park, YELL 42714)

In 1940 Replogle was recruited by the University of Kansas to become part of their football coaching staff. He agreed as long as they would grant him the summers to be a ranger naturalist in Yellowstone Park. They agreed, and he spent forty-three years with the Jayhawks football program as assistant coach, scout, and chief of photography.

Replogle's early assignment as a motorcycle patrolman gave him wide familiarity with most areas of the park. He spent about twenty summers at Canyon Village in Yellowstone, serving much of the time as a naturalist in charge and later at Mammoth Hot Springs as an administrator. He holds the distinction of working in the 1930s with Gerald Ford, who later became president of the United States.[10]

He married Marian Churchill from Chicago, Illinois, and first brought her to Yellowstone in the summer of 1937, where they lived in a tiny, rustic cabin at Madison Junction. Marian developed the same love for Yellowstone as her husband and returned every summer until her death in 1971. Following Marian's death, Replogle married Rebecca Rice McCormick, a long-time friend, in August 1972 at Mammoth Hot Springs.

Replogle was flamboyant and often brash and opinionated. Underneath that brashness was a softness and sensitivity that manifested itself in poetry, art, and the talks he gave as a ranger naturalist. As a coach and leader he was demanding, but also loyal and friendly.[11] Bob Jonas, one of Replogle's naturalists at Canyon, recalled that Replogle's group of ranger naturalists "enjoyed an active social life and real camaraderie. He and Marian had a campfire gathering most nights at their cabin where the naturalists and their families joined together in socializing."[12]

During the 1940s and '50s, Replogle researched and mapped the great Bannock Indian Trail that stretched across northern Yellowstone from east to west. This trail was used by the Bannock Indians for several decades in the 1800s to travel between their ancestral home in Idaho and the buffalo hunting grounds in Wyoming and southern Montana. Replogle's efforts in mapping this trail culminated in the publication of his monograph *Yellowstone's Bannock Indian Trails,* which became part of the Yellowstone Interpretive Series sold during this era.[13]

Replogle served as acting district naturalist and assistant district naturalist of the Northern District of Yellowstone for some years. From 1966 until 1973, when he retired, he served as the management assistant to the park superintendent. For four seasons after his retirement, he continued to serve as an annuitant to the assistant superintendent until his death in July 1977.

GEORGE DEWEY MARLER (1931–73)

Automobiles in Yellowstone were still three years in the future when fourteen-year-old George Marler made his first trip to Yellowstone Park in a neighbor's wagon in 1912. At the West Entrance, he and his sister boarded a Yellowstone Park stagecoach and traveled the lower loop, sleeping under the stars. The entire trip from Thornton, Idaho, to West Yellowstone, around the lower loop, and back home—a distance of approximately 225 miles—took two weeks. It took the party two days just to go from the West Entrance to Old Faithful and another two days to get to the Grand Canyon of the Yellowstone. Their group made camp in the meadows along the Firehole River in the Upper Geyser Basin just opposite Riverside Geyser. Marler noted in his diary that Riverside Geyser erupted at least twice during the night.[14] Little did young Marler realize the prelude this was to his nearly forty years of work with geysers and hot springs in Yellowstone Park.

Marler earned a bachelor's degree in zoology and ecology in 1927. Four years later, he began work in Yellowstone as a ranger naturalist. He was known for his work with geysers, but less known was his passion for birds, which he studied, lectured on, observed, defended, and sketched. His master's degree was in fringillidae,[15] earned from Brigham Young University. During World War II, when naturalist work was dramatically reduced in Yellowstone, Marler lectured on birds for the Audubon Society. He rendered beautiful and detailed drawings of his feathered friends. In the 1940s, when the trumpeter

George D. Marler at Old Faithful, 1931.
(Courtesy of the National Park Service,
Yellowstone National Park, YELL 42690)

swan was endangered through hunting, Marler took up their cause, publishing informative articles in magazines and papers about their plight. Marler
met his wife, Laura Scherberne, while lecturing for the Audubon Society.
They were married in 1947 and had two daughters.

Marler's wife, Laura, perhaps summed him up best: "He was a brilliant
man but a modest man with a broad range of interests. He was much to
himself, didn't like the limelight. He knew a great deal about the animals,
birds, flowers, and, of course, the geology of Yellowstone. He also had a great
interest in park history, and he loved to collect arrow points and other
artifacts."[16]

Marler became a nursing parent to the geysers and hot springs, visiting
them daily over a forty-year span; taking their temperatures; measuring their
ebbs and flows, their moods of spouting tantrums and peaceful quiescence;
protecting them from tourists' mischievousness; curing them from incidents
of vandalism; restoring them from virtual extinction; and extolling their virtues to the world. In addition to his work with geysers, he served as the naturalist in charge at Old Faithful for several seasons and was made a permanent
park naturalist in 1957.

Marler was held in high regard by scientists from the US Geological Survey who sought out his knowledge on park geysers. He eventually joined their team in order to further his research on geysers. His strongest advocates were Dr. L. C. Graton, an economic geologist and professor of mining geology at Harvard University, and Horace Albright, the former superintendent of Yellowstone Park and former director of the National Park Service. Through the influence of these two men, Marler was able to accomplish research that contributed significantly to an understanding of Yellowstone geysers and hot springs, as well as geothermal theory, which was published in respected scientific journals and magazines.

Marler helped plan and develop at least five major self-guided trails in the Old Faithful Geyser Basins during the 1950s when the park was moving toward self-guided discovery. His culminating work was an exhaustive two-volume inventory of all thermal features in Yellowstone Park.[17] In 1962, again due to the influence of Dr. L. C. Graton, Marler received an honorary doctor's degree from Brigham Young University for his renowned work in geothermal geology in Yellowstone. From 1966 until 1969, he worked closely with Dr. Don White of the US Geological Survey, studying topics related to his beloved geysers. Due to failing health, Marler retired from the National Park Service in 1973.

MERRILL DEE BEAL (1939–66)

Merrill Dee Beal was born on November 3, 1898, in Richfield, Utah, the ninth of twelve children born to George and Melinda Beal. The son of a farmer, Beal learned to work hard, but also discovered an early flair for writing and debating. His first introduction to Yellowstone Park came through a geography book he read as a youth. Meager finances and the demands of the farm presented no opportunity for him to visit Yellowstone until after he was married and teaching school. Beal graduated from college and became a teacher after a short stint in the Marine Corps during World War I. He married Bessy Neill in 1923, and they had two children, one (a daughter) who died at age sixteen.

While living and teaching in Rigby, Idaho, the beckoning call of the wild visited him almost every night in the form of the wailing midnight whistle of the Yellowstone Special, a passenger train that rumbled through Rigby on its way north into the high pine plateaus of Island Park and on to the West Entrance of Yellowstone National Park. Later, while a teacher at Ricks College, Beal took students on summer excursions to Yellowstone. However, not

Merrill D. Beal kneeling by a lodgepole pine, June 1956. (Courtesy of David and Jean Beal)

until 1939 did he actually consider applying for a summer position there as a ranger naturalist.

Beal was already forty years of age when he began work in Yellowstone. To that point in his career, he had primarily devoted himself to teaching and public life. Encouraged by his friend Lowell Biddulph, and driven by the need to augment his teaching salary and have a summer break from teaching, Beal accepted a position as ranger naturalist the summer of 1939. He and Bessy enjoyed twenty-six seasons of bliss in Yellowstone. After their first summer in Yellowstone, their daughter suddenly died, but they returned to the park the next year with their younger son, David, who began work as a soda jerk at the Old Faithful Hamilton Store. David joined the National Park Service and eventually became assistant chief park naturalist in Yellowstone and chief park naturalist at Grand Canyon National Park.

In later years, Beal took on the added name of "Sam" or "Samuel." He often signed documents: "Samuel D. Beal" and some acquaintances had no idea that his real name was Merrill D., unless, of course, they read his published books, in which he always gave his correct birth name. Lowell and Ruth Biddulph, close friends of the Beals, once heard Beal defend his choice of "Sam" as a first name. "Why," said he, "Sam is a good name, a biblical name," to which his wife, Bessy, retorted, "Honestly, Samuel means 'asked of God,' and you being the ninth of twelve children, I seriously doubt that your mother was asking God for another child!"[18]

Merrill Beal's gifts were in history, education, and public affairs. His most significant contribution to Yellowstone was in the realm of human history. Notwithstanding the fifteen years he spent at Old Faithful, Beal was most closely associated with Madison Junction and was a champion of the "National Park Idea" canonized by earlier historians, such as Hiram Chittenden. Beal participated in the pageantry that symbolized the historic campfire of 1870 and the articulation of the creation of national parks for posterity.

Beal's most enduring legacy to Yellowstone is his writing, which includes *The Story of Man in Yellowstone* (1956) and *I Will Fight No More Forever: Chief Joseph and the Nez Perce War* (1963). One of the noted historians in the state of Idaho, Beal wrote several books on Idaho history, including a history of the railroads. Beal taught history at Idaho State University in Pocatello for almost three decades. He was active in civic affairs and a member of important historical organizations. Beal retired from park service in Yellowstone at the end of the 1966 season after twenty-six years of service.

★ ★ ★

Thirty years into his service in Yellowstone, Bud Lystrup provided his own assessment of the extraordinary tenure of these Five Old Men and others like them:

> Why do men like Dr. Biddulph, Dr. Beal, Clarence Alleman, Dr. Nash, Ted Parkinson, George Marler, Wayne Replogle and others return season after season after season? It is not because of the remuneration. It is not because of the urban comforts. Primarily it concerns love and respect for nature and the willingness to share such love and respect with people from all walks of life. It concerns the never-ending search for more information about the hidden secrets of nature. It means satisfaction gained from knowing that a visitor (a plumber, a mechanic, a teacher, a bank clerk, etc.) has been made happy because he has learned a little of that intangible thing called "Appreciation for Nature's Wonders." The knowledge that one has helped another to be inspired by a geyser, a canyon, a flower or a bird gives vast inner satisfaction. To have inspired the visitor to relax and linger to learn the way of things is a powerful stimulus to help others. These men return because they enjoy being attuned to nature. More simply put they gain sheer enjoyment out of helping visitors adjust to superlative natural phenomena.[19]

Chapter 4

Early Ranger Life in Yellowstone

The Old Yellowstone days of the army, the horse-drawn tallyhos, and the lunch stations were gone by the advent of the Five Old Men in the park, yet their aura lingered on like the musty scent of old leather and coffee brewing on a cooking fire. Harry Trischman, Sam Woodring, Ted Ogston, Jim McBride, and George Baggley, who had served as army scouts or were among the first rangers in Yellowstone, were still its leaders.

Structural evidence of the past remained in the original soldier and ranger stations, wilderness snowshoe cabins, and the rustic grandeur of hotels, inns, and lodges built at the turn of the century by Robert Reamer. Roads were still mostly dirt and gravel. Horses and a good pair of legs were the primary modes of transportation. Winter patrols were made on skis and snowshoes. The telephone system was archaic and limited. Medical services and other amenities were scarce. Living and working conditions were primitive by comparison to later changes that would erase much of Old Yellowstone.

APPOINTMENTS
Positions of temporary ranger in the 1920s and '30s were filled by appointments made by members of Congress, influential administrators within the National Park Service, or the superintendent of Yellowstone Park. Congressional appointees were typically first in line. If the chosen applicant failed to accept the appointment, the next person on the waiting list was contacted by telegram or letter, and so on, until the position was filled. Appointees for one year were not automatically reinstated in subsequent years but were reappointed based upon their previous season's performance.

Reappointment each year came by letter from the park superintendent, providing instructions on when and where to report for duty.

REPORTING FOR DUTY

Selectees for temporary positions typically reported in late May or early
June to park headquarters at Mammoth Hot Springs, where they obtained
a uniform and were sworn in before being ferried out to their assigned duty
station. The first night in Yellowstone was often spent in the army barracks at old Fort Yellowstone, the same building that now houses the Horace Albright Visitor Center. The barracks had not changed from the days of
the army, consisting of an open room with eighteen iron bunks, one small
wooden table, and a huge round iron wood-burning stove in the center of
the room. The men huddled around this bastion of heat to warm themselves
on cold mornings before the breakfast bell sent them scurrying down the
stairs to the government mess. The barracks was a scene of man talk and
revelry as old and new acquaintances were forged by men assembled from
various parts of the country.

The summer of 1930, Wayne Replogle received a belated three-week-
old telegram from Yellowstone Park offering him a temporary appointment
as a ranger. Afraid that he may have missed his opportunity, he drove nonstop
to Yellowstone, arriving at the East Entrance just at closing time. As he drove
up to the gate, Tex Wisdom, the ranger on duty, laid the pole across the road
and told Replogle to come back in the morning, despite his vigorous protes-
tation. Replogle had no recourse but to spend a cold night in his car at
Pahaska Tepee, a small mountain resort five miles outside the park.

Pahaska was built and once owned by William F. "Buffalo Bill" Cody.[1]
While on a hunting expedition in 1901, Cody marked the location for a
hunting lodge with a hand ax along the bank of the North Fork of the Shoshone River. Cody had Abraham Archibald Anderson design and build the
lodge for him in 1904–5 for the purposes of accommodating hunting trips
and as a financial enterprise to cater to tourists traveling to and from Yellowstone Park. He gave the lodge a Lakota Sioux name meaning "Long Hair."[2]
Pahaska Tepee literally translates into "Long Hair's tepee or lodge."

In 1916, while touring Yellowstone National Park, Stephen Tyng Mather,
director of the National Park Service, in company with Horace Albright and
others, stopped for lunch at Pahaska Tepee. They found the food to be of
poor quality and the waitresses of such demeanor that Mather questioned
whether Cody was running an eating establishment or a brothel. Cody died

a year later (January 10, 1917) in Denver, Colorado, of kidney failure. Today, Pahaska Tepee remains a mountain resort and is open to public tours. It is listed on the National Register of Historic Places (1973).

After spending a bitter cold night in his car at Pahaska, Replogle reappeared at the entrance at seven in the morning none too happy. Tex Wisdom removed the log and allowed him to come in, and Replogle responded, "Well thank you so very much! I've only waited twelve hours." More than thirty years later, Replogle reminisced about this event with a group of young ranger naturalists at Grant Village: "I've been looking for Old Tex ever since and if I ever meet him I'll punch him in the nose."[3] Truth be known, Replogle had met up with Tex, and there had been no bloodletting. It was just Replogle's entertaining style.

Replogle finally made it to Mammoth and reported at park headquarters, which at the time was in the former US Corps of Engineers' building, a pagoda-looking structure with a green roof and gray sandstone block nicknamed by park personnel the "Temple of Truth." At this juncture, his story takes a turn toward the exaggerated. "I entered there and went upstairs to the Chief Ranger's office. I stood at attention for thirty minutes. The Assistant Chief was George Miller. It took him at least five minutes to turn his head and look at me. He said, 'Now what do you want?' I just handed him the telegram and it took him thirty minutes to read one line."[4]

The sleeping quarters for the rangers was in the cavalry barracks of old Fort Yellowstone. In the words of Herbert Lystrup, the barracks area was a menagerie of "impromptu beds made on the floor amidst a confusion of packages, travelling bags, suitcases, clothes, shoes and boots, wrapping paper, magazines, and newspapers."[5] The fact that some brought portable phonographs suggests that they were in for a rude awakening when they discovered that many of the places had no electricity.

Like the other rangers, Replogle took his meals at the mess hall until he was shipped out to his duty station, which turned out to be Canyon that first summer. He made no comment on the quality of the food served by the government mess, but Bud Lystrup was profuse in praise: "Dinner that evening at the Government mess was second to none."[6]

Temporary rangers were sworn in for summer duty by a judge serving as a US commissioner. The swearing in and taking of the oath of office was a solemn event that imposed upon each man the significance of his duty to protect Yellowstone Park, to carry out the policies and regulations established by the Department of the Interior, and to obey the orders of its presiding officers.

Uniform of the Yellowstone Park ranger in 1939. *Left to right:* Merrill Beal, Lowell Biddulph, Harry Truman, and an unidentified ranger. (Courtesy of L. G. Biddulph)

RANGER UNIFORM

The ranger uniform in 1930 consisted of pegged breeches (baggy about the hips and thighs and skintight around the knees and calves) and a Nor-folk jacket made of forest-green serge wool. Cordovan leather riding boots came above midcalf, some with laces and others not, and a broad-brimmed, gray Stetson hat topped it off. By 1928 the original white shirt and black tie worn by the rangers was replaced with a steel-gray shirt and a green tie. Gold-plated collar insignias (USNPS) and the silver badge added an air of authority.

The uniform was required to be worn at all times while on duty, except in backcountry or on horse patrol. Then Levi's could be worn. Rangers desir-ing to attend a social event after six o'clock, such as the dances held at the Grand Canyon Hotel, were required to wear a white shirt. The rangers did their own laundry and ironed their shirts with flat irons heated on wood-burning stoves.[7]

Ranger uniforms were purchased from what was then the Whittaker general store at Mammoth Hot Springs, owned by George Whittaker, a for-mer scout in Yellowstone from 1897 until 1900. The store was originally established in the 1880s by Jeanette "Jennie" Henderson, an early postmaster in the park. Jennie began the general store at Mammoth as a post office and gradually expanded it to include the sale of curios, general merchandise, and ranger uniforms, including boots and hats.

After twenty-five years, Jennie sold out to her brother, Walter Henderson, and an associate named Alexander Lyall in April 1908. Walter sold out to George Whittaker in 1913. In 1932 Anna Pryor and Elizabeth Trischman purchased the store from George Whittaker and managed it for twenty years until they sold out to Charles Hamilton. After buying the Pryor Store, Hamilton, who started his proprietorship in the park in 1915, gained a monopoly on general merchandizing in Yellowstone that lasted for the next fifty years. In 2002 the Delaware North Companies, Inc., won the right to operate the general stores and photo shops in Yellowstone and did so under the title "Yellowstone General Stores."[8] Although some changes have been made to the original Henderson and Whittaker store over the years, it remains remarkably similar to the early one.

In 1929 Bud Lystrup ordered his uniform a month before his arrival. Wayne Replogle had no such forewarning the following year and must have purchased his uniform right off the rack. Both men bought a new pair of the spiffy field boots that proved to be troublesome once on. Lystrup tried every conceivable way to get his off the first night and finally succeeded only with the help of another fellow sufferer, he pulling and Lystrup pushing on his behind.[9] Replogle had no such luck and slept in his.

The following morning at seven Replogle was on the road to Canyon. Fred Johnston, the district ranger that summer, ordered Replogle to go out and walk all the trails and get familiar with the area. Replogle claims that he walked all day and still couldn't get his boots off that night and slept in them again. He thought he was going to have to resign, his feet hurt so badly. He finally succeeded in removing them by soaking the boots in cold water, but it took six weeks for his blisters to heal.

PAY AND BENEFITS

Pay for the seasonal ranger was meager by today's standards, but not unreasonable for the time. A ranger in 1930 was paid about $140 per month. Comparatively, the average annual salary in the United States was $1,368, up from $1,236 in 1920.[10] In 1930 there were almost no taxes, and unemployment was extremely high due to the Great Depression. Teachers' salaries were about $300 less than those for white-collar workers. Replogle remembered his first year's pay in 1930 as being based on a salary of $1,200 per annum: "Your barracks cost $5 a month. Three meals cost a dollar and a half a day. So, when we were paid, your check amounted to somewhere between $50 and $70 a month. And out of that you paid for your uniform, which cost between $75 and $100, and if you had to store a car it cost you $5 a month. So really you never got very rich as a ranger, kind of like now, you don't get very rich. I think it was a little more romantic in those days."[11]

The only benefit to working in Yellowstone in those days was working in Yellowstone. Time off was not heard of in the 1930s. Rangers were on duty twenty-four hours a day, seven days a week. Bud Lystrup provides insight to the mood of these days in Yellowstone:

> While I was idly leafing through my early diaries recently, I noticed that I worked seven days each week during those first few summers in the Park. There were no days off then, no eight-hour days or forty-hour weeks. And yet, you know, it never seemed a hardship. I took my leisure when I could, usually during the rainy days when the tourists huddled in their tents and cabins playing cards and mending fishing tackle. When those days came, damp and gray, I slipped into my oldest clothes, put on my raincoat and set off on foot to explore the nearby hills.[12]

Dances were about the only social recreation for rangers at Canyon, but, according to Replogle, rangers did not go to dances alone at the Grand Canyon Hotel unless they were either crazy or looking for a fight. Apparently, the dances attracted rough characters who did not have much respect or friendliness for the rangers.

Replogle's first day off came during his sixth year in service while stationed at Old Faithful. One day at about nine o'clock in the morning, his supervisor informed him that he had the day off. He claimed he wanted to hide under his bed because he felt like such a derelict. But instead, he rode to the top of Mount Washburn on his national park patrol motorcycle. Sam Beal noted in his memoirs that during his twenty-six years of service in Yellowstone, he never took a day of sick leave.

Eventually, the forty-hour workweek (more or less) was implemented in the park, along with two days off each week—called lieu days—as well as other benefits. The attitude about work was different then. Today, paid time off, sick leave, a forty-hour or less workweek, health insurance, and employer-matched savings have become expected benefits by many workers.

Until the recent economic downturn in the United States, recreation and leisure were emphasized. People lived for weekends and even pushed for a four-day workweek and frequent paid vacations far away from the concerns and tasks of work. Not so with the Five Old Men. They loved their work in the park. Every day in Wonderland was a holiday. Replogle expressed the feelings of all five men when he wrote in his personal log at the end of his forty-seventh season in Yellowstone: "Imagine getting paid for working in Yellowstone. Sure is a fine life!"

TRANSPORTATION

Communication and travel in the early 1930s in the park were limited. Many of the stations around the Grand Loop—the famous ones like Old Faithful and Canyon were exceptions—were one-person posts with primitive facilities and often remote. Outside contact by telephone or radio was practically nonexistent and motorized transportation unavailable. Mail took days to arrive. Travel took forethought and the time to walk the distance or catch a ride with a passing motorist. Although private automobiles were permitted in the park by August 1, 1915, personal cars for employees were not allowed in the park until about the mid-1930s. Those who drove personal cars to Yellowstone were required to park them in a government-provided garage at Gardiner, Montana—just outside the North Entrance.

Lowell Biddulph could not afford a car of his own in 1928, being a new college graduate, so his father drove him to Mammoth Hot Springs from their home in Provo, Utah, in his Model T Ford and then dropped him off at Canyon Ranger Station, where he was assigned. The summer of 1929, Herbert Lystrup caught a ride on a yellow lumber truck from Mammoth to his first duty station at Fishing Bridge, enduring cold rain and intermittent snow by secluding himself under a tarpaulin.

Void of personal transportation, a ranger was resigned to tough it out wherever he was stationed. Government vehicles were scarce in the 1930s and '40s, and most rangers did their work on foot or horseback, occasionally resorting to bicycles. The bicycle was actually the forerunner of the automobile in Yellowstone. A trio of riders was the first to enter Yellowstone in October 1881. In 1892 two men entered Yellowstone via the Northeast Entrance on a high-wheeled bicycle. Another trio of riders toured the park in 1897. Merrill Beal, George Marler, and Bud Lystrup rode bicycles in the early 1940s to patrol the geyser basins along the Firehole River in addition to their daily walking tours and other duties in the geyser basins.

Naturalists Major Walter P. Martindale (*far right*), George Marler (*second from right*), and Bud Lystrup (*second from left*) at Old Faithful, 1931. (Courtesy of George Marler)

Rangers walked distances that would be unthinkable for today's generation. Assignments that included patrols of the popular sightseeing areas along the Grand Canyon and the geyser basins, inspection of thermal features in remote areas, hikes to the summits of Mount Washburn and Purple Mountain for fire lookout, and campground checks were all done on foot.

Biddulph's and Replogle's first summers in service (in 1928 and 1930, respectively) were spent at Canyon. Rangers were posted each day at Inspiration Point, Grand View, Lower Falls, Upper Falls, and Artist Point. In 1928 Lowell Biddulph and a fellow ranger named Paul Wylie[13] frequently raced each other up the 493 steps from the Yellowstone Falls to the parking lot for conditioning and friendly competition. Wylie and Biddulph competed against each other in their college days in football when Wylie played for Montana State University and Biddulph for Brigham Young University.

Replogle's assignment the summer of 1930 was on this same 493-step stairway to the falls: "I handled all the heart attacks. I would walk down and there'd always be some old fat gal passed out or something. And I'd have to shoulder block her back to the falls, and the guy who was on Inspiration Point had to walk about three miles to get to his duty station. If he wanted to eat, he'd have to walk three miles in and then three miles back. That fellow usually did without lunch."[14]

Campgrounds were classified into different designations in those days, and rangers checked to ensure that the campers were in the properly designated camp. Replogle and Gerald Ford did most of the campground checks at Canyon in 1936. They both enjoyed running to keep in condition and began their checks of the auto camps about five o'clock each morning. They ran from one site to another, checked the state of the campsite, and for each car wrote down the number of the license plate, the state, and the make. After completing checks in the auto camps, they ran the half- to three-quarters of a mile to the mess hall just south of the Chittenden Bridge for seven o'clock breakfast. After breakfast, they walked to their duty station for that day.[15]

The major stations on the Grand Loop road were typically fourteen to sixteen miles apart, sometimes more. Rangers usually hitched a ride with a motorist when traveling about, but sometimes they would walk the distance. In the summer of 1929, for instance, Lowell Biddulph spent an evening with a college group from Rexburg, Idaho, led by Merrill Beal. Biddulph even caught and cleaned enough fish to provide the group of students a sumptuous trout dinner. When it was over, he walked back along the Yellowstone River to Fishing Bridge, arriving sometime after midnight—a distance of fourteen miles. Motivation for the hike came in the embodiment of a young female student named Ruth Hobson, whom Biddulph later married.[16]

ACCOMMODATIONS

Until 1935 no architectural prototype for national park structures was extant. Architecture for this period drew heavily from European influence and was inappropriate for the rustic nature desired in national parks. The exceptions were the beautiful trailside museums designed by Herbert Maier and the Old Faithful Inn designed by Robert Reamer. In 1935 the National Park Service published *Park Structures and Facilities,* guidelines for standardizing architecture that was sensitive to a natural landscape. The guidelines emphasized rustic design, using native materials, that "gives the feelings of having been executed by pioneer craftsmen with limited hand tools, and thus achieves sympathy with natural surroundings."[17] This form of natural architecture became known as National Park Rustic, or by a more colloquial term, "Parkitecture."

Living conditions for temporary rangers in the park were not substantially improved until the mid-1950s with the advent of Mission 66. Many of the rustic and primitive structures built in the late 1880s and early 1900s were still in use prior to Mission 66. During the 1920s and '30s, the National Park Service constructed what became known as snowshoe cabins, ranger stations, and fire lookouts throughout Yellowstone and some bunkhouses in the more populous areas such as Old Faithful and Canyon.[18] For the most part, living conditions remained austere. Some shacks donated to the park service by the Yellowstone Park Association were used at Canyon and Lake for temporary summer housing along with tent-top cabins. Most of these were without electricity and indoor plumbing. Other structures and camping facilities were constructed in Yellowstone during the 1930s by the Civilian Conservation Corps (CCC), a part of the Emergency Conservation Work and Public Works Administration program.[19]

Prior to 1940, most bachelor rangers and even some families lived in primitive tent tops and ranger stations that lacked indoor water and electricity. Some seasonal men were assigned fire watch on top of mountains or at backcountry ranger stations far from any roads or human contact, making family life in the park a virtual impossibility.

The early tent tops were one-room structures, identical to those used by the camping companies of the stagecoach era. Floors were made of pine or fir slats resting on wood runners. The walls were framed with two-by-fours upon which were fastened wooden slats. The roof was also framed with two-by-fours and covered with a heavy canvas tarp that draped down and covered the open space above the walls. These structures slept two to four men. The tent tops were flimsy and not animal proof, as George Marler found out his first year at Old Faithful. He reported the following incident: "During the hot period of summer we left the door open each night. On one of these nights I was rudely awakened by a lapping on my face which I knew at once was a bear's tongue, perhaps finding sweets left on my lips from bread and jelly at supper. I jumped up in bed and I shouted. The bear, a black, precipitously left the cabin. The other occupants of the cabin were awakened by my shouting."[20]

Bud Lystrup described the ranger station at Fishing Bridge, where he and Lowell Biddulph spent the summer together in 1929:

> At one side of the room there was a large, old-fashioned [woodburning] parlor heater...a wash basin...a galvanized metal pail hanging from a nail under one of the windows...a crank telephone with a hearing piece attached to a cord and an adjustable speaker...and a pile of cut wood covering an entire wall from ceiling to floor. That was it; not another stick of furniture. The adjoining room...was the living quarters. There were two single beds, all metal, and on each bed was a

The checking station at Dunraven Pass was erected about 1915 to regulate one-way traffic from Canyon to Tower Fall. (Photo by Zaversnick; courtesy of the National Park Service, Yellowstone National Park, YELL 31655)

well-flattened mattress. Folded neatly at the foot of each bed were two olive-drab army blankets. No chairs, no tables, no shades or curtains for the windows.[21]

Water was carried into the station using the galvanized bucket filled from the faucet outside. Any hot water had to be heated on the stove. Summer mornings were often bitterly cold until a fire was built in the stove. There was no electricity, and all lighting was provided by candlelight or lantern. The latrine was an outdoor privy behind the station. This type of living required forethought, preparation, and endurance.

Lowell Biddulph was one of two rangers assigned to the Dunraven Pass[22] the summer of 1930. The pass and nearby peak were named in honor of the Earl of Dunraven (Windham Thomas Wyndham-Quin, Fourth Earl of Dunraven and Mount-Earl), who visited Yellowstone and was so impressed with its beauties that he gave it international publicity in his book *The Great Divide,* published in London in 1876.

A checking station, horse barn, and small auto camp were constructed in this high-mountain pass in 1915 to regulate the one-way traffic between Canyon and Tower Fall. Primitive and isolated at an elevation of 8,859 feet, the setting was one of rugged beauty. Forests of Engelmann spruce, whitebark pine, and Douglas fir stretch across steep mountainsides, twisted and gnarled at timberline where the wind blows incessantly. Tall grass and brilliant wild-flowers brighten the rock-filled slopes. Grizzly and black bear roam the forests, elk and deer graze the high meadows, and bighorn sheep haunt the craggy peaks.

The checking station stood near a mountain spring where a parking area and historical marker are now located. The building was about ten by twenty feet in dimension and was made of wood with a peaked, shingle-covered roof and an overhanging front porch. The station had no electricity or indoor plumbing. When the road between Tower and Canyon was improved and made two-way, the need for a checking station and auto camp was eliminated, and the house and barn were removed.

Rangers were also stationed at Tower Fall, a few miles down the road from Dunraven Pass, and lived in the old soldiers station until a newer ranger station was constructed. Ben Arnold, the head ranger at Tower Fall in 1932, frequently rode his horse up Tower Creek trail onto Prospect Peak and other mountains in the Washburn Range. Replogle and another temporary named George Eckles were stationed with Arnold at Tower in 1932. One day Arnold's horse came into the Tower Station without Ben on it. Certain that Arnold was in some kind of trouble, George Eckles rode his horse up on Prospect Peak and found Ben limping along on a broken leg caused when his horse fell. Tough old Arnold had walked two or three miles by the time Eckles found and brought him in on the back of his horse.[23]

At Canyon rangers lived in a bunkhouse. Biddulph was there in 1928, and Replogle and Ford were stationed there with six other rangers in 1936. The supervising ranger in 1936 was Frank Anderson, and he was the only one of the rangers who had a private bedroom. All the other men slept in a large room. Replogle described the wall construction of the day: "Every few years they moved the walls to fit the needs, and when they rebuilt a wall they usually built it out of half-inch thick cardboard. That was the first type of interior walling they ever built."[24]

Ford and Replogle were coaching football in the winter months, and both men had been football players in their day, Ford an All-American center for Michigan and Replogle an All-Conference running back at the College of Emporia in Kansas. One evening a discussion ensued between himself and Ford about the proper method of tackling a person. Both men had different opinions about how it should be done, so one of the rangers listening said, "Demonstrate." Replogle positioned himself as a running back, and Ford flew into Replogle, driving him through the wall and into the adjoining

Rangers assigned to Canyon the summer of 1936 included future president Gerald R. Ford (*third from left*) and Wayne Replogle (*fourth from left*). (Courtesy of the National Park Service, Yellowstone National Park, YELL 114650)

room where Anderson was asleep. Anderson "jumped up out of his sleep and said, 'What the hell's going on?' Of course, by that time everybody's on their back on the floor; total mirth you know."[25]

DUTY ASSIGNMENTS

Ranger duty was hard, physical labor. If a man was willing to work hard and be taught, he was accepted by the old-timers; if not, he was soon sent on his way. Ben Arnold, head ranger at Tower, had a crotchety reputation among the rangers, and the word was that if you wanted to get into trouble, get assigned to Ben Arnold. Wayne Replogle's and George Eckles's assignment to Ben the summer of 1932 was reason for consternation. Despite their fears, they determined to make a good showing at whatever Ben threw at them. On the first day of work, Arnold assigned them to cut wood as one of their first tasks. The woodpile was Arnold's private boot camp, where he weeded out the misfits from the keepers.

Eckles and Replogle worked like mad trying to impress old Ben, who they knew was periodically watching them from his kitchen window. Finally, about three o'clock, after they had worn a good set of blisters on their hands,

Ben came out to the woodpile and said, "Well, it looks like you have done a pretty good job. At three-thirty there will be a patrol in my kitchen." Sharply at three-thirty, Eckles and Replogle reported for patrol duty at Ben's kitchen, where Ben and his wife, Margaret, had cake and ice cream for them.

Ranger work could also be lonely, especially at smaller stations where only one person was assigned. Madison Junction, located on the west side of Yellowstone, was a one-person station until 1954. Although all tourist traffic from the West Entrance came through Madison Junction, a single ranger without transportation found the assignment there a strange mixture of busyness and loneliness.

Replogle was stationed at Madison Junction the summer of 1931. Each morning after raising the flag, he hiked up Purple Mountain, directly north of Madison Junction, and surveyed the area for forest fires. After about an hour, he returned to the cabin. Most days, when not busy with tourists, he killed time by hiking up the Firehole Canyon to the rapids and falls and looked at flowers. When he needed food, he caught a ride to Riverside (West Yellowstone) and back, about a thirty-mile round-trip.

The first year Merrill Beal was at Madison Junction (1941) he discovered that his job was whatever people needed him to do, and it was not always something for which he felt qualified or comfortable doing:

Sometimes the District Ranger in West Yellowstone telephoned instructions concerning a blockade to intercept a party. That worried me, because I didn't have a gun, and I lacked training in such matters [most naturalists did]. On one such occasion, the party didn't appear. However, I did stop a person in response to a report that he was driving in an erratic manner. He was a cook from Old Faithful Lodge. I accused him of being intoxicated. Of course, he denied being in that condition. But I persuaded him to stay in the parking lot until patrolman Lewis arrived. After quizzing the cook, Lewis allowed him to leave. An hour later, he managed to drive through the Firehole Canyon area without incident (in those days the road through the Firehole Canyon was challenging even for a sober driver). Then, when the way was clear before him, he dropped off a three-foot bank and tipped over in the Firehole River.[26]

The two rangers stationed at Dunraven Pass had two major assignments: to regulate auto traffic between Canyon and Tower Fall and to provide fire lookout and ranger services on the summit of Mount Washburn. It was about a four-mile hike both ways. Lowell Biddulph met the president of the Havana Cigar Company at the summit one day in 1930 and was given a box of his famous cigars as a token of his appreciation. Biddulph did not smoke, but other rangers enjoyed them throughout the summer.

The road crew maintained a string of horses at Dunraven Pass for patrolling and clearing roads and trails. The Washburn Range was grizzly habitat, and bears came frequently to Dunraven Pass, drawn by the aroma of human food and oats in the horse barn. One night Biddulph was awakened by two grizzlies ferociously fighting on a snowbank over scraps of food. One swatted the other, sending him rolling head over heels, and then he swatted the other, sending him rolling.

Grizzlies pulled the planking from the horse barn, trying to get at the oats stored inside, which not only damaged the structure but also endangered and frightened the horses. The road-crew foreman tried everything he could think of to deter the grizzlies, even driving large spikes through the walls of the barn pointing outward, but nothing seemed to stop them. As a last resort, the foreman planted small pieces of dynamite around the barn. When the bears appeared for their nightly foray, the foreman detonated the small charges. They were not large enough to harm the bears, but it frightened them so badly that they were not seen again that summer.[27]

Rangers at Canyon periodically had to rescue people who became stranded in the Grand Canyon of the Yellowstone. Despite its treacherous nature, climbing in the canyon was unrestricted in the 1920s and '30s, and numerous are the personal reminiscences of people who attempted to scurry up its precipitous twelve-hundred-foot walls.[28] As a result, many climbers had to be rescued by the rangers. A stout rope was kept coiled in the back room of the ranger station for such emergencies.

One evening in 1928, Lowell Biddulph was standing duty at the Canyon ranger station, located at the time near the head of Uncle Tom's Trail. An older couple from Chicago came into the ranger station and reported their two teenage grandsons missing. The two boys had gone hiking in the canyon earlier in the day and had failed to return. Biddulph took the rescue rope from the ranger station and followed the grandparents to the head of Uncle Tom's Trail, where the man had last seen his grandsons enter the canyon.[29]

He began his descent along the trail and could soon hear the boys desperately calling for help off to the right side of the trail. The boys had followed Uncle Tom's Trail into the canyon, then had left its safety and tried to scale the steep canyon wall to the top. Dizzying heights and loose rock caused panic, and they sat paralyzed on the steep slope, shouting for help, as the shadows and colder temperatures began to fill the canyon.

With the rope slung over one shoulder, Biddulph cut across the steep canyon slope to a position above where the boys clung to the cliffs. Securing one end of the rope to a tree, he lowered himself down to the first boy, who screamed in fear and pain when Biddulph tried to move him. The boy's legs were almost paralyzed from prolonged squatting, rendering them practically useless and extremely painful. Biddulph remembered, "Only after lengthy massaging of the boy's legs and patient talking was I able to move first one, then the other boy to the safety of the wood platform of Uncle Tom's Trail."[30]

The rescue operation was observed by the grandparents. Once the boys were safely on the platform, the woman threw her arms around Biddulph's neck and kissed his cheek. The grandfather slapped him on the back and pushed a fifty-dollar bill into his hand. Biddulph returned the money, explaining that it was against rules for him to take a reward. After three exchanges of the money, according to Biddulph, the man conceded, but gave him his business card and said, "I'm a prominent attorney in Chicago. If you ever need assistance, you just call me." The next day, when Biddulph entered the ranger station for duty, he found a package addressed to him from the man. Inside were two large boxes of fifty-cent cigars, estimated worth about fifty bucks![31] It seems that Biddulph had a propensity for receiving accolades in the form of cigars.

MAINTAINING THE PARK

Not all ranger work was exciting. In fact, much of it was mundane janitorial work to keep the Grand Old Park presentable to its adoring public. The Five Old Men and their colleagues came to the park as early as their teaching assignments allowed to prepare the stage upon which they would perform that summer.

In May Yellowstone was drowsily awakening from an extended winter sleep. Snowbanks yet covered the grounds and walkways; squirrels, chipmunks, and larger mammals were fresh out of their dens. Birds were returning to Yellowstone's waters and forests, and the early spring flowers and buds began to color the landscape.

Much work was required to open the museums and campgrounds. Walkways had to be shoveled of lingering snow and swept clean of the heavy mat of orange-colored pine needles and cones that had fallen. Tree limbs, broken away by heavy snows, were cut up and removed from paths, trails, and walkways. Wood and kindling for campfire programs and cabin use were split with ax, wedge, and sledge. Shutters on windows and doors and roof support poles were taken down and stacked. Museum display cases and windows were washed, dusted, swept, and polished. Geysers, hot springs, and other famous points of interest were checked to ensure that no damage had been done to them during the winter. Occasionally, carcasses of animals that had fallen into a hot spring had to be removed.

In addition to the manual labor, the senior naturalist at each station had to develop an interpretive plan for the naturalists assigned to the station. Nature walks were scheduled throughout the three months, along with auto caravans to key locations, nightly campfire programs, museum duty, geyser basin duty, Old Faithful cone talks, and Canyon duty. Books, pamphlets, maps, and other supplies had to be picked up from the park headquarters at Mammoth, inventoried, and prepared for sale.

Wear and tear to geysers and hot springs, as well as man-made facilities, was heavy during the summer months. Some damage came from normal use, but other damage was thoughtless and malicious. Each fall, after the hordes of people left the park, it had to be repaired and prepared before the heavy winter snows came. All the buildings that were not inhabited by people during the winter had to be closed and winterized. Electricity and inside water were shut off, roof support poles put back in place so that heavy winter snows did not cave in the roofs, windows shuttered, museum display cases covered, restrooms cleaned and winterized, mouse traps set, and all food or other attractions for mice, rodents, and other creatures removed. Geysers and hot springs were cleaned, and debris that was thrown into the orifices and pools of the thermal features during the summer months was removed. Initials that had been thoughtlessly carved into the delicate algae formations were also removed as best as possible.

By September the animals that had summered in the high mountain cirques returned to the lower plateaus, and soon, long lines of elk were on the move toward the lower valleys where forage was more accessible. Like the animals, the temporary men were migratory, leaving the park in late fall to pursue teaching and coaching assignments and returning with the spring thaw. Fall came with a tinge of regret, but spring always brought joyous anticipation. Bud Lystrup's diary for the summer of 1932 provides a glimpse of the life of the early seasonal ranger naturalist:

May 31: Reported in at Gardner [*sic*], Montana for swearing in, then secured a cot and mattress for the summer and spent a night in the old cavalry barracks at Mammoth before moving on to Old Faithful.

June 1: Travelled to Norris Junction museum via the new road through the Hoodoos just south of Mammoth to wash display cases and prepare the museum for opening.[32]

June 6: Met Jack Ellis Haynes who donated a picture to the museum at Mammoth.

June 9: Harry Trischman—North District Naturalist—reported that a portion of Liberty Cap had fallen off.[33]

June 10: Drove to Soda Butte in the Lamar Valley to observe buffalo and visit the buffalo ranch.[34]

June 12: New naturalists arrived for orientation. They seemed bewildered and lost. They went out into the geyser formations at Mammoth Hot Springs with Mr. Crowe to learn about the geysers.

June 17: Reported to Old Faithful museum for duty. Stayed at the ranger station with three other men.

June 20: Gave the bear lecture at Old Faithful.

June 29: Prepared geyser activity reports for June.

July 2: Gave a flower lecture to an auto caravan of 40 cars.

July 4: Went to Madison Junction and attended a dedication ceremony of the Stephen Tyng Mather plaque.

July 13: Helped rescue and obtain medical assistance for a 3-year old girl who fell into an open pool and was severely burned. (The child was transported to Mammoth hospital and died there.)[35]

July 14: Observed Mortar geyser in action, a geyser in the Upper Basin near Riverside Geyser; named by F. Jay Haynes in 1883, because the eruptions resembled discharge of mortar ordnance.

July 18: Drove to Fishing Bridge, East Entrance, and Pahaska Tepee. Talked briefly at the Fishing Bridge program. The museum at Fishing Bridge is the envy of other stations.

July 25: Grand Geyser erupted; named by Dr. F. V. Hayden in 1871; 160 feet in height.

July 30: Hiked into Lone Star Geyser Basin along the upper reaches of the Firehole River to observe and check things out.

August 1: Searched for a lost woman; found her one mile east of Old Faithful on the road to West Thumb. She was disoriented.

August 3: Conducted auto caravan through geyser basins; saw eruptions of Daisy, Riverside, Lion, Oblong, Grotto, Rocket, and Jewell Geysers.

August 6: Accompanied Geyser Bill [T. J. Onkrom] to the five-mile post toward Madison Junction to check on geysers. Dr. Bauer visited today and spoke to a group on the geology of Yellowstone.

August 12: Giant Geyser erupted; named in 1870 by Washburn Party because of its long duration of eruption (more than an hour in a steady stream about three feet in diameter and average of 200 feet high). Giant plays very infrequently.

August 15: George Marler reported to Old Faithful to take the place of another ranger naturalist who left. [The year 1932 was Marler's second season in Yellowstone Park.]

August 22: Raven Creek fire burning. Assigned to help on the fire for a few days.[36]

August 30: Snowed the entire day.

August 31: Turned books and money for the season over to George Marler. [Lystrup had to return to Wisconsin to begin high school teaching, and Marler could stay longer in the fall.]

September 2: Closed up most activities and facilities. The end of the season is drawing to a close. Regret leaving Yellowstone.

Chapter 5

Family Life in Yellowstone

WOMEN IN A MAN'S WORLD

A gravestone marks the confluence of Nez Perce Creek and the Firehole River about six miles above Madison Junction. On it is inscribed: "Mattie S., wife of E. C. Culver, died March 2, 1889 age 30 years." In 1889 Mr. Culver was working for the Yellowstone Park Association as the winter keeper for the Firehole Hotel, located at Nez Perce Creek near the Lower Geyser Basin.[1]

Culver's wife, Mattie, contracted tuberculosis that winter but delivered a baby girl before succumbing to the disease. The winter was severe, and the ground was frozen solid, prohibiting the digging of a suitable grave for Mrs. Culver. They put her body in two barrels of snow to preserve it until the spring thaw. When the ground allowed, they buried her and placed a marker there. The baby girl was kept alive on a diet of sugar and canned milk.

Each year, at least for many years, someone (perhaps Mattie's husband, daughter, or other relative) came and decorated Mattie's grave with flowers. Nan Weber Boruff has written an interesting account of this woman in a book titled *Mattie: A Woman's Journey West*.[2]

Mattie Culver's gravestone is a memorial of sorts to the spouses and families of those who served in Yellowstone in years when living was hard and accommodations primitive. For decades, ranger life in Yellowstone was almost exclusively a man's world. The women who worked or lived with their husbands in the park had to be as tough as the men, and they lived under conditions that most modern women would find intolerable.

A decade before Mattie Culver's death, Sarah Romrell Marshall gave birth to a child on a bitterly cold January day in 1881. She and her husband spent that winter in an unfinished structure, known as the Marshall Hotel, at the confluence of Nez Perce Creek and the Firehole River, the same location where Mattie would die nearly ten years later. Sarah's fourth child, a baby daughter, was named Rosa Park Marshall. She was the first white child born in Yellowstone Park.

There were others. Jennie Henderson lived and worked in Yellowstone for nearly a quarter of a century as postmaster and owner of the first general store. Twenty-five years took its toll on Jennie, and she finally had to sell out to her brother and retire to California due to failing health. Herma Baggley and Mrs. Ben Arnold both served in the park and lived with their husbands during the early 1900s under primitive conditions.

Early conditions and the nature of the work attracted young bachelors, not so much family men. Strong parallels existed between the ranger corps and the military. Families did not fit the image and conditions of service. The old adage "If the military had wanted you to have a wife, they would have issued you one" was true for the early rangers.

FAMILIES IN YELLOWSTONE

By the late 1920s and early '30s, when the Five Old Men entered park service, living accommodations had not appreciably changed from earlier days. Although adequate family housing for permanent employees was available at Mammoth Hot Springs, housing for families of temporary rangers was not available until the 1930s. By then, an increasing number of married men were hired as temporary or seasonal ranger naturalists. The provision of some type of temporary housing became necessary if the park was to attract qualified men who naturally did not want to be separated from spouses or children for three or four months a year. Moreover, families wanted to share in the excitement of living in Yellowstone despite the primitive and austere conditions.

Facilities and services were drastically cut back during World War II. Gas and tire rationing precluded travel. Manpower was so sparse that many services could not be provided. Most families of seasonal employees who were not drafted into the military and were retained by the National Park Service remained at home, many raising a "war garden."[3] Of the Five Old Men, only Biddulph and Lystrup remained working summers in Yellowstone during the war. Beal obtained a PhD at Washington State University and was the custo-

Merrill, Bessy, and David Beal at Old Faithful, 1939. (Courtesy of David and Jean Beal)

dian at Big Hole Battlefield National Monument.[4] Marler lectured with the Audubon Society in Massachusetts, and Replogle served in the United States Navy.

Other than the war years, family members accompanied the Old Men to Yellowstone each summer. In all, eleven children spent their summer months in the park and became as passionate about it as the Five Old Men. The return to Yellowstone in the summer was as natural for them as it was instinctive for the animals of the park. Anticipation for the trip to Yellowstone began with the first spring thaws and grew into excitement as cars and small trailers were packed with food, utensils, clothing, bedding, and other supplies needed for the next three months. How joyful it was to return to the park each summer after the long winter months of school and work in other parts of the country. The aroma of pine forests was intoxicating. The first black bear and other animals were greeted like old friends. Mountain panoramas, lakes, waterfalls, geysers and hot springs, and the great canyon of the Yellowstone were friendly to the eye and dear to the heart. No matter how austere the living conditions—primitive cabin or tent top—home was wherever the family was, and working together they soon made a cozy dwelling in which to spend many happy hours.

Ranger naturalists served wherever in the park they were assigned, which varied from year to year in the pre–World War II era. After the war, the Five Old Men seemed to settle into a particular station: Lowell Biddulph at Fishing Bridge; Bud Lystrup, George Marler, and Sam Beal at Old Faithful; and Wayne Replogle at Canyon and Mammoth. Sam Beal also spent almost half of his summers at Madison Junction and was closely identified with that station because of its emphasis on Yellowstone history.

During the 1940s, park management began giving naturalists two vacation days each week, called lieu days. These two days were typically filled with family adventures, such as fishing, hiking, horseback riding, or visiting interesting places such as Red Lodge, Cooke City, Cody, Virginia City, or Jackson Hole and the Tetons. For more than a decade, Wayne Replogle and his wife, Marian, who had no children, spent their days off hiking and mapping out the Bannock Indian Trail.

Each family had places in the park and rituals of special meaning, not merely the famous sites but the less obvious, out-of-the-way places not swarming with tourists. Dave Beal, for instance, never forgot the many weekends that Wayne Replogle took him, as a boy, hiking in the Firehole and Gibbon Canyons. Harlequin Lake—hidden in the forest at the foot of Purple Mountain near Madison Junction—was Sam Beal's Shangri-la to which he made frequent pilgrimages. A friend once suggested to Beal that Harlequin be renamed "Beal Lake" because he was so attached to it.

Wayne and Marian Replogle enjoyed camping and tramping the woods. Despite Marian's refined upbringing as the daughter of a Chicago judge and being an accomplished organist, she proved to be a woman of true grit. Specimen Creek campground, located in the northwest corner of Yellowstone Park where Specimen Creek intersects Highway 191, was their favorite place to camp. Late in his career, after the campground had been eliminated, Replogle reminisced:

> From the late 1940s until 50's and even into the 60's, many times a summer we would drive up there after work on the night before our

days off, arriving there sometimes at 2:00 or 3:00 in the morning. We'd fix dinner, go to bed and sleep well, get up the next day and tramp and hike and enjoy the place, and read, and hit the hay that night and get up the next day and spend most of it there, returning to our home in Yellowstone late on the second night. I look back at the disappearance of that famous Specimen Creek campground with some nostalgia.[5]

Tramping through nature with their fathers was a never-to-be-forgotten pleasure for children. Flowers and plants, insects, birds, and mammals were all part of their great study of nature.

George Marler made every trip into nature a learning experience for his two girls, Barbara and Lela. He provided notebooks and pencils for them to record the names of the flowers, plants, birds, and animals that they encountered during their forays. George was not much for words when in nature, and the girls used to ask him questions just to get him to talk.

Lystrup took his daughter, Liz, and son, Tiff, on frequent excursions. Fishing along Sentinel Creek near the Lower Geyser Basin was always enjoyable. Lystrup wrote in *Nature Notes* that they came upon a secluded lake and saw deer grazing peacefully in a green meadow. A great blue heron stood in the shallows on stilted legs gracefully feeding, and the distant howl of a coyote was heard. Simple things were powerful to him. Lystrup had a particular fondness for Hayden Valley. Of this sprawling, sagebrush-covered plain, he wrote, "It was during one of these pleasant rambles that I discovered Hayden Valley, a lovely, unspoiled alpine scene. I've returned there many times since the day I first came upon it, but its charms wear well, they don't diminish. Forever changing, the valley yet remains a retreat of untapped riches waiting to refresh the human spirit."[6]

The hike to the summit of Mount Washburn to watch the sunrise was a ritual common to all five families. Parents and children shivered on the dark, ten-thousand-foot summit as they watched night turn into day. Jagged forms of the Absaroka peaks were silhouetted against the backdrop of changing colors on the eastern horizon: white, rose, orange, and a final blast of brilliance as the sun rose into a cloudless blue tapestry.

The first rays of a new day pierced first the summit on which they stood, instantly warming them, before descending the mountainside and opening to their view an ever-expanding wilderness below. The great canyon gorge erupted into flames of yellow, orange, purple, and brown, followed by the

Tom Collins' Rock is on Yellowstone Lake's shoreline between Pelican Creek outlet and Storm Point on an outcropping of low-lying rocks. (Photo by the author)

emergence of a sea of green lodgepole pine stretching eastward for miles until it butted against the distant Absaroka bulwark.

Far to the southeast, the sunlight danced upon the glass surface of Yellowstone Lake and turned the great river that bore the same name into a silver snake, meandering through the sage-colored expanse of Hayden Valley, until it leaped in foaming emerald shafts into the Grand Canyon of the Yellowstone at their feet. To witness the birth of a new day on Mount Washburn was to be reborn in spirit.

The hike to Tom Collins' Rock on Yellowstone Lake was an annual excursion for the Biddulph family. A cluster of low-lying rocks protrudes into Yellowstone Lake a few hundred yards west of the prominent cliffs of Storm Point and about three-quarters of a mile east of Pelican Creek inlet. Someone had chiseled into one of the flat rock surfaces the name "Tom Collins." The inscription was not dated, but it was obviously old because of the amount of crustose lichen on the rock and the condition of both the rock's surface and the inscription itself.[7]

Biddulph thought that either an early explorer or a visitor to Yellowstone dating as far back as the late 1800s had chiseled the inscription. The name of Tom Collins does not appear in any of the historical records of Yellowstone as a trapper, explorer, member of Hayden's survey party, military person, employee of the National Park Service, or visitor. Most people did not even know that a rock with the name on it existed in Yellowstone. Just maybe there was no such visitor to Yellowstone by that name. Maybe the name of Tom Collins was a hoax.

In 1874, two years after Yellowstone was created as a national park, the name Tom Collins became the subject of a wildly popular hoax perpetrated against unsuspecting souls that began in New York and carried on to other parts of the country. As the hoax went, a person would approach a gullible person and ask them if they knew someone by the name of Tom Collins. The answer was always no, and the trickster went on to say that a man named Tom Collins was in a bar around the corner talking about this person, and in not too flattering of terms. Of course, the objective of the hoax was to get the person riled up enough to charge off to the bar and demand that the insolent Tom Collins show himself and receive his just reward for slandering the person's good name. This joke became so popular that it is remembered in history as the "Great Tom Collins Hoax of 1874" and even had some music hall songs written about it.

In 1876 the first Tom Collins drink was introduced in New York by Jerry Thomas, consisting of gin, lemon juice, sugar, and carbonated water. It is believed that this mixed drink was inspired by the Great Tom Collins Hoax. It is not completely out of the realm of possibility that the Tom Collins engraved in the rock at Yellowstone Lake had some relationship to the hoax. Perhaps it is the epitaph of an early tourist from New York City who found his way to that isolated shore and forever engraved his craving for a cool Tom Collins cocktail in stone.

Mountain peaks were particular treasures to Lowell Biddulph. A child of his could hardly grow up not loving mountains. Annual hikes to the summit of some of the major peaks in the Absaroka Range, such as Avalanche and Top Notch Peaks, and sliding down the steep, snow-laden cirques were experiences never to be forgotten. Biddulph's oldest son, Howard, put this emotion into poetic form with biblical intonations:

"Father's Mountain"
(Isaiah 40:9)
Come up with me
Into the high mountain,
You called to us at early light;
So

Fumbling sleepily
The family dressed
Shivering on the cottage floor.
Climbing steeply single file,
We paused as you identified
Each birdsong, type of tree and flower,
Examined tracks of Wapiti,
And kept a sharp eye out for bears.
Brushing through a sylvan maze,
We soaked up clinging morning dew,
Learned where to safely drink the stream,
Partake a forest berry feast.
On the ridge of timberline,
We rested 'midst Forget-me-nots,
Breathed deeply thin enchanted air,
Rehearsed a plan to climb the peak.
Then laboring perpendicular,
We scaled the ancient altar tall,
And heaped on top our own memorial of shale,
Exalted from the valley low,
Our throne among the great ones set,
You opened to us gifts on high
Of Earth's and Heaven's precious lode.[8]

Places were not the only symbols of affection for the families. Objects also became almost totem-like in significance. One of these objects for the Biddulph family was an imposing lodgepole pine that stood in the forest near the lakeshore not far from their cottage at Fishing Bridge. Unlike most lodge-pole pines, which were typically slender, straight, and limbless for a good portion of their height, this tree was friendly, with great spreading branches within easy reach of even the smallest child. Each child had a branch of the tree that was his or her special branch, and many an hour was spent in the tree playing and daydreaming. The tree became an icon of the family's solidarity and mutual love and was dubbed the "Family Tree."

Yellowstone belonged to the nation and even the world, but for a few days in early summer of each year, before the teeming crowds of tourists poured through its gates, it belonged just to the ranger families. To walk in the hush of the early-summer forest was like entering a sanctuary, void of any human sound other than the soft crunch of feet on the carpet of rust-colored

Bud and Betty Lystrup with their children, Liz and Tiff, en route to Yellowstone, ca. 1942. (Courtesy of Liz Lystrup)

pine needles and the welcoming chatter of a squirrel or the staccato rasp of a raven in a nearby tree.

No matter where assigned or to what dwelling, the families made it their home. Shutters were removed and the windows cleaned, letting in the bright sunlight of another summer. Floors were swept, cupboards and closets cleaned and stocked, and a warm fire built in the wood-burning stove. The cottages, as devoid of modern luxuries as they were, became scenes of great family togetherness, where good meals, games, talks, and fun etched lasting memories into all their lives.

Birds and animals, large and small, came close, many of them losing much of their timidity as the summer wore on. Acquaintances were renewed each summer with squirrels and chipmunks and birds that frequented feeding stations erected by the naturalist families. The squirrels especially became quite demanding, and if not fed, they set up an awful scolding from a nearby tree. The insatiable consumers ran back and forth from the feeding tray to a secluded spot to nibble on a morsel or hide it away in the ground or the root of a tree for winter storage.

George Marler provides an account of his family's interaction with squirrels and other creatures the winter of 1951–52 at Old Faithful:

> All winter we had a squirrel who chattered to be fed on bright days and even ventured into the kitchen when a door was left open. Now we have five squirrels and they set up a terrific clamor each morning at dawn (5:30) on our porch. It takes many pancakes to satisfy them—I have even baked bread for the family. An old beaver built a house and took up his abode near the ranger quarters and we've been giving him a hand. We feel sure he is beaverdom's worst engineer for he has felled five or six trees this winter and every one of them lodged. So we have untangled them, hacked off the upper branches and carried them to his house and even made trails to the big trunks so he could get to them to gnaw off the bark. All of our donations have been received, bark eaten, and bare sticks stuck in mud on the creek bottom.[9]

Families participated in the Yellowstone adventure as much as possible. Spouses occasionally stood museum duty when urgent requirements, such as fighting forest fires, took their men away. Children also helped their fathers with their chores. They built campfires for evening programs, ran slide projectors during campfire lectures, helped with museum duties, performed janitorial work in and around the museums, raised and lowered Old Glory each day, and accompanied the men on caravans, game stalks, and nature walks. The Five Old Men passed to their children a passion for Yellowstone's wonders. From the fathers the children and spouses learned to recognize by sight and sound the birds, plants, flowers, and animals of Yellowstone. School science and biology projects were completed in the park, and even Boy Scout merit badges and rank advancements were earned.

INCIDENT AT TURBID LAKE

A favorite activity for ranger families was evening game stalks. Elk, deer, buffalo, moose, and other animals came into the open meadows to feed at dusk, providing wonderful opportunities for observation. Upon occasion, animals provided more interaction than desirable.

The Biddulph family had an electrifying encounter with a grizzly sow and two cubs while driving on a deserted service road to Turbid Lake near Mary Bay. Biddulph allowed one of his older teenage sons to practice driving a stick shift while he sat next to him. It seemed safe enough with no other cars allowed on the road. Biddulph's wife, Ruth, was in the cab, and three younger children were riding in the back of the open pickup.

As the family puttered around a corner of the narrow dirt road[10] in the deep forest, they suddenly came upon a grizzly sow and two cubs standing on a small embankment overlooking the edge of the road. So startled were the bears that one of the cubs tumbled down the embankment and into the road, directly in front of the oncoming pickup. Before anyone knew what had happened, the little cub was up and running down the road in front of the pickup. The sow, of course, became concerned for her cub and gave chase.

Biddulph yelled to his son, "Step on it," meaning the gas. He did not want the sow to catch the pickup with his three children in the open back. The boy promptly stepped on the brake without clutching, and the pickup came to a jolting stop. The sow angrily attacked the back end of the pickup, delivering a couple of powerful blows that dented the tailgate.

"No! No! The gas!" cried Biddulph to his son. The frightened boy restarted the pickup, ground it into gear, and jerkily accelerated down the road. By this time, the cub had made it safely off the road and back into the trees, and the sow left the pickup to reunite her cubs. But it was too late for the Biddulphs. The pickup was dented, the tension inside the cab was palpable, and the children in the back were hyperventilating.

FRIENDSHIPS TO LAST A LIFE-TIME

Friendships among the naturalist families flourished in Yellowstone. Living under similar circumstances and having much the same experiences each summer, spouses and children shared a bond and supported each other in good and challenging times. While the men worked, the women and children found activities to keep them interested. At Old Faithful in 1939, for instance, the women and children engaged in what they called "geyser chasing." Ruth Biddulph explains this activity:

> Families of naturalists, and the men themselves whenever they had free time, enjoyed the hobby of geyser chasing. We would take our children and some snacks and maybe a book or two and park out in some area where a geyser was predicted to erupt. Some of them, like Giant, erupted very infrequently. Others were more frequent but were quite

irregular, and it was a great thrill to be lucky enough to be on hand for their eruption. Some days we had to go quickly from one lucky eruption to another in a different area. It could be quite exciting. The tourists who saw the eruptions did not know how lucky they were when we had waited perhaps hours for the event. They generally had to have a geyser show within ten or fifteen minutes or they couldn't wait. But we had all summer![11]

Living in the woods surrounded by wild creatures large and small was pleasant, although potentially dangerous. Children often played in the forest with little trepidation for wild animals, despite the fact that bears were frequently in and around their living places. Moose, buffalo, and elk also lived in the vicinity and could be aggressive, especially when young were present. Despite their relative comfort in a wild environment, occasions of crisis did arise for families.

One of those times happened during June 1942, when the three-year-old son of a park ranger couple, Verde and Peg Watson, was grabbed by a black bear. The children were playing by a creek a short distance from the apartments when suddenly the women heard the children screaming, "The bear's got Kent!" The mothers ran out to see a black bear dragging the three-year-old son of the Watsons by the head into the woods.

As the bear dragged the boy across the stream, his clothes fortuitously caught on a wooden water pipe, causing the bear to lose its grip on the boy's head. The brave mothers swarmed upon the bear, beating it with brooms and dust mops and shouting until it slowly retreated into the woods. The partially scalped boy was taken to the hospital in Livingston, Montana, where he healed from his wounds and the trauma.[12]

Another close encounter happened to one of Biddulph's sons while playing in the "Family Tree" near his cabin in Fishing Bridge. One afternoon, while he sat daydreaming on one of the tree's higher branches, a black bear happened by and climbed into the same tree as the boy. The dilemma posed urgent decisions for the boy: should he remain out on the limb and yell for help, hoping that someone in the cabin would hear him? Should he jump? Or should he attempt to quietly climb down without the bear noticing him? No option was without risks. Yelling would only attract the bear to him. Leaping the twenty feet to the ground would likely break bones, leaving him to the mercy of the bear.

Descending was the only option, which was made all the more urgent when the bear suddenly spotted the boy. The bear became somewhat animated and began to position itself to where it could climb up to the boy. Its intentions were not playful. The time to act had come. The boy slid down the limb to the large trunk and speedily descended, passing the bear on the opposite side. As they passed each other, the bear peered around the trunk at the boy with beady brown eyes and reached for him with a forepaw. At that point, the boy leaped the remaining ten feet from the tree and ran to the safety of the cottage.

FAMILY HOUSING

Until the advent of Mission 66, family housing for seasonal ranger naturalists in Yellowstone was fairly primitive. Of course, Mammoth Hot Springs was the exception because that is where the permanent personnel were housed. Wood-burning stoves were used for heating and cooking (some of the fancier stoves were Majestic brand with oven and double warming ovens above the cooking surface). When electricity was available, lighting was often just a 60- or 75-watt lightbulb at the end of an electrical cord hanging from the ceiling. Indoor toilets and refrigeration were luxuries enjoyed by few, and naturalists often used residual snowbanks and ice chests for cooling perishables.

Telephone communication was the old wall-mounted crank type, consisting of a wooden box, an earpiece connected to a cord, a handle to generate an electrical signal, and an adjustable speaker piece. Station telephone numbers were a series of Morse Code longs and shorts cranked out by hand using the crank on the side of the box. When a number was rung, all the phones on the line rang, requiring that one listen carefully to each code that was rung. Later, a telephone central was able to connect the desired station directly. Simple phone lines were run to several of the remote ranger stations as well as major stations. The transmission by wire was weak enough that one had to speak loudly—at times almost shout—to be heard. There was no such thing as privacy in a phone call.

As austere as family housing was in the park in those days, it was not quite as primitive as some people apparently thought. Some visitors from the East or other countries believed that Yellowstone and even the surrounding civilian communities were still part of the old Wild West. A woman from Pennsylvania told Ruth Biddulph that when her husband was transferred by his company from Pennsylvania to Pocatello, Idaho (about 180 miles from Yellowstone), she sold all her electric appliances. The woman's comment may regrettably be a testimonial to the quality of our educational system: "Imagine," she marveled, "I've been a school teacher all my life, and never in my wildest imagination did I think that they had electricity out here."[13]

Other than Mammoth Hot Springs, which was where permanent personnel and their families were housed, Old Faithful was the first station in the park to get modern living facilities. The new apartments were ready for occupancy the summer of 1939 and had the latest conveniences, including electric heat, refrigerators, running water, indoor bathrooms, and new furniture.

The senior naturalist's quarters at Fishing Bridge was a little cottage, built in 1930, and was a miniature replica of the larger museum in rustic architecture. It also served as an office and storage for supplies. The summer of 1938, the Biddulphs and other seasonal ranger naturalists assigned to Fishing Bridge lived in four tent tops at the edge of Yellowstone Lake, approximately 100 yards east of the Fishing Bridge Museum.

Ruth Biddulph described the site:

> I cannot imagine a more beautiful place to live in for a summer than our spot on Yellowstone Lake. There were four tent tops, as I remember, in a row about fifteen yards apart. Today, they are completely obliterated, and it is hard to find the place where they were, but whenever I go there I try to visualize the exact spot. They were on a slight bluff overlooking the sandy beach, and surrounded by the forest pines and firs. One could stand in the doorway of the tent top and look out over the lake and Mount Sheridan rising up through the clouds at the south end.[14]

The floor space in these tent tops was about ten feet square. Heating and cooking were done on a small wood-burning stove, scarcely large enough to hold a kettle of water. Water was piped in, and there was a small sink, a small cupboard, and one uncomfortable bed. Additional needs were augmented with broken furniture from the Lake Hotel and Lodge that had been deposited at the old dump near Indian Pond.[15] Biddulph was a handyman and repaired what was needed. He also built a small trailer on a chassis that augmented their living space.

At night, when the moonlight glistened upon the lake, turning the sparkling quartzite sand and forest into a silver wonderland, the grizzly bears came to fish and swim. The aroma of food drew them to the tent tops. Their large humpbacked silhouettes drifted across the canvas walls, frightening Biddulph's wife and little son. Biddulph frightened them away by banging pans together and shouting at them, a technique that left a lasting impression on their son, as we shall later see.

In 1947 the Yellowstone Park Company donated to Yellowstone National Park several single-room cabins and tent frame structures that were used for seasonal housing at Canyon after World War II. Additional wood shacks built to house families of Chittenden's road crews were also used for housing at Lake. Wayne and Marian Replogle lived in a tiny cabin at Canyon for many years until new apartments were built at the edge of Cascade Meadows during Mission 66.

The six or seven structures at Lake served for many years as summer housing for temporary ranger naturalists assigned to Fishing Bridge. The one-room shanties lined a dirt service road secluded in the forest in front of the horse pasture at the foot of Elephant Back Mountain. Today, the main lower loop road just south of the East Entrance road junction runs precisely where the cabins once stood.

These shacks were made into summer abodes by the creative hands of the wives of the naturalists. The larger cabins were partitioned into two rooms using blankets or sheets stretched across a wire. The cabins were built so flimsily that they shook and trembled when strong winds blew or bears rubbed up against them. The wood floors were elevated a few inches off the dirt on log runners, and the walls were noninsulated clapboard nailed over a two-by-four frame. Three or four small square windows were adorned with homemade curtains strung on wires. Cabin doors had screens, and doors were normally left open during the warm summer afternoons to allow in a cool breeze. Horse flies and common house flies were a constant nuisance, especially around the outside latrines. A sturdy fly swatter was an essential possession.

There were no indoor bathtubs or showers in these shanties. Showers had to be taken at the Lake Lodge. Latrines were the standard "outhouses" shared by more than one cabin. Anyone with a bladder problem had to brave the cold, dark nights with a flashlight and hope that they did not run into a bear or other animal in the process. The cabins had cold water piped into a kitchen faucet, but hot water came only from kettles heated on the wood-burning stove.

Naturalists chopped their own firewood and kindling from blocks of lodgepole pine delivered in large piles near their dwellings early in the season. Mornings were bitterly cold, even in the summer months. Standing water often had a small skiff of ice by early morning, but soon melted as temperatures rose into the seventies. One crank telephone serviced all six of the cabins and was located outside, attached to a telephone pole.

Bachelors and couples without children lived in the tiny studio cabins hardly big enough for a double bed. A bachelor named Frederick Turner,

Howard Biddulph (son of L. G. Biddulph) and Pat Truman (daughter of Harry Truman) cutting wood, Old Faithful, 1939. (Courtesy of L. G. Biddulph)

affectionately named "Frog Turner" by the children of other naturalists' families, lived in one of these studios. Turner was doing postgraduate studies in biology with a specific focus on reptiles and amphibians in Yellowstone. He spent much of his off time in the marshes around the horse pastures, studying and catching western chorus frogs, salamanders, and tadpoles. He turned his studio cabin into a research lab, with dissected frogs and frog skins pinned to the walls and spread about the cabin and small refrigerator. Turner's research was published in 1955 by the Yellowstone Library and Museum Association as number 5 in its interpretive series.[16]

Bud and Betty Lystrup and their children lived in one of these flimsy cabins during the 1943 season while Lystrup was assigned there. Bears persistently came sniffing around the cabin for food and tore at the planking with their claws to gain entrance to the food pantry. So frightened was Betty by the bears that she and her children sat in the car most days.

Shortly thereafter, the family moved to the cottage next to the museum at Fishing Bridge, which was more secure and pleasant, except that it was infested with bats. They successfully drove away the bats with a broom, but not before one had bitten their daughter, Liz.[17] The Biddulphs occupied this same cottage from 1945 until 1968. Although rustic and austere by today's

The cottage at Fishing Bridge was constructed the same time as the trailside museum (1930–31) and housed the head ranger naturalist as well as an office. (Photo by the author)

standards, the cottage at Fishing Bridge was a cozy step up from the other cabins at Lake. It boasted cement floors, indoor plumbing, a bathtub, a large Majestic wood-burning stove with double warming ovens, and a small refrigerator. Best of all, the cottage had a commanding view of beautiful Lake Yellowstone.

In reviewing park history, one is struck by the number of structures that burned down in the early days, some, like the hotel at Norris, multiple times. The little cottage at Fishing Bridge nearly suffered the same fate in the late 1950s. Biddulph had been out fishing with his children on Yellowstone Lake while his wife, Ruth, remained at home reading and preparing dinner. Upon his return, Lowell found Ruth standing in a smoke-filled kitchen, cooking over the hot wood-burning stove. His comment about the excessive smoke initially provoked some ire from his wife, but it was quickly discovered that the smoke pipe from the stove was burning the wall on the other side of the kitchen. Fortunately, the wall was constructed of flame-retardant material that prevented an outright flame, but it would have been but a few minutes before the roof had burst into flame. Biddulph was able to extinguish the fire by running a hose down the chimney before more damage was done.

The incident became a humorous if not exaggerated story among the naturalists at Fishing Bridge of Biddulph's unflappability. While his older son was pouring water down the chimney, Biddulph went next door to the museum to call the fire department at Lake Station. Joseph Catmull was on desk duty at the museum when Biddulph entered. "Hi, Joe," Biddulph greeted him as he walked in. "Need to borrow the phone." Biddulph cranked out the number and waited. "Hello, Charlie? This is Lowell Biddulph at Fishing Bridge. Yes, I'm fine. How are you?" Charlie was the fire marshal at Lake. "Beautiful day today," Biddulph agreed. There was another pause while Joe Catmull listened to what he assumed was Charlie's small talk. "Say Charlie, do you think you could send over the fire truck to our place." Another pause. "Well, we seem to have a bit of a fire in the cottage." Joe Catmull's brown eyes got wide and round. Was it possible that he had just listened to an emergency fire call? His cottage was burning down and he was exchanging pleasantries? Biddulph said goodbye and hung up the receiver on the side of the brown box. "Thanks, Joe, for the use of the phone. I guess I'd better get back and see what I can do." And with that he walked out of the museum leaving Joe with his mouth agape. The fire was put out without considerable damage before the fire truck arrived from Lake, but the siren of the truck brought a crowd of inquisitive tourists, and for years afterward, Joe Catmull shed tears of laughter whenever he told the story of Biddulph's call for help.

THE WOOD TICK INCIDENT

Summer nights in Yellowstone could get bitter. Once the fires were out and one snuggled into warm flannel sheets under heavy wool blankets, only a dire emergency could coax him or her out into the bitter night air.

One cold night Biddulph was awakened by an urgent nudge from his wife.

"Lowell! Lowell! There's a wood tick in the bed!"

"A wood tick?" Biddulph asked in a sleepy voice as he peered disbelievingly from the warmth of the woolen blankets.

"Yes!" she replied, her voice rising with increasing urgency. She was now sitting upright in the bed. "It was a wood tick. I felt it crawling on me, and I brushed it off and it fell down inside the covers. Turn on the light! Quick, Lowell!" Ruth was becoming more animated as she vainly tried to see in the inky blackness.

Lowell moaned and then slowly crawled out of the warm bed into the cold night air and groped for the lightbulb suspended in the middle of the room.

"Calm down, Ruth. Now where did you see the wood tick?" His eyes strained to adjust to the stark brightness of the unshaded light.

"Well, it was right here, and I brushed it like this." She demonstrated with a quick sweep of her hand. "And it fell right down here." She jabbed into the thick wool covers with her finger. Then, realizing the close proximity of the wood tick to her own person, she leaped out of bed and searched her night clothes for the tiny, flat tick.

On hands and knees, Biddulph pulled each cover off and carefully searched for the elusive wood tick. It was not until he had stripped the bed to the mattress that Ruth spoke again, the once urgent tone in her voice now replaced with bewilderment.

"Lowell, how do you suppose I saw that wood tick in the darkness?"

There was only silence as Biddulph, frozen on the bed in a posture of search, tried to comprehend the significance of his wife's question.

"Could I have been dreaming?" she wondered aloud.

A gag of exasperation escaped Biddulph's lips, and without further comment he doused the light and flung himself back into bed, not bothering to straighten the covers, leaving his wife standing in the darkness to ponder.

"I couldn't have really seen that wood tick in the darkness—could I?" she asked herself. "I'm sure it was just a dream." Satisfied with her conclusion, she crawled over her husband and back into bed and was soon in peaceful slumber.[18]

HONEYMOON AT MADISON JUNCTION

Marian Churchill Replogle came to Yellowstone the first time in the summer of 1937, soon after her marriage to Wayne Replogle. Marian was born in Joliet, Illinois, and grew up in a privileged and refined home, much different from the rugged, almost primitive environment of the park that awaited her. This first summer was Wayne and Marian's first real honeymoon together. Wayne came early in the summer, and Marian remained in Illinois until early July to finish up her organ studies.

Meanwhile, Replogle had been scrounging out an existence in a small cabin at Madison Junction where he had been assigned for that summer. He had been doing his own cooking; he had lost some weight, and his stomach's holding capacity had diminished considerably. Enter Marian. The first night of her arrival, she decided to favor her husband with some hot biscuits. They were so very good by comparison to what Replogle had been eating that he overdosed. Feeling rather nauseous and afraid that he was about to throw it all up in her presence and deeply offend her, he excused himself by fabricating a reason for his exodus and went out and lay down under a tree, certain that he was about to die.

However, after relieving himself of the biscuits, he felt somewhat better, and after regaining his strength, he wandered back into the cabin and, of course, lied to his bride, saying that he had been up to the auto camp and had met some friends who wanted some information. Years later, in looking back on the summer of 1937 and the little honeymoon cabin at Madison Junction, he remembered it as a wonderful and beautiful place—with the exception of the first night.[19]

Sam and Bessy Beal lived in the ranger's quarters at Madison Junction, beginning in 1941. Beal described the cottage:

> A nice cottage was built several rods behind the museum, and from that point, the campground extended eastward for several hundred yards. Facilities for a small crew of road maintenance men were hidden among the trees near the forks of the river. We discovered that living in a lone ranger's cabin on the edge of a campground was something else again. The Park Service provided a woodpile, but the ranger had to split stove-length logs. Campers had adequate rest rooms, and the Gibbon River was convenient for bathing purposes. The ranger's quarters had a bathroom. We had a telephone for government business. There was no electricity at Madison until 1960. We brought an icebox from home and purchased ice.[20]

Wayne and Marian occupied a small cabin at Canyon from 1940 until 1959 when new apartments were built at the edge of Cascade Meadows. This old cabin was actually two abandoned visitors' cabins connected together. One cabin was too small to accommodate a naturalist and his family, but two of the cabins, connected, provided a reasonable two-room dwelling that they fixed up cozy each season. Replogle arranged with the manager of the Canyon Hotel to save the cracked dishes and cups, and he stocked his and other ranger cabins with these dishes, which he called "buffaloware."

Bob and Arlene Jonas were assigned to Canyon in the 1950s. Similar to Marian, Arlene arrived at Canyon three days after her marriage to Bob. She knew no one and had not the first clue about "living in the wilderness." Marian became Arlene's special friend. She took her under her wing and showed her how to do things and how to make the most out of an austere environment. She introduced her to the other wives of the ranger naturalists and helped everyone feel like family.[21]

Despite the austere living style, morale and camaraderie at Canyon were good during the years that Wayne and Marian served there. The Replogles frequently held campfire social gatherings at their cabin where all the naturalists and their families joined together in activities. Jonas described Wayne Replogle as "a real character." Both he and Marian had a penchant for pulling practical jokes on other naturalists and each other. Such was the time that Replogle and another ranger placed a dead black bear in a sleeping posture under the Jonases' trailer. Upon returning home, Jonas was rather surprised to find a bear sleeping under his trailer. He tried unsuccessfully to awaken and chase it away, even throwing a firecracker at it. It was then that he heard the giggles of Replogle and another ranger coming from behind a nearby tree, and he knew that he had been duped.[22]

Replogle was a complex man. He possessed a relaxed temperament. He was often jovial and easily made fun of himself. But his leadership style could also be aggressive, and he left no doubt in his men's minds that he was in charge. An incident arose during the 1950s when Replogle had some disagreements with the other naturalists who served at Canyon. Jonas could not remember the details of the disagreement, but it had to do with local procedures regarding interpretation that Replogle enforced with which the others took exception. Replogle apparently breathed out some threatening words to his men that caused them to fear that he would not recommend them to the chief park naturalist for rehire the following summer.

The truth of the matter was that Replogle was not really in charge at all. Marian was. Marian found out about the disagreement through the wives, and knowing Wayne's feelings, she demanded to review all of his evaluations made on the naturalists at Canyon for that summer before he submitted them to headquarters. Marian was not to be trifled with, and all of the men were "recommended" for rehire the following year. It would not have been beyond Marian's temperament to tell Wayne that if he did not recommend her friends' husbands for rehire, he would be enjoying his own cooking again the next summer. The women of the naturalists were a tight group.[23]

PART TWO

Protecting Yellowstone

To understand nature is one of the greatest resources of life.

—John Burroughs, "Leaf and Tendril" (1908)

Chapter 6
Black Alice and Prohibition

PROHIBITION AND THE VOLSTEAD ACT

The Eighteenth Amendment to the Constitution was passed in December 1917, specifically prohibiting the production, sale, and transportation of intoxicating substances within the United States. The Eighteenth Amendment paved the way for the National Prohibition Act, known as the Volstead Act, which was passed by Congress over presidential veto on October 28, 1919. The act established a legal definition of intoxicating liquor and required enforcement by law.

Despite legislation in faraway Washington, DC, alcohol was not swept out the door but under the rug, or, more accurately, underground, to the black market. The illegal production and distribution of alcohol appear to have been at the very doorstep of Yellowstone. The park was surrounded by western communities in Idaho, Montana, and Wyoming that were known for their rough-and-tumble environments with a deeply ingrained Old West saloon culture.

Helena, Butte, Bozeman, Gardiner, Red Lodge, Cody, Ennis, and Riverside were just a few of these enclaves of western culture, and all were in close proximity to one of the park's entrances. Butte was known for its hundreds of saloons. Red Lodge, just outside the Northeast Entrance to the park, grew up around coal mines and was known for a violent history, some of which assuredly related to alcohol consumption. With the Great Depression, several mines closed, and many people turned to bootlegging to survive.[1]

Prior to becoming a township, the area just outside the West Entrance of Yellowstone Park was known by various names, such as West End, Boundary, and Yellowstone. At the time the Union Pacific built a railroad line to the West Entrance of Yellowstone Park, it was known by the name of "Terminus." The town was officially settled about 1907–8 and named "Riverside" because of its proximity to the Madison River. By 1920 the town's official name became "West Yellowstone." However, the name of Riverside continued to be used for several years thereafter.

One source reports that illegal liquor, disguised as "Yellowstone Spring Water," was manufactured and bootlegged at Riverside for a time. According to the source, bushels of feed corn entered into West, while kegs of Yellowstone "Spring Water" departed for speakeasies across the nation.[2]

Speakeasy was the name for black-market establishments that bootlegged alcohol to customers. The name came from the manner of ordering alcohol without raising suspicion about the illegal activity that was going on. A bartender might tell a patron to "speak easy," or quietly, when purchasing the forbidden substance. A speakeasy was typically a higher-class establishment, whereas the lower-class dives garnered a less flattering name of "blind pig" and "gin joint."

ATTEMPTS TO ENFORCE THE ACT

The Volstead Act provided for only fifteen hundred congressionally allocated federal Prohibition agents to enforce the law nationwide. Such a small number of agents to enforce such an unpopular law throughout the entire United States precluded meaningful enforcement in federal preserves such as Yellowstone National Park. Apprehension and conviction of small-time bootleggers were simply not cost-effective. Agents focused primarily on much bigger fish in Chicago, New York City, Los Angeles, and other metropolitan areas.

Complete enforcement proved futile during the Roaring Twenties, although gangsters such as Al Capone were eventually jailed on racketeering charges. Speakeasies became popular and increasingly connected to organized crime. Corruption was rampant, and although police and the Federal Prohibition Agency raided establishments and arrested owners and patrons, bootlegging was a lucrative-enough business that they continued to thrive. Often, police and federal agents were bribed to overlook the establishment or at least give advance notice of their raids.

Of course, Yellowstone Park was not exempt from enforcing the Prohibition Act. Concessionaires were required to cease all sales of liquor and other alcoholic beverages within the park. The obligation to enforce the Volstead

Roosevelt Arch was designed and built by Hiram Chittenden and Robert Reamer as the grand northern entrance to the park. It was dedicated on April 24, 1903, by President Theodore Roosevelt. (Photo by Cogswell; courtesy of the National Park Service, Yellowstone National Park, YELL 28796-3n[1])

Act fell upon the park rangers, and the five entrance gates to Yellowstone were key control points of enforcement. Park rangers who served at the gates were required to inform the public of the law and to enforce it through inspection, confiscation, and prosecution when necessary.

A newspaper article appearing in the *Milwaukee Journal* dated August 23, 1930, noted, "Bootleggers are finding it extremely dangerous and highly unprofitable to attempt to ply their trade in Yellowstone National Park."[3] The reason given was the vigilance of rangers and their unceasing drive on lawlessness. Chief Ranger George Baggley noted that bootleggers received no sympathy from rangers; in fact, they would be treated fairly roughly.

Be that as it may, the system of enforcement at park entry gates had weaknesses that provided opportunity and temptation for those inclined to break the law, especially when a profit could be made. The park had insufficient staff for the task of border patrol. The one or two rangers at each entrance made it virtually impossible to interdict smuggling of alcohol through vehicle inspection, especially during high-traffic times. Weekends saw the heaviest traffic, especially Friday afternoons, when people were anxious to get into the park and find appropriate accommodations or camping sites before the onset of darkness. Mornings and evenings were the busiest times of the day at the entrances.

Another weakness was the lack of police training. Most if not all rangers assigned to gate duty were not trained to be policemen or border patrolmen, especially when dealing with potential criminal activity such as bootlegging. Yet another weakness was the lack of communications and ready transportation. In 1930 entry guards had few if any vehicles to pursue a would-be violator and poor communications with which to garner backup. They could not leave their post to chase after someone and, fortunately for everyone, had no means of applying deadly force. Thus, anyone scheming to escape the ranger(s) at the entry gates without detection could easily determine how best to exploit these weaknesses for their own benefit. That is precisely what happened the summer of 1930.

BLACK ALICE IN YELLOWSTONE

An employee of the Yellowstone Park Company, aided by his wife, decided that the profits were worth the risk and in 1930 began a bootlegging operation at Canyon, where he worked during summer months. His wife, who resided in Livingston, Montana, acted as his supplier, making weekly trips into the park in her car to deliver the liquor. For some time park rangers suspected the couple of running a bootlegging operation, but it was only suspicion, as no one had been able to catch them in the act or bring any substantial proof of their breaking the law.

Black Alice, as she was nicknamed by the rangers, was particularly adept at exploiting the weaknesses at the entry gates. She apparently had some type of seasonal pass through her husband's employment in the park and was apparently well enough known, even regarded, by the rangers on duty that she handled herself with some entitlement. She made her approach only on Friday afternoons, when the lineup of cars was extensive and the entry rangers were busiest. Then, pulling out of line, she bypassed other cars ahead of

Lowell Biddulph in 1930. (Courtesy of L. G. Biddulph)

her and, with the toot of her horn and a friendly wave, swished through the entry gate as if she owned the place.

It seems reasonable that if the apprehension of Black Alice and her husband had been a serious priority for park administrators, surely they could have found a way to get the job done, especially considering Chief Baggley's description of his men's unceasing drive on lawlessness and Black Alice's predictable routine of entering and exiting the park. Whatever the reason, Black Alice had her way with the rangers in Yellowstone. By midsummer of 1930, someone at park headquarters, most likely Chief Baggley, decided to deal with Black Alice once and for all, and the directive came down in no uncertain terms: STOP BLACK ALICE.

In early August 1930, Lowell Biddulph was transferred from the Dunraven Pass checking station to the North Entrance for the purpose of beefing up the ranger force there. Biddulph left his beloved high-mountain post and took up living at the ranger quarters at Gardiner, Montana. The rather bland scenery of Gardiner was not a welcome change for Biddulph from the spectacular wilderness vistas of Mount Washburn.

One Friday afternoon while Biddulph was on gate duty, Black Alice made her usual end run around the gate, tooting her horn and waving affably, as she accelerated up the road toward Mammoth. Determined to accomplish the assigned mission, Biddulph left another ranger to control the gate, and he commandeered the next motorist, ordering him to "follow that car!" The startled driver gave chase, with Biddulph standing on the running board of the car while clinging to the side of the vehicle with one hand and holding on to his broad-brimmed Stetson hat with the other.

Somewhere up the Gardner River Canyon road before reaching Mammoth Hot Springs, Biddulph and the motorist overtook Black Alice and pulled her over. Biddulph approached and asked her to turn around and follow him back to the entrance gate. Black Alice feigned innocence and surprise. She demurely protested that she was visiting her husband at Canyon and that delays would prevent her arrival before the roads were closed. Biddulph apologized for any inconvenience but insisted that she return with him.

Alice complained that she had always been allowed to bypass the check-in procedure and that she was well known and respected among park personnel. Biddulph doggedly insisted that she return to the gate, at which point Alice turned dark, accusing him of "being new around these parts" and "out of touch with her privileges."

Biddulph prevailed, and Black Alice disgustedly returned to the gate. Her car was searched, and several bottles of liquor were discovered concealed in her personal effects. Alice was summarily arrested, and she and her husband were turned over to the judge at Gardiner, thus quietly ending the days of Black Alice and *Thunder Road* in Yellowstone Park.[4]

As a warning to others, the newspaper article of August 23, 1930, noted that within one week, four people had been charged with bootlegging in Yellowstone; two were in jail, and two more were mandated over to federal court. Although names were not mentioned, it is assumed that Black Alice and her husband were among the felons. Three years later, Prohibition died under the Twenty-First Amendment.

Chapter 7

Patrolling Yellowstone's Highways

THE CONCEPTION OF A ROAD SYSTEM

For the first few decades of its existence, Yellowstone Park remained obscure and inaccessible to the public. Not only was the park difficult to get to, sequestered as it was in the rugged Rocky Mountains, but even if people could find their way to its boundaries, there were but rough trails and virtually no accommodations for travel within the park. Yellowstone's obscurity was its salvation. If it had been easily accessible to the public while unprotected by regulations and proper staff to enforce them, Yellowstone's priceless wonders would have surely been irreparably wrecked.

Soon after the park's creation, counterforces of development and protection began to compete. The matchless wonders begged to be discovered and enjoyed by an eager citizenry. At the same time, conservationists petitioned for caution and preservation. Money for development of Yellowstone Park was slow in coming. Park Superintendent Nathaniel P. Langford lobbied Congress for funds to build roads and other accommodations with little or no success.

As early as 1873, individuals operated a primitive pack-and-saddle business out of Mammoth Hot Springs into the park. Even before that, Jack Baronett, the Yellowstone scout who became famous for rescuing Truman Everts from his thirty-seven days of peril, operated a toll bridge near Tower Fall to capture business from hunters and gold miners coming from Cooke City and Red Lodge mines.

In 1873 Gilman Sawtell built a road from Virginia City to the Lower Geyser Basin by way of Madison River, and a toll road was built from

Stagecoaches carrying tourists, called "dudes," and private campers, called "sagebrushers," pass along an old park road, ca. 1900. (Courtesy of L. G. Biddulph)

Bozeman, Montana, to Mammoth the same year. Nevertheless, the interior parts of the park remained inaccessible to all except those willing to travel by horseback or on foot. Superintendent Philetus W. Norris probed the park's interior between 1877 and 1882 and built a road from Mammoth to the Lower Geyser Basin. Norris's roads opened up a stage business between Mammoth and the Marshall Hotel located at the confluence of the Firehole River and Nez Perce Creek.

Nevertheless, it was not until the army came into the park that notable headway was made in building a road system. Army personnel helped in creating park roads, but Lieutenant Dan Kingman and Captain Hiram Chittenden claim the honor of being the principal architects. Hiram Chittenden, the man most credited with designing and completing the road system in the park, foresaw the future challenges roads would bring to Yellowstone, and he cautioned: "While it is true that highways are least objectionable of all forms of artificial changes in natural conditions, still they should not be unnecessarily extended, and the great body of the Park should be kept inaccessible except on foot or horseback."[1] By 1918, when the army left Yellowstone, all entrances and important sites along the Grand Loop were accessible by road.

In keeping with Chittenden's idea of limited accessibility, Chief Ranger Sam T. Woodring and others planned and laid out a 157-mile trail system through Yellowstone Park.[2] The trail was named the Howard Eaton Trail in honor of the celebrated horseman and trail guide who conducted approximately one hundred horseback parties through the park. The trail was mostly veiled from public byways and intersected it at major points of interest. The National Park Service dedicated the Howard Eaton Trail in a ceremony at Sheepeater Cliff on June 19, 1923.[3]

THE INFLUENCE OF RAILROADS

The railroads wielded significant influence on the development of hotels and the road system in Yellowstone. In the 1880s, railroads were advertising Yellowstone as a wonderland and bringing tourists to the boundaries of the park. Those coming by rail were predominantly wealthy folk who were accustomed to luxury and fine food. Most of them found the early condition of the roads and eating and sleeping accommodations in Yellowstone appalling, thus inspiring the construction of large hotels and lodges at Mammoth, Canyon, Lake, and Old Faithful.

The first terminal specifically built for tourists coming to Yellowstone Park was completed in 1883 by the Northern Pacific Railroad (NPRR) in a sagebrush-covered valley along the Yellowstone River, a few miles from the park's Northern Entrance. Cinnabar, Montana, as it was named, became a bustling hamlet of about one hundred souls whose sole industry was to cater to Yellowstone's tourist trade. Tourists disembarked the train at Cinnabar and boarded stagecoaches that ferried them to the hotel at Mammoth Hot Springs. In 1903 the tracks were extended to Gardiner, Montana, and Cinnabar rather quickly became a ghost town. In this same time frame, Burlington Railway ran a line to Cody, Wyoming, fifty miles outside the East Entrance, and the Union Pacific built a line to Monida, Montana, and eventually to "Terminus," later known as Riverside and West Yellowstone.

Although hotels and sleeping accommodations were certainly important, transportation of tourists was clearly the more financially lucrative of the two concessions, and competition swirled for a time around this hot spot of tourism in Yellowstone. The realization of the potential did not waste itself upon the leaders of the NPRR, who used their money and political clout to gain license and to subsidize various hotel and transportation concessionaires in Yellowstone.

The major concessionaires operating accommodations and transportation services in Yellowstone Park during the three decades between 1883 and 1916 included Frank Jay Haynes[4] (known as F. Jay), the Yellowstone Park

Stagecoaches transported early tourists about Yellowstone until the automobile was allowed entry in 1915. (Photographer unknown; courtesy of L. G. Biddulph)

Transportation Company (YPTC), the Wiley Permanent Camping Company, and the Powell and Shaw Camping Company. There were others, but they were mostly gobbled up by the larger concerns.

Competition was stiff, and certain individuals, such as Harry Childs, sought to completely monopolize the transportation and hotel business in Yellowstone. He eventually nearly succeeded in his quest, being elected president of the Yellowstone Park Association in 1901, which later became the Yellowstone Park Transportation Company.[5]

Until the advent of the automobile in Yellowstone, the "carriage trade" was the only mode of travel through the park with the exception of about three parties of bicyclers. Visitors were ferried in various types of stagecoaches and tallyho wagons from the train depots to the hotels and lodges inside the park. By 1911 hotels had been built to accommodate these wealthy folks, including at Mammoth, Canyon, Lake, and the Firehole Geyser Basins. Guests were given the grand tour around the park in an assortment of horse-drawn carriages. These included: 6 six-horse Concord coaches, 29 six-horse tallyho coaches, 165 four-horse Concord coaches, 79 two-horse surreys, 14 formation wagons, 129 mountain spring wagons, and a total of nearly fourteen hundred horses.[6]

Tallyho coaches, built by Abbot-Downing Company of Concord, New Hampshire, were large, open-sided coaches designed to transport large numbers of people. The interior seats looked forward, and seats were also placed on top of the coach with a "boot" in the back for luggage. Lest the reader become naively enamored by the intrigue of traveling through early Yellowstone by stagecoach, let it be remembered that the roads were bumpy and dusty; the passengers were exposed to horseflies, bugs, and uncomfortable temperatures; and natural odors offended delicate eastern noses.

To provide respite from these arduous traveling conditions, the Yellowstone Park Association operated eating establishments at various locations along the Grand Loop. These tent palaces offered lunch breaks to tourists and were managed for several years by an entertaining Irishman named Lawrence Francis Matthews; hence, they became known as "Larry's Lunch Stations." The lunch stations were really nothing more than a canvas rip-off with long tables, wooden benches, and a meager but exorbitantly priced meal. However, Matthews's Irish wit and charm helped to dispel, at least for the brief time visitors were at his station, the weariness, weather, and overpriced food.

Lunch stations were located at Trout Creek in the Hayden Valley, then West Thumb with the completion of the Grand Loop road between Old Faithful and Lake, and later at Norris Geyser Basin when the hotel there burned two different times.

THE AUTOMOBILE CHANGES EVERYTHING

In his final report to the chief engineer upon his departure from Yellowstone, Hiram Chittenden noted that all proposed roads had been built and that the sprinkling system had adequately resolved the dust problem. Chittenden felt that the road system existing at that time was adequate in spite of the increased volume of traffic to the park, but he warned that if traffic continued to increase at the same rate that it had in the past, the road system would need to be rethought.[7] The advent of the automobile into Yellowstone only ten years later changed everything. Not only did it mark the end of lunch stations and the exclusivity enjoyed by the wealthy, but it also forced modifications to the park's road system.

The first private automobiles were allowed into the park on August 1, 1915. Actually, the superintendent issued seven permits the day prior, but August 1 was the official opening day for cars. Rough dirt roads, passable for horse-drawn stage, proved challenging for the more fickle automobile. Gradient as well as surfaces had to be dealt with. High passes, such as Dunraven

Pass, caused problems for cars, although Replogle noted that the Model A cars were better at handling steep grades than the later high-powered engines. Drivers carried water bags on the front of their vehicles to refill the carburetors that steamed like hot springs and spouted like geysers during steep ascents. The little spring at the summit of Dunraven Pass was a popular place because the water bags were bone dry by the time these cars reached the pass.

Early cars used gravity-feed and air-pressure systems for moving gas from the tank to the carburetor. Yellowstone's rather harsh gradients (in places) created significant challenges for these types of cars. After the 1920s, when the first cam-operated fuel pump was invented, cars had to have hand air pumps near the driver for pumping gas to the engine when the automatic one failed, which it often did. George Marler and his father abandoned a fishing trip in the park because their car engine kept dying from lack of gas getting to the carburetor.

Cars entering the park were required to be in good mechanical condition and pass an inspection before being allowed to enter because there were no repair services within the park. Once inside Yellowstone, drivers were left to their own luck, and more than one vehicle was pulled out of the park with a good set of mules. It was also difficult to slow or brake a vehicle when descending a steep grade because early cars used mechanical brakes instead of modern power antilock brakes. Brake pads quickly wore out on steep grades, prompting some folks to chain logs or other heavy objects to the back of their cars to serve as a drag and help preserve the brakes on steep downgrades.[8]

For a period of time, the roads of Yellowstone were shared by both automobile and horse-drawn carriages. The narrow wheels of the carriages grooved the sometimes wet and muddy roads into deep ruts that made travel by automobile untenable. Conversely, the wider tires on larger trucks helped flatten the ruts. To accommodate both modes of travel, some regulations had to be put in place for the automobiles:

- all automobiles entering the park had to be in good mechanical working condition
- cars had to sound their Claxton horns at all blind curves
- cars could not exceed 12 miles per hour when ascending an incline and 10 mph when descending
- when approaching sharp curves, cars were not to exceed 8 mph
- cars were never to exceed 20 mph at any time under any condition

Speed was monitored by measuring the time it took a vehicle to go between checking stations. If a tourist arrived at the next checking station too quickly, he was suspect of speeding. The Grand Loop road through Yellowstone was one-way for several years. The road between Canyon and Tower Fall was one-way until about 1937, and night travel was not allowed. At 6:00 p.m. the rangers placed a log across the road, blocking travel up the mountainside to Dunraven Pass. The last driver allowed in before the log was put in place checked in at the Dunraven Checking Station, and if it was not too late in the evening, the driver was allowed to continue on down to Tower Fall, where he also checked in. If it was too late in the evening, the driver stayed overnight at a small auto roadside camp at Dunraven Pass across from the checking station. In the morning, about seven o'clock, the rangers removed the log and opened the road to traffic. Replogle noted, "About 1932 or 1933, along in there, they began to try to be a little more open about traveling in Yellowstone. So, by that time you didn't have to tell someone you were going to Tower; you just [went]...and if you didn't get there that was your tough luck."[9]

IMPROVING YELLOWSTONE'S ROADS

The roads in Yellowstone were narrow, poorly surfaced, and followed closely the topography of the land. Sharp curves, abrupt hills, and blind spots were frequent. By the time the first of the Five Old Men began working in the park (1928) there were only about four or five miles of true asphalt road, mostly on the west side of the park through Elk Park and Gibbon Meadows. The rest of the roads were graveled, with some light oil spread on top to settle the dust, a process called "dust coating."

The period from 1926 to 1939 was the most significant period of road development in Yellowstone Park. In 1924 the park administration upgraded telephone poles and cleaned up the roads and roadside areas. In the 1930s, roads and bridges were improved. By the end of 1939, the old days of mud holes and dust had been mostly eliminated, and most of the Grand Loop had been covered with a bituminous surface (a tarlike substance found naturally in asphalt). All but one hundred miles of road had been improved to some degree. In the 1940s and '50s, the oiling of roads was continued in addition to improving general safety and parking.[10]

The introduction of private motorized vehicles in Yellowstone also impacted the public conveyance system. In 1916 Frank J. Haynes introduced the first motorized coaches, used by the Cody-Sylvan Pass Motor Company. However, in 1916, NPS director Stephen Tyng Mather forced a merger among

The motorized bus (made by White Motor Company), operated by the
Yellowstone Park Transportation Company, began service in 1916. This bus
overlooks Grand Canyon, 1930s. (Photo by Frank J. Haynes; courtesy of the
National Park Service, Yellowstone National Park, YELL 96222)

concessionaires and gave all rights for transportation within the park to Harry
Childs and the Yellowstone Park Transportation Company with the additional
mandate that within a year they would convert from horse-drawn carriages to
motorized buses. All other transportation concessionaires had to give up their
licenses. Subsequently, the YPTC contracted with the White Motor Company
for the acquisition of 116 motorized buses for touring Yellowstone.

The concessionaires were required to get rid of their huge inventory of
coaches, stock, and tack. By 1936, 27 fourteen-passenger yellow motor buses
(model 706, six-cylinder) were in use in the park. Three years later, a total of
98 of these buses were in use.[11] As noted earlier, park employees were not
allowed to keep personal vehicles in Yellowstone until around 1937.

PATROLLING YELLOWSTONE'S ROADWAYS

The automobile presented new challenges to safety. Roads became more
congested, and tourists often drove faster than the conditions of the road
allowed, resulting in accidents, injuries, and even deaths. Rather quickly,
the park ranger was pressed into service as a highway patrolman in addition
to other protective functions.

In 1919 the Park Service invested in six Harley-Davidson motorcycles for patrolling park highways. "National Park Ranger" was embossed across the crossbar of the bike, and a serial number with NPS was stamped on the front mudguard. The ranger assigned to highway patrol generally wore a leather coat, gloves, heavy pants, knee-high laced boots, goggles, and a ranger hat or, in cold weather, a leather cap with ear flaps.

Riding motorcycle patrol in the park was dangerous. The motorcycles typically had no windshield to protect the ranger from bugs, birds, and other flying objects. Careless drivers coupled with rough road conditions put more than one motorcycle patrolman on the injured list. In 1929, while Biddulph was serving at Fishing Bridge, a ranger known only as "Ranger Ross" rode motorcycle patrol in the Lake area. Ross claimed to be the sparring partner for Jack Dempsey when he was world heavyweight boxing champion. Ross was confined to desk duty later that summer after breaking his arm when he was run off the road by a motorist, an injury the likes of which he never sustained as a boxer.

Wayne Replogle served as a motorcycle patrolman throughout Yellowstone, beginning in 1931 and continuing for three or four summers. At the beginning of the 1932 season, Replogle retrieved the old Harley-Davidson from winter storage at Tower Fall but had difficulty starting it. He finally had to enlist the help of a fellow ranger named Ted to jump-start the bike.

Ted had access to an old Ford vehicle to which the two men attached a rope and towed the motorcycle up to where the petrified tree stands. Here they turned around, and Ted yelled, "Are you ready?" Replogle yelled back, "Yeah!" Ted took off down the hill in the pickup like a rocket, pulling the Harley with Replogle clinging to the handlebars. Eventually, Replogle had the presence of mind to pop the clutch and give it some gas, and the Harley's motor rumbled to life.[12]

Once the bike was running and the rope untied, Replogle took it for a test run out along the Northeast Entrance road. In 1932 the road to Cooke City, Montana, was still a graded dirt road for approximately fifteen miles from the Roosevelt junction to the old buffalo ranch (now the Yellowstone Institute) in the Lamar Valley. The remainder of the road from the ranch to Soda Butte and beyond was what Replogle described as "two tracks that the wagons made."[13]

Wayne Replogle was on patrol one day in 1932 on the road between Mammoth and Tower Fall when he encountered an unexpected flying object. The main road at the time, now called the Blacktail Plateau Drive, wound its way up from the Yellowstone Valley across the Blacktail Plateau. Replogle explained how the UFO dethroned him:

> It was a very narrow section of the road and I was riding motorcycle patrol...and I was riding along around a very sharp curve here in a very narrow space [when] a raven flew out of these trees at just the level of my shoulders and hit me right in the chest, and I fell off the motorcycle. I didn't get hurt except it skinned me up a little. Dale Nuss's father [Dale later worked with Replogle at Canyon for several years] was visiting from Oklahoma and was about 100 yards behind me, and he saw this happen. By the time I got unwound from the motorcycle, he was standing beside me asking me if I was hurt. He laughed very hard and said, "Well, if it had killed you I would still have to laugh because all I could see flying was raven feathers and your arms and legs."[14]

Later in 1932 a motorcycle patrolman was injured at Old Faithful, resulting in Replogle's transfer there from Tower Fall. After completing preliminary morning tasks, Replogle rode from Old Faithful to Madison Junction, where he stopped at the government mess hall to flirt with the woman cook, at whom, in Replogle jargon, he enjoyed "taking a good squint." She must have enjoyed being squinted at because she always had a piece of pie and a cup of coffee waiting for him. From Madison Junction, Replogle rode to the West Gate, then to Norris Geyser Basin, and back to Old Faithful.

Although his primary duty was a highway patrolman, Replogle had other duties, which included hoisting the flag at the museum, checking campgrounds, and scouting the geyser basins and adjacent forests in the evenings for sagebrushers camping illegally and couples who often parked down in the bushes.

One evening, as he made his rounds in the geyser basin, Replogle noticed a car parked about one hundred feet off the road behind some trees. Replogle dismounted his motorcycle and walked over to ask the owner to move his car back onto the road.

> When I got there it was Bud Lystrup, off-duty naturalist...Bud and (Betty) were back there talking, I guess, and he got out and said, "Now, Rep, we've got to work out an arrangement here. When you make your evening patrols down here, I'll be parked back here with Betty and we'll be rotten-logging a bit, and if you see the car why you beep

Bud Lystrup and Betty Pontliana share ice cream on the
steps of Hamilton Store in Lower Geyser Basin, ca. 1932.
(Courtesy of Liz Lystrup)

at me twice with your motorcycle beeper and if I answer twice with the
car horn you know it is I, so please let us stay back there." So, I made a
deal with Bud...and I let Bud and Betty continue their love tryst right
there, and it must have worked out pretty well because Betty and Bud
were married that winter and they raised two fine kids.[15]

The term *rotten logging*[16] was a euphemism commonly used among early
park employees of this era to mean some form of romantic intimacy. Syn-
onyms of the same era are *sparking, spooning,* and *pitching the woo.*[17] Contemporary terminology would include *making out.* This colorful term presents an
image to the mind of the reader of a young couple sitting on a rotting log
somewhere in the seclusion of a forest in the moonlight engaged in some
form of intimacy.

Replogle did some of his own rotten logging. He had an eye for the girls
working at Old Faithful. The girls lived in a dormitory and had a curfew that

mandated the doors be locked by a certain time each night. Any girl not inside at the time of lockup slept elsewhere, unless she had other special arrangements, and she would have some accounting to do if she did.

One night Replogle got his date back after curfew and found the door locked. The girl's room was on the first floor, and she had left the window to her room unlocked, probably anticipating such an event. They determined to sneak the girl back into the dormitory through her bedroom window. It was a sound plan except for one unanticipated occurrence. In the middle of the struggle to get the girl through the window, an on-duty ranger came around the corner of the dormitory and saw the two in the process of entry. Of course, he shouted at the two and came toward them on the run. Fear quickly became the better part of valor, and Replogle bolted, leaving his date hanging half in and half out of the window with her legs flailing. Replogle sprinted around the building and back to the station, and that is all we know of the story.

As a side note, several other slang expressions besides *rotten logging* came into use during the early days of Yellowstone that provide a unique insight into that era. The tough, rowdy breed of stagecoach driver who always had a wild tale to tell in the most colorful of language was a "savage." On the other hand, the wealthy tourists who came by rail and traveled about the park in stage coaches and slept in the fancy hotels were called "dudes" by the savages. More common folk, who drove their own rigs through the park and camped out instead of staying in the expensive hotels, were called "sagebrushers" by the dudes and the savages. A "dude heaver" was a waiter in one of the hotel restaurants. A "biffy queen" cleaned the hotel and cabin rooms and changed the bedding. Many more nicknames are attributable to this age of Yellowstone, and, not surprisingly, some are still in use today.

THE REPROBATE AND THE SCALAWAG

The enforcement of speed limits was the role of the motorcycle patrolman. One day at Norris, Replogle apprehended a speeder who was going 60 miles per hour in a 12 mph zone. It turned out to be a woman named Mrs. Allen with whom he had talked frequently by telephone but had never personally met. Mrs. Allen was the "central" for the telephone company at Mammoth. When someone wanted a connection to a number, they cranked the handle, and the central operator answered and connected them. Replogle's description of Mrs. Allen fits the prototypical personality so often ascribed to central operators of the era: "[She was]...a large red haired lady, a fiery redhead. She was just a marvelous person who laughed and screamed all of the time. Just every day was a party in her life. When you called her on the phone and asked for a number . . . it may take you two or three minutes to get a number, but you had to carry through the conversation as she wished."

For some reason, only known to Replogle, she referred to him as "the Reprobate." She told Replogle one day not to "pinch" (ticket) her if she came out in his district. Replogle said, "Well, Mrs. Allen, I just won't pinch a person so nice as you."

In spite of his promise, here came Mrs. Allen, ripping along past Norris in her car at 60 mph, and Replogle, not knowing who it was, naturally ran her down and pulled her over. When he walked over to the car, Mrs. Allen's eyes got as big as saucers, and she opened her mouth wide and screamed at him, "Oh, you're the Reprobate." And Replogle replied, "Mrs. Allen, you scalawag, I saw you come through here like a maniac. You ought to be in jail." And she said, "Oh, I know I ought to be in jail, but I'd rather be at home having dinner with you." Replogle replied, "Alright, let's make a date." So she invited Replogle to dinner the next day, and he forgot the whole speeding affair.[18]

The era of motorcycle patrolmen ended in 1936 when the Park Service purchased several new Ford convertibles with a V-8 engine, rumble seat in the back, and chrome siren. Patrol cars and pickups were far more functional for the multiple tasks of ranger duties, and they were much safer. The motorcycle nevertheless remains an icon in park history, and rangers like Replogle helped keep Yellowstone's highways safe.

Chapter 8

Protecting Yellowstone's Bears

No other wonder in Yellowstone, other than geysers, is as intoxicating to the public as bears, and no creature was more ruthlessly exploited during the early decades of the twentieth century. The popularity of Yellowstone brought an inevitable collision between man and bear that nearly brought the latter to demise within mere decades after the park's creation.

Two varieties of bears are indigenous to Yellowstone National Park: the American black bear (*Ursus americanus*) and the grizzly (*U. arctos horribilis*). Both species of bear have different temperaments and reacted differently to the incursion of humans into the park region.

Black bears are more social. Omnivorous in nature, the black tends to be a forest dweller, living in the lowlands and meadows where food sources of nuts, berries, vegetation, small rodents, birds, insects, ants, and grubs are plentiful. Inquisitive by nature, black bears are more inclined to enter into camps and places occupied by humans, especially when foraging for food. The black bear is smaller in size than the grizzly and comes in a variety of colors, including black, brown, cinnamon, and blond. They are somewhat timid in nature unless provoked, startle easily, and may quickly retreat up a nearby pine tree to avoid a perceived threat, using their short, curved claws to good advantage. As a result, the black bear quickly adapted to the human presence.

Grizzly bears are more solitary, tending to remain away from human contact unless drawn out by a significant attraction. In comparison to the black bear, grizzlies are also more aggressive in nature, standing their ground and even charging anything that threatens them, especially when protecting their young or a kill.

They are a larger bear than the black bear, with a larger head, wide dished face, and a prominent hump between the shoulders. Grizzly habitat is open range and high mountain terrain, where they use their massive, straight claws and powerful forearms to break up logs, roll over rocks and stumps, and dig in the ground. Grizzlies hunt for grubs, moles, mice, ground squirrels, and other rodents. They are large and powerful enough to take down a deer or larger ungulate, such as elk, moose, and small bison, especially individuals that are weak or injured. Grizzlies get much of the fat and nutrition required for winter hibernation from trout that they find in streams, rivers, and lakes. Although the grizzly typically avoids human contact, unlike its black cousin, if it ever loses its timidity or isolated nature and comes into camps or human-occupied areas, its aggressive temperament makes it extremely dangerous and destructive.

EARLY ATTITUDES REGARDING BEARS

The grizzly did not stoop to begging on roadsides. Its hook was garbage dumps and bear-feeding shows. Dumps were maintained for many years near major installations, such as Old Faithful, Lake–Fishing Bridge, and Canyon. Food scraps as well as junk were deposited in these dumps, and the aroma attracted the grizzlies from miles around. The Trout Creek dump that serviced both Lake and Canyon was a couple of miles south of the main road in Hayden Valley. The open sagebrush hillsides were latticed with paths deeply grooved into the sod by grizzlies coming to feed.

For a few years, a small dump was maintained in the vicinity of Indian Pond (known then as Squaw Lake), east of Fishing Bridge. Garbage from the cabins, lodge, and hotel at Canyon and Fishing Bridge was dumped there. Ten to fifteen grizzlies regularly visited this dump. One particularly large grizzly, named "Ole' One-Ear" by Lowell Biddulph, was king of that dump. The bear had endured many fights over the years, evidenced by large scars across its face and one missing ear. So large was this bear that when it stood erect by the side of the pickup, only its belly was visible in the side window.

Rangers of this era understood the power and unpredictability of bears, but boundaries between the two appeared less defined. Early attitudes and perceptions about these bears placed them and humans in dangerous juxtaposition. The black bear was treated, on occasion, as a pet by early employees and administrators. Early photographs show visitors and even park administrators and rangers standing next to black bears as if they were dogs, or feeding a bear hand-to-mouth while it stood next to them. Even the superintendent of Yellowstone Park Horace Albright is shown in a popular photograph sitting at a table and sharing food with three black bears. One small black bear, named Barney, was kept on a chain like a domestic pet.

In 1928, when Lowell Biddulph was stationed at Canyon, a young black bear took up residence under the ranger station. The bear frequently came out and peered through the front door of the ranger station, perhaps hoping for a handout. The rangers teased it by throwing their wash water at it and chasing it around the station, where it would escape by means of an entry hole in the foundation. As the bear grew during the summer, entering and exiting the hole became more arduous, and the rangers frequently booted the bear on its furry behind as it dove for safety. Once safely inside, it would bear its teeth and growl menacingly.

BEAR-FEEDING SHOWS

In the 1920s and '30s, the Park Service devised a means to showcase park bears, particularly the grizzly, to the public by staging bear-feeding shows. Old Faithful and Otter Creek, near Canyon, were the sites selected for these shows, as both locations drew large crowds of tourists. The shows were hugely popular with the public. Thrilling, entertaining, and educational, yet unhealthy and artificial in their staging, the shows brought large crowds and provided an up close and personal look at the nature and disposition of bears.

Bear-feeding shows began each year at the opening of tourist season and ended immediately after Labor Day. After a winter's hibernation, attracting grizzlies to the feeding stations required enticement. Rangers painted the trunks of the pine trees around the show area with an irresistible blend of honey and molasses. Bud Lystrup wrote, "Once the bears had been persuaded to abandon their haphazard diet of wild berries, ants, and fish for a regular fare of choice garbage from the exclusive Old Faithful Inn…[w]ithout further coaxing, the bears would arrive regularly each evening at the feeding grounds until the program was discontinued after Labor Day."[1]

The feeding platforms were low structures made of wood or cement placed in a ravine or lower terrain. Tourists sat on logs or benches on a hillside behind a small fence or shallow mote where they could see the entire feeding arena. Such precautions provided psychological comfort to the tourists but afforded no real protection from a bear determined to get at the crowd.

Each day, rangers—one of them, Gerald Ford, a future president of the United States—collected about fifteen large cans of table scraps from the

Audience at a bear-feeding show at Otter Creek in the 1930s. (Photo by Danecki; courtesy of the National Park Service, Yellowstone National Park, YELL 27353-7)

hotels, lodges, cabins, and the government mess and delivered it to the bear-feeding platform. "We didn't dare call it garbage," Replogle recollected, which suggests that even during the 1930s, *garbage* was a politically insensitive term to use when making reference to feeding bears. Replogle continues regarding the feeding operation and his famous colleague:

> The truck would drive in approximately at 5 o'clock in the evening and dump these scraps off on this cement platform about 14 by 20 feet down in the meadow. And the bears would start descending about 2 in the afternoon. Jerry had a gun, but he preferred to carry a club. And when an old grizzly would climb up on the truck to get at the garbage, it was up to Jerry to pop them on the snoot. I think when they called Jerry [the bears] backed off because he was about the size of the grizzly bear and about as ornery, too.[2]

The aroma of garbage drew large numbers of grizzlies from long distances. Replogle said that one night he counted 110 grizzlies at Otter Creek (Canyon) and that any given night 50 to 80 would come to the platform to eat. That number of grizzlies staggers the imagination of the modern visitor to Yellowstone who is lucky to see a single grizzly from a distance. Is it possible that 110 grizzlies could congregate at one place in Yellowstone? Or is it probable that Replogle counted the same grizzly more than once? Or exaggerated the number? We don't know, but George Marler and Herbert Lystrup, who gave the bear lectures the summer of 1932, sustain the idea with similar numbers.

A group of 7 medium-size grizzlies, named "the Galloping Seven" by the rangers, frequented the West Thumb area but regularly appeared at the Old Faithful show in time for the evening feeding. Two other large grizzlies showed up one night, their faces still covered in white flour from breaking into a large flour barrel at Lake Station earlier that morning. By seven o'clock the same day, they had made their way from Lake to Old Faithful, a distance cross-country of approximately twenty miles (it was thirty-eight miles from Lake to Old Faithful by way of the highway).

Garbage attracted more than bears. Scavengers, including coyotes, gulls, ravens, and blue jays, flocked to these areas as well. Winged scavengers were as entertaining as the four-legged kind. Ravens and seagulls constantly flew above the crowd of spectators gathered for the show, filling the air with high-pitched yakking and raucous cawing. The gulls in particular were "not too careful about [their] bathroom activities…many a time [letting] go upon some rather proud lady's hat or dress."[3]

Most scavengers gave wide berth to the bears as they competed for the scraps. However, on one occasion Lystrup observed a coyote outwit a large grizzly at the Old Faithful bear-feeding show. The grizzly was jealously guarding a bone that a coyote was diligently trying to steal. The coyote darted in and snatched at the bone, narrowly escaping the swipe of the grizzly's paw. The coyote then ran to another spot on the platform, and the bear chased after it to drive it off, only to have the quicker coyote dart to another spot. The bear finally became so confused and disoriented by the coyote that it sat in a befuddled daze while the coyote simply walked in, took the bone, and trotted away.

Replogle and other rangers had names for as many as 46 different grizzlies, such as Scarface, the Galloping Seven, Caesar, and Henry VIII. The naming of bears suggests that the rangers of the day enjoyed an interesting familiarity with the bears that came each evening to the shows, but it did not diminish in the least their utmost respect for the grizzly. They knew, from personal experience, that these bears were wild and unpredictable.

THE ENTERTAINER

Of all the rangers who ever gave the bear-feeding lecture, none was as colorful and prominent as Walter P. Martindale. Known to his colleagues as "the Major," Martindale became almost a folk hero among the tourists and the rangers during the 1920s. His flair and swagger were those of a proud military officer. He was always dressed for the shows in his immaculate National Park Service uniform with a Sam Brown belt with polished buckle and shiny spurs on his boots. He carried a braid of leather as a "swagger stick" that he slapped against his boots to emphasize a point.[4] A cigar clenched between his teeth was a permanent fixture. He laughed easily and often but commanded respect from the tourists as if he were General Patton himself.

Martindale's showmanship was nearly as riveting to his audiences as were the bears, and probably more entertaining. Martindale cantered into the arena precisely at 6:45 p.m. each evening astride his striking black horse. He wheeled his mount to face the audience, waved his quirt, and then doffed his hat. He dismounted and swaggered back and forth in front of the audience with his hands behind his back while his horse followed his every move. Lystrup thought this an impressive demonstration of animal training until he discovered that the Major hid a lump of sugar in one of his hands.

At 7:00 p.m., Martindale remounted and assumed his position about seventy-five yards from the feeding platform. He glanced with the exaggerated seriousness of a field commander about to order an attack and nodded at the ranger who sat on a nearby stump with a high-powered rifle cradled across his knees. The rifle guard nodded back with equal seriousness. Lystrup noted, "Not a shot was ever fired, and I came to suspect that the Major's dramatic precaution was more drama than precaution."[5]

Wayne Replogle, who actually served as rifle guard for Martindale at times, shed additional light on this melodrama: "It was my job to sit over another fifty feet between the people and the grizzlies with a rifle across my lap on an old stump, and there be the guard on duty. To this day I've never figured just how I would guard the people from 50 or 60 grizzlies with a rifle that was seldom loaded."[6]

As imposing as Martindale was when performing in costume before a crowd, offstage he became, in the words of Bud Lystrup, "a man easily lost in a crowd." He described him as being "thin and slightly stooped with a long nose resting on a somewhat pinched face that always seemed flushed. His mouth was wide with thin lips above a pointed chin." To Lystrup, "He was a showman with only meager knowledge of thermal features and absolutely no respect for nomenclature. Like other rangers, he led geyser walks, but what meager scientific knowledge crept into description of the thermal phenomenon was usually accidental and quickly lost among his jokes."[7]

LYSTRUP GIVES THE BEAR LECTURE

Walter Martindale did not return to the park the summer of 1932, and Chief Naturalist C. Max Bauer assigned Lystrup to do the bear lecture at Old Faithful. Then, partway through the summer, the ranger doing the bear lecture at Otter Creek unexpectedly died—not incidental to the bear-feeding show—and George Marler was assigned to do it at Canyon.

The precedent set by Martindale intimidated Lystrup, and he felt the need to continue the show as best he could. However, he did not know how to ride a horse, and his knowledge about bears was, in his words, "a little more than the average tourist." In spite of the fact that the lack of knowledge had never intimidated his illustrious predecessor, Lystrup nevertheless combed the Mammoth library for any information he could find on bears and fortunately found enough to strengthen his self-confidence. As for the horse, the district ranger taught him how to saddle and mount a horse and the rudiments of riding.

The evening of the first lecture arrived. Lystrup's successful attempt to catch the horse was made possible only because the horse decided, at length, to cooperate. His first attempt to saddle and mount resulted in the saddle and blanket hanging beneath the horse's belly and Lystrup lying on the ground. Finally mounted and with confidence slowly returning, Lystrup maneuvered the horse out of the corral and toward the bear-feeding grounds. Unfortunately, as he passed a row of cabins, a woman suddenly appeared and shook a rug in the horse's face, sending it galloping back to the corral with Lystrup clinging to the saddle horn. After much coaxing, he got the horse to again leave the corral, and he arrived at the bear-feeding grounds just in time for the show, trying to look dignified and confident.

The log seats were packed with visitors, waiting with great anticipation. Although rough and nothing similar to his well-polished predecessor, Lystrup gave what he considered to be a successful presentation. Martindale was a showman, Lystrup an interpreter. Their approaches to the public were very different. Whereas Martindale had been intent upon impressing the crowd, Lystrup focused on educating them about the bears. He let the bears take the lead while he observed and interpreted what was happening:

> I came to realize that I couldn't follow precisely my previously prepared lecture—there were too many interruptions; and I was speedily convinced that the talk would be more interesting if I departed from my standard text whenever there was something of significance occurring

Bud Lystrup delivers the bear lecture at Old Faithful's bear-feeding grounds in 1932. (Courtesy of Liz Lystrup)

in the arena...so, my prepared lecture soon became...an interpretation of the activities that took place on the platform. Thus, if a mother bear came to feed with her cubs, I discussed the gestation period, the birth, care, feeding and development of the young. If a grizzly bear condescended to enter the arena, I had a chance to point to the differences between the grizzly and the black bears. I learned to drop one subject and shift to another as the attention of my audience shifted here and there, from coyotes to gulls, from the raven to other birds and animals that frequented the arena.[8]

The speaker invariably gains more from a talk than the audience that listens, and so it was with Lystrup. He learned something new each time about the subjects of his presentation, both as individuals and as species. Much of this information was new to him that he had not found in books. These tantalizing hints inspired his inquiring mind to further study.

Replogle said that he gave the bear talk at Canyon's Otter Creek the summers of 1936, '38, and '40. He entered the "arena" each day at 4:30 in the afternoon and studied the bears for about an hour. This not only helped him get acquainted with the bears that were at the station that afternoon and develop some interpretive ideas, but it also helped him judge how safe it was going to be for the public. The people were allowed to enter the arena at 5:30 p.m. At 6:15 p.m., Replogle delivered a thirty-minute talk on bears to the first group. The second group came in immediately behind the first, and the talk was repeated. The people routinely saw as many as fifty-eight to seventy grizzlies during a showing. Marler said that he saw one hundred grizzlies at Canyon in 1932.

Marian Replogle had her husband's uniform laid out for him when he came home to change for the evening program. He always wore a clean shirt and carried a handkerchief in his back pocket with which to wipe the sweat from his brow. This observation was not lost on Marian, who was not above playing a dirty trick on her man. One night while giving one of the talks, Replogle retrieved what he thought was the handkerchief only to have one of his wife's brassieres unwind down the front of his face. He admitted later: "When the thundering laughter ended, I can't remember what happened, but I was sure the speech was about over."[9]

BATTLE FOR SUPREMACY

Frequently, bears got into fights with each other on the platform, electrifying the crowd with their terrible ferocity. An unforgettable fight broke out between two large grizzlies one night at Old Faithful while both Replogle and Lystrup were present. Among the bears at that platform this particular evening was a rogue the rangers had named "Caesar." He was a large grizzly, and he proclaimed his dominance among all of the bears present, until the arrival of "Scarface."

Lystrup describes what happened next: "Suddenly loud murmurs from the audience disturbed [Caesar's] reveries. Many tourists rose, unthinking, pointing to the edge of the arena....[S]tanding in the shadows was one of the largest grizzly bears I had ever seen. He stood silently on his hind legs, his huge head swinging slowly from side to side. Scarface had arrived."[10]

How large a bear was Scarface? Replogle suggested that Scarface was immense, measuring eight feet, three inches from nose to toes and weighing about a thousand pounds. He justified these measurements:

One time we saw [Scarface] walk over to a pine tree and mark the tree. And by marking we usually describe it as a bear would back up to a tree and stretch his body as high as he could and stretch his nose as high as he could. And we observed old Scarface that evening do this, and after he left, we measured the spot to where he had measured and it was 8 feet 3 inches. He got his name from the fact that in the many fights to control his supremacy his face was completely chopped up and scarred by other bears. The prognosticators who knew bears, especially one who had killed two grizzlies weighing over 900 pounds in Yellowstone Park in the very early '20s, suggested that probably Scarface weighed well over 1,000 pounds.[11]

Lystrup continues his story of the fight: "The audience was hushed. An eerie quiet enveloped the arena. Scarface growled quietly but with immense authority, and all the bears, black and grizzly, young and old quickly left the grounds. All but one, that is, for Caesar boldly stood his ground. Scarface dropped to the ground on all four feet. Slowly, cautiously, he advanced toward his young challenger. Without warning, Scarface coiled and charged. Just as quickly Caesar moved to meet the challenge."[12]

The two monsters fought mightily before the awestruck visitors, knocking each other down, snarling, and biting. Eventually, Caesar's youthful strength overpowered the size of Scarface, and he lay defeated:

Scarface rose slowly. With some condescension, Caesar stepped aside as the deposed ruler struggled to his feet and moved wearily into the forest. The battle for supremacy was over. The audience was silent, still spellbound by the rare drama they had seen. Then, as Scarface disappeared, Caesar ran to a nearby tree and reared up on his hind legs. Stretching himself, he scratched a mark on the trunk of the tree as high as he could reach. He walked with dignity to the edge of the arena, raised himself on hind legs and roared, loud and ferociously. He was proclaiming himself King![13]

Wayne Replogle said this about the incident:

In all my life I have never seen anything as absolutely terrible in the animal world as occurred then. This fight continued for almost 30 minutes, and they were quite torn up with considerable blood, and when it was all over, they were both exhausted. Scarface sat down and the other bear sat down, and finally Scarface moved away in the forest and the other bear stayed there. It was close to darkness then so we retreated.

The following evening the new bear came in and he was supreme, so we called him Caesar. After a few nights, we heard a noise off in the woods and my attention was drawn to a large bear making his way back towards the feeding spot. He was unsure of where he was going because occasionally he would run into a tree. He moved to the edge of the forest and stopped. When the other bears left the feeding grounds at dark, this old bear made his way in to pick up what little food he could find. We concluded that the fight had blinded Scarface. We saw him maybe three or four times in the remainder of the season, in August and early September. In 1933, when the season began, Scarface never appeared again, so we think that he died in the winter of 1932 and 1933. Now this was the dethronement of the most amazing bear in the history of Yellowstone Park, and Dorr Yaeger wrote quite a story about Scarface.[14]

Caesar reigned supreme for three years, until 1935, when he was dethroned by another bear at the same feeding grounds. The new bear was named "Henry VIII" by the rangers. In the wild, supremacy is fleeting at best.

THE DEMISE OF BEAR SHOWS

The bear-feeding grounds at Old Faithful and Canyon were less than safe. The visitors and the feeding platform were in dangerous proximity, inviting disaster at any given moment. Replogle complained to his superiors of the danger posed by the bears. They responded by digging a waterless ditch about two hundred feet long, which did not help. The bears crossed it whenever they wanted, and once across they were not very disposed to go back to the other side. The rangers built a fence along the bottom of the ditch, but the bears, not appreciating the purpose of the fence, would sometimes get on the wrong side.

The feared finally happened at Old Faithful while Replogle was present:

> One evening, an old bear parked her cubs out near the end of the fence, and she was very nervous. She would run over and get a bite of food and then run back and smell her cubs.... [O]ne time a black bear got in the way and another grizzly got scared, and all hell broke loose. Grizzlies ran and people screamed ... and grizzlies and people were running toward the trees and buildings.... [I]n that melee ... were George Baggley and [Francis] "Babe" LeNoue, the Chief and Assistant Chief Rangers ... and they too had to take for cover, and I well recall that

the next day the Old Faithful bear grounds were closed. This was late August of 1935.[15]

After the pandemonium subsided and some degree of normalcy was regained, Replogle heard a voice calling to him from above. Looking up, he saw a man sitting high in one of the trees where he had scampered for safety. It turned out to be Red Fenwick, who had been the head yell leader of the high school in Douglas, Wyoming, where Replogle had coached in 1926. The two men had a good laugh about the circumstances of their reunion.

The era of showmanship in the park began to die away by the late 1930s, and showmen such as Major Martindale went with it. Bud Lystrup commented on this transition: "The Major was a superb entertainer. And if he frequently got facts and fantasy hopelessly entangled, what did it matter? The boundaries were always vague. But times change, and styles change with them. Major Martindale and the others of his kind gradually disappeared from the park. They were replaced by men trained in the sciences; entertainment ceased to be an end in itself and became instead merely another means to a different goal—an enlightened appreciation of the natural wonders of the Yellowstone."[16]

ROADSIDE JUNKIES

While the grizzly became a connoisseur of garbage, the black became a roadside junky. In the late 1950s and early '60s, a fictional bear character named Yogi and his sidekick, Boo-Boo, were produced by Hanna-Barbera. The picnic basket–snatching bear of Jellystone Park became the darling of the cartoon era and further perpetrated the public's addiction with the begging black bears of Yellowstone.

Unfortunately, quite a bit of Yogi and Boo-Boo were to be found in the black bears of Yellowstone. A minister visiting the park with his family reported to Sam Beal that an "irreverent bear" snatched his meat loaf and vanished at the precise moment they were saying grace. Beal empathized with the minister by telling him that one summer while he and his family were carrying supplies into their cabin at Old Faithful, a bear absconded with a three-pound package of bacon. The minister replied, "Well, the scripture says, watch and pray."[17]

Begging Yellowstone black bears became wildly popular with tourists. Feeding the bears became a national pastime. The bears could look almost human. Some of their facial expressions and body language were so endearing

A black bear begs for handouts along a Yellowstone road. (Courtesy of L. G. Biddulph)

that people could not resist feeding them, and some even had to have their picture taken with them. This was unhealthy for the bears and dangerous for the people. The bear often could not tell where the food ended and the fingers began, resulting in several bitten hands.

One woman was seen pushing cookies into a bear's open mouth while it stood upright on hind legs and forepaws resting on her shoulders. After a short time, the cookie supply ran out, and the woman retreated to her car. The bear followed her inside. She hastily exited out the other side, shutting the door behind her, an unfortunate mistake. The bear virtually destroyed the interior of the car before someone let it out.[18]

A family visiting Tower Fall one afternoon parked their car in the parking lot and walked over to take pictures of the falls,[19] leaving the front windows of their car open. It was a warm afternoon of a very active day of sightseeing. The grandmother was too tired to walk over to the falls and decided to remain in the backseat of the car. She soon dozed but was awakened by a noise, only to discover that a black bear had opened the car door, climbed into the front seat, and was helping itself to some food left by the family. The elderly woman suddenly discovered reserves of energy previously unknown in exiting the car. Older generations of automobiles had pull-down handles, and Yellowstone Park bears quickly mastered the technique of opening car doors.

The presence of bears along park highways clogged the roads, causing dangerous traffic jams. Rangers and naturalists frequently had to break up bear jams and get people to move along. In the 1950s, Lowell Biddulph came upon a jam of cars between West Thumb and Lake. Cars were backed up in both directions for a half mile. Biddulph maneuvered himself forward to see if he could break up the jam and found a large crowd of people standing around a couple who were feeding cookies and meat scraps to a large sow bear.

The woman wanted her husband to take her picture with the bear next to her. She held a cookie high enough that the bear stood up on its hind legs to get it. Half successful, the woman now wanted the bear to look at the camera, but the bear seemed more interested in the cookie than the picture. So, she took hold of the bear's ear and turned its head toward the camera. Remarkably, the bear cooperated. In retelling the story, Biddulph quipped that the woman must have been a schoolteacher.

The woman would have gotten away with the foolish act had her teenage son not suddenly pushed the bear in the back, forcing it down on all fours. It was hard enough for the bear to put up with all the blathering humans and flashing cameras, but a shove in the back pushed the sow over the edge. Instantly, the docile bear became a snarling beast. It whirled about and took after the boy through the crowd of screaming, rapidly scattering onlookers. It caught the boy several yards up the side of the road and gave him one good swat on the seat of his pants with a forepaw, sending him flying into the ditch along the roadside. As he lay whimpering in terror, but otherwise unharmed, the bear walked calmly back to her cubs.

Nothing more really needed to be said to the people, although a stern lecture was delivered by Biddulph. It is doubtful that many heard the lecture as they scurried to their cars and moved on down the road, but for sure they all left the scene with a vivid lesson on the dangers of feeding bears. For sure, one fortunate family better understood the wild nature of park bears.[20]

A woman once asked Beal: "Are bears really dangerous? Why, they are the cutest creatures the way they wiggle their ears and tails."

"That's true," Beal answered, "but you can't believe either end of a bear."

At times, people were loath to obeying the rules and even challenged a ranger's authority. Wayne Replogle reported such a situation at Dunraven Pass:

I remember one time I went up to Dunraven Pass in the 1950s. The traffic was stopped for a half mile each way. I walked up to try to break it up and there was this large lady feeding a bear. I asked her if she wouldn't mind [not] feeding the bear and get in the car and leave. She said, "you mind your business and I'll mind mine." So I said something more to her and she gave me a look or two that I haven't forgotten. I just couldn't get her to quit feeding the bears. Finally, she turned and started toward the car and this big old brown bear that she had been feeding just bit her on the rear end. I could have kissed that bear. Well, she let out a scream and he got a large piece of her pants. And that old gal got in the car and moved it and we broke up the jam.[21]

Replogle's comment about the woman must be taken in context of the circumstances. For the most part, rangers and naturalists were polite and professional with people when enforcing regulations and protecting them from their own stupidity. At the same time, they had to have some backbone to confront visitors who willfully refused to follow rules or who responded with disparaging remarks meant to intimidate, such as: "I am so-and-so, with much political influence. A complaint against you to so-and-so would cost you your job."

This very statement was used against Merrill Beal in 1946 at Madison Junction by a camper. Beal was an old debater and found this grist for his mill. He responded by inviting the man to "produce his credentials and name a great man who would champion his childish position." He said of himself: "I was not constitutionally conditioned to be ingratiating. I was both democratic and Christian in outlook and attitude; a course in public relations would have helped. However, I had little tolerance for deliberate violators, and none for anyone who tried to intimidate me."[22]

CAMPGROUND FORAYS

There was real truth in the popular campfire song:

> *Way down on the Yellowstone River,*
> *Where campers are camped thick as bees;*
> *Along about twelve o'clock midnight,*
> *You can hear this refrain through the trees:*
> *Bring back, bring back,*
> *Oh bring back my bacon to me!*

Virtually every campground in Yellowstone was fair game for black bears and, less often, grizzlies. If you camped out, you could almost bet that a bear would visit you, especially if any scent of food was about. Bears caused untold damage and turmoil in the campgrounds of Yellowstone. Rangers instructed visitors to keep food items locked up in the trunk of their cars. Most were open to suggestions, but some thought they knew better.

Two young men who camped at one of the Fishing Bridge campgrounds in the 1950s decided that raw steak was too precious to leave in the car. They decided to put the steak under one of the men's pillows so that they could ward off any attempts by bears to get it. During the night, a black bear came into their tent, got the meat out from under the pillow, somehow without awakening the would-be guardian, and might have gotten away had it not been in such a hurry to partake of its find.

Unfortunately, the bear sat squarely on top of the man, who awakened to a four-hundred-pound nightmare. He did the first thing that came into his groggy mind; he clobbered the bear on the head with his hiking boot. The incensed bear dropped the meat and mauled the man before exiting the tent.[23]

Food in the trunk of a car was not safe if the car doors were not locked, as a Boy Scout troop from Minnesota found out while camping at Fishing Bridge. The night before they were to return home, a bear got into their car, opening the door by pulling down on the handle. It then dug through the backseat to the trunk and began to indulge itself on the food.

To make a bad situation worse, the car door shut behind the bear, trapping it inside. For a while, the bear was preoccupied with the food, but once the food was devoured and the bear discovered that it was trapped, it became desperate. In its attempts to get out of the car, it completely destroyed the interior, breaking out the windows and windshield, tearing the seats to shreds, defecating all over, and pulling the steering wheel completely from the column. Lowell Biddulph, the senior ranger naturalist at Fishing Bridge, was called to solve the problem. Carefully, the car door was opened, and the bear fled into the forest. In good Boy Scout spirit, the troop hosed out the car, fashioned a make-shift steering wheel, and drove it all the way back to Minnesota! No doubt, they did so with tales to last a lifetime.

A RETURN TO NATURE

Policies regarding wildlife management changed over time. In the early 1900s, the bear was viewed even by park managers more as a tourist attraction than as a unique creature living in a delicately balanced ecosystem. The wilderness, once the habitat of grizzlies and black bears, became a pleasuring ground, and man and beast were brought into dangerous proximity. Tourists often came to Yellowstone with little or no appreciation for the wild nature of park bears. Frequently and carelessly, people transgressed boundaries that left them vulnerable to danger. When bears did something completely consistent with their nature, like destroying human belongings or even physically injuring a human being on occasion, they were severely punished.

For instance, in the 1950s, a black bear sow with two yearling cubs had to be killed with a high-powered rifle because of a young man's thoughtless actions. While near the campground at Fishing Bridge, the young man encountered the sow with her cubs. Rather than retreating and giving wide berth, the boy began throwing wood at the bears. The sow charged the boy. He climbed a lodgepole pine some forty-feet high. The sow was threatened enough that it went up after him. The boy began screaming for help. The rangers were called, and, of course, the only way to save the boy was to shoot the bear. Two cubs needlessly lost their mother, and they had to be captured and sent to a zoo.

Troublesome bears were trapped, their faces painted white, and released deep in the wilderness. Releasing the bears once trapped could be dangerous. Typically, the bear was released while the pickup pulling the trap was moving so that the bear would be less inclined to attack the rangers. One ranger drove the pickup, and the other was in the bed of the truck and lifted the door of the trap using a cable. Once the door was lifted, the bear usually jumped from the trap and ran away.

One of Biddulph's colleagues told him about a near-fatal release of a black bear that he had been involved with. He and another ranger released a large black bear in a meadow. When the door of the trap was lifted, instead of jumping and running, the vengeful bear climbed out and got on top of the trap and started making its way toward the ranger in the back of the truck. The ranger grabbed his lever-action rifle, while the driver (the man telling the story) accelerated. The bear continued to make its way down the trap toward the ranger. So distraught was the ranger that he pointed the rifle at the bear and ejected all of the shells without pulling the trigger once, and the bear fortuitously fell off the trap. Once the escape was complete, the driver of the truck was sworn to secrecy, a promise he obviously failed to keep.

Biddulph was involved with a grizzly release during the late 1950s. The ranger force had acquired a World War II landing craft that they used on Yellowstone Lake for hauling horses and supplies. A grizzly bear had been trapped in a campground and was being hauled across the lake in the landing craft to be released. Unfortunately, they did not quite make it to the other side of the lake before the grizzly began to revive, and they had to make an emergency landing. For a few tense moments, the bear chased the rangers about the landing craft until they hit the beach. The front gate was promptly dropped, and the grizzly charged out and across the beachhead like a true marine.

Bears that persistently returned or proved dangerous by injuring people were exterminated. In the 1930s, bear extermination may have been done with less consideration for extenuating circumstances than it is today. Wayne Replogle claimed that in 1935, while he was stationed at Old Faithful as a ranger, approximately thirty bears were "exterminated as troublesome" by the rangers and dumped in a mass grave. According to him, this place was near the road that ran across the river toward Twin Buttes, just east of Goose Lake near the Midway Geyser Basin.[24] Similar rumors were perpetuated about thirty years later when the park made strenuous efforts to remove the black bears from the roads and campgrounds.

David Condon brought the plight of park bears to the forefront of park management focus during the late 1940s and '50s, but not without significant cost to his career. His warning regarding the possible demise of park bears was not well received by the public or park management, who were loath to remove the black bear from park highways. Eventually, the evidence could not be ignored, and managers began to take the necessary steps to end bear feeding and return it to its native habitat.

Campgrounds at key areas were shut down and returned to the bears. Key wilderness areas throughout the park were established primarily as bear habitats, and human use was restricted in these areas according to numbers of people, length of use, and season of the year. Policies on bear feeding, long established, were finally enforced. Human garbage from campgrounds, hotels, and other lodging was removed from the park each day, eliminating the temptation for bears. Garbage dumps at Trout Creek, Squaw Lake, and Old Faithful were closed. Black bears were forced away from park highways where they had made a living, and they retreated back into the forests and meadows where it was healthier for them.

The policy remained unpopular with many people, and rumors began to surface in the 1960s that park officials were destroying large numbers of bears. It is possible, although not proven, that Replogle's report from 1935 of bears being destroyed as nuisances is true, but the idea of this happening in the

1960s and '70s is false, especially given the ecological principles that governed wildlife management by that time. Paul Schullery, a noted writer and historian on topics of Yellowstone National Park and nature, and Lee Whittlesey, the historian of Yellowstone National Park, noted in 2003 the rise of these stories about supposed bear slaughters:

> In the late 1960's and 1970s, when National Park Service managers undertook the unpleasant and unpopular task of divorcing Yellowstone's bears from garbage and breaking them of their roadside begging habits, it was probably predictable that regional communities would generate rumors of rangers secretly slaughtering hundreds of bears and concealing them in huge backcountry pits. Despite thirty years of unsuccessful search for evidence... of such horrors, those rumors are now firmly ensconced in the folklore of Yellowstone.... It seems probable that when the rumors were first launched more than thirty years ago, they were most popular among people who preferred that the bears remain visible, garbage-fed, and commercially accessible.[25]

None of the Old Men were in the least pro commercialization of park bears during this period. To a man, they strongly supported getting bears off the roads, out of the campgrounds, and back into their natural habitat. They saw bears killed because humans carelessly crossed over into the bears' world. They saw bears seriously and sometimes fatally damaged by bits of glass and tin from garbage cans inadvertently swallowed that caused internal bleeding. They were witness to the troublesome nuisance that addiction to human garbage caused for bears. They knew that the best way to see a bear was in its own natural habitat, not scrounging in a garbage can or eating at some wilderness garbage dump.

Ranger naturalists helped save the bears by bringing the public to an awareness of and respect for the black and grizzly bears of Yellowstone. Through campfire talks, nature walks, museum discussions, and other interpretive methods, these men and women educated the people on the damage being done to park bears.

Yellowstone bear numbers have increased to a point that bear managers say that the Yellowstone grizzlies and black bears are "doing good." As always, good things come with a trade-off. The days of seeing park bears up close and personal are a thing of the past. Visitors today must look long and hard and enjoy some luck to see bears in Yellowstone. The good thing is that there *are* bears in Yellowstone. However, those who remember the days of bear jams, campground forays, and bear-feeding platforms do so with some melancholy, and they never forget the thrill of these close encounters with Yellowstone's bears.

Chapter 9

Fighting Yellowstone's Fires

A PRICELESS NATURAL RESOURCE

Yellowstone's forests are one of its greatest natural resources.[1] The park's extensive forests provide a home for a remarkable variety of plants, birds, and animals. Approximately 80 to 85 percent of the forest plateaus within Yellowstone Park are lodgepole pine, one of three subspecies known as *Pinus contorta*. The lodgepole was named for its usefulness to the Native Americans as poles for their tepee lodges and travois.

Lodgepole forests are unique because of the characteristics of the tree and its growing patterns. The lodgepole pine is typically a tall, straight, slender, thin-barked pine that usually grows in dense populations to heights of fifty to seventy-five feet. A majority of its trunk is void of branches except for short dead shoots. Lodgepole forests are typically void of heavy plant undergrowth because of the thick overhead canopy that precludes life-giving sunlight from penetrating to the forest floor, thereby dissuading new growth. The lodgepole pine lacks a taproot and is thus not well anchored into the ground. Its fairly shallow, spreading root system makes it vulnerable to toppling in windstorms. At times, sections of forest have been blown down by strong winds like jack-straw. As a result of these characteristics, older lodgepole forests tend to become sterile and littered with dead and fallen timber, making it difficult through which to navigate, a fact complained of by early exploring parties in Yellowstone. These dead and fallen trees become dry fuel that allows fire to rapidly ascend to the canopy of the trees, where it can quickly jump from tree to tree, a phenomenon known as "crowning." Fires in lodgepole forests can be almost unstoppable when they crown, especially when driven by wind and drought.

Lodgepole forest with Yellowstone Lake in the background. (Courtesy of L. G. Biddulph)

Lodgepole pine is a fire-adapted tree and relies upon high temperatures, such as those caused by forest fires, to regenerate. The cones are tightly sealed, requiring intense heat to break the resinous seal and disperse the seeds. Newly burned lodgepole forests quickly resurrect with bright-green shoots and brilliant floral colors long inhibited by old greed.

EARLY FIRE POLICIES

During the years of conservation policies, fires were considered the number-one threat to Yellowstone's pristine forests. Fires were quickly engaged and aggressively fought to extinction when possible. Victory over some large fires came only with the help of Mother Nature.

In the 1920s and '30s, fire lookout stations were placed at strategic locations within the park to protect Yellowstone's two million forested acres. Lookout stations were constructed on high prominences such as Mount Washburn (1921), Mount Sheridan (1931), and Mount Holmes (1931). In addition, a fire lookout was maintained on Pelican Cone in the Mirror Plateau and on Purple Mountain near Madison Junction. When a lookout spotted the first thin spirals of smoke rising out of a green sea of forest, he quickly located it as best he could using map and compass and immediately reported it to park headquarters. Park employees, especially rangers and ranger naturalists, were the first line of defense in fighting forest fires. Nothing took precedence over a fire.

The park administration maintained a large number of horses and mules that were used specifically for trail clearing, patrolling, and firefighting. A string of these horses and mules was maintained during the summer months at Lake Station in a large fenced pasture. When fires broke out, these animals were used to pack in supplies to fight the fires.

These horses were conditioned for the backcountry and were not intimidated by bears or other large animals. The aggressiveness of these horses toward black bears was exhibited one day in the Lake pasture as witnessed by some of the naturalist families living nearby. A black bear ventured through the pasture and was immediately accosted by the horses and mules. Unable to attain the fence, the bear ascended a large pine tree for safety. The horses surrounded the tree for about twenty minutes, circling, whinnying, kicking the trunk of the tree, and snorting out threats to the bear. The horses eventually lost interest and paraded off into another part of the pasture. When safe, the bruin wasted no time in descending to the ground and making a beeline for the fence.

SCOUTING FIRES

When a fire was spotted by a lookout, a determination was made as to its size and threat. This was normally done by sending a ranger out to scout the fire. If required, men and supplies followed sufficient to put it out. Reinforcements came by pack horse and on foot. Biddulph and Replogle had several such assignments.

During the summer of 1933, Wayne Replogle was riding motorcycle patrol out of Lake, and a fire was reported in Yellowstone's Central Plateau, the broad expanse of forest stretching from the back side of Elephant Back Mountain to the Firehole Geyser Basins. The chief ranger assigned Replogle to scout the fire.

Replogle rode his motorcycle to the top of Mount Washburn to get a good fix on the fire. He was able to see the smoke from the fire lookout station atop the 10,250-foot summit of Washburn. He estimated that the fire was in the heavily forested timber somewhere near Beach Lake. The fire appeared small, and his supervisor told him to go find it and extinguish it. Replogle got himself a horse, a few supplies, and equipment and set out through the timber.

It took Replogle the entire day to find the fire. After hard riding through heavy timber, he finally found the blaze. Certain that it was small enough for one man to handle, Replogle spent the night and into the next day digging a fire line around the burning area with pick and shovel. Eventually, the fire was extinguished. Hard riding, little sleep, and strenuous physical labor left him nearly thirst crazed. For the next several hours, he vainly tried to find Beach Lake, which he knew was nearby. After several hours of fruitless searching and fighting his horse, which wanted to go in another direction, he finally gave the horse its rein, and within twenty minutes, it was at Beach Lake. Years later, Replogle reminisced, "The horse ran directly into the middle of the lake and began to drink, and I fell off and began to drink, too."[2]

FIGHTING YELLOWSTONE'S FIRES

Firefighting is grueling work. Much like combat, only one inexperienced in fighting a fire would find it exciting or glorious. During the summer of 1932, Bud Lystrup was a relatively new ranger naturalist stationed at Old Faithful and had not had the opportunity to be on a firefighting crew. Hearing the tales of older men who had been on fires, Lystrup actually hoped to be called out on a fire. He got his wish on July 10 of that year when urgent orders came for him to report to the chief ranger at South Gate for fire duty. "Equip yourself with clothes and shoes for fire fighting and bring a bed roll," the order said.

Young Lystrup and other men, laden as if infantry soldiers going to war, excitedly followed their leader through the forest toward Heart Lake, located at the foot of Mount Sheridan in the southern primitive part of the park. Strings of horses and mules brought in the equipment and rations, but the men had a hard ten-mile hike and were exhausted before they even began to fight the fire. Leaving their base camp in a swamp, the men broke into fire teams. Lystrup and his team crossed over a mountain and attacked a new fire that had recently broken out. Time was of the essence in establishing a fire break line to keep the fire contained.

Days of backbreaking work followed with little sleep or food. His hands were blistered; his muscles ached from hacking, chopping, cutting, and shoveling in intense heat; and his face and body were grimy with sweat and smoke. Rations came in sacks labeled USNPS and contained a melted bar of chocolate, a box of crackers, a can of pork and beans, a small can of coffee, and one of bacon. They cooked the bacon on a shovel placed over the fire.

The wind came up and the fire crowned, threatening the crews with intense, almost overwhelming heat. Lystrup wrote of this experience, "Have you ever stood toe to toe with a bursting flame sizzling and crackling as the inflammable pitch oozed out? Have you ever swung an ax into a tree when the very flames seared your face? Have you ever sensed the impact of a huge tree banging to the ground, just missing you by a hair? It takes guts to stand up there in the heat and smoke and take it."[3]

Lystrup discovered upon the parched earth the burned-out nest of a grouse with four scorched eggs and the thoroughly cooked body of the mother hen nearby. He was moved: "Think of the marvelous courage of this mother who couldn't leave the nest with its eggs and the young not even born. There is no mother more vigilant in the care and welfare of her young than the wilderness mother."[4]

One dark night, while Lystrup and another ranger were patrolling the fire lines, they heard the approaching rumble of thunder and saw lightning flashes streak the distant sky. Neither man spoke aloud their prayers for rain, not even when the first big drops splattered on their bare heads. A wind kicked up, and the fire began to flare. They were about to call out for reinforcements along the fire line when a deluge of rain fell upon them in torrents. The two men stood laughing in the rain, relishing its sweet wetness as steam from the dying fire rose about them as if from the very dregs of hell. Lystrup returned to the spike camp, where men were rejoicing with hilarity. Bone tired, he crawled under his drenched, smelly old horse blanket and fell asleep in a puddle of ooze.

The Heart Lake fire scorched seventeen thousand acres and was extinguished only by heaven-sent rains. As Lystrup looked back upon the burned area from a rise during the hike out, he was deeply moved by the scene of carnage caused by the fire: "A graveyard of 17,000 acres filled with charred stumps and snags, remnants of a former luxurious stand; stillness, stark naked trees standing pitifully alone. No birds or squirrels were chirping and singing. Death and destruction were widespread. I turned my back upon the scene, glad the experience was over."[5]

WIVES AS LOOKOUTS AND INTERPRETERS

World War II greatly reduced the manpower in Yellowstone. Only twenty-two men served on the staff in Yellowstone during the war years. The men who remained in the park carried a heavy load of interpretive and protective assignments.[6] The summers of 1942 and '43 were big for forest fires. Several fires caused by lightning strikes during the 1942 summer season required all of the manpower Yellowstone could muster, leaving vacant the interpretive duties and museums. In order to compensate for the loss of available men to fight forest fires, the park hired the wives of some of these men to fill in as interpreters.

The wives of Wayne Replogle and Frank Kowski were hired as "ranger fire lookouts" to watch for and report additional fires that might break out.[7] Marian Replogle was also hired as a ranger at the Norris Museum for two or three weeks during these fires while her husband was out fighting them. Her duties were to open, close, and maintain the museum in her husband's absence. She answered questions posed by visitors and gave directions as best she could. At the end of the summer, Marian received a check from the government for thirty-eight dollars. When the check arrived, she wanted to save it in her scrapbook. But Replogle said, "Oh my gosh! Thirty-eight dollars is a fortune. Let's cash it and use the money."[8] Which of them won that difference of opinion remains a mystery, but safe money goes with Marian.

Bud Lystrup ran the museum at Madison Junction the summer of 1942. In addition to his naturalist duties, he was also the fire watch and climbed up onto Purple Mountain on the north rim of the Madison River Canyon to check for fires each day. When forest fires broke out that summer, Bud was called up, leaving the museum unmanned. To fill the void, Betty Lystrup took over his duties and kept the Madison Museum open for visitors.

LEWIS LAKE FIRE, 1943

Park Superintendent Edmund B. Rogers reported fifteen fires during the summer of 1943, twelve of which were controlled and extinguished through human effort. Lowell Biddulph was stationed at the South Entrance that summer. One morning, he counted nine different fires start up from lightning strikes during a bad electrical storm. There was no one to fight the fires except a crew of Japanese Americans who had been moved to Heart Mountain Relocation Center near Cody, Wyoming, after Japan's attack on Pearl Harbor on December 7, 1941.

Ironically, while Americans fought in the South Pacific against the Japanese, incarcerated Japanese Americans fought the forest fires in Yellowstone Park. Superintendent Rogers noted, "Our most dependable source of manpower for forest fire suppression work was a crew of Japanese from the Heart Mountain Relocation Project who worked five different fires and consisted of a crew of 180 men."[9]

Biddulph was sent to a large fire at Lewis Lake to meet these Japanese American men. He remembered:

These men knew very little English. I was given two hundred of these men to fight this fire. We had quite a time. We couldn't understand each other too well. We had lots of good food, but they didn't like what we had. We had chicken and turkey and beef, the finest food in the world, but they didn't like it. They didn't work; they couldn't work, and finally I said to their leader, "What's the trouble?"

He said, "They can't eat your American food."

I said, "What are we going to do about it?"

He said, "Get them some rice."

So we got hundred pound sacks of rice and boiled it up in wash boilers. Then they wrapped it into balls and they took knapsacks of these balls of rice. Work increased. We got a lot done. When they came back to camp at night they still would eat nothing but rice, heaping their plates with rice and pouring soy sauce over it with a few sardines. That was all they needed.[10]

The fire at Lewis Lake was successfully put out, but not before a considerable amount of forest was burned. The old scars of the Japanese's battle against Yellowstone's fires during World War II were still visible on the hillsides along the Lewis River Canyon in the 1950s and '60s, but were probably almost fully eradicated by the fires of 1988.

CHIPMUNK CREEK FIRE

In the 1950s, a large fire broke out along Chipmunk Creek, which drains from the Two Ocean Plateau into the south arm of Yellowstone Lake near Peale Island. This area is remote, far from any road and deeply isolated in Yellowstone wilderness. The forest in this region was particularly dense and difficult to get through. The Washburn-Langford-Doane expedition of 1870 particularly noted this area as extremely difficult for horses to traverse, some getting high-centered on fallen timber. It was also prime grizzly bear habitat.

Lowell Biddulph was assigned to scout out the fire and determine if artificial suppression was necessary. A government boat transported him across the south end of Yellowstone Lake and dropped him off near the outlet of Chipmunk Creek. Alone and with night setting in, Biddulph pressed into the dense forest. After hours of struggling through uncharted, mosquito-infested forest, Biddulph came upon the fire, which was large and growing rapidly. He sent back a request by radio asking for men and equipment and then turned his attention to marking out a trail from the burn area to the lake. This was not accomplished without some trepidation on his part because of recent grizzly bear activity in the area. A Fish and Game employee, who had been

Photo of the Cub Creek fire on the eastern shore of Yellowstone Lake. (Courtesy of
L. G. Biddulph)

checking the egg-collection station at Peale Island a few days before, was
accosted by a grizzly. The bear chased him around the trap, and he escaped in
a small rowboat, fortuitously tied to the trap, using a paddle made of a broken
piece of planking.

A grizzly so inclined toward mischief could prove deadly. Fortunately,
Biddulph was able to establish a trail and guided firefighters into the blaze
without incident. The blaze was eventually extinguished, but, as was the case
with the Heart Lake fire of 1932, not without the help of nature's
precipitation.

FIRE BOSSES AND TRAINING
In his history, Merrill Beal lamented not being called up to do the "he-
man" work of firefighting:

> Reasonably competent and cooperative employees receive special as-
> signments in Park Service. This rule has applied to seasonal natural-
> ists during serious fire seasons. Some of the veterans, like Biddulph,
> Lystrup, and Replogle, became fire-camp bosses. Others served as fire
> group leaders.

My lieu days were devoted to substituting for them. One season, every naturalist at Old Faithful but me was called on fire service duty. My role, although vital, seemed void of prestige for a couple of days.[11]

Beal did have occasion to work on a fire at Specimen Ridge, but the rain put that one out, and he served as assistant timekeeper on the Witch Creek fire, south of Lewis Lake, which was not quite as glamorous as camp boss. But his friend Bud Lystrup would have gladly soothed Beal's need for "prestige" with the very words he wrote at the completion of his first firefighting experience: "I had the audacity to long for a fire....I thought it would be fun, adventuresome and heroic—it is anything but that....It wasn't at all picturesque. It was real, tough, hard, back-breaking labor."[12] During the 1950s and '60s, the National Park Service spent considerable time and money in establishing more effective firefighting policies and training techniques for those who were called upon to fight the fires, since most men had little practical experience in doing this dangerous work. In order to establish policies and procedures for this training, the Park Service held a conference in Yellowstone about 1960. Between 100 and 150 dignitaries from Washington, DC; the regional office in Omaha, Nebraska; and other places attended. Superintendent Lemuel Garrison assigned his two assistants, Luis A. Gastellum and Julius A. Martinek, to put together a static display of a model fire camp. Gastellum and Martinek drew upon the ample experience of Wayne Replogle and assigned him the task of preparing the camp. Martinek told Replogle that no cost would be spared for this meeting because of the level of dignitaries coming.

Dot Island at the mouth of West Thumb was selected as the site. Replogle assembled a staff of people to help him put the camp together. The meeting was to be held on a Sunday, and by Saturday evening, Replogle and his team had put together what he called a "very beautiful camp" on Dot Island, complete with a fire-camp layout, tables and chairs for meals and discussion, and a liquor bar.

On Sunday, about noon, the guests arrived at Dot Island by park boats. After a period of "imbibing," the dignitaries sat down to a sumptuous dinner that included steaks and fresh-cooked trout. When it was all over, the men loaded in the boats "with some help" and went to shore, while Replogle remained another day to clean up.

No mention was made by Replogle in his memoirs of any actual training or discussion relative to firefighting, only the consumption of fire water.

It must have been a big success—value of taxpayers' money undetermined—because Garrison told Replogle to "please leave this camp alone for future parties. It will be a permanent setup for the future use of government meetings."[13] Thus, it seems that Dot Island became, for a time, the Martha's Vineyard of Yellowstone Park.

TOWARD NATURAL MANAGEMENT

By the mid-twentieth century, principles of ecology began to influence how park managers viewed and dealt with forest fires. Fires began to be recognized as a regenerative force and part of the great circle of life in nature. By the early 1970s, park administrators began experimenting with a more natural fire policy. As many as 235 fires, a majority of which were less than 100 acres in size, were allowed to burn. All were successfully extinguished by natural means; the fire either ran out of fuel to burn or was extinguished by precipitation. But no one was prepared for what happened in the summer of 1988.

Unseasonably wet summers between 1982 and 1987 significantly increased the growth of foliage and vegetation in the park. The year 1988 proved to be the driest summer in the recorded history of Yellowstone. The die was cast. Fires began that season primarily due to lightning strikes. By the end of July, 99,000 acres were in flames. By the early part of September of that year, 36 percent of park acreage had been torched (739,000 of the 2,221,800 acres). Including the greater ecosystem surrounding Yellowstone, 1.2 million acres had burned. Sixty-seven structures were destroyed. An undetermined number of bear, buffalo, elk, deer, and moose had perished, not to mention many smaller mammals and birds.

Given the endangerment to man, one of the biggest firefighting efforts known in the history of the region was assembled to once again do war with nature. But in the end, as it always is, it was nature that decided when the war would end, and man was left with the stark realization of his feebleness in comparison to nature's awesome power.

From an aesthetic eye, the forests appeared devastatingly ruined. Dense green forest had turned to stark, black bones. Yet the plant and animal species in Yellowstone proved resilient and "fire adaptive." The animals continued to flourish despite the blackened forests. Within a short period of time, wildflowers and other plants sprang up on the blackened floor, providing brilliant contrasts of color amid the gray drabness. Seeds from the cones of the lodgepole pine released their precious life, and new green sprouts began to grow.

What seemed to man to be an ugly killing of nature was, from an ecological perspective, but a renewal of life.

With such an understanding, Lystrup's description of a graveyard of dark, naked stillness is given hope with the understanding that forests, like people, grow old and must ultimately die, but death by fire brings a resurrection of new and glorious life. Nature has much to teach man. It helps us focus not on what was but on what is to come. It requires us to see beyond the immediate and understand a more expansive cycle of life, to see decades beyond and realize that fire is nature's way of sanctifying itself. Nature's invariable cycle—a birth, a life, a death, and a reawakening—provides a pattern of hope for mankind.

Lin Yang's assessment of human aging is hauntingly appropriate to Yellowstone's forests and gets the last word:

> I like spring, but it is too young. I like summer, but it is too proud. So I like best of all autumn, because its leaves are a little yellow, its tone mellower, its colors richer, and it is tinged a little with sorrow and a premonition of death. Its golden richness speaks not of the innocence of spring, nor of the power of summer, but of the mellowness and kindly wisdom of approaching age. It knows the limitations of life and is content. From knowledge of those limitations and its richness of experience emerge a symphony of colors, richer than all, its green speaking of life and strength, its orange speaking of golden content and its purple of resignation and death.[14]

Chapter 10

Old Faithful's Best Friend

Merrill Beal was once asked by a tourist if he ever tired of seeing Old Faithful erupt, to whom he replied, "Do you ever tire of seeing the face of your beloved?" Although Beal was not as devoted a geyser observer as was his friend and colleague George Marler, he still found great pleasure in the thermal features of Yellowstone: "I never tired of seeing the old reliable ones, such as Beehive, Castle, Clepsydra, Daisy, Fountain, Grand, Great Fountain, Lion, Lone Star, Riverside, and White Dome. Geysers that played less frequently and regularly had an exhilarating influence on me. These included Giant, Giantess, Morning, Splendid, and Fan geysers."[1]

Few if any people associated with Yellowstone through its illustrious history have equaled George Marler's devotion to geyser study. *American Magazine* referred to Marler as "Old Faithful's Best Friend" because of his long association with the famous geyser.[2] By 1950 Marler had devoted twenty years of his life to geyser study, and he had established himself as the premier authority on park geysers and hot springs. He knew more about their history, evolution, and functioning than any man or woman at the time. Marler found more than pleasure in the thermal features of the park. He literally consecrated himself to their study and protection and became their most ardent advocate.

Yellowstone's geysers and hot springs are international treasures, each year drawing millions of visitors eager to see and explore these natural wonders. Before adequate regulatory processes were in place, or at least enforced, Yellowstone's geysers were severely damaged and some even destroyed by curious visitors. People climbed on, waded in, bathed in, did their laundry in,

The view of Old Faithful Geyser in eruption from the Old Faithful trailside museum, ca. 1950. (Courtesy of George Marler)

carved their initials in, threw debris in, rolled boulders into, and broke off delicate pieces of these features. Some of the more beautiful pools, such as Morning Glory Pool, became Yellowstone's Fontana di Trevi, so laden with coins that it impaired their function and destroyed their pristine beauty.[3] Fan Geyser and Handkerchief Pool became virtually extinct for a time.

The human damage done to Yellowstone's natural resources each summer was of great consternation to Marler and his colleagues. Surely, one of the consolations of Yellowstone was to step back from the roads and view pristine, primitive nature, the same landscape beheld by the Native Americans and first white explorers. Sadly, Marler noted, "it was the geysers, the very objects which furnish the inspiration for the area set aside as a national park, which suffered the most."[4]

Three types of vandalism were particularly destructive to thermal features in the park: removing or defacing of mineral specimens from the geysers and hot springs, misuse of geysers for their intended purpose, and throwing of debris into the geysers and hot springs.

DEFACING THERMAL FEATURES

Marler had early photos of geysers, such as Old Faithful, Castle, and Turban, that were taken by William H. Jackson during the 1872 Hayden Survey. Comparing these early photos with conditions in his day, Marler was able to see the deplorable mutilation of thermal features by souvenir hunters who removed mineral specimens from the delicate formations.

Other visitors felt compelled to record their identity by carving their initials into the delicate sides of the pools and orifices. At Biscuit Basin the hot-water runoffs were beautifully tinted by algae in shades of brown, red, orange, blue, and pink. This natural beauty was often marred by unsightly names, initials, and dates carved into the formations.

One July day in the 1930s, two teenage girls were apprehended by the district ranger while they were carving their names and birth dates into the cone of Old Faithful following an eruption. He brought the two girls into the ranger station and questioned them as to their motives. Bud Lystrup was present to witness the inquisition and noted that both girls confessed that they had done it just for fun. The ranger gave them the option of removing their names with a steel brush or accompanying him to Mammoth Hot Springs to face the judge. The girls chose to use the brush, but the damage had been done. As Lystrup pointed out, "It requires years for the algae to grow over and cover the marks."[5]

MISUSE OF GEYSERS

The only purpose of a geyser or hot spring in the park is as a living, kinetic testimony of the power of the earth's volcanism. Misuse of these hot springs began as early as 1885 when an enterprising but unfortunate Chinese man operated a laundry business at Old Faithful over a hot spring. Will Burdett, a columnist of his day, told the story with humor and a little exaggeration:

> It is written in the Archives of Yellowstone Park that a child of the Flowery Kingdom, wearing the usual smile on his child-like face, and his shirt outside of his trousers, came to the Upper Geyser Basin to establish a laundry, because there was enough hot water there to run a Presidential Campaign. He pitched his tent over a thermal Spring, wrote his name in weird characters upon a sign board, and when the raiment of the native and pilgrim came in, he chucked the whole invoice into the bubbling spring. Then he threw in a bar of soap, and smiled to see the great forces that upheaved mountains and shake continents, and toss the mighty Globe into convulsions most awful, doing plain washing in a Chinese laundry. But this spring was a slumbering geyser. The soap awakened the imprisoned giant; with a roar that made the earth tremble, and a shriek of a steam whistle, a cloud of steam and

a column of boiling water shot up into the air a hundred feet, carrying soap, raiment, tent and Chinaman along with the rush, and dropping them at various intervals along the way. "Hookee-la," said John, when he came down—way down! "Joss he no like washee for China-boy. Too muchee bubblee make." And since that day men have known the way to arouse a slumbering geyser is to give the monster soap.[6]

Through subsequent years, scientists performed experiments with soap, trying to understand its effect on geyser eruptions. They found that soap had no universal influence on thermal features. Some erupted quickly with the addition of small amounts of soap, and other geysers did not respond at all. They concluded that geysers with a constricted throat that had water temperatures close to the boiling point were susceptible to eruption with the addition of soap. Beehive Geyser was one of those. Soap appeared to lower the surface tension of the water and cause it to retain heated air that would normally escape from the surface through bubbles. The increased heat in combination with a reduction of surface tension elicited an explosion of water if the plumbing and temperature of the water were right.[7]

For some time after the Chinese man's unfortunate discovery, soaping hot springs became an intrigue, especially for employees of various concessionaires. Due to the potential for serious damage to hot springs and the inappropriateness of tampering with natural features, soaping was prohibited by park administration. Marler was particularly offended by such behavior, but on at least one occasion he was forced to resort to the use of soap to help save a thermal feature, as we shall see shortly.

Bathing in hot springs was another problem. The water in most thermal hot springs and geysers is superheated and of sufficient temperature to scald human or animal flesh. Unfortunate deaths and serious injuries occurred over the years, usually precipitated by carelessness or disregard for safety rules. In 1932 Lystrup reported having to help rescue a little girl who had fallen into a hot pool. She later died of her burns (see chapter 3). There have been others. Lee Whittlesey, Yellowstone Park historian and archivist, has detailed an exhaustive history of people who have lost their lives in Yellowstone because of such accidents.[8] Animals were also victims of the hot springs. An occasional deer, elk, or buffalo fell into a hot spring or orifice during the winter months, and its carcass had to be removed by the rangers.

Not every hot pool is scalding. Turquoise Pool in Midway Geyser Basin is such a one. In the early 1920s and '30s, park employees frequented this

Marler at Handkerchief Pool in Black Sands Basin in October 1950, after restoring the pool to activity. (Photo by D. Condon; courtesy of the National Park Service, Yellowstone National Park, YELL 35698)

pool for late-night skinny-dipping. In 1932 Wayne Replogle had the assignment to ride his motorcycle down to Midway Geyser Basin and chase off the employees who came there to bathe.

Many years later, he made a comment about an employee, supposedly working at Old Faithful in 1932, who jumped into Opal Pool, mistaking it for Turquoise, and was scalded to death.[9] Park death records provide no evidence of this event, nor does Whittlesey's book on deaths in Yellowstone contain any such event. It is extremely unlikely that such a death would go unrecorded in medical records, and we must assume that Replogle's memory of the event is flawed in some way, at least in regards to the outcome. Regardless, it illustrates an important point that those who violate the laws of nature are often severely punished.

THROWING DEBRIS INTO POOLS

Certain death came to people who threw themselves or fell into boiling hot springs, but hot springs also occasionally suffered death by people throwing debris into them. One victim of human vandalism was a small but very popular spring named Handkerchief Pool, so named because when hand-kerchiefs were thrown into the pool, they were sucked deep into its inte-rior by convection currents and then returned to the surface soaked in hot mineral water. This unique phenomenon made Handkerchief Pool one of the chief attractions to the geyser basins in Yellowstone Park. It was a small, delicately throated pool in the Black Sand Basin, measuring only twenty-four by thirty-six inches in diameter on the surface. The upper basin tapered rather abruptly to a six-inch throat, leading to a second chamber below the first. Water entered the pool from a side vent in the lower chamber in a pulsing fashion that caused convection currents to swirl between the two connected chambers, creating the convection phenomenon so attractive to park visitors.

Unfortunately, people threw more than handkerchiefs into the small pool. Debris eventually choked its tube and filled its lower chamber. In 1926 someone jammed a log into the six-inch throat. Water no longer filled its basin, and its famous convection currents ceased to work. In 1938 nearby Rainbow Pool erupted into a geyser and so completely filled Handkerchief Pool with cemented sand that its location was no longer readily discernible. A beautiful and intriguing wonder of Yellowstone was eliminated by human abuse.

For years afterward, visitors to Yellowstone pummeled naturalists with questions about the whereabouts of Handkerchief Pool. Beginning in the fall season of 1946 and extending through 1950, cleanup work on the geysers was instituted by park superintendent Edmund B. Rogers and Chief Park Naturalist David Condon. In October 1950, Marler was assigned to rejuve-nate Handkerchief Pool. With pick and shovel, he and Granville Ogburn and Jack Heaton carefully removed the cemented sand from its basin and delicate throat. In the lower chamber, they found that the side vent, through which water entered into the pool, had been plugged by a piece of wood. With some effort, the wood was removed, and behold! Water again began to fill the lower and upper chambers. Ogburn suggested that they drop a handkerchief into the pool and see what would happen. Marler recorded the outcome: "Scarcely before it was wet a downward current carried it into the bowl and out of sight. Presto, it shot up to the surface! Further experimentation seemed to indicate that indeed a miracle had occurred; Handkerchief Pool's restora-tion was complete."[10]

Park administration tried unsuccessfully to protect Handkerchief Pool by not advertising it and trying to keep it anonymous. However, word got

Marler removes debris from Teakettle Springs, October 1950. (Photo by Verde Watson; courtesy of the National Park Service, Yellowstone National Park, YELL 33173)

around, and it was not too many seasons before Handkerchief Pool was once again rendered inoperable by human debris. In the words of Jack Ellis Haynes, "A fascinating natural feature at the mercy of sightseers had become history."[11] In 1988 it was determined by some type of experiment that the convection action had returned to the pool. Since then, Handkerchief Pool has vacillated between a quiet pool and a small geyser.

During the summers at Old Faithful, Lystrup observed innumerable people throwing stones, sticks, and other debris into the pools and geysers. He understood children's curiosity, but failed to comprehend adults' thoughtless actions. He came upon Brilliant Pool just as two men and their wives were about to roll a large boulder into its beautiful water. His shout brought them up short. None of the four could explain their intentions, but they were extremely apologetic and rolled the boulder back to its original position. Lystrup concluded, "I suppose that in the history of Yellowstone, tons of materials have been deliberately thrown into the pools and geysers. There is no question that many of the geysers have been irreparably damaged by such thoughtless actions."[12]

Fan Geyser, named by the Washburn Party in 1870 because of the shape of its plume, played only two or three times a year to an average height of 110 feet. At one point, it became fully dormant, and Marler discovered that several hundred pounds of rock and sinter had broken off and rolled into the orifice of this relatively small geyser, along with bottles, sticks, and other human debris. Marler and his crew removed this debris in the late fall of 1950, and Fan Geyser, along with its sidekick, Mortar Geyser, continued to perform for the public.

PRICELESS GARBAGE DISPOSALS

Morning Glory Pool, considered to be one of the most beautiful pools in the park, was another victim of human destruction. Its shape and sinter sides reflect the deepest azure blue of the sky. In earlier days, Morning Glory Pool became Yellowstone's wishing well. Thousands of visitors threw coins into the pool until its sides and lower visible ledges literally glittered with a coating of copper and zinc. Other objects were thrown into the pool as well, and rapidly, Morning Glory Pool lost its beauty and ebullition.

Removal of the coins and other junk seemed impossible. The best rangers could do was reach the visible edges of the pool, and even that was a difficult task for a pool as large as Morning Glory. In desperation, Marler resorted to something he detested: the use of soap. Soap just might induce Morning Glory Pool to erupt and vomit much of the garbage that had been thrown into it.

With approval of park administration, Marler induced Morning Glory to erupt using soap. The pool vomited up only a portion of its contents, but it was substantial, including rocks, money, film cases, flashbulbs, fishing gear, fruit pits, cans, cigarette containers, matches, buttons, telephone wire, bottles, combs, lipstick, nails, an engagement ring, watches, rifle shells, keys, safety razors, seventy-six handkerchiefs (it seemed that tourists wanted to see if Morning Glory could duplicate Handkerchief Pool), towels (if a small pool could do handkerchiefs, maybe a large pool could do towels or sheets), tokens, and a host of other objects.

This sorry display of human disrespect was found in other geysers and hot springs. While on duty one summer morning at the Lower Geyser Basin, Bud Lystrup heard a strange mechanical sound, like a sprocket of a camera turning film, or perhaps bolts and screws loosened on the boardwalk. He hunted around for the noise for some time, finally discovering its source: an empty beer can—Pilsner's Extra Light—bobbing up and down in the boiling water of Jet Geyser. Lystrup wrote in *Nature Notes*, "The can was gingerly removed and natural sounds once again reigned supreme."[13]

Within thirty minutes on a Sunday morning in mid-August, Lystrup
picked up, recorded, and placed in his government truck the following garbage from the Upper Geyser Basin:

> 23 paper cups (conical and cup), 3 paper cartons filled with garbage,
> 2 Ritz cracker boxes, 1 Sun Maid raisin box, 1 U&I powdered sugar box,
> 17 paper milk cartons, 1 Nabisco fig Newton carton, 1 Hamms beer car-
> ton, 1 Nabisco honey grahams box, 6 paper pie plates, 1 cottage cheese
> carton, 29 film cartons of various sizes, 8 blue and white flash bulbs,
> 1 cellophane wrapped Roi Tan cigar, 16 bread wrappers, 1 box F & F
> cough lozenges, 1 round carton Lady Melba sandwiches, 1 broken por-
> celain plate, 1 carton Rockwood mint wafers, 1 carton Tide, 21 cans of
> varying substance (author did not copy Lystrup's meticulous itemization),
> 25 beer cans (all itemized), 33 bottles of beer (all itemized by label), 15
> bottles (all itemized by type), 38 cigarette containers (listing all brands),
> and 18 broken bottles.[14]

PROTECTING THE GEYSERS AND HOT SPRINGS

Marler was vexed by what he considered inadequate protection of the thermal features. He lamented that millions of dollars were spent by the federal
government on roads and facilities in the park so that tourists might be able
to enjoy the world's largest display of hydrothermal features, yet they failed
to adequately appropriate manpower to protect, police, and supervise the
very treasures for which the park was famous.[15]

Marler's vexation was shared by others. The ratio of rangers to visitors
was insufficient to prevent much of the incidental and malicious vandalism
done to geysers during the summer season. Ranger naturalists helped to protect and police the geyser basins as they performed their interpretive duties.
One morning the combined staff of rangers and naturalists, which included
Merrill Beal, George Marler, and Bud Lystrup, had a meeting in the ranger
station near Old Faithful. Art Jacobsen, head ranger, entered in a huff and
confronted the assembly of men with stern words: "You rangers have got to
patrol the basins more regularly. I just came from Black Sand Basin, and I'm
disgusted. They are starting to throw pennies in Emerald Pool; and I found
bacon rinds in several places. The sagebrush campers are washing dishes in
those little hot springs. I want that stopped—do you hear me?"

A young ranger, named Remer, heard loud and clear, and he accepted
Art's challenge. Disguising himself as a tourist in civilian clothes, he stood by

the geysers at meal times, intent on apprehending an offending tourist. One morning, tired of ambling around and waiting, he sat in a shady place and began to doze. Upon looking up, he observed a shining object in the hands of a lady kneeling by a small hot spring. He bounded toward her, saying, "Madam, you are not permitted to wash your dishes in these springs."

Arising with dignity and indignation, the lady said: "Please note that I am not washing anything. I am simply dipping a cup of water for medicinal purposes. In his lecture the naturalist explained that geyser water is super heated and pure."

Remer agreed, but added, "Don't take much, or you may get a mild case of dysentery."

"Young man," said she, "that's exactly what I need."[16]

Preservation of Yellowstone's geysers and hot springs remained a central focus throughout the interpretive era. Ranger naturalists dedicated themselves to raising public awareness of this priceless heritage through campfire talks, geyser walks, cone talks at Old Faithful, and other public forums. The attempt at making sensitive and responsible stewards of the public was a never-ending task that was never truly fulfilled to their satisfaction.

PART THREE

Interpreting Yellowstone

The born naturalist is one of the most lucky men in the world. Winter or summer, rain or shine, at home or abroad, walking or riding, his pleasures are always near at hand. The great book of nature is open before him, and he has only to turn its pages.

—John Burroughs, *Under the Maples* (1921)

Chapter 11

The True Observer

THE NATURE OF OBSERVATION

John Burroughs once described his friend and fellow nature lover President Theodore Roosevelt in terms that speak of the qualities needed by a genuine interpreter: "You may know the true observer, not by the big things he sees, but by the little things; and then not by the things he sees with effort and unpremeditated seeing—the quick spontaneous action of his mind in the presence of natural objects. Plenty of men see straight and report straight what they see, but those who see what others miss, who see quickly and surely, who have the detective eye, who get the drop so to speak on every object, who see minutely and who see whole, are true observers."[1]

Any person can clump about in nature, see little or nothing, and emerge unchanged. But for the true observer, each excursion into nature is a life-changing event. He or she goes quietly and observantly into nature, sees things that dull eyes miss, and hears things to which others' ears are mute. Observers see relationships, small things in the context of the greater whole. The solitary or momentary event is but a blip in a much vaster continuum of time and space. Observers don't just see things; they feel things. They are attuned to the rhythms and beauty of nature, and their reports are descriptions not merely of what they see, but also of how they feel about what they see.

The Five Old Men developed, over time, into worthy examples of true observers. Each came to passionately love the flora and fauna of the park. They took thousands of pictures and kept journals of what they saw and under what circumstances they were seen. They were fully engaged each time they went into Yellowstone's nature. It was not good enough to just see something; they

Five Old Men in front of the Madison Junction Trailside Museum, ca. 1949. (Courtesy of the National Park Service, Yellowstone National Park, YELL 19888-1)

wanted to comprehend it as fully as possible. John Muir's sentiments fit all: "In my love for nature, I have a passion for plant study, especially for flowers and trees, but also for birds, animal life, and rock formations."[2]

FOUNDATIONS OF OBSERVATION

We briefly noted in a previous chapter the use of field observations in laying the foundation of the educational programs in the park. We now examine a few of these observations of Yellowstone through the eyes of the Five Old Men who are representative of many of their colleagues.

Early educational efforts, particularly a publication known as *Yellowstone Letters* and its sequel, *Yellowstone Nature Notes,* helped establish a premium for good observation and field reporting by its rangers and ranger naturalists. *Nature Notes* had a homey quality to it, often with sketches rendered by the observer in pencil and pen of animals, plants, birds, and wilderness scenes. Although comparatively meager in content and scientific rigor by today's standards, *Letters* and *Nature Notes* set the precedent for observation and interpretation in Yellowstone for the next several decades.

Early issues of *Nature Notes,* dating from 1932 to 1942, were edited by the chief park naturalist, Dr. C. Max Bauer. Publication was suspended during 1943, '44, and '45 due to World War II. In 1946, after Bauer left Yellowstone and Dave Condon became chief park naturalist, an editorial board was established composed of the chief park naturalist, chief park ranger, and the management assistant to the superintendent.[3]

REPORTING OBSERVATIONS

A variety of reporting styles emerged in *Nature Notes.* Some entries were what Burroughs called "straight seeing and reporting." Their authors sought to reconstruct the observation as accurately and unbiased as possible. Other observers gave interpretations of what they saw in nature, and still others had a flair for emotional expression.

Some examples of straight reporting follow. One writer reported seeing two loons on Riddle Lake. Another saw two trumpeter swans fly over Mammoth Hot Springs. He followed them to Swan Lake Flats—just south of Mammoth—and found that they nested there. Another reported bald eagles nesting in a large Douglas fir on the east side of the Yellowstone River about a mile below Fishing Bridge.

Such reports might be thoroughly uninteresting to today's reader unless one understands the times and circumstances under which they were written. At one time, swans and bald eagles were endangered species. Swans migrated in and out of the park and were killed by hunters outside the park to such an extent that they were in serious danger of extinction. George Marler took up the cause of the swan by writing articles about their plight. Seeing two adult birds fly over Mammoth and set up housekeeping at Swan Lake Flats was important information at the time.

Equally important was identifying the location, habitat, distribution, and migratory habits of various species of birds and animals in the park; hence, the value of reporting loons at Riddle Lake and eagles along the Yellowstone River. Naturalists of that era did not have the plethora of information about wildlife of Yellowstone that modern scientists now enjoy. Such reports through the years have helped build a lexicon of interpretive information and knowledge from which park naturalists and scientists could draw.

An interesting example of interpretive reporting was made by Riley McClelland and Wayne Replogle of a swan family that they helped rescue. Wayne Replogle made reference to this story in the *Mile-by-Mile* transcript he made of Yellowstone Park in the 1970s. The following report is provided by Riley McClelland in March 2012:

A pair of Trumpeter Swans nested on a swampy pond south of Bunsen Peak in late spring 1964. The nest produced four cygnets. On 5 July, the swan family was seen "hiking" from the pond toward Swan Lake. Wayne Replogle and I were driving south across Swan Lake Flat on the afternoon of the 5th. We saw the four cygnets, barely visible in the Big Sagebrush, on the east side of the main road that crosses Swan Lake Flats. The cygnets seemed very small for the time of year. The adults were on the west side, several hundred feet from the road. The cygnets obviously were wary about crossing pavement for the first time.

After watching from a distance for half an hour and observing the cygnets flee away from the road each time a car drove by, we decided to intervene. The young birds clearly were in jeopardy of being hit by a vehicle. Replogle and I carried the four cygnets across the main road to the Swan Lake side. Perhaps this was contrary to policy, even then, but we decided there was nothing "natural" about swans getting run over by a vehicle. The next day, 6 July, the two adults and four cygnets were observed floating on Swan Lake.

On 12 July, Replogle and Elroy Bohlin observed the swan family back on the nesting pond, south of Bunsen Peak (the distance between the nesting pond and Swan Lake is 1.2 miles). No swans were observed on Swan Lake on the 12th. There are no further records (of which I am aware) until mid-September, when the swan family had again departed the nesting pond and returned to Swan Lake. The family remained on Swan Lake through late September and early October. The final sighting and record of the two adults and four cygnets on Swan Lake was on the evening of 16 October. That night (16–17 October), the Swan Lake surface froze. On the 17th, the swan family was not seen.[4]

Bald eagles were in a similar situation as the swan. Noting the location and presence of a pair of adult eagles allowed naturalists and biologists to track the number of young and even band them for longitudinal studies.

For several years, Lowell Biddulph monitored the bald eagles that nested in the great Douglas fir tree on the Yellowstone River a mile north from Fishing Bridge. Several generations of eaglets grew to adulthood in the massive nest high in its dead branches. Biddulph watched them from the time they hatched until the time they made their first solo flight from the nest. After a few moments of mad flapping, the young eagles caught the air currents and swept across the great river and wilderness landscape on outstretched wings, as if they had done it forever.

Such observations not only taught Biddulph about eagles, but also gave him broader insight into human life. In a talk he gave to students at Ricks College as dean of students, he used the example of a bald eagle that he once saw flying majestically in the sky, only to collapse its wings and plunge to earth. Upon examination of the once-mighty bird of prey, he discovered that it was filled with parasites that had eaten away its life a little at a time. He compared the parasites to bad habits, addictive behaviors, and harmful attitudes that eat away at human character and destroy productive lives.

Naturalists had remarkable opportunities to observe interaction among wildlife in the park. Watching these life-and-death dramas made them better interpreters for the public. Biddulph reported in *Nature Notes* watching an osprey circling high over a river. Suddenly, it plunged some thirty feet straight down into the swiftly moving water, then rose with some difficulty into the air with a wriggling cutthroat trout clutched in its talons. Nature had endowed this bird with eyesight so keen and agility so profound that it could see a fish at great heights in flowing water, plunge into the water without harming itself, and capture the illusive fish in its hook-like talons.

Astounding as that feat was, what followed was even more amazing and served to illustrate how one species benefits from the endowments of another in nature. Biddulph reported that no sooner had the osprey succeeded in getting airborne with the fish than it was assaulted in midair by a California gull. The gull swooped in upon the osprey repeatedly until the struggling and distracted bird lost its grip on the fish. The trout fell to the ground, and the gull promptly broke off its aerial assault and recovered the fish. The osprey returned to fishing.

The casual observer would not imagine a gull capable of such a feat against a much better-equipped bird of prey. But the report showed how a scavenger-like gull can use its intelligence to have a fish dinner without doing the hard work of catching the fish.

Another field observation from *Nature Notes* was reported by a naturalist conducting a nature hike through Minerva Terrace at Mammoth Hot Springs during World War II. In the course of the walk, several bighorn sheep—rams and ewes—bounded directly through the startled crowd of tourists. This surprising encounter was surely as alarming for the sheep as it was for the tourists. Bighorn sheep normally seclude themselves on craggy, higher cliffs and are, therefore, less visible to tourists. No explanation for this unusual encounter was ventured by the reporter, other than to surmise that the sheep had been migrating from Sepulcher Mountain across the canyon to Mount Everts.

Some entries in *Nature Notes* were historical in nature and included observations of both human and geological interest. George Marler, who regularly wrote about his observations of geysers and hot springs, often included historical and geological comparisons to observations made by earlier explorers, as far back as the Washburn Expedition of 1870. These series of observations made through the years helped both naturalist and tourist appreciate the often subtle changes that occurred to the park's geysers and hot springs.

Merrill Beal's and Wayne Replogle's contributions to *Nature Notes* were frequently on topics of human history and Indian lore, although not exclusively so. Beal was particularly interested in the early exploration and discovery of the park and provided entries on findings through his research, whereas Replogle's primary interest lay in the Native American. Much of Beal's work was published in books in addition to *Nature Notes,* and Replogle's search for the Bannock Indian Trail was also published as a book. Later chapters of this book include some of their work.

THE INFLUENCE OF OBSERVATION

Time spent in nature had a transforming effect upon ranger naturalists, which was reflected in their observations. Ted Ogston, the army scout–turned-ranger knew this as well as anyone. His directive to seasonal rangers in the 1920s and '30s was to get out into nature and learn by experience. John Muir, the celebrated explorer and wilderness naturalist, also had a high opinion of wilderness exposure. Although he studied at the University of Wisconsin and received honorary degrees from Harvard, Yale, and the University of California, he noted, "One day's exposure to mountains is better than cartloads of books."[5]

The following example from *Nature Notes,* published in 1947, has an aesthetic quality, despite the scientific jargon, suggesting soul-felt inspiration wrought by a beautiful wilderness scene that the author attempted to paint in words:

> Here, perpetual snow banks feed small rivulets to form alpine lakes in the glacial cirques of these high mountains. Cascading streams flow down precipitous slopes from these sequestered lakes dashing, falling, and leaping to the valley below. Dense forests of Engelmann spruce (*Picea englemannii*) and Alpine fir (*Abies lasiocarpa*) form a most delightful setting along these cool, moss covered streams bordered by colors of pine and blue of the Lewis Monkey flower (*Mimulus lewisii*) and

Mertensia or Bluebell. Pastel shades of lemon colored Columbine (*Acquilegia flavescena*), cream colored Lousewort (*Pedicularis bracteosa*) and ever dainty grass of Parnassia combine artistically with vivid paintbrush reds, deep gentian blues, and the purple of the stately Monkshood (*Aconitum columbianum*).

Following these streams one gets occasional glimpses of Water Ouzel (*Cinclus mexicanus*) as they dip and bob from rock to rock feeding in the spray of numerous little falls. Plaintive calls of the Chickadee (*Penthestes gambeli*) and Junco (*Junco mearnsi*) are heard in their search for food. Not infrequently, the stillness of the forest is disturbed by the rasping, staccato calls of jays and the raucous call of Nutcracker. Following the cascading streams from the glacial lakes to Sylvan Pass one gets a feeling of contentment. The stillness of shady glens, the musical rhythm of the streams and the grandeur of stately evergreens combine for exquisite beauty.[6]

Captured in the author's meticulous and detailed observation of nature is the pleasant familiarity he enjoyed with its wild rhythm and a deep sense of contentment wrought by being in its presence. It is exactly the transformation John Muir found in wilderness when he wrote, "Climb a mountain and get their good tidings. Nature's peace will flow into you as sunshine flows into trees. The winds will blow their own freshness into you, and the storms their energy, while cares will drop off like autumn leaves."[7] It was this type of voyage into the realm of human emotions and intellectual growth that Freeman Tilden conveyed in his popular book *The National Parks: What They Mean to You and Me.*

Although contributors to *Nature Notes* sometimes gave in to their emotions and spoke in poetic prose, nevertheless, their observations reveal the sense of stimulation that these early interpreters deeply felt and were attempting to stir in others. Two short excerpts from Wayne Replogle's entries on the Grand Canyon of Yellowstone drip with sentiment that he felt for this wonder:

GRAND CANYON OF THE YELLOWSTONE

Oh! To behold such elegance—such purity!—such ethereal barbarism of nature, clothed in its robe of a thousand colors; deepest black through all the grays, to pearl, to purest white, cadmium orange to

Wayne Replogle at Lower Falls, the base of Uncle Tom's Trail. (Photo by D. Condon; courtesy of the National Park Service, Yellowstone National Park, YELL 42361)

lemon yellow, ox-blood red to delicate pink, light green of the timber to deep green of the spruce and juniper; blue skies above with lovely tinted clouds floating like massive dirigibles dipping in salute to the mighty chasm. Oh, perpetual wonder carved by the chiming chisel of a wise and skillful God,—live on![8]

SUNSET AT CANYON

A sacred solemnity swept over the Canyon. There was a dead stillness, one almost crushing; a feeling of ethereal depression, something like an hour of prayer. The sun had crept below the broken horizon. The purple green mountains were now in silhouette. The entire western sky was ablaze with harmonious color, changing, swelling and then dying like the tones of a majestic organ in diminuendo. The whisk of a Western Tanager broke the patient silence. Dusk and a breeze had come. Thus ends the day under western skies at the Grand Canyon of the Yellowstone.[9]

THROUGH AN OBSERVER'S EYES

This chapter on observation is concluded with some of Bud Lystrup's insights taken from the 1953 volumes of *Nature Notes*. Lystrup saw minutely and he saw wholly, and his inquisitive mind was always probing, questioning, exploring, and exulting. Lystrup was, until his retirement in 1967, the longest-serving ranger naturalist in Yellowstone.

His observations reflect, perhaps better than most, the gift for seeing and appreciating what others failed to see or dismissed as mundane. They offer the reader a wonderful insight to the world of Yellowstone through this observer's eyes.[10]

Moonlight over Old Faithful

During a moonlight night I stood on the formation west of Old Faithful with a huge full moon low in the sky behind Old Faithful Lodge. The moon shone so brightly that its light almost penetrated the column of water when Old Faithful erupted. At the termination of the eruption a long narrow cloud came sailing swiftly from the north directly in front of the moon. The effect was as though someone turned out the lights. It was most considerate, the manner in which the cloud arrived after the eruption.

Odors

When a geyser or hot spring establishes a run-off channel over an area of vegetative cover the grasses, sedges and shrubs are well cooked. The resultant odor is pungent in a peculiar sweetish yet fetid scent. Such an odor permeated the atmosphere when a group of long dormant geysers became active recently in the Gem Pool region. The odor hung heavily in the atmosphere to an almost offensive degree.

Mid-August along the nature trail affords one the opportunity to appreciate three distinctive fragrant odors: mint, pungent and spicy; ripe huckleberries, lush enough to prompt sampling; and the pine resin, delicate but penetrating.

I marvel at the manner in which a current of air can suddenly, out of a calm atmosphere, grasp a wisp of vapor from a hot spring or geyser and twist it into a perfect whirling cone.

RED-SHAFTED FLICKERS

Two red-shafted flickers are easily observed for they were not in trees seeking food, but were busy picking from the forest floor. Most manifest and striking was the black crescent fitted with precision like a bib on its chest.

BUTTERFLIES

The great influx of butterflies has stirred up much speculation around Old Faithful area. They occur over the entire area. They were first noticed in great numbers August 11–13 and now a week later a second swarm has arrived. The margin of the wings are ragged and uneven. When folded, the wings are mottled with a brown the dominating color though one can find a dash of gray, a little orange, a tiny band of blue. But once the wings are open, the Polygonia wears an entirely different suit. Now he has become a creature in orange and black.

OX-EYE DAISIES

I feel that the welcome nod given by the cluster of ox-eye daisies along the road north of Castle Geyser is almost personal. Each year in August they burst forth and dominate that spot with their cheery yellow and pure white. They grow only there along the road and on the geyser trail over Geyser Hill where hundreds of feet trample them. Why should such a hardy plant with abundant seed dispersal not be much more populated over the entire area?

ALBINO CORALROOT

The talus slopes across the little stream from Emerald Pool, in June, abound in delightful floral displays. Ferns and little elephant-head predominate but Indian paint brush and coralroot splash their colors betwixt to lend a mosaic scheme unmatched on canvas. I tried to grasp the beauty when my eyes beheld a flower breathtakingly different. There, majestically proud among its lavender coralroot friends stood an albino coralroot (*Corallorhiza*); sheer white orchid flowers wore a velvet sheen of the most delicate structure. Awards come when one least expects them—my day was complete.

Blue Flowers

People from New England, especially Massachusetts, have frequently remarked to me that they are most impressed with the blue flowers in Yellowstone. They explain that they have blue flowers but the intense true blue is lacking in New England.

Snails

A man asked me one day if snails are common in the streams around the geyser basins. I [asked] seasonal naturalist Ken Armitage who is doing work in limnology. He has found only two snails and their shells were so fragile that they almost crumbled when he picked them up. Snails make their shells from carbonate, and since there is very little calcium carbonate in the geyser formations it is logical that snails should be scarce.

A Sunday Morning

A Sunday morning in July was a soulful experience for me. I walked through the tourist cabin area on my way to work. In front of a cabin seven children ranging in age from perhaps four to twelve were seated on benches arranged in a semi-circle. A father, Bible held in his hands, was conducting Sunday School. He read passages from a [B]ible and asked questions of the children. Hands were raised in eagerness. I stood there and marvelled at a sight which is all too infrequent in this age of hurry and scurry.

A Grizzly Den

On July 20 of this year [1933] District Ranger Childs, Ranger Dougherty and I hiked to the top of the Madison Plateau, south of the Black Sand Basin to determine the feasibility of a temporary fire look-out station. We took the occasion to visit a rock cave known to be a hibernating den of grizzlies. The outer chamber or entrance was about 20 feet by 20 feet by 10 feet high. Before entering we shouted lustily and tossed in some rocks, but there was no response. We crawled in to find a very comfortable den about three feet high and nine feet in diameter. To my surprise there were no bad odors and no evidence of bear excreta. The

Bud Lystrup with megaphone in hand at the base of Uncle Tom's Trail, with Lower Falls in the background. Naturalists regularly led groups to the floor of the canyon. (Courtesy of Liz Lystrup)

place was neat and orderly and the floor bare and smooth. In the center was a hollowed out nest lined with bits of sticks, grass, withered moss, pine and spruce cones, and some horse dung.[11]

SAND PIPERS

Near Purple Pools across from Giant Geyser, a sandpiper has made its nest on the ground amidst a few twigs and blades of grass. Four large eggs lie in the nest. It is remarkable how little protection is afforded to the nest. The female tries to lure me away from her nest with her plaintive calls, fearful that I will harm them. I continue to visit the nest during the week of 11–17 July. Eventually three eggs hatch, but one never does.[12]

THE END OF NATURE NOTES

Yellowstone Nature Notes enjoyed nearly forty years of publication before dying inauspiciously following the 1958 season, the victim of the emerging age of scientific research and information. The Madison River earthquake of August 1959 interrupted its normal publication for that year, and the editorial board used the lapse in time to retool the publication.

In 1959 the editorial board resolved to change *Nature Notes* into a more scholarly annual publication that would be "respected by scientists and librar-ies."[13] The special edition of *Nature Notes* entitled *Yellowstone's Living Geol-ogy—Earthquakes and Mountains* by Dr. William A. Fischer published in June 1960 announced the park's shift away from the amateur reporting of park employees and reliance upon professional, scientific research.[14] No further publications of *Nature Notes* appeared after the 1960 special edition. When its purposes had been accomplished, *Nature Notes* was retired and remains today a rich resource of historical, cultural, and inspirational literature[15] in which the Five Old Men and their colleagues left an intriguing snippet of their love for Yellowstone.

Chapter 12
Into the Woods

Come to the woods, for here is rest. There is no repose like that of the green deep woods. Here grow the wallflower and the violet. The squirrel will come and sit upon your knee, the logcock will wake you in the morning. Sleep in forgetfulness of all ill. Of all the upness accessible to mortals, there is no upness comparable to the mountains.

—JOHN MUIR, *The Wilderness World of John Muir*

Visitors came to Yellowstone not merely to see its geysers, steaming in great vaporous fields, or to fish its wild streams, but also to partake of its "upness." Most went cautiously into nature, staying close to trails and roadways, and then remaining only briefly. Others wanted to experience more deeply its wild nature and "suck out all the marrow of life."[1] To those who made the effort, Yellowstone opened its most inspiring scenes and intimate encounters with its wild denizens.

Ranger naturalists of Yellowstone ventured into the woods, most out of duty, but some with passion. Some went carefully and superficially; others went deeply. Those with the skills and comfort for backcountry tramping spent much of their free time so engaged. For them, birds and animals became friends among which they felt at home. Bud Lystrup appreciated the call of a little black-capped chickadee along a forest trail: "The simple little song reassures one deep in the forest away from the hustle and bustle of man-made things."[2]

Of course, not all encounters were feathery and lovely. The plaintive call of a chickadee is far removed from the roar of a charging grizzly bear or an irate moose or buffalo. When the Five Old Men went to the woods, anything was possible, especially for those who went deep into the woods and high upon the mountains.

Merrill Beal recorded his feelings of Yellowstone at the beginning of his twenty-six seasons there: "We love Yellowstone and all that it signifies in time and space. We love the glorious air, sunlight, and water; its mountains, valleys, trees, and flowers. We love the animals and birds and especially the great lakes and grand canyons."[3]

By Beal's own admission, he was less comfortable in the backwoods and stayed to the trails when going into the woods. Despite his careful ventures, Beal had a few close encounters.

In 1943, while inspecting and repairing telephone lines in the Mount Washburn area of the park, he encountered a bull moose feeding in the middle of a lily pond. It was an enchanting scene: the great moose with velvet-covered antlers standing in crystal water that reflected the blue sky and pine forest. So captivated was Beal by it all that he guided his horse toward the pond for a closer look. Apparently, he came too close. The moose began to glare at him, snort, and toss water with its antlers. Uncertain as to the speed of his mount in comparison to the moose (some have been clocked at speeds of 40 mph) and his ability to remain in the saddle at full gallop, Beal wisely retreated and avoided possible disaster.

While hiking along the Nez Perce Creek trail from the Lower Geyser Basin, Beal encountered three buffalo bulls in a meadow. Writes Beal, "The bulls challenged me by throwing dirt upon themselves and pawing like mad. I quartered away into a grove of trees, but one of the bulls charged, head bunting a small tree. This pantomime impelled me to spring to a thick grove of trees."[4]

One warm, sunny day, George Marler had an encounter with a bull elk near the first bridge between Mammoth and Gardiner: "About 50 feet from the road a bull elk lay prostrate and gave every indication of being dead. I thought this a good opportunity to get some ivories, or teeth. I walked down to the animal and placed my foot on his shoulder preparatory to getting at his mouth. My foot just about caused an explosion. The elk was not dead, as I thought, but sound asleep. When I stepped on him he came to life and took off like a wounded deer."

The event was repeated twenty years later in almost the exact same spot. Marler was a little more cautious this time, as exploding bull elk leave a lasting impression: "Instead of putting my foot on the neck, I put it on the side but I got the same result of an animal coming to life like a cyclone and taking off for the wide open spaces."[5]

Marler found that cow elk with calves proved to be cantankerous. Once near Castle Geyser while he was trying to photograph a calf nursing from its mother, the cow took after him. He was agile enough to escape into some trees and managed to get a photograph of the annoyed cow glaring at him around the tree trunk with curled lips.

While fishing in the Madison River below Madison Junction, Marler attempted to ascend to the bank so that he could move farther upstream to a better hole. However, his path upward was blocked by a cow elk with a yearling directly behind her. The elk stamped hard with her forefeet, and Marler backed down into the river. After a few minutes, he tried it again with the same results. The stamping was repeated until Marler finally hit the cow on the head with a wobbler that he was using as a lure, and the cow and calf turned and ran away.[6]

Life-and-death dramas were an everyday occurrence in nature. Some were more eventful and obvious than others, but these events left those who witnessed them profoundly moved and deeply respectful of the instinct for survival and natural gifts bestowed upon wild creatures.

Such was the case for Bud Lystrup one day after completing a nature walk in the Upper Geyser Basin. Lystrup was scouting about on his own when he was drawn by a thrashing in the water near the bank of the Firehole River. Upon investigation, he found that a garter snake had coiled itself around a six-inch fish and was attempting to bring it to shore. Surprising as it was that a snake had lassoed a fish in the stream, even more intriguing was the challenge that faced the snake in landing the fish. It was about twelve inches from the surface of the stream to the top of the bank. Lystrup watched with growing interest: "Gradually the fish began to weaken. The snake suddenly whipped its tail up on the bank...coiled it around a bunch of grass...then pulled itself and the defeated trout out of the water. A deft, intelligent and almost unbelievable maneuver....[T]he snake let the victim thrash around in the tall grass until...nearly dead. Then, the struggle over, the survivor slowly ate the fish, head first."[7]

Lowell Biddulph and David Condon, the chief park naturalist, witnessed an animal drama during World War II while driving between Tower Fall and Mammoth Hot Springs. Where the road leaves Pleasant Valley, or what used to be called Yancey's Hole,[8] it ascends onto the high plateau overlooking the deep gorge cut by the Yellowstone River. Across the road at a place called

The Narrows in Yellowstone Canyon, near what was called "Yancey's Hole" or "Pleasant Valley," is formed by vertical basalt columns and steep intervening slopes. (Photo by the author)

"the Narrows," the canyon wall is a few hundred feet of sheer, nearly vertical cliffs composed of alternating layers of vertical, cleaved basalt rock and intervening sediment.[9]

On one of these steep sedimentary slopes between sheer basalt abutments, a bighorn ewe was in obvious distress. Void of her normal agility, she labored vertically up the steep, gravelly slope toward the basalt cliff above, while the two ranger naturalists watched intently through binoculars. After great effort, the ewe gained the top of the slope, pressed her nose against the basalt wall, and gave birth to a tiny lamb. The newborn lamb immediately began to slide down the incline toward the precipice that dropped two hundred feet into the Yellowstone River. The ewe worked her way down the slope below the sliding lamb in enough time to stop it from certain death. Bracing the lamb with her legs, the ewe scraped out a flat depression in which the lamb could rest.

Once the lamb was secure and calm, the ewe once again struggled to the top of the slope and gave birth to a second lamb. The ewe seemed to understand

Lowell Biddulph looks down into "Hidden Valley" at the headwaters of
Crow Creek in the saddle between Avalanche and Hoyt Peaks in the
Absaroka Mountains, ca. 1958. (Courtesy of L. G. Biddulph)

that the full length of the slope was needed to save the lamb's life. The process
of rescue was repeated. With great effort, the ewe moved the two lambs
together and stood over them while they nursed. Darkness overtook the scene,
but the two ranger naturalists returned early the next morning, anxious to see
what had become of the family. To their delight, the two lambs were jumping
about the slope and playfully butting their heads together.

Such events provided lessons for a lifetime. The instinct of motherhood to protect and preserve life, even in peril, is not merely a human quality but is shared by animals. Survival instinct is also a shared quality. The lambs' ability to quickly gain agility was essential to survival in the environment into which they were born. Man, by comparison, is far more helpless and vulnerable at birth, but capable of achieving a higher level of intellectual functioning. Yet we can learn from our animal counterparts important lessons about compassion, sacrifice, and the sanctity of life.

Those who stayed to the roadways and beaten paths in the park saw only a microcosm of Yellowstone's remarkable nature. Those who hiked into mountainous wilderness were witness to some of nature's supreme shows. In the 1950s, during a hike up Avalanche Peak in the Absaroka Mountains, Lowell Biddulph was given an unforgettable performance by some elk.

A small saddle joins the rugged peaks of Avalanche and Hoyt that rise high above tree line immediately north of Sylvan Pass. Accessible only by hard, steep climbing, the saddle presents a view of a seemingly endless labyrinth of mountain peaks, barren ridges, and deep, remote pine-covered valleys.

Directly below the saddle, lying butted up against the backdrop of the sheer eastern side of Hoyt and Avalanche Peaks, is a glacial cirque with two beautiful, sapphire-colored lakes surrounded by grassy meadows and pine forests. The water from the springs, lakes, and melting snow forms Crow Creek, which empties into the North Fork of the Shoshone River near Pahaska Tepee.

Among the herd of elk frequenting the cirque that day were three cows and a calf. These four animals grazed for a while, then moved away from the rest of the herd toward the glacial lake. As they reached the lake, suddenly they commenced to run and jump and splash about in the shallow water. This playing continued for some minutes, after which they retired to the adjacent meadow. While the others watched, one cow commenced a dance routine that has been dubbed in Biddulph lore as the "Wapiti Wilderness Wiggle."

The dance routine began with several jumps into the air, accompanied by pronounced twisting and turning. The cow turned in rapid circles one direction, then in the other, in a stiff-legged motion, with head held high. This was followed by great bounding leaps about the meadow. The routine ended with a fast sidestepping motion, first to the right with head tilted sharply in the direction of movement, then to the left. At the conclusion of this routine, the other elk that had also been observing the show began to

Rangers and Fish and Game personnel banding a young white
pelican on Molly Islands in the southeastern arm of Yellowstone
Lake, ca. 1955. (Courtesy of L. G. Biddulph)

dance and splash in the shallow lake. Sitting atop the wilderness arena, Biddulph had a first-rate show.[10]

The birds of Yellowstone were as delightful as the mammals. Some species live indigenous to the park, but most are sunbirds, migrating from hundreds and thousands of miles away. In the 1930s, Fish and Game personnel
began banding birds in Yellowstone as a means of tracking their migratory
habits. The band was engraved with the date and location of banding.

Annual trips were made in the early summer to the Molly Islands in the
far end of the southeastern arm of Yellowstone Lake where some species of

birds nested. The islands were named by the US Geologic Survey team in the 1870s after the wife of Henry Gannett. They are a small, low-lying outcrop of rock perfectly barren of any trees or vegetation that serve as the ancestral breeding grounds for the white pelican, Caspian tern, California seagull, and double-crested cormorant. Every square inch of the islands is covered with makeshift nests, unhatched eggs, and bird droppings. The birds are not what one would call great nest builders, as is the barn swallow or the robin. They seem to drop their eggs—some quite large—in almost any vacant spot.

The annual banding of birds was done while the young were still unable to fly. Fish and Game personnel, augmented heavily with rangers and ranger naturalists, descended upon Molly Islands by park boat and accomplished the task in one long, exhausting day.

There was no element of surprise in the rangers' approach to the islands. Their arrival turned an already noisy community into wild pandemonium. Baby birds in various stages of development squawked and flapped the alarm as they ran helter-skelter about the island amid generations of feathers, bird droppings, and other debris.

Birds that could fly took to the air and commenced what might have been a plausible reenactment of the 1941 bombing of Pearl Harbor. Adult birds dive-bombed the rangers as they tried to catch little and not-so-little birds. The rangers quickly learned that the white pelican babies were formidable. Adult cormorants and terns swept in and divested rangers of their hats. Others swooped in and delivered smelly splatter bombs that sent whitewash out like napalm. Rangers were hit in various parts of their anatomy, but paused only long enough to utter, "Oh, yuk!" and then pressed on with their mission despite the feathered kamikazes.

CLOSE ENCOUNTERS OF THE FURRY KIND

Encounters with bears were perhaps the most unnerving experiences. Black bears were particularly plentiful around human populations, and rangers frequently had interaction with them. Even with the highest degree of caution exhibited by a ranger, an encounter with a bear was sometimes unavoidable. A first-year ranger naturalist who was assigned to Fishing Bridge encountered a sow with a cub as he was walking to work through a meadow. The bear gave chase, and the young naturalist showed up an hour late for work at the museum, having spent the time running circuitously through the woods, pursued by the bear and her cub.

A sow black bear and her two cubs had been working the roadway at Madison Junction, begging for handouts, for a few days. One day, after a hard morning's work, they entered a shady forested area for a siesta. Beal was innocently exploring a forested area along the Madison River and inadvertently entered the same shady grove where the bears were dozing.

Upon entering the trees, Beal was confronted by the sow in what he described as a "menacing manner," likely with growls, a show of teeth, and perhaps even a mock charge. Beal was understandably alarmed by this confrontation and reported that his automatic response was "an involuntary ejaculation of fear and horror"—in other words, a scream. "It was not a voice of command, but the bear stopped." Beal drew a conclusion from this close encounter: "I think some bears recognize rangers."[11] Possible but not probable; more likely, this sow recognized from his reaction that Beal was of no threat to herself or her cubs. His immediate retreat from the grove of trees provoked no further aggressiveness on her part. It is also probable that the bear was used to humans, having worked the roadways with her cubs for many days, and was not as intimidated by Beal's presence as might otherwise have been the case.

It was a different situation, however, when a human came uninvited into a bear's den. Again we turn to Merrill Beal's memoirs. On a late fall visit to Yellowstone, Beal and his son, Dave, and wife, Jean, visited a bear den in the vicinity of Morning Glory Pool at Upper Geyser Basin. They entered the den, and Sam poked his head into the adjoining chamber, only to discover that a bear had already moved in for the winter, made obvious by what he described as "ominous sounds of growling, sniffing, and clicking of teeth." The Beals' exodus was "precipitous."[12]

George Marler was given a tongue-lapping by a black bear on his first visit to the park as a boy in 1912. Young Marler was sleeping in the open bed of a wagon belonging to his neighbor from Idaho with whom he and his sister were traveling. A bear was attracted to the salty aroma of sweat, and Marler awoke to discover that he had become a human salt lick. It will be remembered that in an earlier chapter, Marler had his face similarly licked clean by a bear while he slept in a tent top his first year as a ranger naturalist (1931). It is always good to wash your face before going to bed.

Grizzlies were an even more fearsome encounter than black bears because of their aggressiveness and destructive power and especially because such encounters typically occurred in deep wilderness beyond the safety of car or building. Marler's first recorded encounter with a grizzly occurred during his first season in 1931 at Old Faithful. Marler and another ranger named Bob Nichols were hiking near a tributary of Iron Spring Creek when they noticed numerous signs of bear. In their progress down the heavily forested creek bank, they encountered a sow grizzly with two cubs. The sow immediately detected their scent and bolted up onto her hind legs about 150 feet ahead of them, mimicked by her two cubs. Fearful of danger, she immediately dropped and started on the run toward the two ranger naturalists. Marler records what happened:

Nichols took off up the hill as only a young man can sprint, while I being more arboreal sought refuge in a Lodgepole pine which had limbs which facilitated rapid ascent. After coming as far in our direction as the tree I had climbed the bear stopped momentarily, looked about, then started back down the gulch where the two cubs were. I stayed up the tree until the bear was well out of sight, and by that time Nichols was coming back down the canyon. We made no further travel in the direction of the grizzlies, but took a circuitous route through the forest.[13]

A second encounter happened the summer of 1946 at a gravel pit just east of the Fountain Group of hot springs near the Firehole River. Marler had taken his new bride, Laura Scherberne, on an evening drive in a government vehicle. The old gravel pit was a deep impression where road crews in the 1920s obtained gravel for road improvements and was subsequently used as a garbage dump similar to the one at Trout Creek in Hayden Valley.

Marler thought he might show Laura some bears. After passing through a small forest of lodgepole pines, they reached the edge of the gravel pit and immediately encountered a grizzly sow with two yearling cubs. The Marlers were riding in an open one-seat Ford government vehicle that offered almost no protection from a hostile bear.

Not wanting to alarm the bear with cubs, Marler immediately stopped the car. However, it was too late; the sow charged their vehicle, forcing Marler to hurriedly back up. Retreat was limited by fallen timber and heavy forest, and Marler had no alternative but to go forward again in the direction of the oncoming grizzly. The moment the car moved forward, the grizzly executed a hasty retreat and ran back to her cubs.

Gaining some confidence from the retreat of the sow but still not out of danger, Marler backed the car up again with the intent of turning around and leaving the area. No sooner did he back up than the sow charged the vehicle, huffing and snorting. As soon as he moved forward, the grizzly retreated. This exchange was repeated no fewer than four times before Marler got the vehicle pointed in the desired direction. By this time, the grizzly had had enough and disappeared into the forest with her two cubs.[14]

A third incident with a grizzly happened when Marler was about sixty years old. The Madison Canyon earthquake of August 1959 brought great attention to Yellowstone because of the fear of damage the quake had caused to the thermal features of the park. A large group of scientists and park officials visited the geyser basins to see what changes had occurred. Among these was the regional-naturalist from Omaha, Nebraska, accompanied by a party of forty or fifty people. Marler was assigned to lead the group to Imperial Geyser.

After noting the condition of the geyser, the party began to return to the parked cars, a considerable distance away. Marler was at the rear of the party, when suddenly he became aware that a grizzly was approaching the group from the rear on the run. Alarmed, Marler shouted a warning to those ahead of him: "A grizzly is coming toward us on the run!" The herd of people took off down the trail, as Marler described it, with the "speed of antelopes," every man for himself.

Marler "got on a trot" but stayed to the rear, not by choice but by age. Within a matter of seconds, a good distance had opened up between him and the thundering herd of fleeing people, leaving him to imagine his fate when the grizzly caught up with him. To his surprise and great relief, the grizzly swerved off the path when it was within twenty feet of Marler and, without slowing its pace, shot past him and the rest of the party. Of the aftermath of this incident, Marler simply notes, "Mental pictures of being chased by a grizzly stay with a person for a long time."[15]

One of Wayne Replogle's first encounters with grizzlies happened on his first date in Yellowstone Park. One summer night in 1931, when the sky was clear and the moon near full, Replogle took Berthina Clon, who was head of the recreation center at Old Faithful Lodge, on a moonlight hike to Observation Point, a prominent pine-covered hill overlooking the Upper Geyser Basin. His intention was to do a bit of "rotten logging" with Berthina.

Details of their excursion are sketchy at best, but, according to Replogle, after a moonlight hike up to Observation Point, the couple "settled up against a fallen tree" where they got "somewhat comfortable," then, strangely, both "went slightly asleep." Things suddenly got quite exciting:

I was awakened by a strange noise, and I looked up just beyond our feet and there stood a very large grizzly. I let out a scream you could have heard between here and Chicago, and my scream, of course, didn't equal the screams that Berthina gave out. . . . The bear gave a strike at me but hit a small bunch of fir trees, and the fir trees hit me and knocked me back over the log, and then, the bear, after a huge growl, fled away. . . . Berthina was crying, and we made our way back to the dormitory behind the lodge and I bid her farewell.[16]

Apparently, Replogle kept track of this girl over the years because he said that she later became a noted soprano who did considerable work in Chicago in entertainment.

Not far from Tower Fall, near Roosevelt Lodge, Replogle was accosted by two grizzlies while hunting for elk antlers with which to decorate their little cabin at Canyon. This time he was with his wife, Marian. The area was a good location to find large single antlers dropped in the winter, or even occasionally a full rack from the skull of a winter kill. It was illegal to remove objects or artifacts of any kind from Yellowstone, but in those days, rangers and other employees could take elk and deer antlers out of the field for use in the park.

Leaving Marian at the car, Replogle climbed a steep slope and scouted about the upper meadows. After a successful search and carrying a six-point antler in each hand, Replogle headed back to the car when he encountered two full-grown grizzly bears. Replogle tells the story: "I went over a little knoll and two grizzlies decided that I looked fat enough to eat, so they took after me and I came running down with the best speed I had toward [the car]. I just gave a great big jump and I rolled and tumbled down about 150 feet before I quit rolling, and the bears turned back at the top and I was saved."[17]

Characteristic of Replogle, he turned this story into a tall tale when relating it to visitors. In showing them the place where the incident occurred, he pointed out the old dead Douglas fir that stood partway down the incline: "I always used to tell the people the story that there was a limb sticking down about 10 feet from the ground and I jumped to grab the limb to get away from [the bears]. I missed the limb completely, but I got it on the way down. After a little while, the joke sinks in and they begin to giggle just a little."[18]

Lowell Biddulph seems to have had more close calls with grizzlies than the others, probably because he spent so much time hiking in the remote backcountry. His numerous encounters with grizzlies began his first summer of 1928, and it was nearly his last. At the advice of his supervisor, Edward E. "Ted" Ogston, Biddulph and a fellow ranger named Arnold Settlage set out one fine June day to learn what nature might teach them. About three miles out into the Mirror Plateau, east of Canyon, they came upon the footprints of a large grizzly in the dust of the trail. So big was its hind footprint, according to Biddulph, that he could almost fit both of his feet—side by side—into the print of the bear. In relating this story about fifty years later, Biddulph reflected that it probably was not smart for them to continue, but they were both young and inexperienced, and they continued to follow the bear's ambling footprints in the dust of the trail for several more miles until they crested a sloping ridgeline.

Suddenly, a few feet in front of the men, a large grizzly reared up from behind a large rock where it had been resting. Size estimates at moments of crisis are like fish stories—almost always overstated. However, the bear was noticeably taller than Biddulph, who stood six feet. The bear's body was covered with brown, matted hair that thinned out on the exposed belly and lay thick and silver-tipped along the arms, shoulders, and haunches. The massive short legs were spread, and it swayed from side to side under the imbalance of its huge frame. Beady brown eyes glared from the broad, dished face, and its heavy jaws hung open, exposing yellow fangs from which drizzled a steady stream of saliva. The rogue opened its mouth in a huge, cavernous flap and roared as it rolled its head from side to side.

The two rangers froze in terror, an involuntary act that undoubtedly saved their lives, for the bear could have easily struck out and killed both of them. Instead, after glaring at the two rangers for what seemed like an eternity, the bear whirled, dropped to all fours, and lumbered off down the slope. For some time afterward, the recuperating rangers could hear the bear crashing through the underbrush while they sat on a log and let their hearts regain a reasonable rhythm. Ogston was dead right. Nature was an excellent teacher, provided the student could survive the class lectures.[19]

In 1938 Biddulph was at Turbid Lake on assignment to obtain small rodents and birds for a museum display.[20] He used a small twenty-two-caliber rifle with bird shot to obtain his specimens. On returning across the meadow to his vehicle, Biddulph encountered a large grizzly in the middle of the meadow about seventy-five yards away. Cautiously, he backtracked and skirted the meadow, keeping close to trees that he could climb for safety if necessary.

It did not take long for his precaution to show its prudence. The rogue suddenly reared up on hind legs and sniffed the air, then walked a few steps in Biddulph's direction while boxing the air and woofing. Presently, the bear dropped to all fours and came at a dead run. Biddulph scampered up a lodgepole pine with peashooter in hand. The bear ran to the tree, reared up, and shook the trunk as hard as it could, all the time roaring its discontent. Biddulph finally fired his puny bird shot at the bear. The sting took all of the spunk out of the bully, and it ran away across the meadow and disappeared into the forest. When he was certain that the bear was gone, Biddulph cautiously climbed down and made a beeline for the car.

As part of his duties to check thermal features, Biddulph often hiked the forests and meadows around Mud Volcano, located along the Yellowstone River on the eastern border of Hayden Valley. While on one of his hikes, he happened upon a small meadow, and to his surprise, a grizzly bear was running full bore across the meadow straight toward him. It was one of those quirky coincidences of being in the wrong place at the wrong time. Biddulph quickly ascended into the limbs of a nearby pine tree. The bear ran to the tree, looked up, sniffed, and then continued on the run in the direction it was going.

That evening, when Biddulph returned to the cottage, he mentioned offhandedly to his wife, Ruth, that he had seen a grizzly that day. Ruth found his mention of such a common thing somewhat akin to a dairy farmer telling his wife he had seen a cow. Nothing more was said about it until the dishes were done and the two were on an evening walk together.

"I saw a grizzly today," Biddulph repeated, as casually as before.

"Yes, you mentioned that earlier," Ruth said, somewhat perplexed.

"Yes, but you didn't ask me where I saw it," he replied.

"Oh, where did you see the bear, Lowell?" Ruth decided to play along.

"From the top of a tree," he said. He now had Ruth's full attention. This was typical of Biddulph's sense of humor.

One day in the 1950s, Biddulph and one of his sons were hiking in this same area when they suddenly heard a sound as if someone was cutting wood with a bucksaw. While his son was trying to figure out why someone was out in the forest cutting wood, Biddulph had already figured out that it was a bear. He ordered his son not to move and to remain perfectly silent. His father's command voice told the boy it was not a time to ask questions or disobey.

The two froze in place. Presently, a grizzly sow and two cubs came huffing and puffing up the hill about thirty yards ahead of them. The sow immediately caught their scent, rose up on her hind legs, and sniffed the air. The cubs did the same. For a few uncertain seconds, father and son froze and looked for a tree to climb just in case. After a moment's pause, the sow dropped, and the three bears continued up the hill.

One of the popular differences given by ranger naturalists to tourists when they asked how to tell the difference between black bears and grizzlies was that grizzlies did not climb trees. Biddulph's many encounters with grizzlies over the years caused him to joke with visitors on such occasions: "Oh!" he would say with a wry smile, "just kick 'em in the ribs and climb a tree. If it comes up after you, it's a black bear. If it doesn't, it's a grizzly."

For several years, the standard reason given by naturalists as to the grizzly's seeming lack of tree-climbing ability was its body weight in comparison to its long, straight claws. Being typically larger than black bears and its claws being much longer and straighter, a grizzly could not sustain its weight in climbing up a sheer, limbless trunk of a lodgepole pine.

In the late 1930s, another intriguing theory surfaced. Bud Lystrup watched Olaus J. Murie, a renowned naturalist and biologist, prepare an adult male, female, and two cub grizzlies for public display in a museum. Murie pointed out to Lystrup that he could not find a collar bone in any of the bears and suggested it as a possible explanation for why grizzlies do not climb trees. Lystrup used this bit of unverified information for years afterward in his nature talks about bears, as did other naturalists.

After Lystrup retired from the Park Service in 1967, he encouraged Ranger Naturalist Dick Townsend to investigate park records to see if there was any information to verify this theory. Townsend could not find any written documentation, and the matter remained unresolved. Later, Drs. John Craighead and Frank Craighead dissected a newly killed grizzly and discovered, after careful examination, that it also lacked a collar bone. The information did not prove anything about tree-climbing ability, but it left the question tantalizingly open.[21]

The belief that grizzlies do not climb trees is not entirely true. Current park biologists state unequivocally that mature grizzlies have been known to climb trees, especially those that have a good limb structure. A four-hundred-pound grizzly has been known to climb as high as fifty feet using nothing but its claws. That said, an adult grizzly is not an agile climber like a black bear, and it is usually loath to climb at all. Its claw structure is designed for grubbing, digging, and tearing, not climbing, and grizzlies are not constitutionally inclined to seek protection by climbing a tree (typically a defense mechanism used by the more timid black bears), but more so to aggress a threat. In his numerous escapes up a tree from grizzly bears, Biddulph never had one come up after him.

A BLACK BEAR NAMED SWEET TOOTH

Yellowstone's natural environment provided ample sustenance for the bear population that inhabited its area. Their numbers and diet did not pose challenges to Yellowstone's plant species. Bears mostly spent harsh winter months tucked away in a hibernating sleep, but spring, summer, and fall were times to fatten themselves and prepare for the next winter. Wild berries, leaves, moles, field mice, grubs, ants, beetles, fish, and other menu items seemed in almost endless supply, but bears also had a sweet tooth. This craving could, depending upon the circumstances, cause damage to trees.

Such a situation occurred on August 6, 1951, while park rangers Roger Contor and Lowell Biddulph were hiking in the Sylvan Pass area of the Absaroka Mountains of Yellowstone. As Contor and Biddulph made their way through the lower alpine forest, they came upon a stand of Engelmann spruce that had been freshly peeled of bark to a height of three to five feet. Biddulph thought it to be the work of a bear, but Contor was not convinced, due to the absence of claw marks.

The two rangers continued their hike into the glacial cirque behind Avalanche Peak, discussing as they went the strange phenomenon as possibly the work of porcupines, beavers, and bears. On their return through the same area later in the day, they heard a peculiar ripping noise. There in a grove of Engelmann spruce was a black bear licking the sugary sap from the freshly exposed trunk of one of the trees. The bear presently discovered that it had been caught with its hands, so to speak, in the honey jar, and it quickly disappeared into the forest. Contor noted, "This apparently isn't a common practice, and fortunately so, for this one animal certainly raised havoc with a healthy stand of spruce in just a few days."[22]

THE RHYTHM OF NATURE

Each of the Old Men found his own rhythm in nature that resonated to his soul in ways unique to his own personality. While this chapter has dwelled primarily on encounters with wild animals, it would be incomplete not to mention the men's encounters with other natural phenomena of Yellowstone, such as the wildflowers, birds, and rocks. To a man, they were in love with the park's flowers and birds. No other statement seems to articulate the love these Five Old Men had for Yellowstone's nature as well as this by John Muir: "There are certain moods that seem to move me; there is a need for loneliness, a hunger for freedom in the out-of-doors. As long as I live I'll hear waterfalls and birds and winds sing. I'll interpret the rocks, learn the language of flood, storm, and avalanche. I'll acquaint myself with glaciers and wild gardens and get as near the heart of the world as I can."

Merrill Beal found symphonies of sound in the waterfalls of nature: "I like the canyon because its water provides a veritable symphony as it tumbles over cascades and waterfalls. It occurred to me that Roger Williams could write a piano composition comparable to 'Autumn Leaves.'"[23]

Bud Lystrup found peaceful, restful sonnets: "The fresh, unfamiliar sounds of the natural world fall upon the ear with surprising pleasure. Flapping wings of birds in flight, the lumbering staccato of the bison's hooves, splashing waters as a trout leaps for an insect, the shrill cry of the gull; all strange sounds, but vaguely, pleasantly familiar."[24]

Lowell Biddulph found in his beloved Absaroka Mountains a feast for the soul: "The mountains are in my blood—they are a part of me. The lonely, windswept peaks, the lovely alpine meadows, plunging white waters, dim, cool, magnificent forests lift and feed my soul, and continually call and beckon to me. Here heaven seems to dip lightly and touch the earth on the jagged skyline where gnarled, twisted trees pierce white floating clouds in fields of blue."[25]

In the magnificent canyon, Wayne Replogle found a world of enchantment: "Almost instantly I felt myself out of a nowhere into a melodious somewhere. Listening, I could hear the passionate roar of the plunging, pure green water far below in a forbidding aisle—on, on it fled!—dashing, splashing, wheeling, surging, falling, tearing, as if it were an endless monster caught in a grip too small to hold it still, yet too grand to free it—rapturous tone it was, held to the rhythm of soft, enchanting breezes dancing over the brink into the Canyon in an endless chain of vanishing nymphs."[26]

Even the pragmatic, scientific mind of George Marler approached romantic prose in describing his beloved geysers in deep winter: "In arctic weather the mist and spray of geysers congeals into crystalline form before it falls, rendering long frost crystals with brilliant, diamond-like luster. The trees are encrusted with ice giving proper adage to the term 'ghost trees.' The entire land is transformed into an ethereal like fairyland, a place of delicate and enchanting beauty."[27]

There was something about this vast beauty that spiritualized a mortal experience for these men and helped them view nature with the reverence and awe of the Native American. The majestic vistas of wilderness broadened a realization of their relative nothingness in comparison to the true magnificence of this earth as a creative masterpiece and man's dependence upon it for sustained life. Whatever it was, they were forever drawn to the woods and the beauties that were to be found there. "The mountains are calling and I must go," as John Muir said.

Chapter 13

The First Naturalist
at Fishing Bridge

THE YELLOWSTONE LAKE ECOSYSTEM

Fate marked the outlet of Yellowstone Lake as a major attraction for tourists. By 1891 a hotel had been built on the hillside overlooking the western shore of the lake.[1] By the 1910s, a boat dock was added below the hotel where steamboats named the *Zillah* and *E. C. Waters* delivered tourists who chose to abandon the dusty, bumpy coach ride from West Thumb to the Lake Hotel and travel the twenty-one miles by water.[2] The boat trip included a brief stop at Dot Island,[3] where the owner of the Yellowstone Boat Company treated the tourists to a display of four buffalo and a few elk that he kept in pens as a kind of zoo.[4]

By 1923 a ranger station was constructed at Lake. Three years later, Robert Reamer expanded the lake lodge located at the edge of the forest at the base of Elephant Back Mountain. The great porch of the rustic lodge looks out upon a scene of singular beauty with a wide meadow, the grand lake, and the Absaroka Mountains rising on the eastern horizon beyond. A fish hatchery was constructed in about 1931 on the lakeshore near the hotel to replace the hatchery at West Thumb. Later, cabins, a Hamilton Store, and a service station were added.

In 1902 Hiram Chittenden built his famous Fishing Bridge[5] (although it really did not receive the name until 1914) just two hundred yards below the outlet of the Yellowstone River to connect the east entrance road with the Grand Loop. Soon thereafter, tourist accommodations began to fill the forest

The famous Fishing Bridge across Yellowstone River, ca. 1935. (Photo by Jack Ellis Haynes, reproduced with permission of the Montana Historical Society Research Center Photograph Archives Haynes Foundation Collection, H-35364)

area on the east side of the bridge between the outlet and Pelican Creek tributary. Charles Hamilton built his largest mercantile store at Fishing Bridge. Other facilities included a cafeteria, Hayne's Photo Shop, a trailside museum, a service station, and cabins. Two sprawling campgrounds literally filled the forest on the lakeshore from the outlet to Pelican Creek.

Long before a road or a bridge was conceived or villages constructed, this area around Yellowstone Lake was home to a rich variety of wildlife. The outlet of the river is an important spawning place of the famous black-spotted trout. A large variety of waterfowl live on the lake and surrounding waterways, including ducks, geese, pelican, seagulls, and cormorants. Eagles, osprey, and other birds of prey nest and hunt along the Yellowstone River. The forests are rich with an abundance of songbirds. Nearby meadows and valleys sustain elk, deer, and buffalo. Marshes and willows along the Yellowstone River and the Pelican Creek tributary are home to moose, otter, muskrats, and beaver. Black bears and grizzlies live in the surrounding forests, and they came to fish in the shallow mouth of the lake's outlet during the trout's spawning season.

These two human populace centers pushed out much of the wildlife, leaving only chipmunks, squirrels, and birds that more readily adapted to human presence. The grizzly's homeland was foreclosed on, while the black bear became a vagabond, stealing at night into the campgrounds to scrounge for garbage.

The Park Service recognized that this area surrounding the outlet of the lake had the potential to become a significant interpretive center. Two full years before the museum was constructed on the shore of Yellowstone Lake, the Park Service began the rudiments of an interpretive program at Fishing Bridge. The summer of 1929, they hired a college graduate with a degree in botany and forestry and assigned him to develop the program.

On a blustery afternoon in late May 1929, a large, yellow truck loaded with lumber stopped at the ranger station at Fishing Bridge. The newly hired ranger naturalist named Herbert T. Lystrup climbed out from under the tarpaulin covering the wood, where he had endured a fifty-mile ride from Mammoth Hot Springs. With duffel bag and leather valise in hand, he jumped to the ground and shook the hand of Francis "Babe" LaNoue, the chief ranger at Canyon. LaNoue stayed only long enough to orient Lystrup to the area and show him around the station. "If you need anything," he told Lystrup, "just call me at the Lake Ranger Station."[6] With that, he left Lystrup alone in this strange, new place.

The ranger station at Fishing Bridge had two rooms: an information room/office and living quarters; it was "spartan," as Lystrup put it. The office was clean but void of furniture. The living quarters had two metal cots fitted with wire springs and two wool army blankets folded at the foot of each bed. The water faucet was at the end of a three-foot pipe near the woodpile behind the ranger station. The latrine was a wooden outdoor privy.

Dusk was coming on, and snow had begun to fall outside with a raw wind. Lystrup shuddered with the cold and felt the first tinges of loneliness creep into him. He built a fire in the wood-burning stove to warm the cold, empty station and filled the galvanized bucket with water to warm for washing. His spirits rising some, he unpacked his few things in the adjoining bedroom and walked to the government mess (about a half mile) for his supper. Upon returning, he found the station dark with no electricity or lantern. By the light of a small candle stub that he found on a shelf in the station, he opened the manila folder and read his instructions and a list of his duties.

His primary assignments were educational in nature. He was to develop and conduct nature walks and give nightly campfire programs for the tourists. The subject of the campfire lectures was "forest trees of Yellowstone National Park." He was also to lay out a nature trail and organize and conduct nature walks to identify plants, trees, and animals in the vicinity. Additional duties

Rangers assigned to Fishing Bridge, summer of 1929. *Left to right:* Herbert Lystrup, an unidentified ranger, and Lowell Biddulph. (Courtesy of Liz Lystrup)

included helping the seasonal ranger control traffic across the bridge each afternoon when the Yellowstone Park buses, filled with tourists, arrived from Cody, Wyoming.

Within a day or two of Lystrup's arrival, he was joined by Lowell Biddulph, the seasonal ranger assigned to Fishing Bridge. It was Biddulph's second summer in Yellowstone, and his duty as ranger was to enforce park rules, regulate traffic across Fishing Bridge, and provide protection and support to the tourists. Lystrup and Biddulph discovered that they had much in common; both were high school teachers in the winter months, and both had a similar love for nature. A close friendship was forged between the two men during this first summer that lasted more than forty years of service. Unbeknownst to both men, Biddulph eventually would lead for nearly three decades the interpretive program at Fishing Bridge that Lystrup began the summer of 1929.

The morning following his arrival, Lystrup went to work laying out a nature trail. His first task was to orient himself to the area, which he did with the aid of a government topographic map that he found in the ranger station. He decided to lay out a nature trail that showcased the variety of the landscape, including the river, the lake, forests, meadows, and the marshy expanses of Pelican Creek that lay a mile east of Fishing Bridge. Each area provided different flora and fauna. Lystrup describes this first nature trail: "Beginning at the east end of [Fishing Bridge], I followed the shore of the Yellowstone River downstream for about a mile to a towering fir. I turned east, walking through beautiful conifer forests, several quiet meadows, and over a gently sloping hill to Pelican Creek. I turned south, following Pelican Creek... until I reached Yellowstone Lake. Then I followed the shoreline west until I reached the campground at Fishing Bridge Village."[7]

Instead of a specific trail, Lystrup marked out only a general route because, in his words, he wanted his "companions to see and sense for themselves the aura of a forest primeval... and to be free to wander where nature offered the greatest rewards on any given day."[8]

Initial participation in the nature walk was meager but grew steadily throughout the summer season. His first nature walk was attended by a husband and wife and their two children. Larger crowds—as many as thirty-five—came later in the season, but the average was nine or ten people. Small numbers did not bother Lystrup: "This [smaller] number of tourists made the walks pleasantly informal—people were less hesitant about asking questions, there was time for unhurried explanations and our discussions wandered far and wide, free of classroom limitations. And, finally, there was the real, if tangible, reward that comes from intimately sharing an experience in a unique, inspired and inspiring setting—Yellowstone National Park."[9]

With the nature trail laid out, Lystrup turned his attention to the campfire program, which proved more daunting than the nature walk. So much of the success of the program or lecture fell upon his skills as a speaker. His first challenge was to select an appropriate location to hold his lecture: "I chose a small opening in the forest, only a hundred yards from the ranger station. Two men from the road crew helped me clear the area and haul in fifteen large logs for seats. We arranged these in a semi-circle, facing a stump, twenty inches high and two feet in diameter that would serve as a platform from which I would deliver my talk. Between the stump and the benches, I scooped out a pit for the campfire."[10]

No stage or amplification system was available, and Lystrup was not a large man—perhaps five feet, nine inches—so a stump was of practical use in amplifying his voice across the crackling campfire. Its obvious limitation was the restriction in movement; Lystrup was confined to the stump. In spite of its limitations, he "stumped" his lecture each evening like an old-time politician.

Even a mediocre presenter today speaking on a moderately boring topic can hold an audience if the PowerPoint is entertaining enough. But Lystrup had nothing but his own charisma and the ambience of the outdoor setting to hold his audience. "Forest trees of Yellowstone National Park" was a topic more suited for a nature walk than a campfire lecture. Other than identifying varieties of conifers and deciduous trees found in the park and describing where they were found and what their uses might be, there was not much to say that would interest the average tourist. His first attempt at a campfire lecture that summer was sobering: "They didn't want to hear a lecture, most of them. They…were more interested in entertainment than they were in education. For me to call the Limber Pine, correctly, a *Pinus flexilis,* only bored them."[11]

Lystrup discovered that he had to rely on his own charisma. As a supporting cast, he recruited "savages" that worked at Fishing Bridge and Lake to perform at his nightly programs. Amateurs all, their enthusiasm and spirit made up for what they lacked in polish. Lystrup frequently arranged for Wallace Wood, the son of a park employee, to slip unnoticed into the woods and play on his cornet the melody to a popular song: "When You Come to the End of a Perfect Day" (1909):

When you come to the end of a perfect day,
And you sit alone with your thought,
While the chimes ring out with a carol gay,
For the joy that the day has brought,
Do you think what the end of a perfect day
Can mean to a tired heart,
When the sun goes down with a flaming ray,
And the dear hearts have to part?
Well, this is the end of a perfect day,
Near the end of a journey, too,
But it leaves a thought that is big and strong,
With a wish that is kind and true.
For mem'ry has painted this perfect day

With colors that never fade,
And we find at the end of a perfect day,
The soul of a friend we've made.[12]

In later years and recognizing the shift away from inspiration toward a more factual-based audience, Lystrup simply noted about these early programs: "It was a more sentimental age." Yet he never ceased to try to stir emotions within human souls who came under his tutelage: "I tried simply in those brief thirty minutes each evening to arouse long-dormant curiosities, stimulate jaded minds a bit and help each member of the audience toward a better understanding of the world of nature, toward a greater and, hopefully, ever-growing appreciation of its unbounded wonders."[13]

In the afternoons, Lystrup assisted Biddulph with controlling traffic across Fishing Bridge. Motorized buses operated by the Yellowstone Park Transportation Company arrived at Fishing Bridge from Cody, Wyoming, with their load of tourists on a strict time schedule. To prevent a bottleneck of traffic at the bridge, the rangers delayed private vehicles from crossing the bridge so that the buses could pass unrestricted.

The delays occasionally frustrated impatient drivers, and rangers had to be patient and maintain cordiality while enforcing the policies. One afternoon when the line of traffic was particularly long, a yellow Lincoln suddenly broke out of line and surged past other cars that were waiting ahead of it. Lystrup was on the bridge at the time and reported what happened:

> I moved to the center of the bridge and held up my hand for the driver to stop. I explained the reason for the traffic line-up. At that moment the passenger in the front seat directed the driver, in no uncertain terms, to turn [around] and return to the end of the line. Later that day, a gentleman called at the Fishing Bridge ranger station and introduced himself as Horace Albright! It was then that I recognized him as the passenger in the car that I had stopped on the bridge. I expected the Director of the National Parks to reprimand me. Instead, he graciously thanked me for "doing my assigned duty." Many years later, after one of the campfire talks, Mr. Albright came to me and said, "You're the man who stopped me on the bridge."[14]

Rangers were both policemen and paramedics of their day. Among other things, rangers became experts at extracting fishing hooks from various parts

The current Fishing Bridge was rebuilt in 1937, and walkways were added for fishermen and foot passage. (Courtesy of L. G. Biddulph)

of a visitor's anatomy. Since there were no medical facilities available at Fishing Bridge, the rangers answered all emergency calls. One such call came at midnight from the tent-top cabins, where a woman was sick. Biddulph dressed and left the ranger station, headed for the tent tops about a half mile away. As he walked along in the otherwise silent night, he heard the rough cough of something inhuman and the click of toenails on the road behind him. He suspected a grizzly before he turned around but was astonished to discover that he was being stalked by three mature bears walking shoulder to shoulder. He walked faster, and the bears picked up his cadence. Finally, he broke into a mad dash, with the bears in hot pursuit.

Biddulph was far enough ahead and quick enough on his feet to make the tent-top cabins ahead of the bears. The cabins offered little protection from the formidable bears; nevertheless, Biddulph lunged against the door of the first one that he came to. It gave way, allowing him to gain access to the dark abyss and slam the door shut. Fortunately, the bears gave up the pursuit. Unfortunately, Biddulph discovered that he was not alone inside the tent top, manifested by the hysterical screams of a honeymoon couple that, until that moment, had been enjoying their recluse.

Explanations came with some difficulty: a well-meaning ranger on his way through the woods to visit a sick woman, being chased by three bears.

Undoubtedly, this was one of the silliest blends of Red Riding Hood and Goldilocks known to man. The only thing missing was a basket of goodies and a red cape.[15] Biddulph's wife, Ruth, a teacher of children's literature, made this delightful connection that has been gleefully canonized into Biddulph family lore.

Grizzly bears were a problem at Fishing Bridge the summer of 1929. A two-year-old orphaned grizzly made a particular nuisance of himself by robbing tents while campers were attending Lystrup's nightly campfire lectures. Biddulph and Lystrup teamed up. While Lystrup gave campfire lectures, Biddulph scouted the campgrounds for the grizzly. Several times he nearly caught the cub, but it escaped by plunging into Yellowstone Lake and swimming about, dodging the small rocks that Biddulph launched at it.

One night, upon returning to the ranger station from patrol, Biddulph was disgusted to see the garbage can turned on its side and garbage strewn about. Obviously, the little grizzly had struck while he was gone. He marched to the can to right it, but instead of grabbing the lip of the can, he grabbed the mangy scruff of the little grizzly lying half-concealed inside the can, which, until that moment, was contentedly munching garbage and had failed to hear the ranger's approach. Biddulph's surprise was exceeded only by that of the grizzly. The grizzly exploded out of the can. Biddulph flew over the can. The grizzly cub fled into the night.

Another of Biddulph's tasks was to monitor safety and compliance with fishing regulations by tourists fishing from the bridge. Until the summer of 1973, when fishing from the bridge was prohibited to protect the spawning trout, people stood almost shoulder to shoulder on each side of the bridge, literally turning the river into a gauntlet of lures and hooks through which fish had to maneuver. Biddulph spent time each day walking along the bridge, talking with fishermen, answering questions, and helping out when needed.

One day a sow black bear with two cubs came across the bridge, precipitating a mass exodus of people, who fled in panic, all but one little old lady who resolutely stood her ground. When the near hysteria was over and the bears safely on the other side, Biddulph approached the woman, who was standing in place with a thirteen-inch trout gripped firmly in one hand and her fishing rod in the other. "Why didn't you run?" Biddulph asked the woman. "Don't you know that bears can be dangerous?"

The little woman looked the young ranger square in the eye and replied, "Sonny, I've been fishing off this bridge for two days straight trying to catch me a fish, and I finally caught one this morning." She waved the fish defiantly

Arthur Nash and Lowell Biddulph at the desk at Fishing Bridge trailside museum, 1938. (Photo by W. E. Kearns; courtesy of the National Park Service, Yellowstone National Park, YELL 38553)

in one hand. "And I'll be damned if any ole bear is going to chase me off and get my fish!"

Interpretive services expanded dramatically with the completion of the museum at Fishing Bridge in 1931. A core of ranger naturalists was stationed there throughout the ensuing years. Nature walks were expanded to include walks along the lakeshore, the Yellowstone River, Storm Point, and even day hikes up Elephant Back Mountain and Avalanche Peak in the Absaroka Mountains. Auto caravans to the fish hatchery at Lake and the Natural Bridge at Bridge Bay were added. An attractive amphitheater, stage and screen, and projection booth were built adjacent to the museum. Campfire topics were expanded to include plants, wild animals, birds, geysers and hot springs, Yellowstone geology, points of interest in the park, and history.

Lystrup was again briefly stationed at Fishing Bridge in 1943, but was primarily assigned to Old Faithful thereafter. Biddulph returned to Fishing Bridge in 1938 and again in '41. In 1945, after World War II ended, Biddulph returned to Fishing Bridge as head naturalist and remained there until his retirement in 1968.

Chapter 14

Trailside Museums

EDUCATION BECOMES A PRIMARY GOAL

Freeman Tilden was right when he envisioned that education begets understanding; understanding, appreciation; appreciation, respect; and respect, protection. The establishment of education as a primary goal for the National Park Service was a tool of protection. That is, educating the public about Yellowstone's wonders was a means of making thoughtful stewards of tourists who came to the park.

As Yosemite and Yellowstone mutually grappled with how to develop their educational programs in the 1920s, a happy resource was found in museums. The charter of the International Council of Museums reflected what the National Park Service sought to accomplish through education: to acquire, conserve, research, communicate, and exhibit the tangible and intangible heritage of humanity and its environment for the purposes of education, study, and enjoyment.[1]

Hermon Bumpus, who at the time was chairman of the American Association of Museums, saw national parks as "roofless museums of nature" with unlabeled exhibits. Museums simply provided the labels. During the 1920s, Bumpus and others began promoting trailside museums as ways to fulfill the educational mandate in national parks. Yosemite had its first museum by 1922, and by 1931, Herbert Maier, in consultation with Dorr Yeager and others, had designed and erected four rustic trailside museums in Yellowstone at Norris, Madison Junction, Old Faithful, and Fishing Bridge.

Earliest attempts at education eventually evolved into interpretation. The terms *education* and *interpretation* are frequently used interchangeably in describing national park policy. Admittedly, each has some of the other embedded within, yet they have subtle but distinct differences. Education is an academic exercise that imparts information or knowledge from a teacher to a student. Education implies a curriculum and syllabus, textbooks, lectures, and a learning environment. Interpretation, as described more fully in chapter 15, is more an exploration or a hands-on discovery—a lab, if you will, where principles are observed in action and even experimented with.

There was more than merely education and interpretation to Yellowstone's program. What might be called naturalism also had a significant influence on education. Well-known naturalists such as John Burroughs and John Muir heralded nature as an enlightened medium. They spoke of places like Yellowstone as sanctuaries of worship where visitors could shake off the natural man and become inspired to a higher sense of purpose and tranquillity. Henry David Thoreau even used the woods around his beloved Walden Pond to formulate ideas on civilized society.[2] Transformation of visitors to the park came not merely with a sprinkling of information or intellectualism; it required a baptism by emersion into nature from which came forth the new and more enlightened being. It was this view of nature that lay at the core of interpretation, at least for the Five Old Men.

The early programs were nevertheless heavy on the education model. Yellowstone's nature was the core curriculum, ranger naturalists were the teachers, tourists were the students, and museums and amphitheaters and geyser basins were their classrooms. Naturalists were required to learn common and scientific labels of all plants and animals, and they sought to educate the public to similar standards.

We are reminded of Lystrup's assignment in 1929 to lecture on the forest trees of Yellowstone at the campfire at Fishing Bridge. Later campfire program topics were plants, animals, birds, thermal features, and history. All of this was educationally focused.

Lystrup quickly learned, as did park administrators, that people did not want to attend summer school in Yellowstone. They came out of intrigue and for recreation and pleasure. National park administrators eventually began to distance themselves from education and move toward interpretation.

The Five Old Men and some of their colleagues, who were hired around 1930 to fulfill these interpretive goals of the National Park Service, embodied virtually all of its characteristics. They were educators, men trained in the natural sciences. They were observers and interpreters whose greatest passion was to introduce visitors to the world of nature and help them discover the

Norris trailside museum, erected in 1929–30, the first of the trailside museums to be built in Yellowstone. (Photo by Russell; courtesy of the National Park Service, Yellowstone National Park, YELL 38705)

wonders to be found there. They were naturalists who resonated to the teachings of Burroughs, Muir, and others like them. They frequently read and quoted these prophets of the wilderness. They fitted perfectly the prototype of the ranger naturalist of their day.

TRAILSIDE MUSEUMS

Few man-made objects characterized the interpretation era in Yellowstone National Park as well as did the four trailside museums that were constructed between 1928 and 1931. They were true interpretive museums. Visitors to these museums entered into an atmosphere of solitude and quiet learning reminiscent of that found in libraries. The museums were filled with what Bumpus called "labels" that could be observed in close detail. A premium was placed on identification or recognition. Old, middle-aged, and young visitors moved about the displays and artifacts in awe, speaking in hushed but excited voices.

Efforts were made by the National Park Service to build buildings that were the least intrusive to the natural surroundings. These rustic trailside museums were constructed inside and out of natural materials indigenous to the park. Roof trusses of these museums were typically of peeled lodgepole-pine logs. The interior was a matrix of lodgepole logs rising in peaks and crossbeams from which hung rustic chandeliers adorned with antlers of elk and moose and the skulls of bighorn sheep. The exterior walls were covered with brown shakes, while the roofs were of thick forest-green shake shingles adorned with an imposing rock chimney. Windows were typically cottage-like and latticed with eight-inch squares of glass. The foundation was made of volcanic rock mortared to a height of four feet that surrounded the entire building. This rustic architecture became known as "National Park Rustic" or, in more colloquial terms, "Parkitecture."[3]

Rooms were adorned with displays of flora, fauna, geology, geysers, and the human history of Yellowstone. Specimens of wildlife were set amid artificial scenes to appear as lifelike as possible. A ranger naturalist, dressed in forest-green uniform and broad-brimmed Stetson hat, counted visitors with a handheld counter and answered questions about a myriad of topics in a quiet, confident tone. When the weather was cold and blustery outside, the trailside museums provided a warm, cozy fireplace with sap-filled pine logs snapping and popping noisily.

THE NORRIS MUSEUM

The Norris Museum was the first true trailside museum constructed in Yellowstone. Of course, the museum at Mammoth, begun by Sawyers in the 1920s, was the first museum in the park, but it was not one of the trailside series. The Norris Museum was constructed in 1929 at one of Yellowstone's hottest and most geothermal-active areas. It is situated on a hill between Back Basin and Porcelain Basin, and it is oriented in such a way that the main interior breezeway looks out upon the brilliant, steaming visage of Porcelain Basin. Steaming pools of brilliant white, hissing ventricles of steam, and pungent odors fill the visitor with a sense of the ultimate thermal power that lies beneath the surface. The intense whiteness of the broad basins is punctuated by encircling deep evergreen forests, offset by distant peaks of the Gallatin Range and skies as fair and blue as the tiny forget-me-not flower.

The museum proper is roughly one hundred feet by twenty feet and consists of two rectangular sections with an intervening breezeway. Its gabled roof is framed with massive logs covered with thick wood shingles, and stone pillars grace its entrance. A stone terrace surrounds the museum.

The displays in the Norris Museum focus primarily on Yellowstone thermal geology, its underworld, and the origin of its geyser basins. In 1995 the

Madison Junction trailside museum, erected in 1930. Persons on steps include M. F. Daum, Kenneth Charley, Herb Maier, and Hermon Bumpus. (Courtesy of the National Park Service, Yellowstone National Park, YELL 38591)

displays were upgraded with more recent information from the ongoing studies of the thermal features and the great heat source lying below Yellowstone's surface. Norris Geyser Basin is the hottest and potentially most volatile place in Yellowstone Park.

Not far from Norris Junction, the visitor finds the Museum of the National Park Ranger. Originally built in 1886 by the army as a soldier station, it was later destroyed and rebuilt to authentic specifications on the original foundation. Park rangers used these stations when they replaced the army in Yellowstone. Although a majority of these old log structures have long since met their demise, some, such as the one at Bechler, continue to live on. Today, the converted museum commemorates the rangers' long service to Yellowstone. It also includes the story of the soldiers who preceded them.

MADISON JUNCTION MUSEUM

The museum at Madison Junction was erected about the same time as that at Norris. It is the smallest of the four original museums. From 1928 until 1954, only one person was stationed at Madison Junction. In 1954 two ranger naturalists were assigned there, and beginning in 1955, three or four served there. Four of the Five Old Men were stationed at Madison Junction, but Merrill Beal is most closely and continuously associated with it, having served there for almost half of his twenty-six seasons in Yellowstone.

Prior to the actual construction of the trailside museum at Madison Junction, a small cabin was made into a one-room historical museum. The north side of the structure was an apartment for the ranger assigned there. Replogle, who was stationed there in 1937, provides a description of the structure: "The small apartment was made up of basically one room with a slight arch division and that was the office and sleeping room and living room, while in the other room was a stove, which was a wood stove, and a basin or place to wash the dishes, and then at the very north end were three tiny rooms. One was a half bathroom, one was a pantry, and one was a storeroom for wood, etc."[4]

The Madison Museum was small and cozy compared to the larger ones at Old Faithful and Fishing Bridge. Its diminutive size was compensated for by its majestic setting. Strategically positioned, the museum sits on a slight rise looking out at National Park Mountain. The view of the historic Madison River winding westward through meadows and flanked by precipitous hills, often spotted with herds of grazing elk, is stunning. The museum's close proximity to the site of the historic campsite of the Washburn Expedition of 1870 naturally focused it on the early history of Yellowstone Park.

A dozen colorful flagstones marked the ascent from the parking lot to the entrance of the museum. A large tinted glass transparency of the Washburn-Langford-Doane campfire of 1870 grandly illustrated the origin of the "National Park Idea." Other pictures of significant historic people and events appertaining to the discovery and exploration of the Yellowstone area adorned the walls, and a series of illustrated placards along the inner eaves briefed park history in a self-guiding fashion.[5] The museum was filled with historic memorabilia, procured and donated to the Yellowstone Park Museum Association by families of individuals famous in the history of the park. A saddle used by Nathaniel Pitt Langford during the Washburn Expedition of 1870 was on display, along with some rifles that he carried. Chairs made of birch by Floyd Bottler, one of the famous Bottler brothers who operated a ranch north of Yellowstone Park, were also on display.

Busloads of visitors came each day to visit the museum on their tour around the park. The ranger naturalist met these tourists daily and provided a tour through the museum. Unlike the Fishing Bridge Museum, which was mostly filled with fauna of the park, the Madison Museum was filled with

Old Faithful trailside museum, erected in 1929–30, removed in 1971. (Photo by
Spranger; courtesy of the National Park Service, Yellowstone National Park,
YELL 38765)

history and garnered many questions about the park's discovery, exploration,
and creation. Browsing through the memorabilia and reading placards whet-
ted the appetite of the guests and prepared them for a short talk by the ranger
naturalist.

OLD FAITHFUL MUSEUM

The museum at Old Faithful was completed in 1929–30 at a cost of eighty-
five hundred dollars and is the only one of the four trailside museums that
no longer exists. The T-shaped building was positioned between Old Faithful Inn and the lodge, about a hundred yards south of the cone of Old Faithful, and was oriented such that the on-duty ranger naturalist could maintain
visual survey of the famous geyser. Lystrup described the old museum:

> The museum was a low building of unique architecture. A huge door
> opened into a large room in which was the information desk, relief
> map, fireplace, and miniature geyser model. The adjoining room con-
> tained a table relief map of the Upper Geyser Basin, and on all the
> walls were display cases pertaining to geysers and history. Open doors
> revealed an open court wild flower garden with a rock garden and pool.
> Along the sides of the court were to be found forestry exhibits and cases
> of pressed wild flowers. In back of the main room was the office in
> which the district ranger had his desk, telephone, files, and a huge map

of Yellowstone. On the other side of the room were the work tables equipped with microscopes, typewriter, plant presses, slide cases, etc. Books and publications were arranged on shelves in closets in the rear of the room. In the rear of the museum was the open air amphitheater with its log seats, fire pit, platform, screen, and projector case.[6]

Visitors to the geyser basins were mostly interested in seeing the geysers erupt. Thus, the ranger naturalist on duty at the museum desk found himself inundated with questions and requests pertaining to their times and patterns. Many of the questions and comments of the day would be considered absurd and naive by today's generation, but people simply did not have the wealth of information that is taken for granted by the present generation.

A few geysers had somewhat predictable patterns of eruption, Old Faithful being the most famous. Endless were the questions posed to the ranger naturalist about its next eruption. Perhaps to aid the visitor as well as save the sanity of the on-duty ranger naturalist, the Park Service placed a large clock in a prominent place in the museum with hands that the ranger naturalist could manipulate to show the next expected eruption of Old Faithful Geyser. This saved a lot of repetitive questions, provided the visitors were observant enough to see the clock. Some were not.

This proved successful enough that during the 1948 season, Chief Park Naturalist Dave Condon had George Marler, who was serving at the time as head naturalist at Old Faithful, add smaller clocks for less famous but popular geysers, including Castle, Daisy, Great Fountain, Beehive, and Riverside. These clocks were not automated, but the hands were manually moved by the naturalists to show the next anticipated eruption of each geyser.[7]

A popular addition to the Old Faithful Museum in the 1930s was "Old Faithful Junior," a replica of the real geyser.[8] This ingenious little replica was built by George Larkin, an employee of Hayne's Picture Shops. Lystrup described Old Faithful Junior: "This base, shaped slightly like a pyramid, was almost four feet tall. A large, round metal saucer, four inches deep and three feet in diameter was securely attached to the top of the base. In the center of this saucer, Mr. Larkin had molded a very clever imitation of Old Faithful Senior's mound and cone, complete with a functional orifice. He used ordinary cement for this, and when it dried it was a light gray color, much like the color and the texture of the natural geyserites."[9]

The replica operated on the principle of a coffee percolator. Inside the wooden base, undetectable to visitors, was a reservoir for heating the water and a coil of copper tubing that connected the reservoir to the orifice. Each morning the ranger naturalist on duty filled the reservoir by pouring about a gallon of water into the large saucer where the water drained into the reservoir concealed within the base. The ranger then turned on the electricity, which heated the water in the reservoir. The copper tubing restricted the normal release of pressure by the heated water, causing bubbles and steam to rise up through the orifice at the top and ejecting a stream of hot water three or four feet into the air. Most, but not all, of the water fell back into the saucer, and drained back into the reservoir and the process started all over again.

Old Faithful Junior was messy but a big hit with visitors, so much so that Bud Lystrup began to wonder "if they were more interested in the capricious imitation than they were in the steady old natural wonder just a few short steps away across the road."[10]

Despite its intrigue for visitors, the ranger naturalists who had to maintain the replica viewed it with contempt, calling it a nuisance or other more colorful descriptions. Old Faithful Junior was fickle and erratic. Its tubing often sprang leaks, and the heating element frequently burned out. It could be hazardous to one's health. Some tourists mistook it for a drinking fountain and got their faces washed with hot water. While Wayne Replogle was on desk duty there, a woman came into the museum, spied the geyser model, and went for it, thinking it was a drinking fountain. Replogle cried out to the woman, "That's not a fountain, ma'am. Don't drink from it." The woman waved him off and bent over precisely as the hot water erupted into her face.

Some tourists thought that the model was somehow connected to the real geyser, acting as some type of gauge that predicted Old Faithful Geyser's eruption. Others were convinced that the real Old Faithful Geyser was nothing more than a large "mechanical monster" and that the rangers primed and controlled the geysers in the geyser basins as they did "Junior."

Practical jokes, like the one played on Wayne Replogle by a couple of employees at the Old Faithful Inn, did not help. Replogle was giving the cone talk at Old Faithful in the 1930s before a crowd of more than three hundred people. A young man who was a "packrat" (bellhop) at the Old Faithful Inn approached him just as Old Faithful was beginning to show preliminary signs of erupting and asked, "Is she about ready to go?" Replogle answered, "Yep, it has spurted quite a bit." The young man turned and looked toward the lodge, put his hands to his mouth, and yelled, "Okay, Joe, let her go!" Sitting out there in plain view of the crowd was another young man whom Replogle knew pretty well. He had taken an old Ford steering wheel with its rod still intact and had punched it into the ground. When his friend shouted for him to let it go, he swiftly turned the steering wheel like a spigot, and as he turned the wheel, up went Old Faithful into full eruption.

The audience screamed and laughed, and after the play was over, a number of people said to Replogle, "Well, we didn't know that you turned Old Faithful on. We thought it was a natural feature." Replogle replied, "Well it is natural. That fellow was playing a joke." And they said, "Oh, no he wasn't." Replogle thought that to be about the finest joke ever to happen to him at Old Faithful. Unfortunately, the naive and the gullible were convinced that it was no joke.[11]

Lowell Biddulph was working the desk at Old Faithful in 1939 when a woman with a thick Swedish accent approached him and asked, "When are they going to flush Old Faithful Geyser?" Biddulph replied that they did not flush it, that it was all natural. He explained to the woman how the water had to be superheated in the ground and pressurized to allow it to rise up through the throat of the geyser until it erupted into the air. The woman listened patiently to his explanation. Just then, Old Faithful began preliminary spurts of water, and the woman cried excitedly as she hurried out of the museum, "Oh! They are starting to flush. Oh! Thank you Mister Ranger!"[12]

Another woman, less humble, asked Biddulph if he would please turn on Old Faithful so she could see it before she had to leave the park. Biddulph explained that there was no way to turn on Old Faithful, that it happened naturally, but the woman would have none of it. "Don't try to fool me," she chided. "I know you have a switch under your desk, and I know that you have big boilers under the ground that you stoke with all the dead wood I've seen piled up along the roadside." Biddulph countered with the truth, but the woman turned up her nose. "My brother-in-law told me that you'd try to fool me," she said. "Please! Don't waste my time. I'm in a hurry and I do want to see it erupt!"

About this time Biddulph was wishing he could get his hands on that brother-in-law. He was about to say, "Lady, if you can find a switch behind or under this desk or anywhere else, I'll happily turn it on for you," when someone nearby shouted, "Old Faithful is starting to go!" The woman gave Biddulph a knowing smirk and marched triumphantly out of the museum.[13]

Ranger-guided walks through the geyser basins occasionally produced strange coincidences that likely contributed to tourists' misperceptions about the geysers. Sam Beal was leading a walk through the Upper Geyser Basin and came to Grand Geyser, which is a fountain geyser that erupts to about

Fishing Bridge trailside museum, erected in 1931, the largest of the trailside series, emphasized Yellowstone Lake ecology and wildlife. (Photo by the author)

two hundred feet. Although its eruptions were somewhat "predictable," it could also be capricious. On this particular day, as the group approached Grand Geyser, Sam was commenting that Grand did not always cooperate with visitors, and he said jokingly to them, "You just kind of have to snap your fingers at it," and, of course, at that precise moment, Grand erupted into a grand show.

A disturbing number of naive tourists believed Old Faithful Junior to be real. Lystrup overheard an older couple discussing the replica one day. The man was miffed that with all the acres of geysers and hot springs they had in the park, why was it necessary to build a building around one. His wife thought it to be a very cute little thing, but as she approached to get a better look, her husband warned her to be careful because it was looking like it was about to blow.[14]

Old Faithful Junior was eventually removed from the museum, perhaps not merely because of its temperamental nature, but also because of its absence of scientific accuracy in explaining geyser theory. In similar fashion, the old museum and its adjacent little amphitheater were replaced by more elaborate facilities and educational programs only dreamed of by the Old Men.

FISHING BRIDGE MUSEUM

Bud Lystrup called the Fishing Bridge Museum "the envy of the Park." The largest of the four trailside museums, the one at Fishing Bridge was erected in 1930–31 and focused on Yellowstone Lake ecology. The museum stands back in the trees about twenty-five yards from the bluff overlooking Yellowstone Lake. A three-foot stone wall made of igneous rock and a cement walkway surround the entire museum. Broad stairs on the south side descend in grand manner to an observation platform, offering an inspiring panorama of all of Yellowstone Lake and surrounding mountains. A large telescope was mounted on a stand, allowing visitors to gain a closer look at the islands and distant shorelines and mountains.

An outdoor amphitheater was constructed a few yards away from the museum where nightly campfire programs were held. Seating was a system of graduated logs, with the largest in the back and smallest in the front, all facing a large stage and screen with a fire ring in the front. A small projection booth, made of the same materials as the museum, was later added to the back of the amphitheater from which naturalists showed slides and films.

The center portion of the museum, the largest of the sections, was wholly devoted to birds of the area. It was open and light, with full-length glass double doors on the north and south sides. The floor space was consumed by several large glass display cases filled with mounted specimens of birds indigenous to the Yellowstone Lake area. Specimens of honkers, tweeters, songsters, cawers, quackers, screechers, and hooters were all to be found there, all labeled.

The west wing of the museum provided displays of smaller animals and plant life found in the vicinity. Two or three corner displays were of aquatic mammals such as the otter, muskrat, and beaver mixed with specimens of squirrel, chipmunk, ground squirrel, golden-mantled marmot, and an assortment of moles and mice.

A botanical display of a variety of freshly picked wildflowers was maintained in an open metal display case filled with water. For several years, Lowell Biddulph gathered a variety of wildflowers every few days and displayed them by common and scientific name.

Unquestionably, the most compelling of all the displays in the museum was the seven-foot mounted grizzly bear, standing erect with snarled face and massive, outstretched forearms. This monster consistently garnered excited cries of horror from visitors

The years took its toll on the old grizzly. Moths, mice, and people's fingers slowly divested the bear of its hair until it looked somewhat like the skin

Mounted grizzly that stood in the Fishing Bridge
Museum for decades, removed in the 1960s. (Courtesy
of L. G. Biddulph)

horse in Margery Williams's *Velveteen Rabbit.* Although a sign, "Please Do Not
Touch," was posted, it was like asking children not to touch a plate of cookies placed directly in front of them. About 1965 the old grizzly was removed
from the museum and replaced with a more subdued grizzly sow and two
cubs. The claws from the old grizzly's forepaws were retained by Lowell Biddulph and eventually donated to the Yellowstone Park Archives.

The east wing of the museum was dedicated to the geology and history
of Yellowstone. A six-foot-square plaster relief map of the park, mounted on
four legs and standing about three and a half feet tall, occupied much of the
floor space. Specimens of various types of rocks of the park were displayed
around the outer walls, similar to that at Norris. Explanations of various geologic epochs were presented, identifying how volcanism, erosion, sedimenta-
tion, mountain building, and glaciations shaped the modern landscape of
Yellowstone.

Skull of Old Tex, an original breeding bison bull brought from the Goodnight herd in Texas in the late 1800s, mounted in the Fishing Bridge Museum; Lowell Biddulph looks on. (Courtesy of L. G. Biddulph)

The far eastern end of the museum was dedicated to a small display of human history. A large stone fireplace with rustic pine mantle occupied the entire northern wall of this comparatively small room. The white-bleached skull of "Old Tex" was mounted imposingly above the mantle.

Old Tex was a significant part of Yellowstone history. This massive buffalo bull was one of three bulls brought to Yellowstone from the Goodnight herd in Texas during the early years of the park and was used to breed a new generation of bison in Yellowstone at a time when the buffalo had almost been rendered extinct. Once the herd in Yellowstone was stabilized and Old Tex had outlived his usefulness, the rangers put him down, but his massive skull adorned the Fishing Bridge Museum for many years.

The fireplace room also had a display case of Native American photographs and paraphernalia collected in the park through the years. Photographs of Chief Sit-Down-Spotted of the Blackfoot Tribe, with one of his many wives, and another of Rain-in-the-Face, a Hunkpapa Lakota Sioux chief who had helped wipe out Custer at the Little Bighorn, were prominently displayed. Both posed with typical sour expression and arms folded as if in insolent mood toward their photographers. Sheepeater Indians posed outside their pole wick-iup, looking like homeless, poverty-stricken vagabonds.

The display also had a variety of Native American implements, including arrowheads and spearheads, bowls, tomahawks, and scraping tools made of stone, flint, and obsidian. There was also a photograph of Bannock Indians quarrying volcanic glass on the summit of Obsidian Cliff from which they made arrow and spear points for their buffalo hunting expeditions to the Crow country in southern Montana and northern Wyoming.

This room of history had a most pleasant ambience made homey with rustic furniture of birch and wicker and a writing table with lamp that filled the room with a soft, warm glow. When days were cold and overcast, as they often were in Yellowstone, nothing was quite as comforting as sitting by the great stone hearth and warming oneself by the crackling, popping fire.

The four trailside museums served as interpretive centers for nearly four decades. By the time the Five Old Men retired from the National Park Service, the term *museum* was being replaced with "visitor center." In 1971 the trailside museum at Old Faithful was torn down and replaced by a visitor center more in harmony with the Mission 66 revisions made in Yellowstone Park (see chapter 21). Then, in 2006, that visitor center was replaced with the current Old Faithful Visitor Education Center, which opened in August 2010. Three of the four original trailside museums yet stand and fulfill their original purpose of interpretation. All are listed on the National Register of Historic Places and together constitute a National Historic Landmark.

Chapter 15

Walks, Talks, and Stalks

THE NATURE OF INTERPRETATION

A granddaughter of Herbert Lystrup observed about his style of interpreting nature:

> The greatest contribution that my grandfather gave to Yellowstone National Park was his ability to communicate the wonders of the Park to anyone—visitor, peer or family. He interpreted, he didn't lecture. He let people make the discoveries for themselves. He knew natural history, biology, and botany, but his gift was allowing people to see for themselves. Interpretation is extremely difficult. Many people in this world don't know how to point people in a direction and guide them in what they're seeing without giving away the punch line. Grandpa did this all the time.[1]

True interpretation is storytelling at its best. A compelling story, honestly and accurately told, elicits in the reader or listener inner emotions and insights that enrich him or her in important ways. Like a good storyteller, a master interpreter does not presume to tell people how to feel or think in the presence of grandeur, but simply guides them into their own intimate experience. Nature is its own ultimate storyteller. No person can reveal the grandeur of Yellowstone with comparable passion and accuracy as can nature. Human language is simply not endowed with the capacity to adequately describe the great canyon, geysers in eruption, beautifully colored hot springs, rugged alpine scenes, or moonlight across a wilderness lake. These things must be

Preseason seminar for new ranger naturalists, 1950s. (Photo by D. Condon; courtesy of the National Park Service, Yellowstone National Park, YELL 19856-7)

seen in their raw beauty to be fully appreciated, and then only by those who are capable of inspiration.

The best interpreters have an instinctive capacity to see what others do not see in nature and to inspire people with their genuine awe for its beauty. Passion for nature comes from deep familiarity cultivated by long and sympathetic intercourse. Inspiring interpreters possess an innate ability to communicate their passion to others. Many men knew the park intimately, but not all had a passion; certainly, not all possessed the ability to share that passion with the visitors and to help them feel the influence of nature.

The Old Men's love for nature seemed to have been a passion that was born early in youth and cultivated throughout their lives, and it was clearly the primary mover for their extraordinary longevity in Yellowstone Park. However, their ability to interpret the passion was a skill that they honed over years of service. Every interaction in nature was an opportunity for them to strengthen those skills as they exposed people to the park's diverse beauty and transforming qualities.

As the public became better informed on subjects of nature, the questions posed to ranger naturalists became more challenging to answer, and the demands placed upon the interpreter's knowledge increased. The simple questions of early years: "What makes the geyser water hot?" or "Why does a geyser erupt?" evolved into more difficult ones: "Can protozoa live and multiply in waters with temperatures as high as those at which algae occur?" or "What is the rate of heat increase in depth below the surface?"[2] Even men with long tenure were challenged by such questions.

Dr. C. Max Bauer worked diligently to prepare his interpreters for the challenge. Each summer was preceded by a three-day annual preseason indoctrination course conducted to prepare men and women as interpreters. Voluminous amounts of information were provided during these classes, more than could be fully assimilated by the average ranger naturalist, yet the interaction with more experienced men was helpful. No doubt with vivid memory of his first season alone at Fishing Bridge, Bud Lystrup deeply appreciated what he called the "intellectual stimulus" gained from the exchange of ideas with fellow seasonal naturalists from all parts of the United States.[3]

Ranger naturalists could not rely solely upon the preseason training to make them adequate interpreters. Nor could they expect to get all they needed by reading the *Manual of General Information* provided by the park administration. Naturalists were expected to become students of nature, as Superintendent Lemuel Garrison wrote in the preface of the 1963 *Manual of Information:* "It will be at once apparent that the whole story is not here but only its bones—a skeleton for the conscientious Interpreter to flesh out through further reading. It is only through a broad understanding, filled in with pertinent details, that the Yellowstone Story can be presented to the park visitor with meaning and accuracy. Thus, much remains for *you* to do."[4]

NATURE WALKS

Bud Lystrup described nature walks as mini excursions into nature that helped each visitor "enjoy and appreciate the great variety of natural phenomena in Yellowstone through the eyes, ears, and mouths of the ranger-naturalist."[5] Visitors found that sharing nature with a ranger naturalist and other people from around the world was an invigorating learning experience, fun yet instructional. Campfire programs and nature walks were as much social events as they were educational. One never knew what would be encountered on a nature walk or an excursion in the geyser basins, and it required a good deal of spontaneity on the part of the ranger naturalist to address whatever was observed.

Preparing for and leading a nature walk was a daunting experience for an inexperienced ranger naturalist. Sam Beal reported his first nature walk at Old Faithful in 1939: "The emphasis of this three-hour walk was botanical. I

Geyser walk at Firehole River in Upper Geyser Basin, ca. 1956. (Photo by D. Condon; courtesy of the National Park Service, Yellowstone National Park, YELL 35666)

enjoyed the nature walk, although my knowledge of flowers was superficial. Not disposed to bluff, I exhibited dubiety. My journal entry of July 24, 1939, states: 'a botanist asked too many questions for my comfort.'"

When a woman asked him why so many of the flowers they saw on the walk were yellow in color: sunflowers, balsamroot, cinquefoil, buttercups, sulfur flower, yellow monkey flower, primrose, arnica, cut-leaf daisies, goldeneye, and goldenrod, to mention a few, Beal had no idea and replied: "Why, madam, this is YELLOWstone!" He hastened to add: "However jocular that answer, I always sought correct information."[6]

Beal remains mute regarding whether he found an answer to the question of color. Available information often came by consulting with a fellow naturalist who had training in the field of concern. Otherwise, information came from guidebooks or field reference manuals. Of course, there was no Internet technology at the time. A review of plant reference books available during Beal's service (*Plants of Yellowstone National Park,* written by W. B. McDougall and Herma A. Baggley and published by the US Department of the Interior in 1936, and even *The Peterson Field Guide to Rocky Mountain Wildflowers,* written by John J. Craighead, Frank C. Craighead Jr., and Ray J. Davis, not published until 1963) provides no discussion of plant genetics related to color variation.

A Precambrian glacial boulder on the west rim of the Grand Canyon of Yellowstone. (Courtesy of L. G. Biddulph)

Yellowstone Park, as a whole, has as many colors of white, pink-red, and blue-purple flowers as it does yellow. More current research has revealed that types and colors of flowers are a function of soil content, plant genetics, and atmospheric conditions. Much knowledge has been gained over the years regarding plant pigments and how soil chemistry (pH and acidic qualities) can cause different colors in plants that would have been unavailable to Beal.

The typical nature walk of the interpretive era was a one- to three-hour excursion led by a ranger naturalist. More rigorous nature hikes, such as to the bottom of the canyon along Uncle Tom's Trail, to the summits of Elephant Back Mountain, and an ascent of Avalanche Peak, were half- and full-day excursions. Tourists and naturalist met at the appointed place and time where they were greeted and given appropriate instruction on the scope and procedures of the walk or hike.

Nature walks took on the focus and personality of the ranger naturalist, who typically invited participants to be observant and stealthy enough to see wild animals or birds along the way. Small groups had an obvious advantage over larger ones. Strung out along a trail, those up front in a large group saw things that others farther back missed completely. Birds and animals were not trained to pose for audiences, although some circumstances might have raised doubts about that in the minds of some.

Ranger naturalists encouraged openness and inquisitiveness among the participants. Frequently rangers said, "There are no dumb questions. A good question is one to which you don't know the answer." On occasion, a visitor would test the credibility of that statement. Lowell Biddulph once had such an occasion while conducting a nature walk near Artist Point. He took his group to a massive glacier boulder in the forest discovered in 1883 by W. H. Holmes of the Hayden Survey Party.[7]

Biddulph explained to his group that the boulder was made of gneiss from the ancient Precambrian era, making it among the oldest basement rock known in Yellowstone. Yet here sat this boulder, measuring approximately twenty-four feet cubed and weighing an estimated five hundred tons atop volcanic earth laid down millions of years later.[8] Biddulph explained how the boulder had been brought by glaciers from the Beartooth Mountains in the northern part of Yellowstone to this unlikely spot near the brink of the canyon.

A woman in the group marveled about this and asked how it was possible that the glacier had been able to drop this boulder among the trees without so much as scratching the bark. For a moment, Biddulph was not certain if the woman was serious or trying to pull his leg. Then, determining that she was sincere, he courteously explained that the boulder was there long before the trees that had grown up around it. The woman responded by asking where the glacier had gone.

"Oh!" Biddulph quipped. "It's gone back to get another load of rock." He then explained that the glaciers, which at one time had covered the entire park in ice thousands of feet thick, had long since melted away with warmer temperatures and were now pretty much confined to small ice fields in mountain cirques.[9]

The nature trail from Squaw Lake, as it was known at the time, to Storm Point on the northern shore of Yellowstone Lake provided an excellent show of animals and flora of the park, as it still does today. Often, bison, elk, deer, and even an occasional bear can be seen during the walk.

Storm Point is a barren, rocky point that rises about sixty or seventy feet above the water. Golden-mantled marmots can often be seen sunning themselves on the rocks. Heavy rains and wind sweeping across the lake from Mount Sheridan invariably crash against Storm Point. Many of the trees exposed on the point are twisted and gnarled by wind and weather. The trunks of some of the trees are clearly twisted in one direction caused as they responded to sunlight moving from east to west across the sky. Biddulph enjoyed showing these trees to his visitors and explaining that trees in the Southern Hemisphere were twisted one direction, and those in the Northern Hemisphere were twisted in another because of the pattern of sunlight.

On one nature walk, a man in his group asked what would happen to a tree in the Northern Hemisphere if it were transplanted in the Southern Hemisphere. Another man in the group spoke up and said, "Mister, it would unwind so fast that it would screw itself right down into the ground!" Everyone in the group had a good laugh.

Bob Jonas and Wayne Replogle once took joking to a bit of an extreme on their nature walk at Canyon, or at least the outcome was more than they bargained for. Their route passed by a cave that was used by hibernating bears during the winter months. While Replogle led the people along the trail, Jonas secluded himself in the cave. When Replogle approached the mouth of the cave, he told the group in a rather animated voice that he was seeing fresh signs of bear and to watch out. That was Jonas's cue to let out a loud growl from inside the cave.

Replogle threw up his hands and shouted, "Run for your lives!" People scattered, and it took Replogle thirty minutes to round them up. He found an elderly lady standing on top of a large boulder where she had climbed for safety. Hopefully, that cured the naturalists from that kind of future prank. The following year at a campfire program, a visitor recalled the bear experience to Replogle and admitted that he "had not seen such a mad bear as the one that was in the cave!"[10]

Apparently, this joke was shared around the ranger-naturalist community with some variation. Lowell Biddulph remembered that when Jonas let out a loud growl from the den and most people scattered, a couple of young men in the crowd picked up rocks and blasted the den, and Jonas's growls quickly turned into howls!

GAME STALKS

Game stalks were motorized versions of nature walks. They were normally held in the early evening when the game animals, such as deer, elk, buffalo, and moose, moved from the shade of the trees into the open meadows to feed, thus making them more visible to tourists. Participants drove their own cars and followed the ranger driving a government vehicle. These game stalks had the potential to create car jams along the roads, and although they got tourists out to see animals, they were not nearly as educational or intimate as nature walks.

The ranger naturalist drove slowly and pointed out the window to the left or right at whatever animal he may have seen. Each driver in the procession of automobiles would also point so that the next person in line could see the animal or bird. There was no way of communicating what the ranger saw, and everyone was left to their own to identify what people were pointing at. One could not really stop in most places when an animal emerged, for fear of creating a road hazard, and the people in the cars in the rear of the caravan were not able to see what was going on ahead of them.

A popular game stalk at Canyon was a drive up the steep mountain road to Dunraven Pass and back. There were some meadows and open mountainsides where elk, deer, bear, and perhaps a moose or even a buffalo could be seen. Of course, ranger naturalists hoped to see a variety of wild animals that would thrill the tourists, and any night that a ranger failed to see a wild animal on a game stalk was considered a very bad night. The rangers at Canyon during Replogle's day had a ruse that guaranteed at least minimum success.

High on the hillside above the road to Dunraven Pass was a brown broken tree stump that, from a distance, looked like a bull elk grazing. As the naturalist came along here, if the animal show had been dismal, he often pointed up the hill to the stump, and each tourist as they passed by looked up there and saw this beautiful brown elk, so to speak. If they got in that night without having seen any other animal, the people always said at least they saw one bull elk. How many pictures of a dead tree stump were passed off as elk is anyone's guess, but that old stump saved a ranger naturalist's reputation more than one night.[11]

AUTO CARAVANS

Auto caravans were conducted to points of interest that were beyond walking distance. Similar to the game stalks, visitors caravanned in their personal cars behind the ranger naturalist to the points of interest, where the naturalist explained the history and interesting facts about the feature. The fish hatchery at Lake Village and the Natural Bridge near Bridge Bay were two popular locations for caravans used by the ranger naturalists at Fishing Bridge.

The fish hatchery building was constructed in 1930–32, using rustic Parkitecture. The building sat near the shoreline of Yellowstone Lake, west of the Lake Hotel and near where the current-day medical facility is located. Up until it closed in 1958, eggs of the cutthroat trout were brought to the hatchery from egg-collection stations at Clear Creek, Columbine Creek,

Fish and Game employee milking a cutthroat trout at one of the egg-collection stations, ca. 1948. (Courtesy of L. G. Biddulph)

Peale Island near Chipmunk Creek outlet in the South Arm, and West Thumb. Visitors learned firsthand about the famous trout in Yellowstone Lake, how they spawned, and the role of the fish hatchery in artificial propagation. They saw how eggs were collected, incubated, and hatched into larvae, helping them better appreciate this unique game fish and its importance to Yellowstone. After the hatchery's closure, the Park Service maintained an aquarium in one of the old hatchery buildings with various live species of fish found in Yellowstone.

The Natural Bridge near Bridge Bay is a unique example of natural architecture. The archway is composed of hard rock more impervious than the softer surrounding volcanic material through which running water has cut a gap. The ravine is filled with rock debris and vegetation. It provided Biddulph a fine visual aid to talk about Yellowstone's volcanic past and the forces of erosion. There were also friendly little golden-mantled ground squirrels and chipmunks that greeted the tourists and willingly partook of food offerings from their fingers.

CAMPFIRE PROGRAMS
Campfires are deeply symbolic to the origin and purpose of Yellowstone. In the early days of interpretation, two campfires were lighted as dark-

ness descended. One symbolized the 1870 campfire at Madison Junction wherein the "National Park Idea" was believed to have been born. The second campfire symbolized the realization of that idea and the friendship and brotherhood enflamed in the hearts of those who came to visit Yellowstone. The early campfire programs in Yellowstone were held in community rooms of ranger stations. Later, clearings were made in the forest, and logs of varying sizes were arranged into a semicircle around a campfire pit. Even later, amphitheaters were constructed adjacent to trailside museums consisting of logs, a screen, and a fire ring.

The logs used in these early amphitheaters were moderately groomed and sized. Despite the outdoorsy feel, they were not contoured to the human body, and they proved uncomfortable and cold to sit on for extended periods unless one had substantial padding. In time, these old, uncomfortable logs were replaced with benches and eventually spacious indoor auditoriums, which lost the outdoors ambience altogether.

Much has happened to media technology since Bud Lystrup stood on a stump in a clearing at Fishing Bridge and lectured on the trees of Yellowstone Park. The first visual technology came in the form of Edmund J. Sawyer's hand-painted slides of plants, birds, flowers, and animals on Forgo glass called "lantern slides." These images were projected onto a screen by use of the Spencer projector, which was heavy, hard to operate, and extremely hot and noisy. The ranger naturalist lectured from the projector behind the audience, where he could change the slides as he spoke. Despite their rudimentary nature, the Spencer projector and Sawyer's hand-painted slides greatly improved the campfire presentations.

Wayne Replogle was fond of neither Sawyer's slides nor the projector. He was a fairly accomplished artist—he had sold his own paintings of Old West scenes—and may have felt that the slides lacked artistic realism. One evening Replogle was giving a lecture on flowers of Yellowstone Park at the little amphitheater located near the old Canyon Lodge and was using the Spencer projector and Sawyer's hand-painted slides.

At the end of his lecture, an elderly gentleman approached him and asked: "How do you like those slides?" Replogle, normally forthright, lied and said, "Oh, they're just fine." The gentleman said, "Well, that's fine because I'm Mr. Sawyer." Replogle concluded, "Well Golly, once in awhile you accidentally do the right thing."[12]

By the 1940s, the Five Old Men were taking their own slides of the wonders of Yellowstone in living color. This new Kodak technology greatly

Campfire program in Yellowstone, ca. 1966. (Courtesy of L. G. Biddulph)

enhanced the campfire presentations. The beautiful pictures of wildlife and wilderness scenes taken of Yellowstone by these men captivated audiences. Nevertheless, one or two of these old Forgo hand-painted slides of flowers and plants still found their way into presentations as late as the early 1960s.

In the 1950s, a few 35mm movies were produced by the park about mammals and geysers and hot springs. They were played on Bell and Howell movie projectors. The film from the feed reel had to be wound through an intricate pathway of loops with careful tolerances, and the film played with a noticeable clicking noise as the tape fed through the projector onto the receiving reel. When finished, the film had to be rewound onto the original reel.

Performing onstage at campfire programs was stressful for some naturalists. The speaker was expected to know his subject and come across as an expert. In the 1930s and '40s, two ranger naturalists did the campfire programs. One was the master of ceremonies, and the other gave the lecture. The master of ceremonies had to be a real showman to break the ice with a diverse audience and get the social juices flowing. Campfire singing was used for this purpose, and some naturalists handled this assignment better than others.

In his first season of service, Merrill Beal practiced diligently and acted sprightly and jocularly by inviting "everybody to pitch his own pitch and pitch in. Sometimes, exceptional spontaneity elicited merriment," he noted, "but the effort was hard on me. During my second season, and thereafter, I substituted nature-oriented poems and commentaries, in lieu of singing. Ample and elegant material was available that conformed to the grandeur of Yellowstone. Kipling, Shakespeare and Wordsworth were splendid sources."[13]

The popular songs of the day included such favorites as "Old MacDonald Had a Farm," "There's a Long, Long Trail a Winding," "Home on the Range," "The States Song," "The Smile Song," "My Bonnie Lies over the Ocean" and a lyrical adaptation of the same called "Way Down on the Yellowstone River," "My Wild Irish Rose," "The Yellowstone Song," "God Bless America," "The Bear Went over the Mountain," and "Row, Row, Row Your Boat."

Some songs, such as "Old MacDonald" and "She'll Be Comin' 'round the Mountain," were fun in nature, getting people to laugh, clap their hands, and tap their toes. A favorite song of the tourists that was unique to Yellowstone was "Way Down on the Yellowstone River" sung to the tune of "My Bonnie Lies over the Ocean." The lyrics are:

Way down on the Yellowstone River,
Where campers are camped thick as bees,
Along about twelve O'clock midnight,
You can hear this refrain through the trees:
Bring back, bring back, O' bring back my bacon to me, to me
Bring back, bring back, O' bring back my bacon to me.

Other songs, like "The Smile Song," built spirit and camaraderie. Still others, such as "God Bless America," "Yellowstone," and "There's a Long, Long Trail a Winding," were more melancholy, almost emotional. By the time the singing was done, people had gone through a range of emotions and were ready for the naturalist's lecture on some aspect of Yellowstone.

Naturalists never knew who or what might show up at their evening programs. Anything was possible, including famous or historical figures, scientists and experts in subjects of nature, park officials, and even animals.

One summer Replogle was assigned to give his first campfire lecture on flowers of Yellowstone at the Canyon amphitheater when, lo and behold, who should show up at the lecture than Chief Naturalist Dr. C. Max Bauer and his wife. Bauer was a superb scientist and very knowledgeable on many aspects of the park, and within a few years he left Yellowstone to become the chief geologist at the National Park Service in Washington, DC. All of the

Five Old Men held Bauer in the highest esteem, and naturally, Replogle was scared out of his wits when he saw Dr. Bauer walk into the amphitheater.

On this occasion, Replogle was serving as both master of ceremonies and lecturer. In the middle of his warm-ups—he was leading the crowd in singing the words to the song "Yellowstone," a song he claimed to hate with a passion—he spied Dr. Bauer and his wife coming up the hill.

"Well, I said I've enjoyed three years as a ranger, but this will end here tonight." Bauer sat on the back log, and Replogle began to talk about flowers. "I didn't know much about flowers," he admitted, "but I was trying. So, I cranked up and I said everything I knew about a flower. I just raved on and raved on.... I knew he'd fire me as sure as sin." When it was all over and the crowd dispersed, Mrs. Bauer came up to Replogle, and he got ready for the blow. To his surprise, she said, "Well, that was a fine talk."

"I said, 'Oh thank you Mrs. Bauer, Oh thank you.'" Dr. Bauer marched over; he was a small man with a little mustache, but Replogle was shaking like a leaf in an October windstorm. Bauer shook Replogle's hand and said, "Rep, that's the best flower talk I ever heard."

"Praise God!" Replogle cried within. If Replogle is to be believed, it was probably the worst lecture on flowers that Bauer had ever heard, but after that Replogle never feared giving a flower talk.[14] In fact, in later years, the two campfire talks that he enjoyed giving most often at Canyon were "The Color and Beauty through Flowers" and "Yellowstone Plants and Their Uses." The latter subject came from his extensive study of the Bannock, Shoshone, and Sheepeater Indians in Yellowstone.

Occasionally, at some evening campfires, living visual aids appeared unrehearsed. A bull moose walked into the Canyon amphitheater the summer of 1942 while Herbert Lystrup was giving the campfire lecture. The press memorandum from the park superintendent, released to newspapers, said:

Ranger-naturalist Herbert Lystrup had just completed the title of his talk, "Yellowstone, An Animal Sanctuary," when who should make an auspicious entrance but a large bull moose. He paid no attention to the visitors who were wide-eyed with amazement, but walked up to the edge of the log seats and proceeded to eat the grass as though no one was present. Mr. Lystrup forgot about his prepared talk for the evening and took advantage of the opportunity to describe to the audience the habits and characteristics of the moose. It seemed that every time the ranger-naturalist made a particular flattering point about the uninvited guest, the moose would lift his head and bow his long velvet-like antlers. He seemed to sense the talk was about him and enjoyed the crowning glory he received.[15]

After such an event, it was difficult for Lystrup to convince tourists, especially children, that the "tame" moose was not a planned event and could not be reproduced in following lectures. The moose did not accommodate the public again, although in other summers, coyotes, bison, elk, deer, and bears dropped in as visual aids to his talks.

The campfire helped to provide the desired ambience for these programs. Often laid in tepee style and doused with kerosene to ensure failsafe lighting, the burning wood filled the dark night with hundreds of swirling, dancing sparks. Flames danced merrily upon the sap-filled wood, silhouetting shadows of people against the forest wall like flickering ghosts in the night. People from all walks of life and all areas of the world laughed and sang together, then listened with rapt interest to the naturalist's intimate stories of nature.

When the lecture was over and the people drifted through the pine trees to their campsites, their flashlights and lanterns bobbing like fireflies in the darkness, the naturalist often stood alone for a moment or two, warming himself by the tiny blue and orange flames that yet danced merrily among white-hot ashes. Perhaps with some reluctance, he poured water on the embers, listened to the hiss of cold on hot, and watched the luminous steam cloud rise against the black sky as the dark night wrapped its cold arms around him. Another day in Wonderland was over.

THE NATURALIST'S REWARD

"The wonder of the world, the beauty and the power, the shapes of things, their colours, lights, and shades; these I saw. Look ye also while life lasts."[16] This epitaph, written upon an old gravestone in Cumberland, England, suggests the sentiment behind the work of the Five Old Men in Yellowstone. Tourists rushed through the park, catching only fleeting glimpses of its wild nature. Humanity seemed to be rushing furiously toward some uncertain end with increasing noise, confusion, and vanity. The men's objective was to slow people down and help them feel the inspiration of natural beauty that comes only by sustained exposure and quiet reflection.

Bud Lystrup put it in the form of questions in a 1953 *Nature Notes* article:

Has the art of relaxation become one of the lost ideals? Have people forgotten how to appreciate, in quiet and rest, the beauty, simplicity and intrigue of nature? Are our national parks really observed or are they superficially scanned in haste? What percentage of our visitors takes the time to accompany a naturalist on a nature walk? Rewards: naturalists are rewarded in their efforts every time they can help people to relax. They are rewarded when people come to them after a walk to tell of their enjoyment and appreciation. It is good to know that people have been helped in a busy, nervous, hurried age.[17]

PART FOUR

Discovering Yellowstone

I feel my love for nature is deep and abiding. Not every student of nature succeeds in making birds, plants, flowers, and rocks a part of his life. Not until you have had long and sympathetic intercourse with them, in fact, not till you have loved them for their own sake, do they enter into and become a part of your life.

—Lowell G. Biddulph

Chapter 16

Discovery

Yellowstone has been repeatedly discovered throughout history. Native Americans lived in and around Yellowstone long before white men came. Indians had summer camps on the shores of Yellowstone Lake. They knew of the geysers and were familiar with the bright sulfurous tones of the canyon. Their name for the river that flowed from its belly was roughly translated as "yellow rock." The French equivalent was Roche Jaune. John Colter may have been the first white man to travel through Yellowstone in 1807–8 and see some of its wonders. During the later 1800s, trappers, mountain men, and other parties explored Yellowstone and made its wonders known to the world. Scientific groups followed the explorers, surveying, measuring, analyzing, and naming most of its features. Since the park's creation in 1872, millions of people have visited Yellowstone and discovered its wonders.

One might reasonably ask, "Is there anything left to discover in Yellowstone?" The answer, of course, is yes. Everything! Each soul that comes to Yellowstone for the first time makes his or her own unique discovery, and each time he returns he finds something he had not seen before. There will always be something new or unique to discover in Yellowstone because nature is always changing. Discovering Yellowstone does not mean to merely see places and objects; it means to discover the remarkable history of these places and objects, how they were formed and how they relate to each other.

Few places on earth have such a varied and dynamic history of change as Yellowstone. Some changes have come with the violent suddenness of earthquakes or exploding volcanoes, others with the subtleness of silt settling on shallow sea beds, the carving of a canyon by flowing water, or the imperceptible cutting of striations across a mountain face by glacial ice. In whatever form that changes come to this land, people will discover anew its charm and beauty.

In the years between 1930 and 1970, places in Yellowstone still existed that had not been photographed or thoroughly explored. Some of the wonders were not nearly as well known and thoroughly researched then as they are today. The Old Men had the privilege of searching and discovering portions of the park.

BLACK DRAGON'S CAULDRON

Imagine the emotions of the members of the Washburn Party as they rode their horses along the Yellowstone River in Hayden Valley on September 2, 1870, saw clouds of steam rising from a pine-covered hillside about a half mile away, and heard loud explosions like that of a cannon's report. Nathaniel P. Langford, a member of the party, described the scene: "Our ears were constantly saluted by dull, thundering, booming sounds.... [T]he ground beneath us shook and trembled.... The cause of the uproar was found to be a mud volcano—the greatest marvel we have yet met with.... [T]he lower side [of] its crater, thirty feet in diameter, rises to a height of about thirty-five feet. The explosions are not uniform in force or time...[and] are distinctly heard at the distance of half a mile, and the massive jets of vapor which accompany them burst forth like the smoke of burning gunpowder."[1]

These thermal features described by Langford were collectively named Mud Volcano and include several cauldrons and mud pots; among the more famous are Mud Volcano and Dragon's Mouth. What appeared to these early explorers to be boiling water, thick bubbling mud, and vapors that smelled like burning gunpowder, we now know, were predominantly escaping hydrogen sulfide and carbon dioxide gas.

Now jump forward in time seventy-eight years to June 10, 1948. Ranger Naturalist Lowell Biddulph, who was serving as the head naturalist at Fishing Bridge at that time, was responsible for interpretive programs at Mud Volcano. Part of his interpretive duties was to observe the thermal features in this area and keep a record of their function and change. Biddulph was about to have a remarkable experience of discovery on that June day in 1948, similar to that of the Washburn Party.

Yellowstone was known to have had significant volcanic activity in its past. The geyser basins gave ample evidence of the tremendous heat source that yet underlay Yellowstone. Although the caldera and hot-spot theory had not been developed in 1948, it was no mystery to geologists that the crust immediately below Yellowstone Park was much warmer than other places[2] and that much of the heat transmitted to the surface, especially in geyser basins, was done so by hot gases. Yet an uncertainty persisted in the minds of those who worked in the park and studied its geology as to its potential volatility in future years.

The uncertainty was fueled during the 1946 and '47 seasons by a mysterious increase in thermal activity occurring in the greater Mud Volcano area. Virtually every spring and vent in the vicinity showed an upsurge in thermal energy. Ochre Springs, located on the pine-covered flank of Elephant Back Mountain, a mile or two removed from Mud Volcano, became violently active during these years, expelling large volumes of water ten to twenty feet into the air. Biddulph noted in a 1946 report to headquarters, "Mild noises, similar in nature to those of Dragon's Mouth, accompany the steam action. This reactivation is in keeping with the stimulated activity of Mud Volcano, Dragons Mouth, Big Mud Pot, the Mud Geyser, and others in the same locality."[3]

At first it seemed as if underground temperatures were increasing, portending the potential for even more violent eruptions. However, upon investigation, Biddulph found that the water temperature of the springs was below boiling (199° Fahrenheit at an elevation of eight thousand feet). He concluded that the boiling action was caused by escaping carbon dioxide gas and steam, not superheated water.

Ochre Springs was not alone in activity. In a ravine some distance south of the main Mud Volcano complex, a cauldron belched thick, gray mud, coating lodgepole pines thirty-five feet away on the hillside. The ground shook with loud thumping noises, and large dome-shaped bubbles formed in the thick mud as gas forced its way to the surface.

A quarter mile away from this cauldron, another feature that Biddulph called the "Devils Ink Well" boiled violently as if it were superheated. The blue-black water was thrown some fifteen feet into the air. As with Ochre Springs, Biddulph found that the water was not at boiling temperatures and that the tremendous bubbles were caused by hot gas escaping from below.

Yet another quarter mile from this cauldron, he came upon a large turbid-looking lake that measured 150 yards long and 75 yards wide. In another report he described the activity of this lake: "This lake might well be called Boiling Lake for the entire surface is in constant motion due to escaping steam and

Black Dragon's Cauldron at Mud Volcano, ca. 1951. (Courtesy of L. G. Biddulph)

gases. In two places near the center the boiling action reaches a peak where large cones of water twelve to fifteen feet in diameter boil up several feet above the surface of the lake, then break into a myriad of bubbles which float outward into riffles."[4]

The increased violence posed intriguing questions for Biddulph. What were the origin and cause of this increased activity? What major changes, if any, would this increased pressure cause on the existing features? And did this portend the eruption of new features?

The answer to these questions came on June 10, 1948. As Biddulph entered the parking lot at Mud Volcano to begin another season of monitoring, his ears were saluted by a sound similar to what Langford described in 1870. Explosions of sound were coming from the pine-covered hills immediately above Mud Volcano. Surely with the same wonderment as filled the minds of the Washburn Party, Biddulph scrambled up the hillside toward Sour Lake and the source of the sound.

Achieving the top of the hill, he stood stunned by the scene before him. Near Sour Lake, in an area that had once been open meadow spattered with small lodgepole pines, there loomed an open cauldron of exploding black mud that measured forty feet by seventy feet in diameter. Thick, black mud was ejected onto the surrounding landscape in booming explosions so violent that mud flew twenty feet into the air and covered trees seventy-five feet away. Virtually every lodgepole pine within the cauldron's circumference had been obliterated.[5]

Biddulph immediately reported this new feature to park headquarters and continued to monitor the new feature daily throughout the summer season. The new cauldron was eventually named "Black Dragon's Cauldron," and with its emergence, attention was turned to Sour Lake, just two hundred feet away.

Sour Lake is a large body of murky green water caused by a concentration of sulfuric acid from the presence of microorganisms and sulfur. Scientists speculated whether the new cauldron would grow in size and what effect it would have on Sour Lake. No one knew the answers to these and other questions. Nature was in full control, and all man could do was stand by and watch the outcome. The area was blocked off to visitors until adequate stability and assurance of safety could be assured.

Although the initial violence of Black Dragon's Cauldron subsided slightly over time, it remained robust. Meanwhile, the spring that fed Sour Lake diminished in size, and for a time it appeared that Black Dragon's Cauldron was robbing from the energy source that fueled Sour Lake. Then, beginning in 1951, Black Dragon's Cauldron began to migrate, advancing along a southwest fissure directly toward Sour Lake. Of course, the question of the day became what would happen when and if the two actually merged.

The surface of Sour Lake was sixteen inches above that of Black Dragon's Cauldron, but the water level in the lake had begun to drop. By 1954 it had dropped thirty-seven inches. In 1961 the two thermal features merged. Unexpectedly, the merger energized Sour Lake; its water level began to rapidly rise, causing its acidic waters to overflow into Black Dragon Cauldron.[6] Now, more than fifty years later, Sour Lake and Black Dragon's Cauldron still coexist on the pine hill overlooking Mud Volcano. However, Black Dragon is no longer a cauldron of thick black mud but a thermal lake of gray-colored water that bubbles at one end.

Geologists have learned much about the forces below Yellowstone Park since 1948. They tell us that a plume of molten lava rose from the core of the earth through the mantle and rests under Yellowstone Park. This molten lava fueled the ancient calderas and makes possible the geysers and other thermal features unique to the park. We now understand that the great geyser basins and many of the other thermal features of the park lie on or near the ancient crack rings of the most recent caldera that exploded across Yellowstone some half-million years ago and formed its interior plateaus. Geologists continue to measure this part of Yellowstone to try to predict if the roof of this caldera is once again rising under extreme subterranean pressure, portending another cataclysmic explosion similar to that which occurred 640,000 years ago.[7] Measurements made between 1923 and 1985 indicate that the surface of Yellowstone is slowly (one yard in sixty years) being pushed upward by subterranean pressure. The apex of the dome lies very close to the Mud Volcano area.

Several mild earthquakes occurred near the Mud Volcano in the 1970s. The highest number of tremors occurred in 1978 and generated significant heat fluxes, increasing the thermal activity of these features. Vegetation was killed off in the immediate area due to increased ground temperatures. Sizzling Basin and Churning Cauldron became superheated, killing off the microorganisms that once grew there. After 1979 the temperatures began to decrease and return to their previous levels.

THE YELLOWSTONE CALDERA

The mountains of Yellowstone are the elders that sit in a great arc surrounding a fire that has burned beneath its surface for millennia. In their faces are etched the stories of creation: great mountain swells; erosion; ancient seas filled with long-extinct fish; trilobites and crustaceans pressed into stone sediment; forests of sequoia-like deciduous trees growing in tropical environments; volcanoes and calderas covering the land with thick molten vomit, entombing trees and leaves in stony epitaphs; and glacial ice thousands of feet thick, etching their hieroglyphics upon the mountains. Forces

Petrified tree stumps on Specimen Ridge in northern Yellowstone, ca. 1957.
(Courtesy of L. G. Biddulph)

of nature have always been in conflict in Yellowstone, pushing up, wearing
down, creating, and destroying.

The most violent of Yellowstone's creative stories speaks of volcanoes
and calderas that formed the Yellowstone plateau and covered great forests of
trees with volcanic ash hundreds of feet thick. Yellowstone Park is one of the
only places on earth that petrified trees have been discovered standing

upright, evidencing the suddenness of their entombment. The petrified tree near Tower Fall is one of the well-known examples of petrifaction, but there is more. Specimen Ridge, on the northern rim of Yellowstone's Mirror Plateau, contains more than twenty layers of petrified forests that have been opened up on the face of the mountain and stand as monolithic testaments of the volcanic forces that shaped Yellowstone.

There are other testimonies of Yellowstone's volcanic past, albeit originally discovered in unexpected places. In the summer of 1947, Lowell Biddulph discovered the stumps of petrified trees high in the Absaroka Mountains above ten thousand feet. These were stony remains of huge, redwood-like trees, one stump measuring ten feet in diameter. One side of the stump stood fifteen inches above the ground, while the opposite side was slightly buried in the soil. Several other stumps of varying diameters were found on the south slope of Top Notch Peak and on the ridgeline running toward Doane Peak. These massive fossil trees were predominantly of agate and were deciduous trees that are no longer found in Yellowstone.[8] In addition to the petrified stumps, Biddulph also found fossilized imprints of leaves, twigs, small fish, trilobites, and shells in the shale rock on the summits of Top Notch and Avalanche Peaks.

These fossils and stumps collectively tell a story of extreme change: of ancient seas and sediment turned to shale in which creatures were impregnated, of a time when forests of huge deciduous trees covered the land, of volcanoes and calderas that covered the landscape suddenly with immense amounts of lava and hot volcanic ash, of great upheavals of earth's crust that broke up the shale sediment and heaped them, along with the fossils and petrified stumps, high upon these mountain peaks.

In June 1964, nearly twenty years after his first discovery of the petrified stumps on Top Notch Peak, Biddulph led Dr. Erling Dorf of Princeton University, who was at the time studying Yellowstone geology, to the summit of Top Notch Peak to study the tree stumps.

The view of Yellowstone from ten thousand feet presented Biddulph with an extraordinary vision of its geologic past. Below him lay the whole of what would eventually be known as the Yellowstone caldera. Yellowstone Lake, lying like a stunning sapphire amid the vast emerald pine-covered plateaus, had once been a barren, frothing moonscape of ash and fiery lava. A mountain range that once filled the thirty-seven-mile panorama from Mount Washburn near Canyon southward to Mount Sheridan had vanished into the frothing caldera.[9] The flow patterns of these great lava fields that formed the

Pitchstone and Mirror Plateaus were clearly visible from the summit of Top Notch. The abrupt edges of these flows, where cooling lava had congealed, dropped precipitously into the Lamar Valley in the northeastern and the Bechler Valley in the southwestern parts of Yellowstone. Long ago, rivers and streams carved beautiful tapestries into the thick volcanic landscape, and lakes and rich forests brought life to the land.

Biddulph recorded his vision from the summit of Top Notch in a 1947 article in *Nature Notes:*

> Great were the reverberating blasts of the volcanoes that belched destruction upon Yellowstone, and massive were the trees that stood the assault. Bombarding missiles stripped these giant trees of their limbs and burned the bark crisp; still they stood proudly erect to be buried in ash and other volcanic debris. Later, percolating water laden with dissolved mineral came in contact with the woody structure changing them to stone. The petrified remains of these giant trees can now be found on the slopes of Top Notch Peak standing erect in stratified ash and cemented breccias. Descending the ridge to the circular valley below, it is easy to imagine the happenings of the past. Layers of breccias suggest tremendous volcanic explosions; layers of ash suggest fine suffocating dust suspended for days in a laden atmosphere covering and preserving leaves, cones, and stems of ancient flora. Perpendicular walls of the cirques suggest giant rivers of ice scouring and gouging at the earth.[10]

Although evidence of the Yellowstone caldera had not been discovered by 1947, Biddulph was not far astray in his thinking when he envisioned "tremendous volcanic explosions" that suffocated the surrounding forests.

The discovery of welded tuffs in the central Yellowstone plateau by Francis R. Boyd, a Harvard postgraduate student, in the 1950s opened up an important new understanding of Yellowstone's recent past.[11] By analyzing the chemical composition of soil in the central interior plateaus of Yellowstone, Boyd discovered that the lava flows there were much younger in age than the older rocks found in the surrounding mountains. This proved conclusively that the lava flows in the lower plateaus came from a different and later source than the rocks found in the Absaroka and Red Mountains.

Further, Boyd found siliceous (containing high percentages of silicon dioxide) lava in these younger plateaus that was welded or fused to

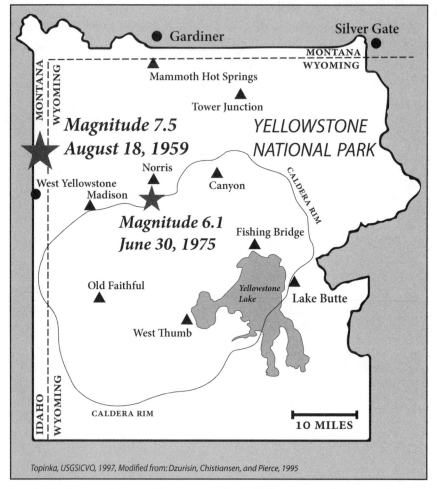

Map 2. The largest of three calderas to erupt in the Yellowstone region occurred some 640,000 years ago and expelled more volcanic debris than any eruption recorded in human history. The map also shows two major earthquakes that have occurred in the recent past. (U.S. Geological Survey Map 1997)

surrounding rock, called "welded tuff." This could happen only with lava that was superheated and rapidly dispersed across the surface of the land. The welded tuffs found in Yellowstone and surrounding areas suggested a more recent and cataclysmic event of explosive volcanism, as recent as 640,000 years ago, much later than the Absaroka volcanoes of some 50 million years before. This frothing, swirling, superheated mixture, called "pyroclastic material," quickly covered vast areas of the Yellowstone plateau.[12]

After Boyd's discovery, the US Geological Survey mounted a study of Yellowstone's flows and plateaus and discovered two welded tuffs of different ages in Yellowstone and a third just west in Idaho. These tuffs reveal that at least three calderas have erupted much more recently than was previously believed. A large caldera of molten lava lay under the south-central part of Yellowstone Park, including a portion now occupied by Yellowstone Lake. Pressure from the gas and hot lava pushed upward, warping and cracking the crust of the earth until the caldera violently exploded, releasing massive amounts of gas, dust, and lava.

The largest of these explosions produced seventeen times more volcanic rock than the Mount Tambora explosion in Indonesia in 1815, which was heard 840 miles away. It expelled twenty-four hundred times more rock than Mount St. Helens in Washington in 1980.[13] The liquid rock and gases covered the Yellowstone plateau and solidified into pumice, ash, and welded tuffs.

With the release of the inner lava, the roof of the caldera collapsed several hundred feet. Like a freshly gouged wound, the cavity partially filled again with hot lava until it eventually solidified. Yellowstone Lake, which did not exist at the time of the eruption, was formed as part of this depression. Heart, Lewis, and Shoshone Lakes in the southern part of Yellowstone lie within the caldera's footprint and are also believed to be part of this great depression.

SPURGIN'S BEAVER SLIDE

In addition to their interest in the emerging discoveries of Yellowstone's geologic past, park administrators were also anxious to recapture physical evidence of early park historical events, many of which had become obscured or lost in the first several decades since Yellowstone's creation. Mapping the Bannock Indian Trail through northern Yellowstone and establishing the validity of John Colter's visit to Yellowstone during the winter of 1807–8 were two such endeavors, discussed in subsequent chapters. Another historical event of interest was the flight of the Nez Perce Indians through Yellowstone in 1877.

In the late summer of 1877, about eight hundred members of the Nez Perce Tribe, living in western Idaho and eastern Oregon, broke away from the reservation and fled across parts of Idaho and Wyoming, seeking refuge among the Crow Nation in Wyoming territory. Their flight took them through Yellowstone Park, which had been a national park for five years at the time of their passage. Pursued by General Oliver O. Howard, the Nez

Perce entered Yellowstone by way of the Madison River at what is now the West Entrance (West Yellowstone) and followed the Madison River to the Firehole River and on to the Lower Geyser Basin.

On the evening of August 24, 1877, the Nez Perce captured George Cowan, his wife, and a group of tourists from Radersburg, Montana, who were camped at the Lower Geyser Basin. Mr. Cowan was shot three times by the Indians and left for dead. His wife and others were taken prisoner but later released. Cowan survived and was discovered by General Howard's scouts; he was eventually returned to his home and reunited with his wife.

The Nez Perce, meanwhile, followed what is now known as Nez Perce Creek through Hayden Valley, crossed the Yellowstone River, and eventually exited the park at its northeast corner. However, the Crow refused asylum to the Nez Perce, and the beleaguered band of men, women, and children turned north toward Canada. On October 5, 1877, after a bitter five-day battle in the Bear Paw Mountains of the Montana Territory, with most of the war chiefs dead and the women and children scattered into the winter mountains, Chief Joseph—whose Nez Perce name was "Thunder Rolling Down the Mountain—surrendered to General Nelson A. Miles just forty miles from the US-Canadian border.

Captain William F. Spurgin, the engineer officer with the ominous task of moving General Howard's supply wagons through Yellowstone, crossed Hayden Valley and then was forced to lower his wagons down a steep six-hundred-foot slope, using ropes wrapped around lodgepole pine. The location became known to the soldiers as "Spurgin's Beaver Slide."[14]

Spurgin's column crossed the Washburn Range at Dunraven Pass and then dropped down into Carnelian Creek drainage and on to Tower Creek. Hiram Chittenden predicted in his history that "the traces of this old road will not disappear except through a forest fire, for centuries to come."[15] In 1901 Captain Spurgin revisited the entire route in company with Hiram Chittenden and identified important locations. Their hope of permanently marking key historical sites was not fulfilled, and assuredly the forest fires of 1988 eliminated any sign of their passage along Carnelian Creek.

During the summer of 1937, Wayne Replogle was assigned by Chief Naturalist Dave Condon to investigate the beaver-slide area in Hayden Valley to discover what signs might yet be discernible. On July 3 of that year, Replogle made his investigation of Spurgin's Beaver Slide and gave the following report in a 1937 article in *Nature Notes:*

The "skillets" who made the roads through the dense Yellowstone forests under the leadership of Captain Spurgin, while General Howard pursued Chief Joseph, certainly deserved the name "engineers" with highest honors.[16]

On July 3, I sought out this section of road leading from the terraces west of Alum Creek across the short section of the plateau which was the only means at that time of getting from Hayden Valley to the Otter Creek Valley, some distance above Chittenden Bridge. It was the section traversed by Captain Spurgin and his wagon train.

My findings were tremendously interesting. The train having ascended the terraces and on to the plateau, found the going hard, no doubt, for a great number of trees were necessarily cut with what appeared to be four inch blades, none too sharp. Most stumps left standing were about three feet in height, which probably permitted the high-axle wagons to pass over them without trouble. Several shallow gullies were crossed and in each case they had been crudely filled with dirt with a stone center for drainage purposes. In one or two places there had been some grading done to insure a safer descent or ascent from a gulley fill.

The trail was marked by long narrow blazes, ten to twenty inches long, cut by an axe, and I presume the same type of axe used to blaze the trees as was used to fall them. The old blazes are in many cases obliterated save for a slight bark scar, while others are from one to four inches in depth. The blazes are followed from east to west and may be traced in a continuous line although the trail is overgrown and in many cases trees have reached a diameter of eight inches or more.

Having followed the trail to the brink of the plateau above the famous slides, I then began the search for the famous rope burns, which resulted from the wrapping of ropes around trees to slowly let down wagons some 600 feet below, by slipping the rope "dallies" (wrappings). I found eight prominent trees with well-preserved burns, stationed from top to bottom some 75 to 150 feet apart. Some burns had been eradicated by the growing of uninjured bark but for the most part there were as many as three circle burns on each tree. The living trees with burns are from ten to twenty inches in diameter with burn marks apparently having been made by one-half or three-quarter inch ropes. In the descent many adjacent trees were scarred or bent as the many wagons were let down over the lengthy precipice. It must be remembered that the feat was one of the most remarkable in early Yellowstone history and although given a peculiar name by the soldiers for no particular reason at all, we should remember that Spurgin's Beaver Slide is yet traceable and has not completely degraded into the long list of early history mysteries.[17]

During the 1950 season, Replogle met Lewis Redhorse, an eighty-two-year-old Nez Perce man who was visiting Yellowstone with his daughter and granddaughter. Lewis had been a young boy in 1877 (Replogle said five years old, but the math would suggest more like nine or ten) and had come through Yellowstone with Chief Joseph on their flight to Montana. Replogle noted in his *Mile-by-Mile* narrative of park history about this meeting: "I had probably the last remaining person to ride over the retreat here when he came through the Park…and I brought him out here and he well remembered this valley [it is assumed that the valley referred to was Hayden Valley because Replogle was serving at Canyon during this time]. It was quite a moment for me to stand there and talk to this person."[18]

It would have been a wonderful thing to have had Lewis Redhorse's personal memoirs of his entire experience, including the flight to Montana and the final battle at Bear Paw Mountain. Unfortunately, we have nothing more on this subject. Redhorse may possibly have been the last of Chief Joseph's band to visit Yellowstone, but he was not the first or only survivor to revisit a tragic and difficult past. In 1935 two members of Joseph's band, White Hawk and Many Wounds, visited Yellowstone.[19]

LOST DIARY OF THE WASHBURN EXPEDITION, 1870

In 1964 Robert G. Johnnson and Lowell Biddulph, serving respectively as district and assistant district naturalists for the South District, were assigned to verify the contents of an old diary of an early prominent exploration party that had been recently found. Biddulph explained the occasion for this task:

The Washburn-Langford-Doane party was the official exploring party of Yellowstone and had as their scribe a young lawyer who kept a diary of their trip through Yellowstone in the back of an old law journal. It was lost for a long time. In 1964, it was found in the Law Library in Helena, Montana. The diary was duplicated and sent to Yellowstone.

Two of us had the experience of following their route through the south-eastern section of the Park by canoe and horseback, going down the east side of Yellowstone Lake and through the whole south-eastern part of the Park.... Our job was to follow through and verify all the names, the distances, the elevations, climb all the peaks and go into the back country. We had a most interesting time.[20]

In seeking verification of this report, the author was unable to find any current park personnel who remembered or had knowledge of this circumstance, including the park's current historian, Lee Whittlesey, or John Good, the past chief naturalist in Yellowstone at the time. Although Biddulph was adamant about the journal and the circumstances of its discovery in Helena, Montana, and their subsequent assignment to verify its contents, there remains no validation.

The journal kept by Cornelius Hedges appears to be the only one to which Biddulph could have made reference.[21] Hedges was a young lawyer at the time of the expedition (1870) and later served as probate judge in Helena. Aubrey Haines states in the foreword to Nathaniel Pitt Langford's book *The Discovery of Yellowstone Park, 1870* that Langford was the expedition's "effective scribe," but also notes that Cornelius Hedges and Walter Trumbull were also journalists of the party. Other than Lieutenant Gustavus Doane, whose superb journal was well documented, no other member of the party fits the description. Langford published his journal of the discovery, so it was never lost, and Walter Trumbull was not a lawyer. So, it is possible that the lost diary was that of Cornelius Hedges. Its discovery would have been important, and the Park Service would naturally feel it significant enough to verify its contents. For this reason, it would seem realistic that they would make a copy of it for that purpose. Such an opportunity for these two ranger naturalists would have been like stepping back into history and joining up with the Washburn Party.

The foregoing is just a sampling of the opportunities these Five Men had to help explore, discover, and verify important historical events in Yellowstone's human and geologic past. The next two chapters deal in greater detail with important discoveries made by two of the Old Men pertaining to early human history of the park.

Chapter 17

Fact or Fancy

EARLY YELLOWSTONE HISTORIES

The emergence of Merrill D. Beal on the Yellowstone scene was destined to impact the development of the historical portion of the park's interpretive program. The naturalist division in Yellowstone was just being developed in 1939, and with Beal's background in western history and teaching, he became an important addition to the staff. He was the only ranger naturalist on staff the summer of 1939 who had formal training in history. During the nearly three decades of his service in the park, Beal helped write and solidify the human story of Yellowstone, and he would eventually become part of a historical firestorm of controversy.

At the time that the interpretive program was launched in 1938–39 in the park, only two major histories of Yellowstone National Park were extant. The first was written by Hiram Martin Chittenden—the celebrated architect of Yellowstone's road system—and published by Stanford University Press in 1895 with subsequent editions following. The second prominent history was not written until thirty-seven years later (1932), when the Department of the Interior published Louis C. Crampton's *Early History of Yellowstone Park and Its Relation to National Park Policies.* Other than these two histories and Nathaniel Pitt Langford's journal of the Washburn Party's trip through Yellowstone in 1870, published in 1903 under the title *The Discovery of Yellowstone Park, 1870s,* almost all historical resources were unpublished personal diaries, journals, autobiographies, government reports, and a few magazine articles.

During Beal's first summer in Yellowstone, he read and mastered all three of the aforementioned historical references on Yellowstone's discovery and creation in preparation for his interpretive work. Beal noted that in time he developed at least six different history talks on Yellowstone to use for his campfire presentations, as a means of "sustaining [his] own interest in Yellowstone history."

Beal was not merely a history teacher but foremost a historian, and his inquiring mind compelled him to add his own interpretations to Yellowstone history. In 1940 he was asked to write a proposal for a shortened monograph of Hiram Chittenden's more exhaustive history of Yellowstone National Park. The pamphlet was to provide a condensed version that would be more attractive to the visitor who was loath to read heavy history books.

By 1941 Beal's monograph, *The Romance of Yellowstone National Park,* was prepared and sent to Chief Naturalist C. Max Bauer. Bauer saw its merit and forwarded it to Jack Ellis Haynes, the prominent publisher of *Haynes Guide: Handbook of Yellowstone National Park.* He, too, praised the monograph, as did Carl P. Russell, supervisor of interpretation. All agreed it would be an excellent addition, provided that it could be further compressed and the cost kept to one dollar or less. Only one person gave a negative review: Isabelle F. Story, Chittenden's editor, who understandably defended the Chittenden history as "sufficient."

The Romance of Yellowstone Park was short-lived. World War II broke out in 1941, and everything in the park was put on hold. Beal accepted a teaching fellowship at Washington State University, enabling him to complete a PhD in history by 1945. The monograph was never published, but the research done by Beal in preparing the monograph provided much of the meat for his doctoral dissertation and for future books that he would write.

THE STORY OF MAN IN YELLOWSTONE

Beal's most important written contribution to the history of Yellowstone Park was *The Story of Man in Yellowstone,* published in 1949 by the Caxton Printers of Caldwell, Idaho. The more than three-hundred-page book covered a wide swath of Yellowstone's history, from early Indians, trappers, and explorers, through its discovery and creation as a national park, to more contemporary issues. Well documented and researched, the book was a product of the altruistic age. Its writing style frequently carried grand, almost romantic, prose, describing majestic mountain backdrops, the "silvery Madison River gliding in the foreground," and the symbolic campfire

Early explorers Cornelius Hedges and Charles W. Cook meet
with Park Superintendent Horace M. Albright in Yellowstone. (Courtesy of the National Park Service, Yellowstone
National Park, YELL 37153)

scene: "The last scene was being enacted—the curtain was about to fall. It
was an hour of recapitulation. The question was posed, 'Men and brethren,
what shall we do?' 'Why,' said Smith, 'we'll fence it in; give me Old Faithful.' 'I'll take the falls,' echoed another. Whereupon the inspired mind of
Cornelius Hedges proposed and explained an idea that marked him as one
of the far-sighted men of his generation."[1]

By 1939 the legend of Madison Junction and its prominence in the
founding of the "National Park Idea" was strongly entrenched. Madison
Junction was fast becoming its mecca and its trailside museum the temple to
which faithful pilgrims annually trekked. National Park Mountain, rising
prominently from the Madison Plateau, became its shrine.

Hiram Chittenden felt it necessary in the interest of history to bestow an
exact source from which the idea for a national park sprang; that source, in
his belief, was the Washburn Party of 1870. Although acknowledging that the

idea for such preservation originated from several independent sources, as had also Louis Crampton, nevertheless, Chittenden concluded: "Inasmuch as the development of the project must have started from some one source…we find it to have been the Washburn Expedition of 1870."[2] The wellspring of Chittenden's belief came from the journal of Nathaniel Pitt Langford, dated September 20, 1870:

> Last night, and also this morning in camp, the entire party had a rather unusual discussion. The proposition was made by some member that we utilize the results of our exploration by taking up quarter sections of land at the most prominent points of interest, and a general discussion followed. Mr. Hedges then said that he did not approve of any of these plans—that there ought to be no private ownership of any portion of that region, but that the whole of it ought to be set apart as a great National Park, and that each one of us ought to make an effort to have this accomplished.[3]

This statement established Yellowstone as the place where the "National Park Idea" was first articulated, and it enthroned men like Hedges and Langford as its seers. For the first several decades during the 1900s, a body of lore with accompanying pageantry, rituals, and shrines arose that institutionalized this belief. The campfire story was a beautiful story, articulating the desired nobility of the human spirit to protect the wild and pristine creations of nature from the profit-hungry mind of man.

Beal's book *The Story of Man in Yellowstone* fully accepted the Langford-Chittenden version of the "National Park Idea" and did much to fuel the tradition. His book received commendation from the National Park Service. Merrill J. Mattes, regional historian for the National Park Service, wrote a fine review of the book, and it took its rightful place alongside histories written by Chittenden and Crampton.[4] In 1956 Beal transferred the copyright to the Yellowstone Library and Museum Association, and it was published as number 7 in the park's Interpretive Series. Second and third editions were published in 1956 and 1960.

WINDS OF CONTROVERSY

By 1957, at the zenith of the campfire story era, park staff began staging a pageant at Madison Junction called *The Birth of Yellowstone,* reenacting the Washburn campfire of 1870. The pageant served to further hallow

The Birth of Yellowstone, celebrating the "National Park Idea," was held at Madison
Junction from 1957 until 1964. (Courtesy of the National Park Service, Yellowstone
National Park, YELL 143037)

Madison Junction as the place of origin and institutionalize the creation of
the National Park Idea. According to Replogle, the script for the pageant
was written by Bert Hansen, a professor of speech and drama at Montana
State University. Starring roles for the pageant were played by rangers and
ranger naturalists. For a number of years, Replogle was the voice for General Washburn and Beal for Cornelius Hedges.

Replogle provided some insight into how the pageant was carried out:

> It was so arranged... that the men rode their horses in and acted out
> their parts while the group of speakers with the equipment were hid-
> den back in the trees. Each particular one had a script to follow and
> the voices were coming from the woods and not the men on the horses
> and in the camps. The pageant usually took an hour and benches were
> placed in the meadow just below the museum across the Gibbon River.
> The pageant was conducted on the south side of the Gibbon at the
> confluence of the Gibbon and the Firehole. It was a very beautiful place
> for staging the actual pageant. In 1964, the pageant was discontinued
> because it was too expensive to operate for the number of people that
> came to watch it.[5]

There was more to the demise of the pageant than expense. Forces were at work, casting a heavy pallor of doubt upon the validity of the entire event, indeed upon its very claim to authorship of the "National Park Idea." The conflict reached critical mass in June 1963, when Aubrey Haines, park historian, sent a memo to the park administration, criticizing the pageant's script as seriously flawed in accuracy and in need of revision or complete discontinuance.[6] Attempts to enshrine Yellowstone—specifically Madison Junction and the Washburn campfire—as the birthplace of the "National Park Idea" were, in Haines's opinion, being untrue to history, and such efforts were misleading and would result in unending and unprofitable argument.[7]

Haines openly challenged the credibility of Langford's claim because he found no evidence that such a conversation ever took place around the campfire on September 19, 1870, or that Hedges had actually made the statement attributed to him by Langford. Nothing in the journal writings of other members of the Washburn Party corroborated Langford's claim, and Haines all but accused Langford (posthumously) of inventing the entire thing to bring unwarranted credit to himself and others in the Washburn Party for the conception and creation of Yellowstone National Park. Haines's deep dislike—perhaps *disdain* is not too harsh a word—for Langford was evident.

Haines's controversial approach was not kind to anyone, himself included. Going against cherished tradition never is. Deep division and angry feelings arose between the Langford faithful and the so-called new apostates. Questioning the reality of the campfire was for the believers like questioning the validity of George Washington's heroic crossing of the Delaware River at the Battle of Trenton. Discrediting Langford and others was like denouncing the virtues of the founding fathers.

Aubrey Haines was discredited by many from the old school for his beliefs. He experienced serious repercussions to his career in the park service because of the influence of others in high places. In fairness to Aubrey Haines, it was never his intention to create controversy but only to be true to history. He served Yellowstone Park with distinction and integrity, and his contributions to history are many and significant. Any harsh criticism he received from others only serves to illustrate the deeply held feelings and unfortunate animosity that this controversy sparked among people who were all loyal to the Grand Old Park.

Despite the firestorm of controversy, park administrators came down on the side of Haines. The pageant was discontinued after 1964, and the recommendation for the Madison Museum to be turned into a "shrine for the

National Park Idea" was turned down. Beal noted the obvious: "Perhaps the Madison Junction shrine idea did not fit the times."[8]

In December 1965, E. T. Scoyan, former assistant director of the National Park Service, requested that Beal write a letter honoring Horace Albright on his eightieth birthday. In response to Beal's gesture, Albright asked him if he was aware of the controversy that the opinions of Aubrey Haines had stirred up. Albright considered the comments of Haines to be "speculative, even debunking," and he was disturbed by the number of people in the National Park Service who accepted these speculations. "Of course," he wrote to Beal, "such a position makes a liar out of Langford and discredits Chittenden not to mention yourself."[9]

Beal was all too aware of the controversy mentioned by Albright. The winds of change were beginning to blow stiffly across Yellowstone, not only toppling the Madison Junction pageant but also challenging the legitimacy of parts of the histories written by Beal. It became increasingly evident to Beal that his written historical contributions were being pushed aside.

In 1958 Beal had been commissioned by the National Park Service in cooperation with Idaho State University to write a history of the Nez Perce War of 1877. As noted earlier, the Nez Perce uprising directly involved the park—at least for a few days—in the nearly four-month-long run-and-gun chase from Idaho into the Bear Paw Mountains of Montana. A sum of fifty-six hundred dollars was granted Beal for this manuscript. With the encouragement of Chief Naturalist Dave Condon, Beal took a leave of absence from his teaching at Idaho State and his summer work in Yellowstone in 1958 and went to work, with his wife, Bessy, serving as editor and typist.

A year later, Beal submitted the completed manuscript to Lon Garrison, superintendent, who noted, "Beal has done a good and faithful work. The Park Service has received the value of the $5,000 grant-in-aid, and then some."[10]

The one notable critic of the manuscript was Merrill J. Mattes, who found flaws in the manuscript and took exception to various judgments made by Beal. Mattes later repented of his criticism with a letter to Beal: "If you were annoyed by the rather extensive and detailed comments made re: your manuscript by this office, that reaction would be understandable. It was an example of incorrect information on our part. I regret that it was handled in that fashion."[11]

Beal's book was published by the University of Washington Press in 1963 under the title *I Will Fight No More Forever: Chief Joseph and the Nez Perce War*.

However, by the time the book was ready for sale and distribution, personnel and attitudes had changed in Yellowstone. Dave Condon, who had faithfully championed Beal's work, and Beal's son, David, had been transferred out of Yellowstone. Superintendent Lon Garrison was also on his way out,[12] and new personalities unfamiliar with Beal and his contributions were in control.

When the University of Washington Press solicited the Yellowstone Library and Museum Association for an order of Beal's book, shockingly, the park declined, saying that the book was "irrelevant to Yellowstone and that it was too expensive (cost $6.00 per book)."[13] Despite the stunning rejection by Yellowstone Park, Beal's book went through fourteen subsequent printings and enjoyed great success, if not relevance.

The rejection of the Nez Perce book deeply disappointed Beal, but it was not to be his last disappointment. In August 1965, Beal was informed that his book *The Story of Man in Yellowstone* would no longer be printed by the Yellowstone Library and Museum Association because the bid was too high, this despite the fact that the book had been a best seller for many years. Chief naturalist John Good suggested, instead, that the book be compressed into a one-dollar pamphlet, shades of *The Romancing of Yellowstone* that Beal wrote twenty-five years earlier. Similar to Ms. Story, Beal gracefully declined to "turn a high-powered history into a pamphlet," and *The Story of Man in Yellowstone* was discontinued.

Beal suspected that there was more to these rejections than mere cost. Rumor had it that Aubrey Haines had written his own extensive two-volume history of Yellowstone that was to be published in cooperation with the National Park Service. However, sensitive to the firestorm surrounding the Langford-Haines controversy, the Park Service shelved Haines's history for more than a decade.

Beal had no illusions that his history books would remain infallible forever. He understood that more current histories would eventually be written about Yellowstone. Yet it was not easy for him to see his works discontinued and have cherished beliefs of historical importance reinterpreted as false or misleading. Beal clearly felt Haines to be too rigid in his judgments, as is noted in his response to Haines's new history: "I have not read the Haines Yellowstone Park History, so I will not judge it. However, I reviewed his edited account of *The Valley of the Upper Yellowstone* by Charles W. Cook, David E. Folsom, and William Peterson, for the *Utah Historical Quarterly.* The review appeared in Volume 34, 1966. Actually, I detected the same revisionary tendency in this work."[14]

The revisionary tendency referred to by Beal was his feeling that Haines too quickly threw things for which he had no absolute proof into the box marked "speculative" and "a curious mixture of fact and fantasy." It is not known if Beal ever did read Haines's history; likely, he did not, due to the failure of his eyesight at the age of sixty-four.[15] What is clear is that Haines's standard for historical accuracy did not allow for unqualified speculation. He was unwilling to take the words of Langford or Chittenden on their own merits, especially when there was no other corroborating evidence, even when it meant going against cherished tradition. There was no sacred cow for Aubrey Haines.

For decades, the Washburn Expedition of 1870 had been the prominent body in the exploration and creation of Yellowstone Park. The story of the campfire and the advent of the National Park Idea was spoken of at campfire programs around the park, written in history books and pamphlets, and became a household name in park parlance. The Hayden Survey Party that surveyed and documented the park's features in 1871 and 1872 was readily recognized as a scientific body that surveyed and verified many features in the park, but it did not hold the prominence of the Washburn Expedition with most ranger naturalists of Beal's day.

With the renunciation of the National Park Idea and the discrediting of Langford's version, the tables turned. The Hayden Survey Party took center stage as the prominent body in the park's development, relegating the Washburn Party to distant anonymity. The altruistic romance of Yellowstone was decisively being replaced by scientific rigor.

In June 1965, descendants of General Henry D. Washburn, the leader of the exploration party of 1870 of which Langford had been a member, bequeathed General Washburn's papers and journals to the Yellowstone Park Library. They requested that this be done ceremoniously at the dedication of the West Yellowstone airport. The most politically correct choice of someone to represent Yellowstone Park in accepting this valuable gift would be the park superintendent, chief park naturalist, or the park historian, Aubrey Haines. To the contrary, Washburn's descendants requested that Merrill D. Beal be the recipient.[16] Would it be speculative to suggest that the Washburn family appreciated Beal's position on the campfire controversy?

JOHN COLTER AND YELLOWSTONE NATIONAL PARK

Merrill Beal's doctoral thesis was entitled "John Colter's First Discovery of Yellowstone: The Problem of Colter's Route in 1807."[17] For four sum-

Merrill D. Beal, interpreter and
writer of Yellowstone history, served
in Yellowstone from 1939 to 1966.
(Courtesy of David and Jean Beal)

mers, Beal had studied and lectured on Yellowstone history, and an important part of its history had to do with the early discovery of Yellowstone. Hiram Chittenden identified John Colter, a Virginia-born trapper, as the first white man to pass through Yellowstone Park.[18] This supposition was made by Chittenden based on Colter's irrefutable reputation and the testimonies of early writers like Henry M. Brackenridge, John Bradbury, and Thomas James. Nevertheless, no proof positive existed in the form of eyewitness accounts or tangible evidence to substantiate the claim that Colter was the first white man in Yellowstone.

Beal and other historians of his day debated Colter's visit to Yellowstone in 1807–8, for reasons Beal notes in the opening lines of his thesis:

> It may seem unfruitful at this time to attempt a solution of the problem of John Colter's 1807 route of discovery in Yellowstone. Many people require no proof of anything cited in the records of such great scouts as Jedediah S. Smith, Kit Carson, and John Colter. Their integrity need not be questioned. Still, it is within the province of the historian to sift and test all of the evidence until the truth falls into place. Even myths and legends should be examined for any implications and bearing they might have upon a fact.[19]

Why was Colter's passage through Yellowstone so significant? It was a matter of historical interest if not importance to know the facts, if possible, about the park's discovery and to know who the first Euro-American was to see the wonders of this land, much as the Adam and Eve story is important to the Christian or creation stories are important to primitive peoples.

Some facts about Colter were substantiated. Colter had been a hunter and scout for the Lewis and Clark Expedition of 1804–6 to explore the headwaters of the Missouri River and find a route to the Pacific Ocean. On the expedition's return trip, Colter received permission from Lewis and Clark to remain in the Yellowstone area and do fur trapping. Eventually, Colter joined up with the famous fur trader Manuel Lisa[20] and helped to build Fort Raymond at the confluence of the Yellowstone and Bighorn Rivers.

During the late fall and winter of 1807–8, Lisa dispatched Colter on a five-hundred-mile trek to promote trade with the Indians of the region. Here things become more speculative. Colter was believed to have left Fort Raymond alone and proceeded south along the Bighorn and Shoshone Rivers, the latter also known as Stinking River because of thermal springs found along its banks. He purportedly traveled along the base of the Absaroka Mountains, up the Wind River, then turned west and followed the Gros Ventre River over Union Pass into Jackson Hole at the base of the Grand Tetons. From there, he is said to have crossed over the Tetons into Pierre's Hole on the Idaho side of the range, where he fought on the side of Crow Indians to defeat a band of Blackfoot Indians. Despite being wounded in the leg, he made his way north over Conant Pass and back to Fort Raymond.[21]

Colter described passing through a land of sulfur and brimstone that became known as "Colter's Hell."[22] For many years, people mistakenly thought that Colter's Hell was Yellowstone and that this was proof positive that Colter had, indeed, been the first Euro-American to see the geysers.

The event that ultimately drove Colter from the Rocky Mountains never to return was a near-death encounter with Blackfoot Indians in the Three Forks area of Montana.[23] Although Colter was the only living soul at the time to corroborate his story, it was a very popular one told by Beal and other naturalists at many campfire lectures in the following manner.

Colter and his companion, John Potts, were checking traps by canoe in the Jefferson Fork not far from its confluence with the Madison Fork when they were discovered and captured by a large war party of Blackfoot Indians. Potts tried to escape in a canoe but was killed by a flurry of arrows, leaving Colter alone to face the bloodthirsty Indians. Stripped naked and forced to run for his life, Colter raced six miles across the flats toward the Madison River, chased by the pack of howling warriors.

Adrenaline, sprinting capacity, and stamina allowed him to outdistance all but one warrior. The strain burst blood vessels in his nose and covered his naked chest with crimson. In this gory state, he suddenly stopped, whirled about, and faced the Indian, who was so staggered by the unexpected sight that he stumbled and fell prostrate. Colter grabbed the warrior's spear and plunged it into him and then ran on until he came to the Madison River, where he secluded himself within a nearby beaver hut.

Later that night, when the enraged Indians gave up the hunt and departed the area, Colter left the hut and made his way over the mountains, some two hundred miles, to Lisa's fort, arriving there in almost unrecognizable condition. Having promised his God that if he were allowed to escape the wrath of the Blackfeet he would leave the mountains and never return, Colter kept his word, returned to St. Louis, married, and settled down to farming.

In 1810 Colter gave Captain William Clark a map that he had personally drawn of his route to the Indians during the winter of 1807. Colter's route was included on the *Map of the West* made in 1814 by cartographer Samuel Lewis and William Clark. However, Lewis's *Map of the West* had distortions, especially the lakes in the Yellowstone and Teton area that were confusing to historians, leaving them uncertain as to whether Colter actually entered Yellowstone at all. In his thesis, Beal took exception to the length of Colter's route ascribed by most historians, believing that it was simply too far for even the venerable Colter to travel in the dead of winter. Beal suggested a much shorter route, confining much of his travel to areas now within Yellowstone National Park.

Merrill J. Mattes, a regional historian for the National Park Service, published his own research on the subject of Yellowstone and John Colter. In 1949, the same year that Beal's book on Yellowstone was published, Mattes published a small account titled Behind the Legend of Colter's Hell: The Early Exploration of Yellowstone Park. In 1962 Mattes also published *Colter's Hell and Jackson's Hole.* These two volumes helped dispel the erroneous belief that Yellowstone Park was the same as Colter's Hell and more accurately established the thermal features along the Shoshone River as the latter. Evidence of Colter's passage through Yellowstone Park remained unverifiable.

Besides the 1814 Samuel Lewis map, two other pieces of tangible evidence surfaced that shed light on Colter's route. The first of the would-be evidence was the discovery of initials reportedly carved into a tree found on Coulter Creek[24] about three-quarters of a mile above its confluence with the Snake River along the southern boundary of Yellowstone Park. In 1889

Merrill and Bessy Beal at their home in Pocatello, Idaho.
(Courtesy of David and Jean Beal)

three hunters claimed to have found an *X,* some five inches in height, carved into a tree above the initials *JC* (hypothetically for John Colter). The blaze appeared to be approximately eighty years old based upon tree-growth studies of the time, which fitted nicely with the timetable of Colter's supposed passage through the park.

This find was supposedly reported to the government (the army at the time). The tree was cut down in 1890, and the blazed section cut out to be placed in a museum. Alas, the blazed section became lost in transit if, in fact, it ever existed.

The second piece of evidence was what became known as the "Colter Stone." In the spring of 1930, a fourteen-year-old boy named William Beard unearthed a stone while plowing his father's field in the Teton Basin of Idaho, originally known as Pierre's Hole. The stone was about the size of a human skull and was inscribed with the lettering "John Colter 1808." The stone was supposedly purchased by a neighbor named A. C. Lyon, who presented it to Grand Teton National Park in 1934, where it remained for several years. The value of determining the authenticity of the stone is self-evident.

In 1957 Merrill Mattes assigned Beal to investigate further the "Colter Stone" by personally interviewing William Beard. On August 21, 1957, Beal and his son, David, who was the assistant chief ranger naturalist in Yellowstone at the time, traveled to West Yellowstone and arranged an interview with William Beard, who was working on a road construction project.

Beard confirmed the story and told the Beals that his father, John W. Beard, had not sold the stone, but had agreed to loan it to the Park Service for study. He never saw the stone again. Beal reported back to Mattes that he had found Beard's testimony sound and Beard a reliable informant. What motive would there have been for Beard to fabricate such a story? At the time of the stone's discovery, the Beards knew little of John Colter and nothing about his possible presence in that area in 1808.

Based on Beal's report, Mattes authorized the "Colter Stone" to be placed on exhibit in the Moose Visitor Center in Grand Teton National Park in 1959.[25] The authenticity of the stone and the date of its inscription were disputed. Fritiof Fryxell, a geologist and Grand Teton National Park naturalist, believed the stone had weathering consistent with the approximate date inscribed on it. Others thought the inscription to be old but not as old as 1808.

The haunting question that no one successfully answered was, how could someone as uninformed as an Idaho farmer fabricate such a hoax? Pure coincidence seemed ludicrous. To this date, the stone has not been officially verified by authoritative means.

Yet another stone surfaced that provided an intriguing connection to the "Colter Stone," although it had nothing to do with Colter's route through Yellowstone. The year before the Colter Stone surfaced in the Teton Basin, Beal and a group of students from Ricks College in Rexburg, Idaho, where Beal was teaching at the time, were excavating an old trapper's fort on the Teton River, a few miles from current-day St. Anthony, Idaho. The fort on the Teton River had been built by Andrew Henry and his trapper brigade in 1810. In 1811 Wilson Price Hunt and the men of the Astoria Expedition wintered in the fort.

By a strange twist of fate, it was the same Captain Hunt who attempted to persuade John Colter, then married and living with his wife, Sallie, near St. Louis, to join him and his expedition into the Rocky Mountains. Though severely tempted, Colter stayed with his wife, remaining true to his promise that he would never return to the Rocky Mountains. His death of unverified cause, perhaps jaundice, in about 1813 sealed his promise.

In excavating the burned foundation of the fort, Beal's group unearthed a river-worn basalt rock about eighteen inches by twelve inches that bore the inscription "Fort Henry 1811 by Cpt Hunt."[26] What became known as the "Hunt Stone" was turned over to the Park Service, and eventually it and the Colter Stone were placed together in the Madison Junction trailside museum for a time. Perhaps the two old explorers were rejoined in the museum more than a hundred years later in the form of stones that were found about fifty miles from each other. The authenticity of these two stones was later questioned by park historians, and they were removed from the Madison Museum. In 1959 Yellowstone transferred the Hunt Stone to Grand Teton National Park.[27] In 2009 the Colter Stone was placed in the Teton County Museum on indefinite loan.[28]

ALL'S WELL THAT ENDS WELL

As early as the mid-1960s, it was clear to Beal that a new day was dawning in Yellowstone, one that left him feeling antiquated and out of step with the current administration. His literary contributions to Yellowstone history superseded, the pageantry at Madison Junction discredited, and the memorial to the formulation of the National Park Idea removed, Beal summed it up this way: "Every dog has its day."[29]

Yet a silver lining manifested itself in the dark cloud of controversy and rejection. In July 1972, six years after Beal had retired from the National Park Service, Superintendent Jack Anderson invited the Beals to attend the dedication ceremony of the "Explorer's Museum" at Madison Junction as part of the park's centennial celebration.[30]

An Explorer's Museum at Madison Junction! It was almost as good as the "National Park Shrine," and it gave Beal deep satisfaction to see a "shrine" to the early history of Yellowstone officially realized. It was a pleasant trip down memory lane made doubly enjoyable by the presence of their son, David, who represented the Midwest Region at the event.

In 1977, when the controversy over the "National Park Idea" had sufficiently died down, Haines's two-volume history, *The Yellowstone Story,* was published by the Yellowstone Library and Museum Association in cooperation with the Colorado Associated University Press.[31]

Chapter 18

In Search of Ghosts

Yellowstone Park was surrounded by several Native American peoples, among them the Bannock. The Bannock Indians were a seminomadic people who ranged over a large area that included parts of Oregon, Idaho, Wyoming, Nevada, and Montana. They are part of the Shahaptian language family and thus related to the Shoshone linguistically under the Uto-Aztecan language group, shared also by the Comanche, Hopi, and Ute, but in physical characteristics they resemble more closely the Nez Perce. They enjoyed a reputation of being generally friendly to the whites, although occasional conflicts did erupt, culminating in the 1878 Bannock uprising brought on by restrictions on their land and abusive behavior by the government.

"The People," as they called themselves, were primarily hunters and gatherers who moved with the seasons. They hunted buffalo and wild game; they gathered seeds, camas roots, and other food; they fished for salmon on the Snake River; they traded horses with the Nez Perce and were excellent horsemen and skillful warriors. Each group called themselves by the name of what they principally ate, such as buffalo eaters, salmon eaters, and so on. They were in alliance with the Shoshone and Crow Indians and were not known to wage aggressive warfare on other tribes. A large group of Bannock Indians lived in the Upper Snake River Valley and the broad camas meadows around Henry's Lake, west of Yellowstone Park. The broad prairies and Snake River plains of southeastern Idaho sustained the Bannock for centuries. However, by 1840 the bison in that region had been reduced to low-enough

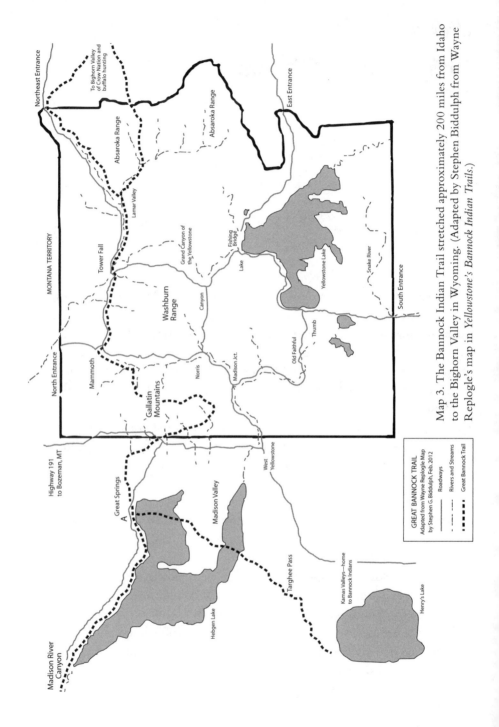

Map 3. The Bannock Indian Trail stretched approximately 200 miles from Idaho to the Bighorn Valley in Wyoming. (Adapted by Stephen Biddulph from Wayne Replogle's map in *Yellowstone's Bannock Indian Trails*.)

numbers that the Bannock Indians were forced to expand their buffalo hunt eastward into the Bighorn Valley of Wyoming.

THE GREAT BANNOCK TRAIL

The Bannock Trail was a creation of both necessity and alliance. The trail across northern Yellowstone provided the safest and most direct route for the Bannock Indians to reach buffalo hunting grounds in the Bighorn Valley of Wyoming. It also provided an important link of protection and alliance between the Bannock and the friendly Shoshone and Crow Indians. The immense area north of Yellowstone—now the state of Montana—from the headwaters of the Missouri to the Saskatchewan River in Canada was the territory of the Algonquian Confederacy.[1] Generally known as Blackfeet to the white people, they were bitter enemies to the Bannock, Crow, and Shoshone tribes, and travel north of the park, especially with women and children, was hazardous. A route to the south was equally untenable due to the greater distance required to travel and the potentially hostile nature of some tribes in that area. Thus, the trail through the northern part of Yellowstone was the safest and most direct route.

Between 1840 and 1878, the Great Trail was used as a regular thoroughfare between Idaho and Wyoming.[2] It passed through the Madison Valley west of Yellowstone Park; crossed over two major mountain ranges, the Gallatins in the West and the Absarokas in the East; and crossed the northern part of Yellowstone before descending into the Bighorn Valley in Wyoming. Two major trails led into the Madison Valley on the west boundary of Yellowstone. One trail left the camas valleys around Henry's Lake, passed through a tree-covered gap now known as Targhee Pass, and descended into the broad, green Madison Valley where current-day West Yellowstone is located. The other trail came up the Madison River Canyon and into the valley where Hebgen Lake is now situated.

The view coming into the valley was both expansive and beautiful. The broad, green Madison Valley was dissected by the glistening, winding ribbon of the Madison River. Vast green carpets of pine forests swept upward from the valley floor toward snow-covered barren peaks rising more than ten thousand feet in elevation. Game and fish were plentiful, and travel was easy in the land of the Sleeping God.[3]

In the northeast part of the Madison Valley, at a place called "Great Springs," the Bannock held important ceremonies to invoke the Great Spirit's blessings upon their journey before launching into the rugged and often dangerous high country of Yellowstone. For decades this broad valley echoed with the sound of pounding drums and eerie songs of a people trying to protect their beloved way of life.

The trail left the valley of the Sleeping God and ascended the forested craggy Gallatin peaks that flank the northwestern boundary of Yellowstone Park. Five major creeks flow down from these high mountains to the valley below: Campanula, Gneiss, Maple, Duck, and Cougar Creeks. The Bannock Trail crossed all five of these creeks in its ascent through thick coniferous forest of lodgepole, fir, spruce, and aspen. The trail followed gradients that were least demanding for their horses pulling travois laden with supplies, buffalo meat, and small children. Undergrowth held feasts of serviceberries, wild strawberries, currents, and huckleberries in season. The forests provided birds and mammals. The travelers camped and traveled by lakes and streams where water and grass were plentiful for their horses and least stressful for their people.

Leaving the lower forests behind, the trail ascended into a world of quaking aspen, Douglas fir, and whitebark pine. "The People" walked and rode through peaceful meadows of green grass and brilliant wildflowers, crossed ridges well above timberline, and descended down into the Indian Creek drainage on the east side of the Gallatin Range.

The view in all directions from the peaks of the Gallatins is spectacular. From these high eminences, the Bannock people surely looked back upon the valley of the Sleeping God and the camas prairies of their home with great fondness. Ahead of them stretched the rolling and deeply grooved plateaus of the Yellowstone River, and on the far horizon, the jagged peaks of the Absaroka Mountains over which they must cross. Beyond these distant prominences lay the Bighorn Valley of the Crow Indians and the precious buffalo.

Upon descending the Gallatin Mountains into what is now known as Swan Lake Flats, the Bannock frequently diverted to nearby Obsidian Cliff to quarry the essential black, volcanic glass from which they fashioned arrow and spear points, knives, and scrapers to be used in their hunt. Obsidian is a volcanic substance found in rhyolitic flows. Its high levels of silicon dioxide make it hard and glass-like. When heated, the Indians were able to flake and shape it into sharp edges for knives and arrow points. Obsidian is still used today in scalpel knives.

Between the Gallatin Mountains in the West and the Absaroka Mountains in the East lay a ruggedly beautiful land of rolling forested terrain, intermittent grassland, deeply grooved canyons, and glacial moraine. The Bannock built coverts (hunting blinds) along the way, from which secluded hunters shot deer, elk, and antelope to sustain them on their journey. The trail stayed along the higher benches, providing pleasing vistas of the beautiful land and surely filling the Indian heart with gratitude and peace. As far as the eye could see, the land swept upward into high overlooking hills covered with distant, mystic forests and wild streams and, beyond, always the mighty mountain peaks.

Although the trail had several alternative routes used depending upon time of year and weather conditions, the more prominent trail dropped from the plateau to the Yellowstone River, crossing it at the confluence of Tower Creek where the water depth was sufficiently shallow for fording, especially in the late fall. At this juncture, the trail left the Yellowstone River and continued an eastward course up the Lamar Valley directly toward the peaks of the Absaroka Range. The secluded Lamar Valley provided lush grass, vibrant river and streams, and big game animals. It was the last rest stop until they gained the Bighorn Valley.

As was the case with the Gallatins, the trail across the Absarokas was carefully chosen by the Bannock. On the north side of the Lamar Valley, the trail forked at a place called Soda Butte.[4] One trail followed Soda Butte Creek northeast up the canyon, tracing the current northeast entrance road to the park. From thence, the trail descended the Clark's Fork of the Yellowstone River to the Shoshone River and into the Bighorn Valley.

Another fork of the trail continued east up the Lamar River, then made a gradual ascent up the high ground between Cache and Calfee Creeks. At the summit where Canoe Lake—at least it was so named in Replogle's day— rests in a narrow defile, the trail left the park and followed Timber Creek, eventually joining the Clark's Fork and the Soda Butte trail. The last of the two mighty mountain ranges conquered, anticipation for the reunion with friends and the impending buffalo hunt must have filled them with eager anticipation.

The journey along the Bannock Trail presented danger of death and injury to these people. Blackfoot war parties, exposure to the elements, and injury from accident or wild animals were realities with which they lived. Warriors continually scouted ahead and behind the caravan, watching and warning of potential and real dangers. Along the hilltops of the Absaroka Mountains, the Bannock built signal cairns from which they could survey the area and build signal fires.[5]

When the buffalo hunt was finished, the Bannock retraced their path across the shining mountains to their homeland. Descending from their path in the clouds back into the valley of the Sleeping God, they camped again at Great Springs and held thanksgiving ceremonies with drum and dance and song before returning to their camas prairies in Idaho.

THE SEARCH FOR THE TRAIL

Sixty-eight years after the Bannock Indians were forced onto Idaho reservations and the Great Bannock Trail across northern Yellowstone Park had been lost to antiquity, Chief Park Naturalist David Condon assigned Wayne Replogle the daunting task of finding the lost trail and mapping it for history.

At the time of the assignment in 1946, firsthand knowledge of the trail was sparse. Much of the trail proper west of Yellowstone was consumed by homesteads, cattle ranches, Hebgen Reservoir, and recreational property. The once-busy thoroughfare across the Gallatin Mountains and northern Yellowstone had vanished in more than a million square acres of forest and rugged landscape.

No man at the time was better suited for the tough detective work required for such a task than Replogle. Although lacking in formal training in anthropology and archaeology, Replogle brought to the task a deep passion for the Native American that he had acquired as a boy from his father's farmhands named Christopher "Kit" Carson and John LeBar. Carson was the grandson of the famous Indian scout Kit Carson. LaBar was a full-blooded Cherokee who had been an army honorary guard for the president of the United States and friend of the famous Jim Thorpe.[6] LeBar was the one who told Replogle the story of the Indian and left him with a feeling of love and kindness toward that race.

Little about the trail or its location and description had been written down at the time Replogle began his search. Superintendent Norris made mention of the trail in some of his reports, and he even sketched a portion of the trail in the vicinity of Indian Creek. Hiram Chittenden also provided a brief description of the trail in his history of the park. However, for the most part, no definitive description of the trial existed.

Replogle's task of finding the trail proved daunting.

"Early in my reading and studying on this subject I discovered a disheartening fact. Mention of the Bannock Trail was not easy to find. Often, when it was mentioned scarcely more than a sentence was devoted to its general route. And in the few cases where its course was described the information was so broad and general that it was not of much help. Furthermore, no two maps or reports ever truly coincided."[7]

Wayne Replogle stands on a section of the Great Bannock Trail. (Photo by D. Condon; courtesy of the National Park Service, Yellowstone National Park, YELL 37839)

Nearly three-quarters of a century had elapsed since the trail was used by the Indians, and their pilgrimage had been one with no permanent lodgings and few objects left to mark the path. The area through which the trail extended was hundreds of thousands of square acres of rugged landscape. The only signs of passage were a few stone implements, arrowheads, scrapers, and chips of obsidian left around remnant campfires. Nor was the search for the trail Replogle's primary assignment during these years. Five days out of seven, he performed his normal duties as head ranger naturalist at Canyon. Only during his two days off did he engage in searching for and mapping out the trail. The quest became a joint effort by both Replogle and his wife, Marian.

Replogle sought out residents of the area who reputedly had knowledge of the trail. With the help of people such as Jimmy Spray, Alex Stuart, Billy Marshall, Billy "Pea Soup" Myers, George F. Henderson, and Sam Eagle, pieces of the lost trail began to emerge. Jimmy Spray, an old-time resident of the area, filled Replogle with fascinating tales of his family's interaction with the Bannock Indians, including chiefs such as White Bear, Tansy Hansy, and Tendoy, perhaps the last of the Bannock leaders to cross the Bannock Trail to buffalo lands. Spray told Replogle about a trail west of Yellowstone that came up the Madison Canyon. Billy "Pea Soup" Myers had driven cattle over the Gallatin Range from West Yellowstone to the Indian Creek slaughterhouse at Swan Lake Flats in the late 1890s.[8] Billy Marshall, who worked in Yellowstone in 1906, knew a fellow named Pete Grossmaker, who also drove cattle up the old Bannock Trail to the slaughterhouse.

Alex Stuart of West Yellowstone helped Replogle get a general idea of the route of the old trail from Henry's Lake through Targhee Pass and on to Mammoth Hot Springs. G. F. Henderson told Replogle about the Great Springs camp down near Hebgen Lake and the many artifacts and arrowheads to be found there. Sam Eagle, who helped pioneer West Yellowstone, Montana, helped Replogle envision some of the best places to look for evidence of the trail through the Gallatin Mountains. He remembered the old-timers saying that the Indian trail followed in such a manner as to avoid the spring runoff of melting snow and the prevailing winds. All of this information was but pieces to a much larger and obscure puzzle.

Unless one knew what he was looking for, evidence of the trail remained invisible yet in plain sight. Once Replogle was attuned to the signs that marked the trail, he was amazed how little difficulty he had in recognizing clear traces of the trail. At times, the trail through Targhee Pass and across the Madison Valley to the ancient ceremonial site at Great Springs was as clear as an old drainage ditch where trail ruts and worn pathways were yet visible in the hillsides. Even after nearly seventy years, the trail across the sagebrush flats was traceable by a richer growth of grass and foliage from the fertilization of horse droppings. In other places, it was less noticeable, and in others entirely invisible. But always when the door of evidence seemed to close, invariably another window opened not far away, leading Replogle onward.

The most difficult search came through the Gallatin Mountains on the west side of the park. The vast forests with downed timber and the extensive mountain peaks presented many false starts and dead ends. But the trail beyond the Gallatins was easier to find, and it was here that Replogle focused his efforts first. He had little trouble finding the trail across northern Yellowstone. The trail through Swan Lake Flats, Bunsen Peak, and across the Gardiner River was obvious to him once he understood what to look for. Trails followed up both sides of the Yellowstone River and forded near the confluence of Tower Creek. From the ford he followed the trail across the old hay fields of the Lamar Valley and up Soda Butte Creek.

The trail that ascended the high ridge between Cache and Calfee Creeks in the Absaroka Mountains was well worn and obvious to his view. He used

Wayne Replogle stands by a Sheepeater Indian wickiup near Bunsen
Peak, ca. 1955. (Photo by D. Condon; courtesy of the National Park
Service, Yellowstone National Park, YELL 37836)

a horse to trace the trail over the Absaroka Mountains and down Timber
Creek. Abandoned coverts along the trail and cairns on the high mountains
ridges appeared undisturbed, as if they were still used by the Bannock.

The National Park Service authorized Replogle rights to conduct limited and careful excavations in various campsites along the trail. His searching
yielded a rich number of artifacts and implements. The number of artifacts
found during the summer of 1950 and turned over to the Mammoth
Museum was a source of considerable encouragement to him and proved
that he was on the right trail.

By the summer of 1951, Replogle had mapped the Bannock Trail from
west to east, except through the Gallatin Mountains. That summer he con-
centrated his efforts in these high mountains along the western border

of Yellowstone. In previous years, his search from the Madison Valley into the Gallatin Mountains had proved fruitless. In the summer of 1951, he decided to work backward, starting amid the high Gallatin Peaks and working down toward the Madison Valley. He began in the White Peak area, and what a difference this change in perspective offered. The great Bannock Trail suddenly appeared, as if a revelation had opened to him. He was able to trace the trail with far less difficulty back across the lower benches and foothills of the Gallatin Peaks and out into the Madison Valley to Great Springs.

END OF THE TRAIL

The trail was now fully connected from Henry's Lake to the Bighorn Valley. With great satisfaction Replogle reported:

> What a journey! Once the Bannock travelled [the trail] in reality, while today most of us will...dream our way along its route through printed pages and following a plotted map. Anyone actually making the trip over it now must be prepared for a pleasant and expansive solitude, broken only by the distant bark of the coyote, the soft sound of the heron in flight from the many swamps along the way, by the feel of rain and sun, and the song of the wind. Perhaps he will be most thoughtful as he sits at a small campfire somewhere along the way, envisioning the passing of a scene in history.[9]

With the trail proper mapped out on paper, Replogle and Marian spent another summer verifying and writing up their findings. Days were spent in the Mammoth library studying historical documents. Many nights were spent in their little cabin at Canyon checking and rechecking findings to ensure that he had correctly established the trail and its many branches. By 1953 Replogle felt that the mission given him by Chief Condon was complete. With deep satisfaction he recorded, "Thus was concluded the exploration for the trail proper. I have followed every foot of it from west to east, over plateau, down valleys, through passes and streams, over mountains. It moves forward, 'going somewhere,' following natural passes and easy contours. The Yellowstone Bannock Trail has been found and traversed, and as one walks down its peaceful ribbon he can almost hear the soft step of those Bannocks who long ago left the area to pursue a new way of life."[10]

In 1956 the Yellowstone Library and Museum Association published the results of his search as number 6 in its series of interpretive books under the title *Yellowstone's Bannock Indian Trails.* It provides the student of history a unique glimpse of the rediscovery of the trail, the country through which it passed, and the people who once trod its path. In 1964 Aubrey Haines wrote a nine-page pamphlet by the same title, which may have been an attempt to synthesize Replogle's book into a more succinct history.

On the eve of publication, while Replogle slept, his wife, Marian, added her own final epitaph of her contribution to the project, something that her husband had promised to do but obviously failed to dictate:

He was going to say—I may not get it just right—After many, many long days of very long steps by his very long legs over very long distances—and many short breaths—when he finally stumbled home I always managed to have the house locked up tight with no way in the world for him to get in until I returned from some little errand.

On all of his short hikes I would stop the car, wave a fond farewell—then review his directions, study maps, compute distances, study his diagrams (usually sketched in the dirt at my feet), drive exactly to the spot and wait. And it was always the wrong spot. Often I have waited for hours at one rock by one stream while he was waiting hopelessly by one rock on another stream. Our faith that someday we would really meet at the right time at the right place kept us going.

Then there was the "research." Many a night our Coleman lamp has burned low while I hunted up a few scientific names. But in the cold light of day they resembled nothing but flagrant typographic errors, and it took a session in the Mammoth Museum to straighten them out.

However, I have helped even more. I have accompanied him a number of times on one of the longest treks through the wilderness—from the west boundary, through the Mt. Holmes region, to the Mammoth area—a 2- or 3-day trip of, perhaps, 60 miles. And I carried my own pack—my sleeping bag. He carried his and a few other small items, such as all the food and utensils for 3 days, the cameras, axe, medical supplies, flashlight, extra articles of clothing, etc. He may not have realized my assistance. Every time that I got myself hung up on a fallen tree and he had to come back and pick me off he had extra time to scan the ground for arrow points or chips. Every time that he could not leave me completely behind and had to wait I am sure that the delay preserved his health and gave him time to practice what he calls "Indian language." When darkness finally overtook us and we had to make camp it was, I, squaw-like, who had to do the work (after he had built our wickiup, chopped wood for the entire night, built the fire, chased away the wild animals I could hear and unpacked the stores). I am still trying to figure out why he calls me "Hazard No. 1." I am waiting with excitement and anticipation to learn what the next big job will be. I am ready and anxious to help again.[11]

GHOSTS ALONG THE TRAIL

The mapping of the Bannock Trail was ultimately more than finding a path in the woods; it was a search for the ghosts of those who once walked the path. Replogle was as determined to learn about the people and their culture as he had been to find their great trail. For more than a decade, he studied their physical, social, cultural, and religious way of life. He came to admire and love the people of the trail.

By the time Replogle's monograph was published, the Bannock Indians, as a distinct people, seemed to be vanishing, as had their trail. In 1829 Jim Bridger reported as many as 8,000 souls among the tribe. Fifty years later, 600 Bannock Indians were reported to be at Fort Hall, with 200 more at the Lemhi reservation in northern Idaho. In 1953 the census from the Indian agent showed only 196 full-blooded Bannock Indians on the reservation. Today, just over 5,600 Bannock and Shoshone people live together on the Fort Hall Reservation near Pocatello, Idaho.

Replogle studied their culture and learned about their dress and grooming customs, mode of travel, how they made their implements and weapons, their wickiups, and especially about their knowledge and use of plants for food and medicines. With the help of Mrs. Ben Arnold, Herma Baggley, and Billy "Pea Soup" Myers, Replogle became quite knowledgeable about natural plants and herbs found in and around Yellowstone and used by the Bannock for dyes, medicines, and supplements. He gave campfire lectures on the subject.

Replogle visited Fort Hall Indian Reservation in Pocatello, Idaho, and found to his delight that the Bannock culture had not died out, despite their dwindled numbers. He watched their sun dance and war dance and famous old stick games with awe. He saw cradle boards yet being used as well as the long braided hair, customary for the Plains Indian. They spoke their language in preference to English and still secured native plants to augment their diet, particularly the camas root and the onion. He saw tepees and other shelters made out of willow, elder, cottonwood, and cattail leaves. He noted with

Painting by Frederic Remington of a Bannock hunting party.

great satisfaction, "It proved that the ancient Indian culture is not dead and that the Indian and his ways have not yet been absorbed by the white man. Our method of living, somewhat forced upon the Indian, has not completely withdrawn from him those ways taught him by his ancestors."[12]

After the publication of his *Yellowstone's Bannock Indian Trails* monograph, Replogle received a kind letter from Henry Old Coyote, a Crow Indian from the Crow Agency in Montana. Henry wrote the following, "It is seldom that one ever finds anything on Indian historical material written by a white man with as much painstaking care and feeling for the Indian people as you have done in your book."[13] Replogle found his beloved ghosts. White Bear, Tansy Hansy, Tendoy, and other Bannock chiefs of the past became real to him in his search, arising out of an obscured past—all part of an ancient trail that once guided Native Americans across the shining mountains of Yellowstone.

Chapter 19

The Science of Geysers

Imagine the wonderment of the first explorers of Yellowstone's geyser basins when they broke from dense forests into a sterile, Dante-like inferno of alkaline whiteness with jets of hot water bursting skyward from weird-shaped orifices. Brilliant sapphire and emerald springs steamed like a witch's brew; cauldrons of thick, gray mud bubbled; steam vents whistled shrilly; and rivulets of tepid water flowed over tapestries of orange, green, yellow, and brown algae.

Joseph Meek, a member of the Rocky Mountain Fur Company, had such an experience in 1829 while hunting in the Yellowstone area. After becoming separated from his associates after a surprise attack by Blackfoot Indians and wandering in a southerly direction for five days, he came upon a scene that reminded him of the city of Pittsburgh as he had once seen it on a cold morning: "Being desirous to learn something about the progress he had made, he ascended a low mountain in the neighborhood of his camp, and behold! The whole country beyond was smoking with vapor from boiling springs, and burning gases issuing from small craters, each of which was emitting a sharp whistling sound."[1]

Early fantastic descriptions were followed by decades of scientific study on Yellowstone's thermal wonders. Theories relative to thermal dynamics have been around since the early 1800s (Mackenzie, Krug von Nidda, Lang, and Bunsen). However, these theories were formulated without access to Yellowstone's incomparable thermal features and unique environment. The park's geyser basins hold the most prolific conglomeration of geysers and hot springs known on earth and are located in one of the coldest and most variable climates in the lower forty-eight states, thus making them prime objects of study.

Ferdinand V. Hayden's survey party of scientists systematically studied the geysers during the 1870s, followed by the eminent Dr. Arnold Hague, whose studies lasted from 1883 until his death in 1917. The unpublished information from Hague and his associates (geologist Walter H. Weed, physicist William Hallock, and chemist F. A. Gooch) was used by Eugene Thomas Allen and Arthur L. Day of the Carnegie Institution of Washington, DC, in their decadelong study of Yellowstone's hot springs from 1925 to 1935.[2]

Until Marler's entry into the National Park Service, field studies in Yellowstone were mostly confined to summer and early autumn, as the winters in the park were entirely too harsh for research. As no satisfactory study of geyser theory could be complete without the observation of seasonal influences of temperature, barometric pressure, wind, and precipitation, Allen and Day arranged with Park Superintendent Albright to have four rangers (Phillips, Baker, LaNoue, and Hanks) make monthly reports on observations during their winter patrols to geyser basins along the Firehole River. These winter observations were carried out for five years, between 1925 and 1930.

Allen and Day's studies helped advance geyser theory related to superheated water and geyser eruption. However, in their final analysis, even they concluded that the cause(s) of geyser fluctuation or, in other words, the irregularities in the beginning and ending of a geyser's eruptions remained "an unsolved problem."[3]

Enter George Marler. Until Marler, no one had conducted a systematic, long-term, all-seasons study of these thermal features. By the mid- to late 1940s, after nearly two decades of detailed study of geysers and hot springs in the park, Marler was developing his own theory about irregularity in geyser eruption patterns.

Allen and Day based their conclusions of the effects of the atmosphere—internal and external dynamics—on geyser eruptions on what Marler believed was "poor scientific evidence."[4] He felt that further systematic research was needed on most or at least many thermal features before coming to a universal geyser theory because each geyser had its own unique characteristics that could cause variations in the findings. Scientists agreed with Marler, including Dr. L. C. Graton, a professor of mining geology at Harvard University.

With the approval of his wife and the encouragement of Dr. Graton, Marler decided that there was great merit in spending an entire winter at Old

Faithful, where he could more closely study the effect of cold weather on geyser function. Marler justified his request to park administration as follows:

> It was due to the fact that no systematic observations had ever been made in winter of any of the geysers except Old Faithful that Dr. Graton recommended that I undertake this project. Whenever I had the opportunity to delve into Park literature pertaining to geyser observations that might have been made in winter, I found the only accurate observations on record were made in the winter of 1949–50 by Ranger Ruben Hart, on Old Faithful Geyser only. It was due to this lack of observational data that I was extremely interested in making systematic winter observations of the geysers and hot springs in the Upper Basin.[5]

Horace Albright, who was then retired from Park Service administration, added his influence to prevail upon Yellowstone administration to obligate funds for Marler to spend the winter of 1951–52 at Old Faithful doing cold-weather research. Dave Condon supported the proposed research and provided funding through the Yellowstone Library and Museum Association.

On November 1, 1950, Marler, his wife, Laura, and two young daughters (Barbara and Lela) settled into the Old Faithful ranger station while the snow fell deep and silent around them. The roads providing access to the outside world were shut by blizzards, and the Marlers found themselves snowbound in wonderland.

The winter of 1950–51 proved severe. In the middle of January, Marler measured the snow level at seventy-two inches in back of the Old Faithful Museum. The tracks he made with his snowshoes in the morning across the flats by Hamilton Store in the Lower Geyser Basin were covered by the time he returned. To keep from getting lost in a whiteout, Marler followed the channels where the hot water ran from the hot springs and geysers. Temperatures descended as low as -67° Fahrenheit. Condensation of steam from geysers and hot springs was pronounced throughout the basins. Fine spray congealed into crystalline form even before it hit the ground, coating all surrounding objects with diamond-like frost crystals and transforming them into an ethereal-like fairyland. The cold was so intense and the ice so massive that even the hottest steam vents were invaded by ice, providing for Marler a true paradox of hot and cold.[6]

Marler focused his attention on two types of geysers: cone and fountain types. Cone geysers have a cone of some shape projecting above the ground

The Taylor Maximum and Minimum Thermometer was used at Giant Geyser, 1959. (Photo by Hewitt; courtesy of the National Park Service, Yellowstone National Park, YELL 20036-7)

that protects the geyser orifice against the elements. Beehive Geyser is an example of a cone geyser. Fountain-type geysers, on the other hand, are unprotected and have large, open surfaces or pools. Fountain Geyser is a good example. Marler hypothesized that cold temperatures, influenced by wind and low barometric pressure, would affect the two types of geysers differently. Theoretically, cone geysers should be less susceptible to external elements than an open, unprotected surface. This, in turn, might affect temperature and patterns of eruption.

To test his hypothesis, he observed selected thermal features throughout the winter and measured temperatures using a Taylor Maximum and Minimum Thermometer. He compared his data with data he had taken during the summer, spring, and fall periods and found that of the 138 hot springs that he had measured during the winter months, 48 had actually increased in temperature and 12 had declined in temperature an average of 4.8° Fahrenheit, while the eruption intervals and frequencies of play remained essentially unchanged.

Marler concluded in an article published by the Yale Geology Department that external factors of temperature and wind have no significant limiting effect on geyser eruptions and that the primary factors influencing a geyser's pattern of eruption and interlude were mostly internal.[7]

Marler felt that his observations of the geysers during the winter of 1950–51 came at a fortuitous time because of the unusual activity of several previously dormant geysers. His work was not complete, however, and he sought to spend a second winter at Old Faithful. The naturalist staff agreed to this proposition, but it was not to be. By January of the second winter, Marler experienced health problems that necessitated evacuation of him and his family to Mammoth for medical care.

THE HISTORY OF OLD FAITHFUL

No other thermal feature in Yellowstone garnered the fame of Old Faithful Geyser. Its very name, "Old Faithful," suggested age and consistency. Marler, Dr. Bauer, and later, Dr. Donald White of the US Geological Survey did considerable studies of the famous geyser, seeking answers to questions that had puzzled tourists and scientists alike for years: What makes Old Faithful so regular in its eruptions? How old is Old Faithful? Has it always been such a predictable geyser?[8]

Geologists tell us that Yellowstone's thermal features are a mild stage of past volcanism and an indication that intense heat yet lies close to the surface in Yellowstone. The latest caldera to explode in the park happened approximately 640,000 years ago. Sometime after the molten roof of the caldera congealed into rock, thermal features began appearing in the circumventing cracks. The dispersion of major geyser basins (Firehole, West Thumb, Norris, and Mud Volcano) in Yellowstone follows roughly the outline of the caldera. Surface water and groundwater and the configuration of the cracks in the earth contribute to form Yellowstone's various types of features that include hot springs, erupting geysers, mud pots, and fumaroles.

In trying to establish an estimated age of Old Faithful, Marler studied its mound and foundation in great detail and concluded that "students of Old Faithful have postulated its age since 1870 without taking into consideration numerous aspects of its mound by which alone the geyser's age can reasonably be determined."[9]

By core drilling in the geyser basins, geologists discovered that the foundation upon which Old Faithful's mound or cone rests is a bed of gravel presumably laid down during the glacial age estimated by geologists to be approximately 30,000 years ago. Although it was known that volcanic activity had occurred at the same time that ice covered Yellowstone, it was evident that Old Faithful's mound was formed after the ice age. Dr. Kenneth Pierce of the US Geological Survey has estimated that the sediment deposits underlying the Upper Geyser Basin are about 14,000 years old, although no conclusive dating has been made. The gravel underlying the Upper Geyser Basin is what geologists call kame deposits, which occur at or near the margins of ice sheets. It is also possible that this gravel was laid down by streams from the melting ice glaciers that once covered all of Yellowstone.[10]

Marler focused on the mound because that feature alone was capable of approximating the geyser's age. He did this by measuring the amount of sinter that had been deposited over time during eruptions. Studies showed that geyserite (called siliceous sinter) was deposited at a rate of between 0.1 to 2.7 millimeters per nine-month period. Given the size of Old Faithful's mound (almost 12 feet tall and 615 feet in diameter at the base) compared to the rate of growth, one might estimate that Old Faithful was several thousands of years old.

Marler disagreed. He discovered what appeared to be large stalactites of geyserite where the falling water was eroding Old Faithful's mound. These exposed formations turned out to be approximately forty tree stumps and pieces of trees encased within the geyserites of the mound. These stumps proved to be lodgepole pine, and the carbon-14 dating showed the trees to be an estimated age of 730 years, plus or minus 200 years.

Of course, it was highly unlikely that trees could grow on an active geyser mound. The presence of the stumps suggested to Marler a period of quiescence prior to the emergence of the current geyser—a long-enough time for a stand of trees to grow over the area. With the reemergence of thermal activity, the trees were killed off, and the stumps and roots were encased by the geyserite. The age of the pine stumps suggested to Marler that the current Old Faithful Geyser was likely only 200 or 300 years old.

Most people assumed that Old Faithful Geyser had created its mound from which it erupted. However, Marler was convinced that the mound from which Old Faithful now erupts was, in fact, not created by Old Faithful Geyser, but that it took over a house that had already been built by an earlier thermal feature.

Old Faithful's mound under a relatively thin veneer of geyserites is decidedly terraced and was created by a pulsing type of activity caused by repeating heavy surges of water that rolled from the vent in all directions. Only a fountain that dispersed sinter-laden water in a flowing, uniform manner could form such a pattern. Marler concluded that the terraces were formed by hot springs occurring at two distinct periods of time that expanded and built the mound until a disturbance, such as an earthquake, altered the internal piping and turned the spring into an erupting geyser.[11] The erupting action of Old Faithful Geyser was eroding part of the mound and building it in other places.

Marler's studies on Old Faithful resulted in the publication of *The Story of Old Faithful Geyser* by Yellowstone Park in 1961.[12] The publication was an excellent resource for interpreters, scientists, and tourists and helped everyone better understand the science and geology behind this most famous geyser.

Interestingly, his theory regarding Old Faithful still holds up pretty well today. Improved technology, including 3-D laser imaging, electron microscopy, and video cameras unavailable in Marler's day, has provided geologists more accurate methods of studying thermal features in Yellowstone.

Recent carbon-14 dating and 3-D laser-imaging studies conducted by Duncan Foley of Pacific Lutheran University in Tacoma, Washington, on Castle Geyser have provided similar findings as Marler and White back in the 1960s. Dating shows that there is a difference of approximately 8,000 years (plus or minus a few hundred years) in the age between Castle's cone and the terrace or shield upon which it rests. Carbon-14 dating estimated the age of the shield at 10,000 years and the cone at approximately 1,000 years.

Foley suggests that the cone was formed by pulses of activity followed by periods of inactivity. Such a "pulse and pause" phenomenon is common with other geologic systems, such as volcanoes. Foley's findings are remarkably similar to those of Marler and White that terraces were built by hot springs followed by geyser activity. Instead of a uniform, consistent thermal development of Yellowstone's geysers—at least Old Faithful and Castle Geysers— they were formed by pulses of activity.[13]

EXCHANGE OF FUNCTION

The regularity or irregularity with which geysers erupt has been a source of interest to visitors and scientists alike since they were first discovered. Significant geologic studies on geyser interconnectedness had not been done until Marler's work. For years Marler suspected that a kind of subterranean ecology existed between geysers that shared the same proximity with one another. He was almost certain that these geysers shared some type of underground connection that influenced each other's performance. He believed that the sharing of heat and water sources between geysers caused thermal energy to shift back and forth from one to the other. The shifting of energy caused periodic and noticeable irregularities in geyser eruptions. However, his evidence at the time was not conclusive enough for publication. Marler called his underground connection theory "exchange of function."[14]

Underground connections between geysers were joked about by early employees of Yellowstone but hardly taken seriously. Geyser Bob (John Edgar) was a classic example of subterranean humor. A woman tourist once asked Geyser Bob, a stage driver back in the late 1880s, how he got his picturesque name. "Well," said the old stage driver, "I clum up on Old Faithful one day and got too near the crater and fell in."

"How interesting!" responded the woman. "What happened?"

"Why," said Bob, pointing to the Beehive Geyser across the Firehole River, "I came out of the Beehive—over there."

"Well! Well! How long did it take?" asked the woman.

"Oh," said Bob, "if I had come straight through it would have taken about ten minutes, but I stopped on the way for a haircut and a shave!" Another and more expansive version claimed that he fell into Old Faithful and emerged nineteen months later in Mud Geyser, away across the mountains and the woodlands.[15]

Determined to find answers to his exchange-of-function theory, Marler selected several groups of geysers to study, including Grand and Daisy in the Upper Geyser Basin, Kaleidoscope and the Fountain Group in the Lower Geyser Basin, and Rainbow Pool and Green Spring in the Black Sand Basin. An eruption of Fountain Pool on June 19, 1947, convinced him that he was right.

Fountain Pool was one of four thermal features in the Fountain Group, the others being Fountain, Clepsydra, and Spasm Geysers. Fountain Geyser had become dormant during the 1920s, and it had not been known to erupt in the ensuing twenty-five years. Many people feared that it might never erupt again, until it did in 1944 and again in 1946. Then, in the summer of 1947, Marler was given a show of a lifetime, as he reports:

As I drove into the Lower Geyser Basin parking area at 8:40 a.m. on June 19, the gods of fortune must have been riding with me and my companion [unknown]. Almost immediately following our arrival at the curb a large fountain of water spectacularly domed up above all surrounding objects. For the following 18 minutes, from 8:42 until

9:00 a.m., I was a spectator of a display of power and beauty for which
Yellowstone alone is famous. With scarcely a pause, explosion followed explosion. The water in the large pool would suddenly con-
vex in a manner to make one marvel at the cohesive forces manifest.
This bluish dome would instantaneously burst into a crystalline mass of
water....Throughout the huge dome-like mass of surging water superheated nuclear masses of water could be seen to explode, bursting out
rocket-like jets at various angles from the main body.[16]

In eighteen minutes, Marler counted 81 eruptions or surges, the average
height being nearly 50 feet with occasional bursts reaching seventy-five feet
or more. The massive column of water was fully 60 feet across the base. No
diminution of force was manifest until the very last burst. When the activity
abruptly ceased, all of the water in the large bowl completely emptied within
thirty seconds.[17]

To his surprise, Marler noticed that the water in nearby Fountain Geyser
and Spasm Geyser also emptied or significantly dropped during the eruption
of Fountain Pool. About twenty minutes after Fountain Pool's eruption
ceased, water began again to flow steadily back into the empty craters. A full
hour after Fountain Pool's eruption, Clepsydra, which played quite infrequently, erupted into a powerful show. Instead of playing for its typical three
hours, it played fully six hours. During these six hours, water poured at a
steady rate from Fountain Pool into Fountain Geyser. However, the water
level in Fountain Geyser did not rise but seemed to be draining out as fast as
it entered. It was obviously going to feed another source.

Marler postulated that the water in these other features was going to support Clepsydra. As he suspected, when Clepsydra ceased playing, the water
immediately began to rise in both Fountain Pool and Fountain Geyser. Marler concluded: "The ebbing of the water in Clepsydra at the time of the
Fountain Pool's eruption, its protracted period of play, plus the immediate
effect on the Fountain system following Clepsydra's action left no room for
doubt as to subterranean connections between these geysers."[18]

Four years later, on May 11, 1951, Marler was studying the Giant Group
(composed of Giant, Mastiff, Bijou, and Catfish Geysers) and witnessed an
unexpected eruption of Mastiff Geyser. This was the first time in his twenty
years in Yellowstone that Marler had seen Mastiff erupt. In fact, Mastiff, Bijou,
and Catfish all erupted simultaneously that day, followed immediately by an
infrequent eruption of Giant Geyser.

Bison winter in Old Faithful Geyser Basin, ca. 1950. (Photo by George Marler, courtesy of George Marler)

The eruption of Mastiff Geyser prompted further historical research on the part of Marler. He discovered in the Hayden report of 1872, written by E. J. Stanley, that a similar event had happened at that time. Mastiff—then unnamed—had surged, followed by Catfish, and then became quiescent as Giant Geyser erupted, in Stanley's words, "as if showing reverence to the grand chief of the realm—Giant. With a terrible rushing and rumbling behavior that caused the earth to groan, Giant came forth."[19]

An even more convincing show came later that same summer on July 18. Marler and Merrill Beal had just arrived at the Giant Group when almost immediately Mastiff Geyser exploded into a colossal display of power, sending water torrents into the air equal to that of Old Faithful. Simultaneously, Catfish played to double its normal height. Ten minutes later, Giant exploded into a two-hundred-foot column of water. Instead of bowing out at the eruption of Giant, its normal tactic, Mastiff held her own, playing a full five minutes and equal in power to that of Giant. In fact, Mastiff was more impressive than Giant by lifting two huge columns of water, the north vent shooting up at a fifteen-degree angle.

At the first eruptions, Dr. Beal ran around behind Mastiff to get a better view of the spectacle and became somewhat trapped when Giant unexpectedly erupted. Between towering water explosions, he caught periodic glimpses of Marler running back and forth to the car and from side to side, feverishly taking photos of the once-in-a-lifetime thermal show. He last saw Marler rushing off toward Old Faithful Museum to spread the word. He had totally forgotten about Beal in his excitement.

Marler's theory of exchange of function provided an important advancement in geyser theory. At the recommendation of Dr. L. C. Graton, Marler published a paper through the Yale Geology Department on the subject of exchange of function as a cause of irregularity in the performance of hot springs and geysers. His article concluded: "All geysers play irregularly, and some with great irregularity. Many geysers showing great irregularity are connected subterraneous with other springs and geysers. After more than 50 months of seasonal observations for over twelve years, many geysers show a shift in direction of the flow of thermal energy from one orifice to another. Irregularity in eruption and quiescence is a natural property of all hot springs."[20]

His article was heralded by prominent scientists, such as Dr. Chester Longwell at Yale. Dr. Graton of Harvard wrote to Marler upon the publishing of his paper: "Your article has shed more light on the causes of irregularity of Yellowstone's geysers than any previous investigation."[21]

THE BONITA POOL EXPERIMENT

After the 1959 Madison River Canyon earthquake, Daisy Geyser, which is part of a group of geysers that included Bonita Pool, Splendid Geyser, and Brilliant Pool, abruptly stopped erupting.[22] Marler had observed this group of geysers since 1938 and was familiar with their patterns. Daisy played regularly every one and a half to two hours, and the eruption was accompanied simultaneously by a rise in the water level of Bonita Pool. When Daisy stopped erupting, Marler noticed, upon closer observation, that some of the water in Bonita Pool's basin drained out of the basin because of a low breach in the wall.

Marler believed that the loss of this water had something to do with Daisy Geyser's dormancy and that if the water level in Bonita Pool was allowed to rise a little higher without breaching the dike, it would provide sufficient energy to stimulate Daisy Geyser out of dormancy. In other words, Bonita Pool was stealing the water that provided the thermal energy from Daisy Geyser, thus preventing Daisy's eruption.

Marler first tried a small, secret experiment. Undetected by others, he repaired the small breach in the dike using sinter, thus allowing the pool's water level to rise about one-half inch higher than normal. The action made all the difference. Presently, the water in Daisy Geyser began to rise, then to surge, and within thirty minutes it erupted in its normal pattern.

The 1959 earthquake had caused unique changes in many hot springs and geysers in the Firehole basins, and Marler wanted to do further studies to determine how and to what degree behavior of hot springs that had changed in their patterns since the earthquake was affected by other springs with which they shared an underground connection. Marler felt that the time immediately following the earthquake presented a unique window of opportunity to study these changes in light of his theory and that additional aftershocks from the earthquake could at any moment cause thermal shifts that would eliminate the opportunity for further meaningful study.

Time was of the essence, but he knew that he needed permission; he could not, on his own volition, tamper with the thermal features. On August 3, 1960, he made a written proposal to West District manager Oscar Dick, proposing damming Bonita Pool's dike, as he had done previously, for only three days to allow for further observation and research on exchange of function. Sensitive to the need to respect naturalness, he noted the following in his request to Dick: "The process of damming Bonita Pool is scientifically sound because the shift in thermal energy [in this case man-made] is the same as nature does. The man-made, temporary dam will allow us to discover and gain knowledge that otherwise, would require a life-time of boardwalk observation."[23]

Opportunity presented dilemma. Marler was keenly aware of the tumult his artificial manipulations of geysers would likely cause among some park personnel who were strictly hands-off when it came to tampering with geysers. Some would indict him on charges of making the geysers his own personal laboratory. They would demand that Yellowstone be kept pristine and one of the few places on earth that man's meddling hand was not allowed. Yet this once-in-a-lifetime opportunity seemed justified, especially when it would cause no harm to the hot springs and could actually rejuvenate one of the important geysers at Old Faithful.

Assistant District Rangers E. L. Robinson and B. R. McClelland soon provided a staunch rebuttal to Marler's plan. They cited a growing concern over scientific research in the basins and proposed that such research was damaging to the natural condition of the geysers. They concluded: "The nat-

George Marler observing a thermal feature in Firehole Geyser Basin, ca. 1958.
(Courtesy of George Marler)

ural beauty and undisturbed natural behavior of their (the basins') features are
our greatest assets. Any research methods which would in any way disturb the
naturalness of the beauty or behavior of any feature are not justified in Yellowstone National Park. If measurements cannot be obtained without alter-
ing a feature, then the measurements are not important enough to obtain."[24]

Battle lines were drawn. Some stood firmly on the side of absolute protection of naturalism, and Marler and a few other naturalists stood on the side of
scientific study and learning. What appeared to be a division really wasn't. Marler was as committed to preservation of naturalism and conservation as anyone
because he understood hot springs and their delicate natures even more than
the rangers or any naturalist of his time. He viewed the dam as more of a restoration than an alteration, with the benefit of knowledge added in.

Reinforcements to Marler came by way of Merrill Beal, who was acting
as head ranger naturalist at Old Faithful at the time: "If management is the
National Park Service's keynote for controlling animals, fish, fowl, forests and
people, why shouldn't thermal features have benefit of similar wisdom?"[25]

Beal's point was taken. Why be selective in how you manage nature?
Why should animals and forests be managed but not thermal features? Of

course, the answer is that animals are numerous and can be reproduced; the loss of some can be replenished. Geysers, on the other hand, are comparatively few in number, unique, and irreplaceable. The elimination of a thermal feature by nature is acceptable, but not by the hand of man. After all, one cannot simply drill a hole in the geyser basin and fill it with water and have a geyser. Mother Nature had unique specifications for geysers that only she could create.

Beal ended his appeal with a passionate extolling of Marler's devotion to park policies and geyser protection, and he recommended approval of the proposal. Oscar Dick agreed with Marler and Beal. Protection was important, but study, provided it did not harm the geyser, was also important, especially when such action could feasibly restore one of Yellowstone's prized geysers to full activity. Dick's approval was not an indictment against the rangers but a vote of confidence in Marler and a realization of the importance of the window of opportunity.

Dick's endorsement was forwarded to park headquarters on August 15, 1960. Chief Naturalist Robert McIntyre generally recommended approval of Marler's three-day study to Park Superintendent Lon Garrison in a memo dated August 19, 1960, with the careful stipulations that nothing be done that would permanently destroy or harm the hot springs.

In spite of the endorsements by top park officials, no official action was taken, so the pleasure-giving potential of Daisy Geyser remained fallow for a few seasons. This passive status made Marler restless.[26] In the summer of 1964, Marler arranged for a demonstration to be given to park administration on Bonita Pool. Anticipating their arrival, Ted Parkinson, a colleague of Marler's at Old Faithful, prepared the dike at Bonita. Hopes were high for showing the top brass from Mammoth the phenomenon of exchange of function and that Daisy Geyser could indeed be resurrected with a simple and unobtrusive modification to Bonita Pool.

Unfortunately, Parkinson was discovered in the act of preparing the dam at Bonita Pool by a ranger who raised heaven and hell. Despite the hullabaloo, Marler retained hope that a demonstration would vindicate them. In fact, the brass did come, in the persona of John Good, the new chief park naturalist who had taken the place of Robert McIntyre upon his transfer out of the park. In Beal's words, "No hearing was held, but Chief Naturalist John Good came to Old Faithful and disciplined Ted [Parkinson] in two ways. His termination date was advanced, and a decree was announced that Ted would never be stationed at Old Faithful again."[27]

Naturally, this was deeply humiliating to Parkinson, who rightfully felt like a scapegoat. He considered resigning and not returning to the park. Fortunately, he decided to face it and stay on. He served out the remainder of his years in Yellowstone at Canyon and Fishing Bridge and eventually became a supervising naturalist. By 1982 he was the senior seasonal naturalist in Yellowstone. Beal noted, "His tenure has outdistanced them all and he is a credit to the service."[28]

Daisy Geyser was restored to full operation, and today it remains one of the more predictable geysers in Yellowstone Park. Its interval was disrupted for a few weeks after an earthquake in Alaska in 2002, but the geyser has regained its normalcy. It is known to be influenced by nearby Splendid Geyser and, to a lesser degree, by Brilliant Pool and Comet Geyser. Exchange of energy or function is an established principle within geyser theory, thanks, in part, to pioneering work of George Marler.

Chapter 20

Earthquake

THE NIGHT THE MOUNTAIN FELL

Three minutes before midnight on August 17, 1959, the fourth largest earthquake in the history of the United States at that time struck in the Madison River Canyon just west of Yellowstone Park. The quake's epicenter, which registered 7.5 on the Richter scale, was below Hebgen Lake in both the Gallatin and Beaverhead National Forests, not far from the old Bannock ceremonial camp at Big Springs.[1]

Hebgen Lake was created in 1914 by the damming of the Madison River with an earthen dam eighty-five feet high and seven hundred feet long. The resultant lake is fifteen miles long and four miles in width with a sixty-five-mile shoreline that encompasses nearly 525 million cubic yards of water. In addition to providing valuable water resources to the surrounding areas, the lake has become a great natural recreation area, surrounded by recreational property, campgrounds, lodges, and water sports. Highway 191 runs north and south, connecting West Yellowstone with Bozeman, Montana. A few miles north of West Yellowstone, Highway 287 breaks west and skirts the northern edge of Hebgen Lake before following the Madison River through the canyon to Ennis, Montana.

The 1959 seismic activity rocked a five-state area and severely fractured the earth's crust along the western boundary of Yellowstone National Park and into the mountains surrounding Hebgen Lake, sustaining in places an average vertical displacement of ten to twenty feet. Simultaneous with the drop in some places, the eastern side of Hebgen Lake (closest to Yellowstone Park) was pushed up as much as eight feet while the middle part of the lake settled. The result was a series of tidal waves or seiches that breached the earth-filled dam. The dam fortunately held, although its core wall structure sustained multiple fractures. Large amounts of water from the overflow of the dam rushed down the Madison Canyon, prompting the evacuation of Ennis, Montana, several miles below the canyon.[2]

The south side of the Madison Canyon above Rock Creek campground is composed of stratified schist rock containing considerable amounts of mica. This highly unstable rock was held in place by a dolomite or quartzite formation that crossed the slide area diagonally. The shock caused this hard, brittle dolomite buttress to snap, sending forty million yards (eighty million tons) of mountainside down into the canyon and Rock Creek campground, burying nineteen campers while they slept. The Madison River was instantly dammed by the slide that measured four hundred feet above the floor, forming what became known as Earthquake or Quake Lake. Fish were discovered in isolated pockets of water as high as two hundred feet above the Madison River.[3]

Throughout the area, roads were badly broken up, buildings destroyed or ripped off their foundations, cars and trailers swept into the river and lake, and, most tragically, at least twenty-eight lives were lost.

DAMAGE IN YELLOWSTONE PARK

The grinding of the earth's fault lines was heard throughout Yellowstone. Old Faithful Inn, the Soldier Station at Norris Geyser Basin, and other structures in the park sustained damage. Park roads at Silver Gate, between West Entrance and Madison Junction, Gibbon Canyon, and other areas in the park sustained damage and were temporarily closed by large boulders and debris that fell from the steep canyon walls.

A portion of Obsidian Cliff fell away due to the tremor. Some of the old quarrying places on the cliff where the Bannock Indians obtained their obsidian were obliterated. The cracks that had been filled with countless obsidian chips left by the long-ago craftsmen were gone forever. This was a particularly disappointing loss for Wayne Replogle, who had studied the Bannock and this quarry site.[4]

Across Yellowstone, campers and employees were jolted from their sleep. Lodgepole pines swayed as if under hurricane gale, many of them crashing to the ground like jackstraw. The waves on Yellowstone Lake crashed against the shoreline with power never before seen. There was even a report that a black bear had become entombed in a cave for a time until rescued by a park ranger. Tourists hurriedly packed their belongings and left the park in mass

Boulders on the road near Madison Junction from the 1959 earthquake. (Photo by Boucher; courtesy of the National Park Service, Yellowstone National Park, YELL 20893-1)

exodus by whatever route was open. Long lines of cars quickly formed at service stations around Yellowstone, and by morning Yellowstone was eerily vacant.

The bears of Yellowstone received the initial blame for the shaking. Tourists' first thoughts, when awakened by the shaking, were that a bear was rocking their tent, cabin, or trailer. Howard Biddulph, son of Lowell and Ruth Biddulph, who was working road crew that summer, lived with his wife and infant daughter in a flimsy cabin at Lake. Awakened by the shaking, he was certain that a bear was trying to get in. Determined to save his family from a would-be bear attack, he jumped out of bed and immediately began clanging pans together as he had witnessed his father do twenty years earlier on the shores of Yellowstone Lake. With each aftershock of the earthquake, Biddulph clanged the pans and shouted at the top of his lungs, "Shoo! Get out of here!" When his parents arrived at his cabin a short time later to check on his safety, Biddulph was actually relieved to learn that it was *only* an earthquake!

Another of Biddulph's sons, David, was running the power plant at West Thumb. That same night the Biddulphs drove to Thumb to check on him. He thought the Russians had attacked the United States and were bombing Yellowstone Park (this was at the height of the Cold War). He, too, was relieved that it was only an earthquake.

ASSESSING THE DAMAGE

Try to imagine the trepidation that filled the hearts and minds of park administrators and staff in those first harrowing hours after the quake. In addition to the safety of Yellowstone's tourists and employees, the concern for the effects of the earthquake on the park's wildlife and famous attractions was profound. Knowing that much of Yellowstone sat on top of a volcanic heat source, fears of a new awakening must have been substantial. Of greatest concern was the effect the shifting of the earth's crust would have on the geysers and hot springs. Would Yellowstone be changed forever?

At Old Faithful, rangers and ranger naturalists were virtually rolled out of their beds by the first shocks. While rangers tried to manage traffic and safety, Beal, Marler, Lystrup, Parkinson, and other naturalists took off toward the geyser basins to check on things. "It was as if a giant hand had pressed down [on the geyser basins]," Marler later described the scene, "forcing water out of all of the springs like a great sponge almost simultaneously."[5]

After a cursory inspection by Marler and others of the geyser basins, he submitted a written report to park headquarters noting the significant activity: "With only seven exceptions, all springs went murky. The majority of the geysers, those that played regularly and the more infrequent ones, plus countless springs with no record of eruptions, had erupted. Some were still in a state of eruption. Geysers that were active in the early history of the Park and had become dormant, resumed activity."[6]

The need for a more thorough inventory of all thermal features in Yellowstone was obvious. Park officials approved the "Emergency Interpretive Study of Earthquake Phenomena" and placed Chief Park Naturalist Robert N. McIntyre in charge. McIntyre assigned Marler to compile a thorough inventory of all thermal features and immediately transferred ranger naturalists from other parts of Yellowstone to Old Faithful as part of the team. Biddulph sent his family home to Idaho, and he reported to Old Faithful. He was sent into the backcountry of the park to look for signs of lava that might have been released by the earthquake and to observe thermal features there. This included Heart Lake, Shoshone Lake, and Lone Star Geyser Basins.

Merrill Beal in front of Sentinel Valley earthquake boulder, 1959. (Courtesy of David and Jean Beal)

The team of naturalists estimated that nearly three hundred springs and geysers erupted in the Firehole Basin as a result of the earthquake. One hundred and sixty of those springs had no history of past eruption. The average rise in temperature of hot springs was more than five degrees Fahrenheit. Cascade and Economic Geysers—dormant for more than forty years—were rejuvenated.[7] Some eruptions were so violent as to break loose large fragments of sinter and blow them out of the orifices and craters. Most of the regular geysers played with markedly shortened intervals, and some played continuously.

Hardly a day passed without the development of new fumaroles and the eruption of previous quiescent springs. A cumulative total of two miles of cracks and breaks in the ground were evidenced in all of the geyser basins. Fumaroles formed in some of these cracks, venting steam and heat in loud, hissing noises. Five hundred and ninety springs turned murky, caused by water action on the sediments in the pools and underground channels. Water levels in several pools dropped measurably from a few inches to a few feet. It is no wonder that Marler saw the period immediately following the earthquake as a prime opportunity to experiment with his theory of exchange of function.

Eruption of Sapphire Pool after the 1959 earthquake, September 1959. (Courtesy of L. G. Biddulph)

On September 15, more than two weeks after the earthquake, Sapphire Pool suddenly erupted with enormous violence. Prior to this eruption, it had been a large, beautiful hot spring with ebullitions of massive silver bubbles that rose beneath its ledges and gently domed on the surface in millions of bubbles. Sapphire Pool was named in the 1880s because of the large biscuit-shaped nodules of geyserites that lined the edges of its basin and its clear, sapphire-colored water. But on that day in mid-September, it had something else in store.

Just after lunch, Biddulph approached Sapphire Pool in Biscuit Basin (a part of Upper Geyser Basin), and he saw a young honeymoon couple standing arm in arm on the boardwalk, looking at the pool. As Biddulph approached the couple that day, loud thumping noises shook the ground beneath them, and he knew that something very dangerous was about to happen. "I said, 'We've got to get out of here.' We ran for the Firehole River, and just as we got there the pool erupted in a huge geyser of over 300 feet. A tremendous explosion! We got doused with water, but I had a raincoat on. They got wet, but we were far enough away not to receive any injuries."[8]

Huge masses of water rose vertically to a height of about 150 feet, while at the same instant, two large arms of water shot out at forty-five degree angles to the east and west. For a period of six months, Sapphire Pool remained a powerful geyser. Eruptions occurred about every hour and started without preliminary warning. Eventually, it stopped erupting and returned to a steaming hot pool that bubbles and occasionally surges.

Until the earthquake, George Marler was disgruntled by what he perceived as apathy on the part of park officials toward his work on the thermal features of the park. His studies and observations seemed to sustain little enthusiasm or momentum with administrators, whose priorities seemed to be elsewhere. The events of August 17, 1959, changed everything literally overnight. Marler noted in his history, "After the earthquake, instead of being the spurned derelict, I suddenly found my company and opinion being sought."[9] His friend and mentor Horace Albright noted that the earthquake not only shook loose rocks and trees, but also shook loose any complacency for Marler's work with the geysers.[10]

Marler provided written reports to park administrators that, in part, resulted in the publication of *Professional Paper no. 435* by the US Geological Survey in cooperation with the US Department of the Interior and the National Park Service. The publication analyzed all physical data from the earthquake. Marler authored the section on the effects of the earthquake on Yellowstone Park's geysers and hot springs.[11] The earthquake drew *National Geographic* magazine to Yellowstone in 1959, and Marler worked closely with the photographers and writers, providing technical information and sixteen valuable photographs of thermal features for their articles.[12]

This inventory of the thermal features of Yellowstone made by park naturalists after the earthquake allowed Marler to compile his most definitive written work on Yellowstone's famous geysers and hot springs. *Inventory of Thermal Features of the Firehole River Geyser Basins and Other Selected Areas of Yellowstone National Park* was published by the US Geological Survey and National Park Service in June 1973.

Ever since exploration parties came to Yellowstone in the late 1800s, the region has been known as a place of rumbling and shaking of the earth. The Hayden Party reported numerous earth tremors during their summers in Yellowstone while surveying and exploring the region. Today, scientists say that there are as many as three thousand earthquakes each year centered in Yellowstone. These "swarms" are not the strong type of the 1959 quake, but they indicate both the presence of magma (molten lava) in the crust of the earth underneath Yellowstone and that pressure is building and being released by the caldera that yet underlies the park. The earth beneath Yellowstone neither slumbers nor sleeps.

PART FIVE

Good-bye, Yellowstone!

As a man gets older he feels different about things in other ways. He likes the hills and to travel the streams, but half the pleasure is in the remembering mind. A place doesn't stand alone after a man has been there once. It stands alone with the time he has had, with the thoughts he has thought—willing to send your mind back to the mountains, the lakes, and the streams.

—Personal *Nature Notes* collected by Lowell G. Biddulph

Chapter 21

Mission 66

YELLOWSTONE'S CRUMBLING INFRASTRUCTURE

Forty years before Yellowstone was created as the first national park, a farm boy—turned trapper—from Maine named Osborne Russell watched the sun set over the Lamar Valley and felt the spirit of this unspoiled wilderness: "There is something in the wild romantic scenery of this valley which I cannot...describe; but the impressions made upon my mind...were such as time can never efface from my memory. I almost wished I could spend the remainder of my days in a place like this where happiness and contentment seemed to reign in wild romantic splendor."[1]

In the fall of 1869, David Folsom foresaw the future popularity of Yellowstone. Upon ascending the Continental Divide west of Yellowstone Lake on his way to the Firehole Basin, Folsom cast one final look back upon Yellowstone Lake and recorded: "This inland sea, its crystal waves dancing and sparkling in the sunlight as if laughing with joy for their wild freedom, is a scene of transcendent beauty which has been viewed by few white men, and we felt glad to have looked upon it before its primeval solitude should be broken by the crowds of pleasure seekers which at no distant day will throng its shores."[2]

As Folsom predicted, the untamed scenes of solitude witnessed by early explorers did not long remain so but were soon teeming with tourists drawn by the park's fame and beauty. The summer of 1948, one million visitors came through the gates of Yellowstone, fueled by the ending of World War II in June 1945. Deeply wounded and numbed by the second extreme violence and loss of human life within a half century, people were desperate to regain

some normality to their lives and sought respite from trauma. The beauties of
Yellowstone and other national parks replenished deep spiritual and emotional wells depleted by world chaos. The Biddulphs (1938) and Beals (1940)
both found solace in Yellowstone from the sorrow of losing children to death.
Others would do the same.

People came in ever-increasing waves, and all of the national parks were
ill-equipped to handle the masses. Little if anything had been done during
the war years to prepare Yellowstone for the masses of people who flooded
through its gates. Campgrounds, cabins, and other accommodations could
not meet the demand of the public. Narrow, winding roads of the park were
jammed with traffic, and the protective and interpretive staff was woefully
inadequate in numbers and ineffectively organized to handle the burgeoning
crowds. The park's infrastructure was crumbling, and National Park officials
struggled to find a solution. Should Yellowstone be refitted to accommodate
public demand, or should the park be kept pristine?

Conrad Wirth, then director of the National Park Service, was resolute in
his belief that national parks were purposeless if they could not accommodate
the public demand. In order to add maximum benefit to the public's enjoyment, he felt it necessary to expand the parks' infrastructure—roads, facilities,
and educational interpretation programs—in bold, new ways. In 1956 Wirth
announced a ten-year initiative called Mission 66 to improve the infrastructure of national parks. Completion was to coincide with the fiftieth anniver-
sary of the National Park Service (1916).

Those who subscribed to the National Park Service Act of 1916 argued
that Yellowstone's natural resources should be so managed that its qualities
remained unimpaired. To cater to the demand for increased highways and
public accommodations was contradictory to the very purpose for the park's
creation. This sentiment was found in a letter written to Bud Lystrup by his
old boss at Hayne's Photo Store the same summer that the park hit one million visitors: "I keep in touch with the Park of yesterday—that part that has
been kept free of the millions who visit it annually—by seeing it through the
eyes of those who disregard the million in their writings. I am sure that I
would not like the Park of 1948."[3]

Through the years, Hayes enjoyed reading in *Nature Notes* the descriptions of intimate and tranquil scenes of Yellowstone as he had known it
before it became overcrowded. When a person such as Hayes had witnessed
Canyon, the lake, the geysers, and many scenes of grandeur in their earlier
solitude, he or she could never view them again surrounded by noisy crowds
of people with the same sense of awe.

Yellowstone's growing popularity was indeed a dichotomy for rangers and naturalists such as the Five Old Men. They knew firsthand of the problems facing Yellowstone. The large crowds at the museums and on nature walks were less rewarding than intimate groups. The Old Men had experienced the park when its beauty was unsullied by masses, when it was yet unburdened with restrictions and regulations brought on by later circumstances, and when one could visit the grand sights and still find quiet solace. Yet they were teachers by nature. They recognized the value of sharing the beauties of nature with the public. They relished each opportunity to take people into nature and teach them of the beauty to be found there. Beal wrote some years after his retirement, "As an educator, I cherished smaller, really interested groups. They are the ones who are thrilled to learn something about 'The Story Behind the Scenery.'"[4]

Achieving a balance between the two competing goals of interpretation and conservation was a paradox for which the Old Men never truly found an answer in their lifetimes. If there was a side to be taken, they were in favor of keeping the park limited and restricted in its use. It was not necessary to let everyone into the park at the same time who wanted to come. As Beal put it to his son, David, when asked to respond to the question of how the park's environment could be less impacted by visitation, "The key to impacting Park visitation is a better distribution of vacations. Public enjoyment did not warrant the spoiling of Yellowstone."[5]

Mission 66 targeted three major upgrades in national parks: roads and bridges, tourist and staff accommodations, and management and staff. Lemuel Garrison, who had helped develop the Mission 66 plan within the National Park Service, was the man chosen by "Conny" Wirth to implement it in Yellowstone Park. In November 1956, Garrison took over as superintendent of Yellowstone National Park and brought with him a plan for change.

PARK ROADS AND BRIDGES

By mid-1950 many of Yellowstone's roads and bridges were inadequate, dangerous, and crumbling. Nevertheless, Mission 66 planners were mindful of Hiram Chittenden's earlier warning not to extend road systems into pristine wilderness any more than necessary. There were no plans to create a scenic drive around Yellowstone Lake or along the primitive Lamar River drainage. Yellowstone's wilderness was sacrosanct.

However, some road sections desperately needed improvement. For instance, the highway at Virginia Cascades between Norris Junction and Canyon was originally built as a narrow, one-way road with blind curves and an unprotected, precipitous edge. This was turned into a one-way scenic drive while the main loop road was moved onto higher, safer ground. Similarly, a section known as the Firehole Canyon Drive between Old Faithful and Madison Junction was made into a scenic drive.

Improvements were also made to the section of road behind Mount Washburn between Dunraven Pass and Tower Fall. The old labyrinth of logs used by Chittenden to reinforce the road surface was replaced with steel girders. Roads were widened in places and resurfaced with higher grade asphalt, helping them endure the harsh winters and temperature fluctuations found in Yellowstone. Blind curves and dangerous hills were smoothed out. Turnouts at key locations were improved along with expanding the shoulders of the roads. Several bridges were widened, strengthened, or replaced, notably the Chittenden Bridge across the Yellowstone River just above the brink of the Upper Falls at Canyon.

The northern section of the original Chittenden Road to the summit of Mount Washburn was reopened and dedicated for visitor use.[6] The southern portion of the road from the summit to Dunraven Pass had so badly deteriorated and was so dangerous in places that it was never reopened and was made into a hiking trail. On July 1, 1959, Wayne Replogle gave the dedicatory address at ceremonies attended by four busloads of dignitaries and guests. The morning was cold and blustery on Washburn's summit; snow was driven almost horizontal by the bitter wind. However, as the buses arrived and the ceremony began, the sky opened up, the sun came out, and it was clear and beautiful, although cold. Replogle concluded his remarks with these words: "I like to think of Yellowstone as a great sanctuary, a place of retreat, a temple of the out-of-doors in the wild country. I like to think of Mt. Washburn as the dais of that temple—the throne from which one may gaze at rare beauty only given to those who choose to share the gift of God-given splendor. Let this almost incomprehensible and illimitable scene burn itself deep into the mind of every observer here today and he will long cherish the true wonder of this country's infinite…beauty."[7] At the conclusion of his remarks, the sky closed up, and it began to rain and snow again.[8]

The improvement to park roads and bridges was an important and useful safety feature for Yellowstone, especially considering the number of cars on the roads and the fact that at the time park bears were still begging on the roadsides and causing heavy traffic jams. Other changes, such as to accommodations and staff reorganization, came with less enthusiasm.

TOURIST ACCOMMODATIONS

Original plans for Mission 66 included upgrading and expanding existing tourist accommodations within the park. The then existing accommodations were considered to be inadequate and inefficient in meeting the demand of visitors. Campgrounds were to be built to double the camping spaces. Lodging facilities that had haphazardly sprung up around what were "sacred sites" around the Grand Loop were to be consolidated into "villages" away from these delicate natural areas. New villages were planned at three locations: Canyon, south of West Thumb, and the Firehole Basin.

The Canyon area was arguably the second most popular place in Yellowstone next to Old Faithful. Construction of buildings and tourist accommodations throughout the years had been haphazard. The old Canyon Lodge was on the east rim, the Grand Hotel was on the west rim, and the ranger station, campgrounds, amphitheater, and other structures were randomly spread about the canyon area.

The vision of Mission 66 planners was to consolidate and upgrade these amenities into a large village at Cascade Meadows, away from the canyon rim. The old lodge was removed from the east rim in 1956, and a modern one was constructed at the new village site, including modern cabins, laundry facilities, a cafeteria, general store, campgrounds, a service station, and a visitor center, all with little resemblance to the rustic Parkitecture of the past. What became known as "National Park Modern" began appearing on the scene. The modern architecture was designed for efficiency and had a commercial appearance created by the use of modern materials and open interiors. The new architecture symbolized a new era in the National Park Service.

The Grand Canyon Hotel, located on the hillside near Cascade Creek, remained a monstrosity of wilderness luxury.[9] Designed and built by Robert Reamer in the early 1900s (the grand opening was held on June 15, 1911), its red birch–paneled walls, polished oak floors, leather and wicker furniture, French plate-glass windows, porte cochere, hydraulic elevator, and grand ballroom were what Wayne Replogle, the head naturalist at Canyon at the time, described as an eyesore of extravagance and luxury that was completely out of touch with the rustic nature of the park. He often said to colleagues that he wished the darn thing would burn down.

The hotel was closed during the 1918 season because of World War I and again in 1943–44 during World War II. Little was done to maintain the hotel during these years. Weather, neglect, and the unstable foundation upon which the hotel rested began to cause structural failure.

The Grand Canyon Hotel opened in June 1911 and was closed in 1958. It burned to the ground in August 1960. (Photo by Frank J. Haynes in 1914; courtesy of the National Park Service, Yellowstone National Park, YELL 29647-3)

Original plans called for the retention of the famous Canyon Hotel, but two circumstances resulted in its ultimate demise. The first and most damaging circumstance was that it ultimately became unsafe for human occupancy. The hotel was built on an unstable hillside that caused the foundation to shift and the infrastructure to crumble.

The second circumstance was directly related to Mission 66. The new lodge and cabins built in the new Canyon Village during the 1950s created a need for additional revenue to pay for their construction. The hotel was stealing from that revenue. Thus, priority was shifted to filling the lodge and cabins with visitors at the expense of the hotel. These two considerations caused the park to permanently close the Canyon Hotel at the end of the 1958 season, and bids for its demolition were received the following year.

On August 17, 1959, the Madison River Canyon earthquake struck, and many people thought that the quake was the reason for the hotel's closure, but the decision to close the hotel had been made prior to that event. By 1957–58, after an assessment by engineers proved the structure to be unsafe, the decision was made to demolish the hotel, and it was closed after the 1958 season.

Demolition began in 1960. Late one evening in August of that year, Replogle got his wish. A fire of unknown origin broke out in the hotel, and

it burned to the ground. The night that it burned was bitter, with temperatures around 22 degrees Fahrenheit. Perhaps as just reward for his disparaging
remarks about the hotel, Replogle was called out of his warm bed at midnight to direct traffic along the highway near the fire. Retribution or not,
Replogle became the brunt of many jokes by his colleagues that he had
started the fire himself.[10]

The problem at West Thumb was different from that at Canyon. Tourist
accommodations at Thumb became so congested about the delicate hot
spring and mud basins that the basins were becoming worn down and endangered. In 1955 an area two miles south of West Thumb was designated as the
location for a new village that would replace West Thumb. First named
Thumb Bay, the complex eventually was given the name Grant Village in
honor of Ulysses S. Grant, hero of the Civil War and eighteenth president of
the United States. The village was to be done by 1966 in celebration of the
ending of Mission 66. Parts were completed as early as 1961, but various
phases of building were not completed until about 1980. Grant Village
became a large, modern complex with a marina, campgrounds, a store, a visitor's center, and more on the shore of Yellowstone Lake.

Meanwhile, a village in the area of the Lower Geyser Basin was on the
planning boards to remove tourist congestion around Old Faithful and restore
it to a more natural appearance. Originally to be named "Wonderland," it was
eventually named "Firehole Village," and original plans called for the demolition of the famous Old Faithful Inn and Lodge. The very name suggested
some type of Disneyland theme park. Fortunately, better thinking prevailed,
and the plans for the village were scrapped about 1964.

CAMPGROUNDS AND OTHER ACCOMMODATIONS

Plans for increased campgrounds and picnic areas were pursued at Fishing
Bridge, Grant Village, Canyon, Indian Creek, and Madison Junction. A
marina, campground, and amphitheater were built at Bridge Bay just south
of Lake Village, not far from the Natural Bridge. A small primitive camp
was also opened at Pelican Creek in 1959. Lowell Biddulph lived close to
this camp and noted that it had frequent problems with bears, as it was in
close proximity to prime grizzly bear habitat.

One summer a sow grizzly with cub came into the camp and terrorized
tourists with its destructive forays. Rangers trapped the sow and captured the
cub. Once the bear was trapped, tourists in the camp fomented its rage by
their senseless harassment, so much so that it began to rip the steel brackets

out of their frame in the trap door. Campers fled, terrorized by the possibility of the fearsome bear freeing itself and taking revenge upon them. Rangers were forced to shoot the bear while it was yet inside the trap. This grizzly was so large that it took a winch to remove its body from the trap. The camp closed soon after that. Days later, Biddulph inspected the empty campground and found that the in-ground garbage cans had become entrapments for chipmunks. Biddulph rescued sixteen chipmunks that nearly perished and removed the bodies of several others for which rescue came too late. The chipmunk community in that vicinity had come dangerously close to being eradicated.

MANAGEMENT AND STAFF REORGANIZATION

Yellowstone experienced two different management structures through the decades of the 1900s. Horace Albright, who became superintendent in 1919, created three ranger districts: North, South, and West. Each district was supervised by an assistant to the chief ranger. Major stations within each district were under the charge of a first-class ranger who answered to the assistant. Many of the initial district and station leaders were seasoned men of the army era in Yellowstone, such as Harry Trischman, Edward "Ted" Ogston, Charles J. "White Mountain" Smith, James P. Brooks, and Harry J. Liek.

In the 1930s, the three-district structure was expanded into nine districts that were more closely identified with important geographic areas of the park: Mammoth, Tower Fall, Lamar River, West Yellowstone, Old Faithful, Canyon, Lake, Bechler (southwest corner of Yellowstone), and Snake River (South Entrance). Each district was supervised by a district ranger. This structure remained until the advent of Mission 66.

Despite its heavier burden placed upon the park's chief administrators, the nine-district organization of the 1930s and '40s provided a more intimate relationship between line personnel and chief park officials. Leadership styles played a role in morale. The chiefs were frequently out of their offices and visible in the various districts. They showed up at museums, occasionally on a nature walk or auto caravan, and often at nightly campfire lectures. The men enjoyed a close and direct camaraderie with their bosses and felt that their opinions were solicited and valued.

While Max Bauer served as chief park naturalist (1932–46), he and his wife sponsored annual picnics for the naturalist families throughout the park. Ruth Biddulph said that her husband had tremendous respect for Dr. Bauer

Group photo of ranger naturalists and families taken July 11, 1951. All Five Old Men families are represented. (Photo by Verde Watson; courtesy of L. G. Biddulph)

and learned much about Yellowstone geology from him. Beal summed up Bauer's leadership style: "He was a scholar and a gentleman. He was always helpful and gracious. He solicited questions and gave personal encouragement. He expected worthy efforts and received good results. He made suggestions when they were needed and offered compliments if indicated. His authority was tempered by sensitivity."[11]

David Condon, who succeeded Bauer as chief park naturalist until 1959, when he was transferred to Great Smoky Mountains National Park, continued these family events. Condon had a special talent for developing rapport with his naturalists, and he gave special attention to his Five Old Men by giving them special assignments within their areas of expertise. He personally encouraged Replogle to explore the Bannock Indian Trail, George Marler to spend a winter at Old Faithful and publish his works on geysers, and Beal to research and write on the human history of Yellowstone Park.

The personnel working in Yellowstone during this era enjoyed a unique spirit of friendship with each other. Naturalist and ranger families became close-knit and formed friendships that lasted lifetimes. No matter where they worked in Yellowstone, from top to bottom, they were one large family enjoying a once-in-a-lifetime experience living in Yellowstone.

The restructuring of the park management for purposes of greater efficiency brought about by Mission 66 ultimately changed the spirit that had existed among the personnel. In place of the flat management structure, Garrison created a deeper layered organization along functional lines. Three districts in the North, South, and West were re-created, reminiscent of the old 1920s but with major differences. A district manager was placed in charge of each district with a district ranger to oversee protection and enforcement and a district naturalist to administer interpretive services.

Greater autonomy and increased authority were given to new district managers. As Garrison described it, each district became a miniature park in itself. District managers had broad operational and administrative control to manage the protection, interpretation, maintenance, budget, and manpower within their districts. The park superintendent administered park-wide policies through a chief park ranger, chief park naturalist, and a chief park engineer, each of whom administered policies and procedures through their counterparts at the district level.

Until permanent men could be identified and transferred in to fill the newly established district naturalist positions, three seasonal naturalists were assigned as acting district naturalists. Wayne Replogle was acting district naturalist in the North District, Lowell Biddulph in the South District, and Bud Lystrup in the West. They filled these positions for three or four seasons and then reverted to assistant district naturalists when permanent men took over.

Garrison felt that the system worked well by putting the decision making where the problems were. There were trade-offs, though. What the Mission 66 three-district structure enhanced in efficiency, it sacrificed in intimacy. Naturalists and rangers who had enjoyed a park-wide brother-sisterhood found themselves isolated into districts with little or no interaction. They felt compartmentalized and muffled under layers of administration. Their input regarding park-wide issues was unsolicited. The park took on an efficient and bureaucratic aura; it was not an easy change to embrace for those who were used to Old Yellowstone.

About the time Garrison was transferred out of Yellowstone in 1963, the management structure that he had put in place was abolished for reasons that remained unclear to him, other than that the regional director told him it was heavy on overhead. It appears that the former director of national parks, Horace Albright, felt the same way. At a meeting with Merrill Beal on August 24, 1962, at Madison Junction, he called the three-district plan of administration an example of "bureaucratic proliferation and extravagance."[12] Despite the abolishment of Garrison's organization at the end of Mission 66, the spirit that existed in the park during the 1930s and '40s was gone, never to return.

STRUCTURES AND EMPLOYEE HOUSING

Director Wirth and his staff were focused on efficiency, modernity, and cost-effectiveness rather than preserving the past when it came to structures. Mission 66 was an era of tearing down the old to make way for the new.[13] Not everything went to the scrap yard. Some effort was made to preserve important historical structures, but some also perished. The more important ones that could not be preserved were to be memorialized with historical markers.

Many improvements in housing were needed, but they came with melancholy to the Old Men, because change meant the loss of a beautiful, rustic way of living and the advent of a new and unwelcome age of modernity and efficiency. At Madison Junction an apartment building was built to house five families, and another building was designed for district offices and a dormitory for other workers. Water and sewage resources were installed, and the Montana Power Company connected all improvements with underground lines. A newer, more modern amphitheater replaced the small, intimate one. Restrooms and a picnic area were completed. The little ranger cottage that had been home to Bud and Betty Lystrup, Wayne and Marian Replogle, and Sam and Bessy Beal through the years was razed. Beal pled to spare it, but to no avail. "We almost wept when it was demolished," Beal noted.[14]

The cottage that the Biddulphs occupied for twenty-five years at Fishing Bridge was fully renovated. Ruth Biddulph wrote in her journal the summer of 1963: "If our lives have changed, so also has the cottage. A year ago it was completely remodeled and modernized. The huge old black woodstove that we used to huddle around and keep stoked with logs of pinewood on rainy days like today is a thing of the past. Gleaming white electric stove, water heater, refrigerator, modern sink and cupboards, have transformed the frontier cottage to urban convenience. Clean, polished linoleum hides the cold, gritty cement floors."[15]

Wayne Replogle expressed his and Marian's feelings when they had to relinquish their little primitive cabin and move into a modern apartment: "I loved this way of living, as did my wife who...had never experienced living like that. And I've never found anyone in my life that loved and enjoyed living under those circumstances as I did other than my wife Marian. She, in all those years, never complained one word about anything, and the year that we were forced to live in the apartment, I well remember when we arrived there and went into the apartment, she sat down and cried because she wanted so much to live in the little old cabin."[16]

THE ADVENT OF VISITOR CENTERS

The park was moving decisively away from formal interpretation toward a more efficient way of disseminating information. The new age introduced by Mission 66 demanded new centers of information, not museums of interpretation. The visitor center in Yellowstone became the icon of the post–Mission 66 era, just as the trailside museum had been for the era of interpretation. All aspects of tourist support and control were consolidated under one roof: information center, ranger station, administrative offices, and comfort stations. Director Wirth settled on the term *visitor center* to describe the evolution toward modernization and efficiency that he sought.

Visitor centers were built at Grant Village, Old Faithful, and Canyon to augment and, in the case at Old Faithful, to replace the interpretive trailside museums. These modern centers were outfitted with the latest technology to effectively and efficiently disseminate information to visitors by movies, sound bites, and electronically animated displays. The Old Faithful trailside museum was demolished in 1973 to make a place for the new visitor center. In 2006 the visitor center was removed and replaced with a larger and better-equipped visitor education center with an auditorium where films, presentations, and ranger-naturalist lectures are presented on Yellowstone. The visitor center at Canyon was later renovated and expanded into a visitor education center similar to the one at Old Faithful.

The original plan was to also demolish the Madison Museum and build a visitor center in its stead. Beal petitioned to save the museum in a memo to park headquarters dated June 15, 1963: "The consensus of opinions expressed here would support the preservation of the building. I should like to suggest that the museum might be converted into a Park Art Gallery. It has admirable nucleus in the 'Founding Fathers Campfire' picture…It would appear that such a gallery could be administered as an adjunctive unit to a new center with ease and satisfaction to all concerned."[17]

The Madison Museum was saved and in July 1972 was dedicated as an "Explorer's Museum." A wayside exhibit just outside the museum commemorates the "campfire story," and a commemorative plaque honors Stephen T. Mather, the first director of the National Park Service. As Beal suggested, the museum housed the Arts Yellowstone Program for a time, and for some years it sat abandoned. In 1995 it became an information station with a small bookstore operated by the Yellowstone Association. The three remaining trailside museums in Yellowstone are memorials to the era of interpretation and education that is now a part of Yellowstone history. Each is listed on the National Register of Historic Places, and together they are a National Historic Landmark.

CHANGES TO INTERPRETATION

Burgeoning crowds, rising costs, and new technology inevitably changed how the National Parks viewed interpretive services. Increasing numbers of tourists overwhelmed the intimate teacher-student methods of interpretation of the past. Nature walks, campfire programs, and game stalks became unwieldy, although Merrill Beal said that he handled one-hundred-person geyser walks with no difficulty. Tourists wanted faster service and became increasingly impatient with slow-moving campfire lectures and nature walks. Cost was also a factor. Old methods of interpretation required more ranger naturalists if the park was to keep up with the growing crowds, and the Park Service was mandated to find more cost-effective ways of servicing tourists.

Park leaders embraced scientific research in Yellowstone and increasingly turned to professional field scientists to provide information about Yellowstone and its natural wonders. A flood of new information was beginning to flow, and tourists were better informed than earlier generations. New technology revolutionized the way this information was disseminated. The old methods of walks, talks, and stalks were viewed as too inefficient and not nearly as captivating as were film documentaries and electronic presentations.

These demands caused a shift to occur in national park philosophy regarding interpretation. It remained the politically correct term in park parlance into the 1980s as "an educational activity which aims to reveal meanings and relationships through the use of original objects, by first-hand experience, and by illustrative media, rather than simply to communicate factual information."[18] However, the methodology necessarily shifted from ranger-naturalist guided tours and lectures to technological information and self-discovery.

Yellowstone had in fact become the roofless museum foreseen by Herman Bumpus that now needed no artificial labels. Yellowstone was the ultimate living museum and the proliferation of information helped tourists become better informed and more inclined to get out into it on their own terms. Visitors were invited to experience nature for themselves with a good pair of binoculars rather than to see it through the eyes, ears, and mouth of a ranger naturalist. Research and photographic technology brought remarkable footage of wildlife and geology to the public's fingertips that they could not hope to obtain on their own or, for that matter, on a nature walk or game stalk.

George Marler, Bud Lystrup, and Sam Beal, among others, were assigned in the mid-1950s to develop and lay out self-guided tours at Fountain Paint Pot and a written guide to the Upper and Lower Geyser Basins, including a map and explanation of geology. They helped to create signs and information placards to be placed along the boardwalks in the geyser basins at strategic positions and foldout maps to guide the visitors from station to station.

Marler helped to write a twenty-three-page brochure published by the US Department of Interior Geologic Survey called *Geysers*. This and other brochures helped provide interpretive literature about geysers and hot springs to be used in conjunction with visitor centers and self-guided tours. Biddulph and Replogle were similarly involved in their districts, helping to prepare information signs and laying out self-guided walks to points of interest around Canyon, Mud Volcano, and the Yellowstone Lake area. Biddulph also laid out hiking trails in the South District.

Information and technology came at the expense of personal communication and intimate interaction. In the face of these technological changes, the Old Men remained nostalgic for the old days when nature walks and campfire programs were small, intimate settings. In July 1963, Bud Lystrup met with Howard Stagnel, the chief naturalist of the Division of Natural History within the Department of the Interior, who visited Yellowstone and attended Lystrup's campfire lecture. For two hours Bud stumped his opinions with Stagnel, expressing his feelings about the loss of contact with visitors. Lystrup argued that visitors needed to receive a stimulating experience instead of a stilted lecture. The true heart of the Yellowstone experience, in Bud's view, was the intimacy and solitude that a visitor experienced, and the development of friendships that occurred during campfire lectures and in other intimate settings. Lystrup encouraged Stagnel to continue personalized lectures and singing that brought a spirit of unity and friendship to those who came to Yellowstone from all over the world.[19] However, the die was cast and change inevitable.

THE DEMISE OF MISSION 66

As villages, campgrounds, and other improvements were being developed, attitudes about expansion began to shift. The prevailing attitude had initially been that every tourist who wanted to visit Yellowstone should be allowed to do so and be guaranteed a place to stay. The insatiable growing demand for accommodations convinced Park Superintendent Garrison that to continue on course would ultimately result in a ring of campgrounds stretching around Yellowstone Lake from Mary Bay to Grant Village, a distance of thirty-three miles and that they would be full every night. It seemed apparent to Garrison that the balance between use and preservation was being tipped too heavily toward the side of use, and the imbalance would seriously jeopardize the preservation of Yellowstone's priceless solidarity.[20]

In the persistent conflict between nature and pleasure, nature was about to win a major victory or at least a compromise. The Park Service and Yellowstone administration began to revamp their plans for development. Garrison and his staff continued with the building of Canyon and Grant Villages, road improvement, and staff accommodations. However, they scratched plans to place a campground in Hayden Valley, and they decided not to expand further campgrounds and, in fact, eliminated some.

Campgrounds in key locations were closed because they were intrusive to bears and other wild animals. The large campgrounds at Fishing Bridge and West Thumb were closed, and the cabins behind Hamilton Store were removed along with other amenities. A modern RV trailer park was developed in the forest on the north side of the road to the East Entrance. The small campground on the east side of Pelican Creek was also closed.

The decision to not increase the numbers of campgrounds and other tourist accommodations was fortunate, for which the Old Men were grateful, as it would have returned the park to a human playground instead of leaving it a natural preserve. The elimination of existing and planned public camping returned important habitat to the bears and other animals. The restriction of powerboats to the southern reaches of Yellowstone Lake protected the fragile beach lines and nesting grounds of water fowl. The eventual elimination of bear feeding and access to human garbage allowed the black and grizzly bears to readapt to their natural habitat, thus saving them from extinction in the park. These were all wins in the eyes of the Old Men.

Some of Mission 66's achievements were positive. The improvement of roads without invading primitive areas allowed a safer and smoother flow of visitors along Yellowstone's byways. Improved housing for employees was for the most part needed and appreciated. Yet it also facilitated the end of a treasured way of life for the Old Men that would never return.

In August 1964, Mission 66 passed quietly from the Yellowstone scene when the secretary of the interior defined "the road to the future," de-emphasizing construction and emphasizing "preserving scenic and scientific grandeur of our Nation."[21] Despite the changes that came to Old Yellowstone, many things did not change, as noted by Ruth Biddulph: "The beautiful lake is the same—the lake and the sky, the mountains and the Lodgepoles, the sense of peace and quiet and serenity and well-being; these priceless gifts remain here and will always be associated with this spot for us."[22]

Chapter 22

Ambassadors of Yellowstone

By the summer following the 1959 earthquake, all of the Old Men were in major leadership positions within the park. Their accumulated over 139 summers of service made them extraordinary ambassadors of Yellowstone and provided opportunities for them to give back some of the rich rewards they had received from the Grand Old Park. Perhaps recognizing that their time in Yellowstone was drawing to a close, park administrators took advantage of their knowledge and experience before it was gone.

VIP TOURS IN YELLOWSTONE

The Five Old Men were frequently called upon to give tours around the park to visiting special interest groups and VIPs. These men were well acquainted with the major features of Yellowstone and could speak about them in an authoritative and interesting manner. The men enjoyed giving tours, as it gave them an opportunity to speak with large groups of people and share with them the special aspects of Yellowstone. Intimate nature walks were the preferred genre for most, Replogle being perhaps the exception (he was a showman with a flair for being in the public eye), but the Old Men had fun with the groups and got them to loosen up and taste of the spirit of friendship that Yellowstone offered.

The Seattle World's Fair in 1962 brought large groups of world travelers to Yellowstone that summer. The administration provided bus tours for many of these groups, and the Old Men helped escort these groups around the park. That summer three busloads of representatives from the International

Foresters visited Yellowstone in conjunction with their world conference. Fifty-five nations were represented in the tour through the park.

Replogle helped with the tours along the northern loop of the park, and the other Old Men helped out in their districts. Beal was asked to be a commentator on one of the buses and to make appropriate comments concerning the principal features along the lower loop road of Yellowstone. All of the visitors on the bus had some grasp of English, and Beal was instructed to speak slowly and loudly and to point and gesticulate freely.

Things went pretty well until bears were spotted. The grandeur of the lake and the canyon were all appreciated, but bears really excited the visitors. As the bus was leaving West Thumb headed for Old Faithful, several black bears were positioned along the highway, so Beal focused his comments mostly on them, as did the bus driver. Beal soon discovered that the driver had given each bear the name and identity of rangers and ranger naturalists serving at the time at Old Faithful. "He described Dick, Bud, Sam, George, and so-forth. Finally, he said, 'Now Millie is coming up.' Mildred Ericson was our only female naturalist. I said, 'Oh, listen, you can't tell the males from the females.' He said, 'Yes, I can.' I said, 'Tell me how.' 'Why' said he, 'I watch which can they come out of!'"[1]

FAMOUS PERSONALITIES

Wayne Replogle excelled at public relations, and he was called upon in this regard especially in his final years as an assistant to the assistant park superintendent. At various times in his career, he personally escorted through "his park," as he called it, well-known personalities such as Lily Pons, Will Rogers, Gary Cooper, ZaSu Pitts, Edgar Bergen, Wallace Beery, Crown Prince Frederick of Germany, Madame Indira Gandi of India, Vice President Hubert Humphrey's sister, and the governors of at least five states. In 1976 Replogle hosted President Gerald R. Ford, who shared a tuna fish sandwich with him at Canyon as they reminisced on their ranger service together in Yellowstone forty years before.

In 1939 a famous personality from France named Lily Pons and her husband toured Yellowstone. Replogle did much of the VIP touring for Pons. She fell in love with the delicate purple harebell flower that she saw blooming all over the park, and she asked Replogle if she could pick a bouquet. Despite the prohibition of picking flowers, Replogle decided to please her by picking a bouquet himself and grandly presenting them to her at her departure from the park. "I bowed and scraped and waved to her goodbye."[2]

President Gerald R. Ford visits with Wayne Replogle and park staff at Canyon, August 30, 1976. (Photo by Jack Richard, used with permission of Buffalo Bill Historical Center, Cody, Wyoming, USA, PN.89.74.13104.77)

Within two weeks, a letter arrived from Lily Pons with a beautiful hare-bell glued to its page. Replogle described the letter as "warm and friendly," something he would have enjoyed more had he not been married. He knew that his wife of two years would not appreciate such a letter, so he kept it a secret from Marian, only to receive another and another in the weeks to come, each warmer than the last. By now he was frantic that Marian would find out, and he could not, for the life of him, figure out how to keep the cat from coming out of the bag.

Then one day, after reading the latest love letter from Pons, he turned it over and found written on the back: "How do you like my Lilly Pond love letters?" It was signed Marian. She had been writing the letters all along, and when it all came out in the wash, Replogle discovered that Marian had been perched on a rock at a distance, watching the bowing and scraping incident through a pair of binoculars.

No group was too small or insignificant for Bud Lystrup, who hosted everything from VIPs and special educational groups to Boy Scout troops. Lystrup was pressed into service by his leaders because of his long service in the park and encyclopedic knowledge of nature.

One summer George Marler and Wayne Replogle were assigned to escort a noted scientist from India through Yellowstone's thermal geyser basins. They arrived at Norris Geyser Basin in a government truck that Marler was driving. He parked the old truck just off the main road on the hillside, and the two naturalists and the scientist walked down the hill about a hundred feet to a spot not too far from the Valentine Geyser and the Black Growler. Marler and Replogle were facing downhill, and the scientist was facing uphill toward the road.

All of a sudden the Indian threw his arms in the air and shouted, "Cluck cum, Cluck cum." Marler and Replogle turned around, wondering what was exciting the man, only to see the old pickup truck coming rolling down the hillside toward them; over the barrier it jumped and plunged into a small hot pot just above where the men stood. George had forgotten to set the brakes, and they spent the rest of the day getting the truck out of the mess.[3]

WILDERNESS TALKS

For several years, the Trail Riders of the Wilderness, an affiliate of the American Forestry Association and a forest conservation group active in support of Yellowstone since 1882, took horseback trips into the southern wilderness area of Yellowstone.[4] The purpose of these horseback trips was to expose members, many of whom came from the larger cities of the East, to the wonders of this great park. Lowell Biddulph was asked to meet these groups of conservationists at Heart Lake near the base of Mount Sheridan and provide nature hikes and campfire talks on various aspects of history, flora, and fauna of the park. The trip normally included an ascent of Mount Sheridan.

This was a choice assignment for Biddulph. Deep wilderness was his preferred setting. His ability to communicate natural beauty to his listeners was not lost on James S. Eddy, the president of the Trail Riders, who praised Biddulph for his knowledge and skill in presenting his material. In his letter to the secretary of the Department of the Interior, Eddy noted that Biddulph's lectures were "among the highlights of his visit to Yellowstone."[5]

HISTORICAL PERSONALITIES

The era of the Old Men was not far removed from the days of exploration and discovery. Many visitors to Yellowstone in those days had a close association with the history of the park. Meeting and hearing personal accounts of Old Yellowstone were choice experiences for these men. Merrill Beal recorded some of these people he met at the Madison Museum:

George Langford: "On July 28, 1946, George Langford, a nephew of Nathaniel P. Langford [a prominent member of the Washburn Expedition of

1870], gave me two guns for the museum. They were carried by his uncle during the 1870 tour of discovery. We removed his uncle's saddle from the showcase, placed him astride, and took his picture."

Fred Meek: "When Fred Meek, a grandson of Joe Meek, came, I introduced him to a group and he talked about his grandfather. We exchanged books and correspondence."[6]

George F. Cowan Jr.: "I had an interesting dialogue with George F. Cowan, Jr. of Spokane concerning his father's 'days of peril,' when he was taken hostage by Nez Perce Indians. He received several wounds, but he escaped and survived great hardship in the Yellowstone wilderness."

Cowan must be viewed as one of the most bedeviled yet enduring men in Yellowstone history with the exception of Truman Everts. Shot three times by the Indians and left for dead, Cowan survived and crawled on hands and knees three days and nine miles down Nez Perce Creek, avoiding close calls with Indians serving as the rear guard for Joseph's band, and without food. He made a small fire to warm himself, but desperately tired, he fell asleep, only to awaken to discover that the dried moss upon which he lay had caught fire and he was severely burned. The next day, he was discovered by General Howard's scouts, placed in a wagon, and carried along with the column until they reached Bottler's ranch, just north of the park.

Meanwhile, Cowan's wife returned home, thinking her husband was dead. When the news of his survival reached her, she hastened to his side. One might think that no man should have to endure more. Not so! On the wagon trip home, while he lay on heavy blankets in the wagon bed, the neck yoke broke, the horses ran away, and the wagon turned over on the steep mountain road. Once again he cheated death, thanks to the insulating effects of the heavy blankets upon which he lay.

An ambulance wagon was dispatched from Fort Ellis, and the Cowans eventually arrived safely in Bozeman. He was put to bed in a hotel, where friends and others rushed to greet and congratulate him on his survival. So many people sat on his bed that it gave way and crashed in a wreck on the floor. "The proprietor jokingly threatened to expel the wounded man, as he could not afford to have such a Jonah on the premises."

Among his callers was an importunate minister who, after tiring Cowan with his overzealous questioning, asked, "Mr. Cowan, during all this…did you not frequently think of your God?" Cowan answered, to his admitted future regret, "Not a d–n sight. I had too many other things to think of."[7]

Floyd Bottler: The son of one of the famous Bottler brothers, who owned and operated Bottler's ranch north of Yellowstone Park, visited the

Madison Museum on August 15, 1952. He identified some chairs on display in the museum made by his father and corrected the information on the sign that said the chairs were made of willow. They, in fact, were made of birch.

White Mountain Smith: "[Charles J. Smith] drove stage and delivered mail [in the park] between 1908 and 1916. Later he served as a park ranger, patrolman, and assistant to the chief ranger. He was the superintendent at Petrified Forest National Monument, Grand Teton, Zion and Bryce Canyon National Parks."

Johnny Hepburn: "Johnny Hepburn had a home for fifty years down the Yellowstone River from the park. We had a pleasant visit with him, and learned about his activity as pilot on the steamboat 'Zillah.'[8] Hepburn said that he once met Beaver Dick [Richard Leigh], a famous old-time trapper in the Snake River area, and his squaw fixed a meal for him."

Beal met other men. C. C. Broadwater witnessed the eruption of Excelsior Geyser in the summer of 1890, its last known eruption at that time.[9] Frank H. Dashback was one of the soldiers stationed in Yellowstone; later, he served as a patrolman during 1902 to 1905 at a salary of thirteen dollars per month. W. W. Lockard of Rawlins, Wyoming, was a soldier in the park, a member of Troop D, Third Regiment, Sixth Cavalry. He was acquainted with Buffalo Jones, who had lived in a small cabin about one mile south of Mammoth, near the Hoodoos.[10] He said Jones used to rope bears and mountain lions for zoos, and he also roped bison calves for roundup. Another unnamed old gentleman told Beal that he had been a cowboy in Buffalo Bill Cody's Wild West show and related some of his experiences.

Wayne Replogle recorded some of the famous historical personalities that he had met in the park:

William H. Jackson: In 1931 he met the famous photographer who accompanied the Hayden Survey Party in 1871 and '72 into Yellowstone and took many of the first famous photos of the park.

Hiram Chittenden Jr.: In 1936 Replogle met Hiram Martin Chittenden Jr., the son of Hiram Chittenden, the famous army captain who planned and constructed the Grand Loop road system in Yellowstone.

Will Rogers: of Rogers Replogle said:

Will Rogers and I had become real good friends, especially on his trip to Yellowstone . . . when he was shooting the movie called "Mr. Skitch." The Gibbon Falls area was the scene of a little love tryst between a young man and a young lady who went swimming in the pool at the

A tallyho carriage on display at Mammoth Hot Springs was a famous touring coach in the 1800s. (Courtesy of L. G. Biddulph)

base of the falls. When one looks down at the pool now, he is aware of the fact that it is completely full of debris and rocks, but at that time, prior to 1932, and a few years afterwards, before some rocks were rolled in there by nature, this was a rather interesting swimming hole. I was on the cone [Old Faithful] the morning in August 1931 when Frank Sartino, the famous musician, walked out to me and said that Will Rogers had just been killed in a plane crash at Barrows, Alaska.[11]

Truman C. Everts Jr.: On August 15, 1961, Replogle and Aubrey Haines (park historian) met with the son of Truman C. Everts, who, of course, had been a member of the Washburn-Langford-Doane Expedition of 1870. He became separated from his party on the southeast part of Yellowstone Park and was lost and alone in the wilderness for thirty-seven days before he was found on a cold October day, nearly dead.

PUBLICATIONS

As discussed in prior chapters, Merrill Beal, Wayne Replogle, and George Marler made important written contributions to Yellowstone Park. In 1968 Lystrup also published two volumes: *Shavings Off the Stick: True Stories of Yellowstone Park Told by a Veteran Ranger* and *Hamilton's Guide to Yellow-*

stone National Park. A later version of the latter was coauthored by Alan W. Cundall.

Lowell Biddulph wrote no books or major articles of his own about Yellowstone. He said that he was too busy enjoying himself. Biddulph's interest was not the written word. He left that to his wife, Ruth. The power of his expression came in more intimate settings while on nature walks and wilderness treks. However, he collaborated with authors on books. In 1970, one hundred years after the Washburn Expedition of Yellowstone, Orrin H. Bonney and Lorraine Bonney published the three-volume *Battle Drums and Geysers.* These volumes provide an interesting look at the history of the exploration of Yellowstone Park and surrounding areas through the writings and life of Lieutenant Gustavus Cheyney Doane, a military officer and member of the famous Washburn-Langford-Doane Expedition of 1870.[12] At the request of Bonney, Biddulph read and critiqued their manuscript for the portion dealing with the discovery and exploration of the Mud Volcano, of which Biddulph was as knowledgeable as anyone of his day.

MEDIA PRODUCTIONS

Yellowstone Park was a popular place for documentaries and educational films. As an assistant to the park superintendent, Replogle was often given this type of assignment. In 1962 Replogle assisted the New York Zoological Society in making a movie called *A Safari in Yellowstone,* about a ranger who takes an African boy through Yellowstone. The boy's name was "Onesmo Mayoi." The producer wanted shots of a bald eagle while they were down in the Madison River area. Luckily, Replogle was able to spot a bald eagle sitting in a tree in the Madison River meadows, and the eagle sat quietly long enough for the crew to film it.

In 1964 *National Geographic Magazine* came to Yellowstone to film, and Replogle was assigned to assist them in finding good places to photograph. He also assisted the British Broadcasting Corporation in shooting a series of Yellowstone scenes and animals for a thirteen-minute television show on BBC-TV that winter.[13]

Centron Corporation made five sound filmstrips called *Learning from Yellowstone National Park* designed for junior and senior high school classes in geography, botany, science, history, and geology. Again, Replogle was the go-to man.

He also completed personal slide sets for use by Yellowstone National Park that included a one-hundred-slide set on flowers of the North District, a forty-eight-slide set for narration on the Grand Canyon, and a ninety-set-slide set on Mission 66. He also made a series of seventeen oral tapes called *A Mile-by-Mile History of the Grand Loop* that, despite the rather personal narrative style, provide interesting insight to some of Old Yellowstone.

PUBLIC-ISSUE CAMPAIGNS

Challenging issues arose in Yellowstone during the Mission 66 era. Superintendent Lemuel Garrison was forced to make difficult decisions regarding park management; some were not well received by the public. Some key issues of the day were campground and facility development, the removal of black bears from the highways and campgrounds, returning prime habitat to grizzly bears, the restrictions on boating on Yellowstone Lake, and the management of the northern elk herd. Men such as Merrill Beal helped promote understanding and consensus with outlying communities on some of these issues.

George Marler promoted the cause of the trumpeter and whistler swans that were on the endangered species list. Marler wrote an article addressing the plight of these beautiful birds entitled "Is the Trumpeter Swan to Remain Only a Refuge Bird?"[14] His article suggested legislation and other restrictions to allow the swan to successfully breed outside of Yellowstone and enable their numbers to be rejuvenated. His conservation work helped to restrict hunting areas and raise people's collective awareness of the plight of the swan. Today, the trumpeter and whistler swans are still found in Yellowstone Park during the summer seasons, in part because men like Marler spoke up.

High-powered motorboats disturbed the primitive areas of Yellowstone Lake. Their noisy motors interfered with the solitude of the wilderness. Their wakes washed onto the low-lying Molly and Peale Islands, threatening the welfare of birds that nested there. It was feared that boaters would begin to trash the pristine beaches and the primitive area.

To protect these pristine areas, the park administration proposed a zoning plan for Yellowstone Lake that imposed speed limits on boats and restricted them from certain parts of the lake. Enough opposition was fueled by special interest groups and biased newspaper articles to force the initiation of a public relations program.

Oscar Dick, the West District manager, asked Merrill Beal, a resident of the Upper Snake River Valley in Idaho and a prominent historian, to visit several of the communities in the Upper Snake River Valley where much of the opposition originated. Beal was a debater possessed with a passion for public affairs. He met with constituencies and explained the rationale behind the need for restrictions. As a result of such efforts, the zoning plan was unanimously accepted and placed into operation. Garrison's memo of appreciation follows: "Sam—I appreciate that most of the favorable showing at IF [Idaho Falls, Idaho] was due to your personal interest. Thanks very Much! This kind of help is surely loyal to the highest degree and Yellowstone will be better forever for your own dedicated service."[15]

The northern elk herd of Yellowstone was a contentious issue for several years because of biological studies that suggested that elk were stripping the park of its range resources, thus causing a danger of soil erosion. Not all scientists or conservationists accepted the proposition that the range was being significantly defoliated. In fact, some studies suggested that no evidence existed to support such a view or that it was necessary to interfere with the number of elk in the park. Advocates of natural ecology insisted that nature will achieve balance without man's interference, provided that man does not act in a manner that seriously threatens nature's ability to regulate.

Be that as it may, park officials pursued solutions to reduce the number of animals. They tried trapping and shipping elk outside of Yellowstone to zoos and other locales, but it was woefully inadequate and very inefficient. Outright slaughter of thousands of elk during the winter months to prevent them from starving only fueled the ire of animal rights activists. Political pressure was brought to bear by hunters to open Yellowstone to public hunting to help reduce the large numbers of animals. Park administrators were opposed to this proposal and took steps to defeat it as an option.

Beal was called upon again to help. On December 11, 1962, he received a rush request from Chief Park Naturalist John Good to obtain letters in support of the park elk reduction policy for the hearing being held in Bozeman, Montana, the following week. Beal secured many letters and a petition in time for the meeting. Good responded, "Thanks for the yeoman's service on the elk hearing. Your speedy action was very helpful to the cause. The hearing established definitely that there was no interest in opening Yellowstone to public hunting."[16]

LECTURES AND TALKS

The Old Men were called upon to give talks and other formal presentations on Yellowstone topics related to their areas of expertise. Biddulph, who both studied and taught Yellowstone geology at the college level, was invited by a naturalist colleague, Samuel Ellison, to teach for the 1957–58 school year at the University of Texas at Austin on the subject of Rocky Mountain and Yellowstone geology.[17] For many years, Biddulph was asked to lecture to various groups in Idaho, Montana, and Wyoming on Yellowstone geology and the cause and effects of the 1959 earthquake. Marler and Lystrup were also asked to give lectures to various groups in Montana, Wyoming, and Idaho. Beal's expertise in regional history, as well as his university teaching and publications, offered him ample opportunity to address public gatherings on topics related to Yellowstone.

LEADERSHIP ROLES

Studies of the history of Yellowstone's interpretive programs suggest that ranger naturalists were out of the administrative mainstream and received few opportunities for middle- and high-level park management.[18] Most ranger naturalists of the era were seasonal, making them ineligible for permanent positions. The position of district naturalist was a career position held by a permanent man who advanced through the ranks by being appointed to positions with ever-increasing responsibility and prestige. Nevertheless, Bud Lystrup, Lowell Biddulph, and Wayne Replogle were selected to temporarily fill the billet of district naturalist for the three districts until permanent men could be appointed. Perhaps it was also a way for the National Park Service to show their vote of confidence and appreciation for the long service given by these men.

Wayne Replogle moved to Mammoth and oversaw interpretive services for the North District, including Tower Fall, Mammoth Hot Springs, the Roosevelt area, and the Lamar Valley. Bud Lystrup was placed over the West District, overseeing services at Old Faithful, Madison Junction, West Yellowstone, and Norris. Lowell Biddulph oversaw the South District, with services at Canyon, Fishing Bridge, West Thumb, Grant Village, and South Entrance. This work entailed considerable traveling and responsibility for several museums and visitor centers as well as supervision of interpretive programs at these locations. These three men served in their new assignments for approximately four seasons until permanent ranger naturalists were installed in their place; they then assumed the position of assistant district naturalists.

In 1960 Merrill Beal was asked by Robert McIntyre to be the senior naturalist at Old Faithful and in 1962 as senior naturalist at Madison Junction by new Chief Naturalist John Good. George Marler was made a permanent park naturalist in 1957 with primary responsibilities for the thermal geology of the park, including geysers and hot-spring monitoring. Subsequent to the earthquake of 1959, Marler remained occupied with observing and inventorying Yellowstone's thermal features and working with the US Geological Survey on research projects.

The permanent district rangers who were brought into Yellowstone to fill the district naturalist positions were relatively new to the park. Beal observed, "Having seasonal veterans such as Messers Replogle, Lystrup and Biddulph, these imported district supervisors had wonderful opportunities to learn about the park. In some cases horses were made available for that purpose."[19]

Although the Old Men proved to be good administrators, their forte was interpretation and teaching. They loved being in nature with people. Merrill Beal's observations about his colleague Bud Lystrup offers some insight into the frustration that perhaps came with turning a solid teacher into a principal: "Bud's training, school teaching and temperament made him a splendid naturalist. He was quite out of character as an assistant to [the district naturalists]. He seemed cast in the role of a 'side kick.' Their service toward Madison [Junction] consisted of delivering books to sell and receiving funds from sales and contributions for Lower Geyser Basin pamphlets. They monitored campfire talks. Perhaps Bud took an increasingly dim view of this activity. He delighted in direct public service."[20]

All of the Old Men, save Marler, who was working more directly with the USGS on studies of the thermal features, were obligated to spearhead program development that ran counter to their true interests. Much of their time was spent monitoring campfire programs and museum services to ensure that quality interpretation was being provided by others. Although Lystrup was obliged to enforce views that were divergent from Beal's on some issues, such as the Bonita Pool experiment issue, their friendship remained steadfast. In his memoirs, Beal remembered, "Whether as senior or district seasonal naturalist, he [Bud] always left me a hand-written letter of appreciation. The salutation of his last one to me follows: 'Sam: Each year it is increasingly difficult to say goodbye....Thanks, Sam, for your cooperation. You operated an excellent program all season. Bud.'"[21]

Fortunately for Biddulph, much of the time he spent as assistant district naturalist was doing what he loved most: exploring the backcountry, taking pictures, and laying out hiking trails. Robert G. Johnsson was appointed district naturalist of the South District and took full advantage of Biddulph's knowledge and experience of the backcountry of the park.

For the few seasons that these two men served together, they spent a great deal of time hiking and riding horseback into the backcountry of Yel-

Lowell Biddulph on a government horse at Hayden Valley. (Courtesy of L. G. Biddulph)

lowstone. Biddulph shared with Johnsson the knowledge he had gained from men like Ogston, Trischman, Coleman, and others over more than thirty years. Biddulph wrote about this period of service with Johnsson, "I also had the privilege of doing a lot of photographing with another ranger of unusual features in the backcountry that had never been photographed before. I had two wonderful summers doing that. Then, I had one summer laying out trails in the backcountry."[22]

A helicopter was made available to help Biddulph mark potential routes for hiking trails. Once he had marked the route on the map by a flyover, Biddulph hiked the ground and laid out the routes that were later developed into trails and are now used by hikers in Yellowstone. All of these trails are in the Southern District and include the nature trail to Storm Point, the trail to the summit of Avalanche and Top Notch Peaks in the Absaroka Mountains, Riddle Lake, Flat Mountain, and other trails south of Yellowstone Lake.

Biddulph's wife, Ruth, wrote about this time of his life in Yellowstone: "He enjoys his work a good deal, especially as he is able to make many trips into the back country, plotting out new trails and hiking or horseback riding over unexplored territory. He can still out hike the younger men and I am sure has been over more of the primitive park territory than any man here—or likely anywhere, for that matter."[23]

Wayne Replogle would provide friendly dispute to that claim: "I've hiked over more of Yellowstone than any living man, so says 'Ranger Rip,' as he is known in the Park. He has hiked thousands of miles through the Park, taken 20,000 pictures, guided VIPs from all over the world and written a book about the Park."[24]

Chapter 23

End of an Era

The picture of the Five Old Men taken the summer of 1960 in front of Old Faithful Geyser was more than a celebration of their long service to Yellowstone; it foreshadowed the ending of an era. Within a few years of the photograph, all five veteran naturalists transferred to the retired list and left active duty, and the purposes and means of interpretation changed.

Timing was kind to the Five Old Men, as it had been throughout their distinguished service. They were the right men at the right time for the right job. This great "roofless museum of nature" no longer required artificial labels that were found in the trailside museums. The Old Men's intimate teaching style and personalized interaction that had educated and inspired a nation—indeed a world—were replaced with an era of mass information and high technology. Educators who once served as naturalists were being replaced by scientists and researchers. Films, documentaries, and information pamphlets were being substituted for the simple nature walks and campfire programs of the past. Tourists, armed with a plethora of information, were enjoined to explore this vast, living museum and interpret for themselves.

The men had grown old in the service of Yellowstone. It was time for a new generation to add upon what they and others had built, just as the Old Men had built upon a previous generation of army scouts and "spread-eagle" men. Perhaps they could better empathize with Harry Trischman, who left his simple but eloquent epitaph on the wash stand of the Crevice ranger station the morning of his last day in Yellowstone: "31 December 1945, they won't let me sleep in their cabins anymore."[1] It was time for the Old Men to say good-bye.

Five Old Men at Old Faithful Geyser, August 7, 1960. *Left to right:* Wayne Replogle, Lowell Biddulph, Robert N. McIntyre (chief park naturalist), Herbert Lystrup, Merrill Beal, and George Marler. (Courtesy of L. G. Biddulph)

Lystrup, Beal, and Marler left service because of failing health. Biddulph's collegiate administrative duties, which he had successfully balanced for thirty-three years, finally demanded his year-round attention. Only death could end Replogle's service. In ending their active service careers in Yellowstone Park, none of the Five Old Men really left Yellowstone, at least not in their minds. Their final departure is covered in this chapter in order of their retirement.[2]

MERRILL D. "SAM" BEAL (1966)

Merrill Beal spent his last five seasons as the head naturalist at Madison Junction. The season of 1966 was his and Bessy's final one in Yellowstone. It was an appropriate location to end his service because of his close associa-tion with this place that was the cradle of discovery and legend in the park. Yet the final years at Madison Junction were strained due to misunderstand-ing and personality conflicts with district supervisors.

At the 1966 preseason naturalist conference, John Good, the chief park naturalist, expressed appreciation to those men who were serving as senior

Merrill D. Beal at Grand Canyon National Park about 1988. (Courtesy of David and Jean Beal)

naturalists in charge of stations. Unfortunately, he overlooked some who headed up smaller stations, like Beal.

Given the earlier discontinuance of publication of his historical books, the termination of the Madison Junction pageant, and the repudiation of the "National Park Idea," Beal may have felt that the oversight was one more indication that he was politely being shown the door. However, Park Superintendent John S. McLaughlin addressed the group after Good concluded and redressed the oversight. "I have been thinking how lucky we are to attract such a distinguished citizen as Dr. Beal to our service."[3] He then withdrew along the aisle and reached over and shook Beal's hand.

The gesture meant much to Beal. However, he and Bessy had already decided that it was time for them to leave Yellowstone. It was more than a mere feeling of irreconcilable change; health was involved. Both physically and emotionally, it was time for him to leave Yellowstone. Surely with some melancholy, he wrote to John Good expressing his intention to retire following the 1966 season. Good replied cordially:

> Dear Sam:
>
> You have always pulled your weight and more, Sam. I want you to run Madison as long as you feel up to the job and enjoy it, but I don't ever want you to return to the job because of a sense of duty to the Service. If you would simply rather stay in Idaho next summer, or if some health problem should develop, then by all means sit tight. On the other hand, should spring find you champing at the bit to return to Madison, come along; the mosquitoes and I will be waiting. Again, let me say we want you as long as the job is fun and not too wearing. But, if it becomes a chore, or if you would rather do something else, then let's call it quits.[4]

Accordingly, Beal closed the Madison Museum and his career on Labor Day, 1966.

Beal's contributions to his professorship, the state of Idaho, and Yellowstone were many and significant, and in his waning years, accolades flowed to him. Beal wrote eight major volumes of distinguished publications and numerous articles and papers in his life of service. Among those associated with Yellowstone stood the following preeminently: *The Story of Man in Yellowstone* and *I Will Fight No More Forever: Chief Joseph and the Nez Perce War*. He also wrote *A History of South-Eastern Idaho; Intermountain Railroads, Standard and Narrow Gauge;* and the three-volume *History of Idaho*. Although his personal interpretations of Yellowstone history were superseded by more contemporary approaches, he had helped create a solid historical foundation upon which others could build.

Beal was a lifetime member of the Oregon Trail Memorial Association and gave important leadership to the American Pioneer Trails Association and the American Historical Association. He served as a member of the board of directors of the Bannock County Historical Society for better than twenty years. In 1963 Idaho Governor Robert E. Smylie honored him with a certificate of appreciation for his work for the Idaho State Centennial. In 1970 he received the Governor's Award for excellence in literary arts.

Beal's teaching career, which included several years of high school teaching and thirty-eight years of college and university instruction, spanned

nearly sixty years of educational endeavors.⁵ He established himself as a leading historian in the state of Idaho during his tenure of teaching at Idaho State
University. In 1968 Beal received the Distinguished Service Award from
Ricks College (now Brigham Young University–Idaho) for his lifelong service to and interest in the little college on the hill overlooking the Upper
Snake River Valley. On May 30, 1971, he had conferred upon him an honorary doctor of humane letters from the University of Idaho.

His park service totaled twenty-six years between 1939 and 1966. During that time, he never took a day of sick leave, and he received no royalties
for his publications written for Yellowstone. On November 7, 1967, Secretary
of the Interior Stewart L. Udall signed the department's Meritorious Service
Award, and it was brought from Yellowstone to the Beals' home in Pocatello,
Idaho, by Park Naturalist Stanley Canter. It came as a complete surprise to
Sam, and he simply responded to the recognition by saying, "My cup runneth
over with affection for the ideals of the National Park Service."

Beal retired from Idaho State University and lived on in Pocatello, Idaho,
until the death of his beloved Bessy in July 1988. Due to poor health and failing eyesight, he spent the last few years living with his son, David, and daugh-
ter-in-law, Jean. He kept the photograph of the Five Old Men, taken at Old
Faithful on August 7, 1960, close to him as a cherished token of memory. In
1980 he wrote in his journal, "Only Biddulph and Beal were living when this
was written. Meantime, my daily glance at the photograph yields pleasant
memories."⁶

Merrill Dee Beal died in 1990 in Tucson, Arizona, and was buried in
Rexburg, Idaho, beside his beloved Bessy.

HERBERT TSCHERNING LYSTRUP (1967)

Arthritis and a tumor in the back of his lower neck had made it increasingly
difficult for Lystrup to perform the duties of a park naturalist. Each year had
become more difficult until finally it was too much to endure. Following
the 1967 season in Yellowstone, Lystrup retired from park service.

In 1968 Stewart L. Udall, secretary of the interior, bestowed on Herbert
Lystrup the Meritorious Service Award. A portion of the citation reads, "He
possessed an encyclopedic knowledge of the park and his interpretive skills
and ability to help visitors see what they wanted to see were unsurpassed. His
enthusiasm for Yellowstone's wonders was infectious and inspired all persons
with whom he had contact. In recognition of loyal and devoted service as a
valued seasonal employee over many years and his diligence in doing all

Herbert T. Lystrup. At the time of the photo, he was the longest tenured naturalist in Yellowstone, serving from 1929 through 1966. (Courtesy of Liz Lystrup)

within his power to make every Park visitor's stay a little more enjoyable, Mr. Lystrup is granted the Meritorious Service Award of the Department of the Interior."[7]

The same year that he retired from park service, Lystrup retired from teaching at Memorial High School in Eau Claire, Wisconsin. He was recognized by the Wisconsin School Board with the Wisconsin Service Award for thirty-nine years of teaching.

Lystrup was a teacher both in the classroom and in nature. His quest was always to educate and inspire those who came under his influence. He witnessed nearly the entire evolution of the interpretation program in Yellowstone and played an integral role in its conception and development. He was an extraordinary observer and interpreter of nature. His interests were eclectic, his passion for inspiring and enlightening visitors to the park legendary.

At the conclusion of the 1967 season, Lystrup had accumulated thirty-eight continuous seasons of service to the park and was the longest tenured ranger naturalist serving in Yellowstone at the time. He served most of his years as a senior naturalist and was stationed at almost all the major interpretive stations in the park. His longest time of service was at Old Faithful, and his knowledge of the geysers and hot springs of the Firehole Basin was exceptional. During the last several years, he was called upon to serve in major leadership positions within the West District, and for the last few years, he and Betty resided during the summer months at West District headquarters in West Yellowstone.

His love for Yellowstone did not wane with retirement, nor did his interest in teaching, especially young people. For the remaining summers following retirement, he and Betty returned to West Yellowstone to live out their final beautiful days, and Betty continued to work for Hamilton Stores. Family members loved to visit them at West, and Bud passed on his great love for nature to his grandchildren. Many former colleagues—some who yet worked in Yellowstone—stopped in to visit and talk about the old days. This was a source of great satisfaction to him.

His daughter, Liz, noted:

My father remained interested in Yellowstone Park until the day he died. When his grandchildren came to visit during the summers, he delighted in conducting nature hikes with them. They were very young at the time but remember those visits vividly. He held them spellbound. It was a mutual admiration society. I believe my father considered himself the luckiest man in the world. He absolutely loved both of his jobs. When you think about it, the two are somewhat analogous. I would say teaching is the common denominator. High school biology is what he taught. I once asked him which part he liked best: flora or fauna. He said if he had to choose, it would be flora. He was passionate about wildflowers.[8]

Herbert Tscherning "Bud" Lystrup died of cancer on March 15, 1977, at the age of seventy-six in Eau Claire, Wisconsin. Yellowstone lost one of its great advocates and most effective interpreters. Betty, his companion and fellow-adventurer for forty-five years, died seventeen years later.

LOWELL GEORGE BIDDULPH (1968)

After thirty-three summers of service in Yellowstone, the demands of academic administration finally caught up with Lowell Biddulph. He retired from park service in September 1968, having served twenty-five years as the senior naturalist at Fishing Bridge and eight years in leadership positions in the South District. At the time of retirement, he was still serving as dean of students and director of the Division of Physical Education, Health, Recreation, and Athletics at Ricks College. He also taught classes in geology, hiking, and fly-tying.

Biddulph was a naturalist of the order of John Muir and John Burroughs. He was a wilderness trekker. His eye was keen in nature and his knowledge of all aspects of Yellowstone superb. He was a fine lecturer and interpreter, possessing a calm, quiet demeanor that drew visitors to him. His greatest love was the unbeaten path and the thin, enchanted air of high mountain peaks. He liked to view the world from the top down.

In 1973 he retired from Ricks College after accumulating forty-three years of academic service. Biddulph was presented with the Service Award by the Rexburg Kiwanis Club (1972), the Ricks College Distinguished Honorary Alumnus Award, and the Distinguished Service Award (1974) and was inducted into the Ricks College Athletic Hall of Fame (1982).

Lowell G. Biddulph with the author (age five) at Fishing
Bridge Museum. (Courtesy of L. G. Biddulph)

Biddulph's entire adult life was occupied as a teacher, coach, college
administrator, and ranger naturalist. Whether in the classroom, on fields of
competition, or in nature, all pursuits were directly involved in developing
the intellect and character of men and women. He summed up his life of service this way:

> All of my life I have been involved with athletics and nature. If I had
> ever been forced to choose one over the other, I feel strongly that I
> would have chosen nature study and naturalist activities. I have been
> a devoted nature lover all my life. Fortunately, I have been permitted
> to do both.
>
> Even though I feel that my influence has been positive in both
> activities, still there is no quantitative measure which can be applied in
> conducting a nature walk, an auto caravan, an all day hike to climb a
> mountain, or a lecture at a campfire program. Perhaps my satisfaction

came because of a pause, a meditation, a look of understanding, or a happy expression when deep inner feelings surface for a fleeting moment, as people go away built up and elevated in their feelings about themselves and their natural surroundings.

I can leave you with a more quantitative measure of my success as a coach in the athletic field, for records of contests are established and preserved, for just what purpose I am not sure, except possibly for the survival of the coach. I have felt, however, that to have the proper influence upon the players is the most important outcome of athletics. To teach them honesty, fairness, devotion to a cause, teamwork and dedication, and patriotism, these are the real values to be derived. Winning is the name of the game, but not the only measure of success.[9]

Nature was a deeply spiritual experience for Biddulph. In one of his final speeches delivered to the student body of Ricks College, he compared life to his beloved mountains of Yellowstone:

Have you ever stood on the top of a mountain and viewed the landscape below? It is so quiet and peaceful. Christ went to the mountain to pray and meditate. We can do the same thing when temptation bothers us or when the pressures mount. Climb a mountain. Seek solitude in nature. It is good to be apart for a while from the pressures of life, to gain perspective and find anew life's meaning in God. The mountains in their seeming unchanging serenity are vast silences—ideal for deep thoughts and life changing meditations. Visions can be ours if we lift our eyes beyond the horizons of self and dedicate ourselves anew to God's purposes.[10]

Lowell George Biddulph died on March 10, 1985, at the age of seventy-eight. He was buried in Provo, Utah, at the foot of Timpanogos Peak, where his first love for nature was kindled as a youth. At his funeral, one of his former high school athletes sang "I Hope They Have Pine Trees in Heaven." On his headstone is inscribed, "Come with Me into the High Mountains."[11]

GEORGE DEWEY MARLER (1973)

It was sickness, not age or lack of interest, that took George Marler away from Yellowstone. It came like the ending of an eruption of one of his beloved geysers. The influx of disease sapped and eventually exhausted the

George D. Marler, Yellowstone National Park naturalist. (Courtesy of George Marler)

energy that had driven him to remarkable heights. By 1965 sickness forced him to resign his permanent park employment and return to seasonal work. Problems began in his esophagus when it became impossible for him to swallow or generate saliva. He went months with tubes down his throat. This effectively eliminated any lecturing or public performances.

By 1966 Marler had a portion of his stomach removed due to ulcers. His wife, Laura, noted, "It was difficult for George to grow old. He was a very active man with many interests, and to lose that was very hard. But activity became very hard on George during this time, and he spent much of his time reading and labeling slides and working on professional papers."[12]

For three years prior to retirement (1966–69), Marler worked with the US Geological Survey. His old friend and colleague Donald White solicited the National Park Service to allow Marler to work with the USGS, although he was still technically a park naturalist. The transfer was agreed upon, and his salary was paid by the USGS through the National Park Service. It was partially the encouragement of Don White that inspired Marler to compile and have published the two-volume, 639-page *Inventory of Thermal Features of the Firehole River Geyser Basins and Other Selected Areas of Yellowstone National Park*. This work, published in June 1973 by the US Geological Survey and the National Park Service, indisputably placed Marler as one of the most knowledgeable individuals of Yellowstone thermal features of his time.

After three years, Marler made a complete break from the National Park Service and worked exclusively with the US Geological Survey. He remained an observer of geysers until the end and was reporting eruption data for geysers to park headquarters until his retirement. Again, Laura: "George was always very interested in the hot springs at Norris Geyser Basin. If he had gone back one more year, he would have done an inventory of the Norris Geysers. George saw most every geyser and hot spring in Yellowstone play. He knew them all, but he never got to see Steamboat Geyser erupt at Norris, and that was always a disappointment to him."[13]

Marler's lifelong work with geysers and hot springs of Yellowstone brought to him appropriate recognition and respect. In 1962 Marler received an honorary doctorate from his alma mater, Brigham Young University, for his outstanding work in geothermal science in Yellowstone National Park. On the occasion, his friend and mentor, Horace Albright, wrote: "As the former director of the National Park Service, I am very proud of you, and your friendship I highly value."

On June 8, 1967, at the Thirty-Fourth Convocation Ceremonies of the Department of the Interior in Washington, DC, George Marler was awarded the Distinguished Service Award by Secretary Stewart L. Udall in recognition of his distinguished work in the field of hydrothermal geology in Yellowstone National Park.

Marler spent the last years of his life at his home in Thornton, Idaho. He was in and out of the hospital so many times that both he and his wife were exhausted. In 1978 their daughter Lela brought them to her home in Layton, Utah, but Marler's health did not improve, and he again had to be hospitalized. Unhappy and in great pain, he requested that his family take him back to Thornton. The doctors agreed that there was nothing more they could do for him.

There was a gleam in his eye the day they told George that he was going home to Idaho: home to the broad, green valley where the Snake River twisted through cottonwood trees and ripening fields of grain and potato vines, where fluffy clouds drifted aimlessly through blue skies, and distant mountains of the Tetons, the Sawtooth, and the Yellowstone lay beckoning within view.

He was gone perhaps even before the car crossed the Utah-Idaho border. By the time they reached Thornton, Idaho, George Dewey Marler had slipped the bonds of earth and lay in peaceful quiescence. The eruption of life was over, the energy expended. It had been beautiful. Spectacular!

Wayne Replogle. (Courtesy of the Wayne Replogle Collection, American Heritage Center, University of Wyoming)

George Dewey Marler died on July 10, 1978, at the age of eighty. He was buried in the Annis Butte Cemetery not far from his boyhood home in Thornton, Idaho.

WAYNE FORDYCE REPLOGLE (1977)

Marian Churchill Replogle died in the spring of 1971, and Wayne Replogle lost his camping buddy, prankster, and cherished companion with whom he had shared the Yellowstone experience for forty summers. That same year he received the Meritorious Service Award from the Department of Interior and an Outstanding Alumnus Award from the College of Emporia, where he had been a standout athlete.

Replogle did not remain single long. In August 1972, in the home of Park Superintendent Jack Anderson at Mammoth Hot Springs, he married Rebecca (Rice) McCormick, whom he had known before he was married to Marian. Replogle wrote their ceremony, which was titled "Slow Me Down, Lord." A snippet is quoted here: "Slow me down Lord—Ease the pounding of my heart by quieting my mind—steady my hurried pace—give me calmness amidst the confusion of the day—teach me the art of taking a minute vacation—of slowing down to chat with a friend—to read a good book—to take a walk in the meadow—to look at a flower."[14]

A year later, Replogle retired from active park service but stayed on as an annuitant in Yellowstone, serving as a special assistant to the superintendent for four more years. In this new capacity and free from the pressures of past years, Replogle had an opportunity to slow down a little and savor the autumn of his Yellowstone experiences. Much of his time was spent in reminiscing about the past and in gathering and recording information about the park's history and geographical locations.

He continued to take VIPs on tours around the park, and he met with important people who came to Yellowstone. He assembled a vast collection of slides for park archives that he had taken throughout the years. He also taped an extensive history of Yellowstone in what he called his *Mile-by-Mile* narrative. This was made with a handheld tape recorder as he drove around Yellowstone, reminiscing on everything he could remember or had heard about. Some of it is inaccurate—time does that to memories—but it provides an up-close and personal snapshot of Yellowstone's past. He and Rebecca took leisurely drives to various places within and without the park, such as Livingston and Cooke City, Montana. He enjoyed visiting with friends and associates and did so frequently.

In the winters, Replogle continued as the official cameraman for the Kansas Jayhawks' football program. Replogle had never operated a movie camera before, and some of his films were classics. He became so animated at the kickoff that he often forgot to capture on film the footage of the special teams' play. "Ol' Rep did it again," Jack Mitchell would say at booster-club meetings when Replogle's camerawork failed to show the ball carrier on the kickoff. Replogle admitted, "I still get a thrill out of the damn kick-off. I get to jumping around, and the camera gets to shaking. That kickoff is something else!"[15]

He wrote in his last season in Yellowstone, "This is my forty-fourth year in Yellowstone and what a glorious way to spend a summer." His entry in his journal dated July 3, 1977, reads:

55 degrees at 7:00 a.m.
  PC [partly cloudy]—windy—sprinkling
  5:00 a.m. Went early to get the guests on the road and checked out. Later, drove with Becky to Tower on old road and out to Cooke. Returned and visited the ... Hodges near Silver Gate and then came on home. Checked for orders at main office and found none. Went home and finished the day.[16]

Early the next morning of July 4, 1977, Wayne Replogle died in his sleep at Mammoth Hot Springs. Ranger friends drove his body and Rebecca back to Kansas. He was buried in his National Park ranger uniform with full honors

Photo taken July 8, 1977, at Replogle's funeral in Coldwater, Kansas. *Left to right:* David Beal, Walter Herriman, Robert Jonas, Dale Nuss, and Rebecca Replogle. (Courtesy of David and Jean Beal)

in Coldwater, Kansas, on July 11, 1977, at the age of seventy-three. The National Park Service sent a special envoy of rangers to signify the loss of one of their own. Four of those rangers were old friends from Yellowstone days: Bob Jonas and Dale Nuss of Yellowstone, Walt Herriman (superintendent of Chaco Canyon National Monument), and Dave Beal, deputy regional director of the Midwest Region of the National Park Service in Omaha, Nebraska, the kid Replogle used to take hiking in Monument Geyser Basin so many years before. Testament to his loves, Wayne drove a Mercury automobile with a large arrowhead on the grill and Kansas plates that said "RANGER."

Notes

INTRODUCTION

1. Lowell Biddulph and his three sons all earned their eagle rank in scouting. Biddulph's mother-in-law noted, "We have a big eagle (Howard who stood 6'5"), a middle-sized eagle (David, who was just over six feet), a little eagle (Stephen was fourteen at the time), and a bald eagle (Lowell)."

2. According to Dr. Merrill Beal, the original photo was taken on August 7, 1960. A newspaper article with the photograph was published in the *Salt Lake Tribune* under the title "5 Tally Park Duty, Sum 139 Seasons" sometime after that (no date is available on the clipping). A similar but earlier article was printed in the *Tribune* on March 11, 1952, under the title "5 Rangers Total 85 Seasons Duty" with a picture of the same men. Both clippings with original photographs and news releases are in possession of the author.

3. James A. Pritchard, *Preserving Yellowstone's Natural Conditions*. This book provides an excellent history of park management policies and procedures. Three other sources pertinent to the rise of education in Yellowstone and other national parks are Barry Mackintosh's *Interpretation in the National Park Service: A Historical Perspective;* Denise Vick's unpublished dissertation, "Yellowstone National Park and Education of Adults"; and William B. Sanborn's master's thesis, "The Education Program of Yellowstone National Park."

4. By 1948 most if not all of the old army scouts and forest rangers who first worked in Yellowstone had moved on to other national parks or retired from the park. For example, Harry Liek and Ted Ogston transferred to Mount McKinley National Park, Frank Oberhansley and Fred Johnston went to Hawaii, Sam Woodring (chief park ranger) became the first superintendent for Grand Teton National Park, and Charles J. "White Mountain" Smith, who had been a stage driver in Yellowstone for nine years and an extra army scout and eventually a park ranger, transferred to Grand Canyon National Park in 1921.

CHAPTER 1

1. Elliott West, *The Last Indian War: The Nez Perce Story,* 82.
2. Invocation offered by Chief Jasper Saunkeah of the Kiowa Tribe of Indians during a tribal council meeting. Date and actual authenticity of this invocation have not been verified, nor its actual origin determined. Several copies of this invocation were in the personal Yellowstone files of Dr. Lowell G. Biddulph and titled "Invocation Given by Chief Jasper Saunkeah of the Kiowa Tribe." Information about tribal councils held at various times was obtained from sources at headquarters in Yellowstone Park, and the actual prayer has some semblance of authenticity.
3. Hiram M. Chittenden, *Yellowstone National Park,* chap. 10. See also Louis C. Crampton, *Early History of Yellowstone National Park and Its Relation to National Park Policies,* 28.
4. Freeman Tilden, *The National Parks: What They Mean to You and Me.* Chapter 1 offers an interesting discourse on the value of national parks.
5. Crampton, *Early History of Yellowstone,* appx. A, 76; the Yellowstone Park Act of March 1, 1872, chap. 24.
6. Crampton, *Early History of Yellowstone,* 1.
7. Nathaniel Pitt Langford, *The Discovery of Yellowstone Park, 1870,* 179–80.
8. Bison, elk, and other ungulates migrate to valleys outside of Yellowstone in winter and compete for food with domestic herds of cattle and sheep. Predators, such as the grizzly bear, gray wolf, coyotes, and mountain lions, also take a toll on domestic animals. Bison are accused of spreading brucellosis to domestic herds, but there is also evidence that the disease was originally given to the bison through domestic cattle that were kept in the early days of the park for milk and other purposes.
9. Aubrey L. Haines, *The Yellowstone Story,* 2:417n33.
10. Ibid., 354n55. Haines notes that Wonderland came as a sobriquet from an article, "Our National Park," *Helena (MT) Daily Herald,* published February 28, 1872, relating it to Charles Ludwig Dodgson's *Alice in Wonderland.*
11. H.R. 764 and S. 392 were simultaneously introduced in both houses of Congress in December 1871. and passed into law in February 1872. The bill creating Yellowstone National Park was signed by President Ulysses S. Grant on March 1, 1872.
12. Philetus Walter Norris was the second superintendent of Yellowstone Park from April 1877 until February 1882. Born in Palmyra, New York, in 1821, he later served as a captain in the Ohio Infantry during the Civil War. He made the first attempts to build crude roads and trails in the interior of the park.
13. William F. "Buffalo Bill" Cody is said to have killed forty-two hundred buffalo in an eight-month period while working for the Kansas Pacific Railroad for which he was to provide buffalo meat for the workers.
14. Fifteen buffalo cows were purchased from the Allard herd in northwestern Montana and three bulls from the Goodnight herd in Texas, and this captive (domesticated) herd was kept in the enclosure near Mammoth. The herd soon

outgrew the Mammoth enclosure and was moved to a corral at Rose Creek in the Lamar Valley. Eventually, this became known as the Buffalo Ranch, and the herd was fed, inoculated, and cared for by rangers who raised and cut hay in the Lamar. The buffalo ranch was closed in 1952, and the herds were turned free in Yellowstone and have thrived ever since, with particularly large herds in the Lamar, Pelican, and Hayden Valleys.

15. Harry Yount served with the infantry and cavalry during the Civil War. Subsequent to his discharge in 1865, Yount served as a buffalo hunter, trapper, and bull whacker for the army and as a guide for the Hayden Party that surveyed Yellowstone in the 1870s. Superintendent Norris hired him as a gamekeeper in June 1880, and he resigned in 1881 after only fourteen months of service. Horace M. Albright, the second director of the National Park Service following Stephen T. Mather, called Yount the "father of the ranger service and the first national park ranger." Yount's stout self-reliance in nature and woodsman skills became the idyllic qualities against which future rangers were measured.

16. Captain Moses Harris and fifty cavalry from Fort Custer, Montana Territory, assumed duty in Yellowstone on August 17, 1886, and established Fort Yellowstone at Mammoth Hot Springs.

17. Sixteen soldier stations were built in Yellowstone between 1886 and 1912 to house contingents of soldiers for protective services. These locations included Soda Butte, Grand Canyon, Norris, Riverside (West Yellowstone), Lower Geyser Basin (Fountain), Upper Geyser Basin (Old Faithful), Lake, Snake River (South Entrance), Thumb Bay, Tower Fall, Gardiner, Sylvan Pass, Cooke City, Gallatin, Bechler, and Crevice. With the advent of the National Park Service, some of these became known as ranger stations and are still operative today.

18. Tamsen E. Hert, "Luxury in the Wilderness: Yellowstone's Grand Canyon Hotel, 1911–1960," 21–36.

19. Stephen Tyng Mather was born in 1867 and became a wealthy industrialist. In 1915 he worked to influence the federal government to create a National Park Service to oversee the several national parks and monuments that were, at that time, being managed by the army and political appointees and were said to be in a deplorable state. Through his efforts, Congress created the National Park Service in 1916, and Mather was appointed as its first director, with Horace Albright as his assistant.

20. Haines, *The Yellowstone Story,* 2:91, 413–34. The name is taken from the spread-eagle badge worn by early park rangers. The earliest badge worn in Yellowstone was that of the Yellowstone Park scout and was a silver round with a cut-out star in the center (much like the Old West marshal badge), with "Yellowstone Park Scout" stamped around the edge and the number of the badge in the center. The original national park ranger badge was composed of two parts: a federal shield and a soldered-on eagle with outspread wings. Later, the badge was cast in one piece. See also Jack R. Williams, "National Park Service Insignia and How the Uniform Grew," 2–3.

21. Tilden, *National Parks,* 2.

22. "Management of Yellowstone's Northern Elk Herd," in *A Manual of General Information on Yellowstone National Park,* by Division of Interpretation, 162.
23. James R. Simon, *Yellowstone Fishes,* 13.
24. Tilden, *National Parks,* 1.
25. Pritchard, *Preserving Yellowstone's Natural Conditions.*

CHAPTER 2

1. *National Park Service Historical Handbook Series,* http://www.nps.gov (online books).
2. Paul Schullery and Lee H. Whittlesey, "Yellowstone Nature Notes: A Neglected Documentary Source," *Yellowstone Science* 8, no. 1 (2000).
3. Haines, *The Yellowstone Story,* 2:310.
4. Ibid., 294–95.
5. Roger Wolcott Toll was potentially a future director of the National Park Service until his untimely death. He was born in October 1883 in Denver. After World War I, he entered NPS service as superintendent of Mount Rainier National Park. About a year later, he was transferred to Rocky Mountain National Park, where he also served as superintendent. In 1929 he was transferred to Yellowstone National Park to replace Horace M. Albright. He was killed in an automobile accident on February 25, 1936, in New Mexico.
6. Haines, *The Yellowstone Story,* 2:296–297. Haines cites an undated form letter signed by Superintendent Roger W. Toll, Yellowstone National Park Archives. The secretary of the interior originated the first cautionary letter that was undoubtedly passed on by park superintendents.
7. Herbert T. Lystrup, foreword to *The Ninety-Day Wonder: A Diary of a Ranger Naturalist in Yellowstone National Park, Wyoming.*
8. Kiki Leigh Rydell and Mary Shivers Culpin, *Managing the Matchless Wonders: A History of Administrative Development in Yellowstone National Park, 1872–1965,* 152–53. Freeman Tilden was born in Malden, Massachusetts, and was a novelist and playwright. In the 1940s, he began writing about national parks and wrote several important books about the subject, including *The National Parks: What They Mean to You and Me.* He died at the age of ninety-six in 1980.
9. Frank C. Brockman, "Park Naturalists and the Evolution of National Park Service Interpretation through World War II," 28.
10. Lystrup, *Ninety-Day Wonder,* 8.
11. Division of Interpretation, *A Manual of General Information on Yellowstone National Park,* in possession of the author.
12. Edmund Sawyer hand-painted images of flowers, animals, birds, and more on glass slides, also called "Forgo" slides, which were distributed to and used by ranger naturalists in their early programs.
13. *Naturalist Division Report* 1 (March 1930): 2.
14. Edmund B. Rogers, superintendent of Yellowstone Park, "Memorandum to Park Rangers and Ranger-Naturalists," June 10, 1939. In addition to giving estimated numbers of bears and big game animals, it provides a three-year comparison of actual and estimated animals.

15. Haines, *The Yellowstone Story,* 2:307.
16. Chittenden, *Yellowstone National Park,* 41.
17. C. Max Bauer was a park naturalist and chief park naturalist in Yellowstone from June 15, 1932, until November 15, 1946, when he was transferred to NPS headquarters in Washington, DC. The title of chief park naturalist first appeared on October 1, 1943; prior to that the title was park naturalist. A graduate of the University of Chicago with a PhD from the University of Colorado, he served as the director of geology in the Directive Branch of Natural History of the National Park Service.

CHAPTER 3

1. Haines, *The Yellowstone Story,* 2:304. See also Wayne F. Replogle, *Mile-by-Mile: An Auditory History of Yellowstone Park,* and the transcription of a talk given to ranger naturalists at Grant Village on August 11, 1965, 31–33.
2. *Yellowstone Nature Notes* 16, nos. 5–6 (1939).
3. Eugene Lusk Roberts was born and raised in Provo, Utah. He was on the faculty of Brigham Young University and coach from 1910 to 1928. He reintroduced football at BYU and named the team "Cougars." While on the faculty at BYU, Roberts began hikes to the top of Mount Timpanogos in 1912. The hikes became regionally famous, and Roberts became so closely associated with the mountain that he was nicknamed Eugene "Timpanogos" Roberts.
4. What became known as the "Timp Hike" began through Brigham Young University and was an ascent of the 11,700-foot Mount Timpanogos. This was an organized group hike led by an experienced leader that typically began at Aspen Grove and led to the summit and then back down by way of the glacier. Sometimes these hikes were made in the moonlight to watch the sunrise over the Uintah and Wasatch Mountains.
5. Personal history of Lowell G. Biddulph (unpublished), hereafter cited as Biddulph history.
6. Herbert Lystrup, "How I Became a Naturalist," used with permission of Liz Lystrup.
7. Jack Ellis Haynes, *Haynes Guide: Handbook of Yellowstone National Park.* It was first copyrighted in 1910 by Frank Jay Haynes, Jack's father, and went through at least sixty-one revised editions.
8. Wayne F. Replogle, *Yellowstone's Bannock Indian Trails,* 2. Replogle notes, "My interest in the Indian and the general history of the frontier goes back to my childhood days. Working for my father was a young man whose grandfather, Christopher Carson, carved quite a name for himself in the annals of the West. This young man was Christopher Carson II. We called him Kit. He was a soft-spoken, shy man, if not quite retiring. But one thing he did well was to tell me the stories of his grandfather and of the Indians. He opened my mind to the romance of it all and I've never lost one bit of my love for the old Wild West."
9. Wayne F. Replogle, Grant Village talk, given to a group of ranger naturalists at Grant Village on August 11, 1965, hereafter cited as Grant Village talk. A full transcript of his talk is found in the Yellowstone Park Archives and

provides an interesting account of several incidents in Wayne Replogle's career in Yellowstone.

10. Gerald R. Ford, thirty-eighth president of the United States, worked as a temporary ranger in Yellowstone Park for a summer in 1936. He was twenty-three years of age. His assignment that summer was at Canyon, where he performed duties such as campground checks, guard on the truck that gathered garbage for the bear-feeding shows at Otter Creek, and helping greet VIPs at the Canyon Hotel. Ford never forgot his summer work in Yellowstone and returned to the park in 1976 while serving as president, where he met with his old colleague and friend Wayne Replogle.

11. "Sport Talk" by Bill Mayer, *Lawrence Daily Journal-World,* July 11, 1977: "Among his greatest admirers are the men whom he scared the hell out of as freshman footballers at [the University of Kansas]. In the next four or five years, they learned and always remembered what a loving, gentle person he was. Most notably, Rep was a first-class human being.... Some will say his greatest gift was the ability to make people laugh. He often accomplished this by poking fun at himself and his own alleged shortcomings. The sight of a man of his stature laughing at himself gave others a little more confidence in themselves."

12. Letter from David Beal and Bob Jonas, November 2002.

13. Replogle, *Yellowstone's Bannock Indian Trails,* was published in 1956 as number 6 in Yellowstone's Interpretive Series by the Yellowstone Library and Museum Association, a nonprofit organization whose purpose is the stimulation of interest in the educational and inspirational aspects of Yellowstone's history and natural history.

14. George Marler's personal history, Brigham Young University, L. Tom Perry Special Collections Library, MS 2171, box 6, Provo, Utah, hereafter cited as Marler history.

15. Fringillidae is the study of small birds, particularly those that are finch-like in appearance and habits. Marler's focus was particularly in bird life in the state of Utah.

16. Laura Marler, interview with the author, 2003.

17. Marler history, 66.

18. Ruth H. Biddulph, interview with the author, 2003.

19. Herbert T. Lystrup, "Personal Reflections," *Yellowstone Nature Notes* 31, no. 3 (1957): 27.

CHAPTER 4

1. Buffalo Bill earned his nickname by providing buffalo meat for the Kansas Pacific Railroad. His international fame came from his famous Wild West shows. Cody was a soldier in the Civil War and the chief scout for the Third Cavalry during the Plains Indian wars. He was a scout for Johnston's Army sent to Utah to quell what was thought to be a Mormon uprising. He was also

known as an "Indian fighter," which he said began during his sojourn with Johnston's Army into Utah.

2. The name "Pahaska" was bestowed upon Cody by the Plains Indians out of their deference to and respectful association with him and other such men. While serving as an army scout, Cody and others chose to wear their hair long out of deference to this relationship.

3. Replogle, Grant Village talk, n.p.

4. Ibid.

5. Ibid.

6. Lystrup, *Ninety-Day Wonder*, 8.

7. Biddulph history.

8. Robert V. Goss, "Yellowstone's First General Store: A Legacy of Jennie Henderson and Her Family," 16–28.

9. Replogle, Grant Village talk.

10. http://www.lonestar.edu/library/research-guides-kingwood. Kingwood College Library is part of the Lonestar College System of Houston, Texas.

11. Replogle, Grant Village talk.

12. Herbert T. Lystrup, *Shavings Off the Stick: True Stories of Yellowstone Park Told by a Veteran Ranger*, 46.

13. Haines, *The Yellowstone Story*, 2:136. Paul Wylie was a grandson of William Wallace Wylie from Bozeman, Montana, who formed the Wylie Permanent Camping Company in the park about 1883. He provided guided tours, meals, and camping facilities.

14. Replogle, Grant Village talk.

15. Ibid.

16. Lowell Biddulph, interview with the author, 1984.

17. National Park Service, *Park Structures and Facilities*, 3.

18. Rydell and Culpin, *Managing the Matchless Wonders*.

19. The National Industrial Recovery Act of 1933 was designed to create jobs, upgrade America's housing and infrastructure, and increase national pride. The CCC camps were a component of this program and brought young people from the inner cities to federal preserves for work experience and jobs.

20. Marler history, n.p.

21. Lystrup, *Shavings Off the Stick*, 2–3.

22. Haines, *The Yellowstone Story*, 1:208.

23. Replogle, *Mile-by-Mile*, 33.

24. Ibid.

25. Ibid.

26. Beal history. The road in those days from Madison Junction to Old Faithful included a dangerous route through the Firehole Canyon. The road was narrow with some blind curves and precipitous drop-offs into the canyon below. The road is now a scenic loop away from the main road.

27. Biddulph, interview with the author, 1984.

28. The steep canyon walls were eight to twelve hundred feet in depth and made of decomposing lava rock. Some 640,000 years ago, the Yellowstone caldera filled the area with thick layers of molten lava, geothermally softening the existing rock. The current Grand Canyon of the Yellowstone is believed to have formed approximately 14,000 to 18,000 years ago by erosion cutting through these layers of weakened volcanic rock. Torrential floods of melted ice water eroded the canyon, and the river that cascades in two beautiful waterfalls today continues its erosive action.

29. Prior to the building of the Chittenden Bridge (1903) across the Yellowstone River, H. F. Richardson (Uncle Tom) obtained a permit to guide people down into the canyon to the base of the Lower Falls. Uncle Tom boated people across the river above the falls where the water was slow, then led them through the forest to a gully where they descended on wooden ladders and ropes to stand in the misty spray of the thunderous waterfall. The trip ended with a campfire supper before boating back to the west side of the river. In 1903, with the building of the Chittenden Bridge, Uncle Tom had his permit revoked. Later, wooden steps and landings were built down into the canyon near the same spot, and the trail was appropriately named "Uncle Tom's Trail."

30. Biddulph, interview with the author, 1983; Stephen G. Biddulph, *The Yellowstone Years,* 16–17.

31. Ibid.

32. The early road constructed by the Army Corps of Engineers also went through part of the Hoodoos. Silver Gate is found there and is part of the original old road built in 1899. In Lystrup's time, the road across Golden and Silver Gates had been recently improved.

33. Liberty Cap was named by the Hayden Survey Party in 1871. It is a column of travertine (lime) deposited by a thermal spring that was once active there and built the cone to a height of thirty-seven feet. In earlier years, it was feared that the Liberty Cap was going to topple over, and an attempt was made to support it with wood poles. But it has survived. On June 9, 1932, or thereabouts, a piece of the cone did break away and fall to the ground.

34. Buffalo were moved to the buffalo ranch on Rose Creek in the Lamar Valley and maintained there until 1952, when all operations were ceased and the ranch closed down. The old ranch is now the Yellowstone Institute.

35. See Lee H. Whittlesey, *Death in Yellowstone: Accidents and Foolhardiness in the First National Park,* 12. The little girl was Joy Hanny from Firth, Idaho. She died at the Mammoth Hospital.

36. Raven Creek is a small tributary to Pelican Creek, which drains into Yellowstone Lake.

CHAPTER 5

1. The Firehole Hotel was built in 1880 as the park's first lodging facility. It remained in use until 1891 when the Fountain Hotel was completed on the east side of Fountain Flats just north of Fountain Paint Pots.

2. Nan Weber Boruff, *Mattie: A Woman's Journey West.*

3. War gardens were encouraged throughout the United States during World War II. Families planted gardens of berries, vegetables, and fruits in whatever space they had available to augment the limited foodstuffs available through the commercial sources.
4. Big Hole National Battlefield is a 655-acre preserve in western Montana where the Nez Perce Indians fought a delaying action with the Seventh Cavalry of General Oliver O. Howard on August 9–10, 1877. It was established as a military preserve in 1883 and designated a national monument in June 1923. In May 1963, it was redesignated a national battlefield. During the time Beal was custodian, the battlefield was under the administrative control of Yellowstone National Park.
5. Replogle, *Mile-by-Mile* tape transcript, n.p.
6. Lystrup, *Shavings Off the Stick,* 46–47.
7. Crustose lichen is one of three types of lichens in the park, characterized by a thin and crust-like growth on naked rocks. It grows very slowly and gradually disintegrates the rock surface. Crustose lichen is often brown or yellowish brown in color.
8. Howard L. Biddulph, "Father's Mountain," unpublished.
9. Marler history (see chap. 3, n. 14).
10. The original road to the East Entrance, constructed by Hiram Chittenden in 1903–5, left the current-day road at Indian Pond and stayed back in the forest, bypassing Mary and Sedge Bays and Steamboat Point. It skirted the southern edge of Turbid Lake and then followed southeast into the foothills of the Absaroka Mountain Range, reconnecting with the current-day road just east of Lake Butte Point. The current road that follows the lakeshore at Mary Bay and Sedge Bay was constructed sometime after 1930, and the old Turbid Lake Road (as it was called) became a restricted service road.
11. Ruth H. Biddulph, *Remembering Lowell G. Biddulph,* 38.
12. Ibid.
13. S. Biddulph, *The Yellowstone Years,* 73.
14. R. Biddulph, *Remembering Lowell G. Biddulph,* 36.
15. Lee H. Whittlesey, *Yellowstone Place Names.* Indian Pond is a small body of water located adjacent to Yellowstone Lake just west of Mary Bay that occupies an ancient volcanic crater. In 1880 Philetus Norris named it Indian Pond because of the Indian tribes that had summer camps nearby. In the 1920s, it was renamed Squaw Lake and remained so until 1981, when its original name was restored.
16. Frederick B. Turner, *Reptiles and Amphibians of Yellowstone National Park.*
17. Liz Lystrup, letter to the author, 2002.
18. S. Biddulph, *The Yellowstone Years,* 79–80.
19. Replogle, *Mile-by-Mile,* tape 13.
20. Beal history.
21. Bob and Arlene Jonas, letter to the author, July 2003.
22. Bob Jonas, letter to the author, November 2002.
23. Ibid.

CHAPTER 6

1. http://www.yellowstoneparknet.com/red_lodge_montana/.
2. http://www.westyellowstonenet.com/.
3. "Bootleggers Find It Tough in Yellowstone," *Milwaukee Journal,* August 23, 1930.
4. R. Biddulph, *Remembering Lowell G. Biddulph,* 33. This incident is also told in S. Biddulph, *The Yellowstone Years,* a copy of which was placed in the Yellowstone National Park Research Library.

CHAPTER 7

1. Chittenden, *Yellowstone National Park,* 240.
2. Samuel T. Woodring was a former army pack master and veteran of the Spanish-American War. He came to Yellowstone in 1921 and was promoted to chief ranger a year later. In 1929 he was appointed the first superintendent for Grand Teton National Park.
3. Chittenden, *Yellowstone National Park,* 258.
4. Frank Jay Haynes was born in 1853 and died in 1921. Haynes was a professional photographer from Minnesota who helped document the development of Yellowstone Park in pictures. He became the official photographer for the Northern Pacific Railroad and for Yellowstone National Park. He and his son, Jack Ellis Haynes, eventually got out of the transportation concession business and focused entirely on photography. The Haynes Photo Shops throughout Yellowstone during the 1900s were an icon of the park, and Jack even published *Haynes Guide,* which was a best seller for years. Hamilton Stores eventually published its sequel through Herbert T. Lystrup and Alan W. Cundall.
5. Richard A. Bartlett, *Yellowstone: A Wilderness Besieged.*
6. Haines, *The Yellowstone Story,* 2:258–59.
7. Mary Shivers Culpin, *The History of the Construction of the Road System in Yellowstone National Park, 1872–1966,* http://www.cr.nps.gov/history/online_books/roads/shs2.htm.
8. Biddulph, interview with the author, 1984. He described chaining a log to his car in the 1930s while passing over Teton Pass near Jackson Hole.
9. Replogle, Grant Village talk, 6–7.
10. Culpin, *Construction of the Road System,* chap. 9.
11. Haines, *The Yellowstone Story,* 2:273, 275, 420–14.
12. Replogle, Grant Village talk.
13. Ibid. Soda Butte is located in the Lamar Valley about six miles northeast of the Yellowstone Institute headquarters on the road to the Northeast Entrance and Cooke City, Montana. Soda Butte is the core of a once much-larger cone formed by a hot spring. It is mostly dormant and marks where Soda Butte Creek joins the Lamar River, eventually flowing into the Yellowstone River. Gray wolves were exterminated from the park in this area in the 1920s and '30s and have thrived again since their reintroduction to Yellowstone in 1995.
14. Replogle, *Mile-by-Mile,* tape 1, side 2.

15. Ibid., tape 16, side 1.
16. Haines, *The Yellowstone Story,* 2:102.
17. *Dictionary of American Regional Language,* s.v. "Rotten Logging."
18. Replogle, *Mile-by-Mile,* tape 12, side 2; tape 13, side 1.

CHAPTER 8

1. Lystrup, *Shavings Off the Stick,* 7–8.
2. Replogle, Grant Village talk, 11. See also Replogle, *Mile-by-Mile,* tape 16, side 2.
3. Replogle, *Mile-by-Mile.*
4. Colonel Robert D. Heinl Jr., US Marine Corps (Ret.), *The Marine Officer's Guide,* 166. The origin of the swagger stick originated in the British army as early as 1790 and was carried by mounted officers of the eighteenth century.
5. Lystrup, *Shavings Off the Stick,* 9.
6. Replogle, *Mile-by-Mile.*
7. Lystrup, *Shavings Off the Stick,* 8, 10.
8. Ibid., "The Bear Talk," 14–15.
9. Replogle, Grant Village talk.
10. Lystrup, *Shavings Off the Stick,* 17.
11. Replogle, Grant Village talk.
12. Lystrup, *Shavings Off the Stick,* 14–15.
13. Ibid., 20–21.
14. Replogle, *Mile-by-Mile* transcript. See also Dorr G. Yeager, *Scarface: The Story of a Grizzly.* This book tells a fictional story based upon this remarkable bear. It is now considered a rare book.
15. Replogle, *Mile-by-Mile* transcript.
16. Lystrup, *Shavings Off the Stick,* 11.
17. Beal history, chap. 4.
18. Biddulph history.
19. Tower Creek and the Yellowstone River converge about six miles above Roosevelt Junction in the northern part of the park. Tower Creek plunges 132 feet amid majestic rock pinnacles from which it derives its name. A portion of the Great Bannock Trail crosses the Yellowstone River at Tower. John Colter may have crossed in this vicinity in 1808. The Folsom Party explored this area in 1869, followed by the Washburn Party in the fall of 1870, and in 1879, the Nez Perce crossed here on their flight to Montana.
20. Biddulph history. See also S. Biddulph, *The Yellowstone Years.*
21. Replogle, *Mile-by-Mile* transcript.
22. Beal history, 11.
23. Biddulph history.
24. Replogle, *Mile-by-Mile,* tape 16, side 2.
25. Paul Schullery and Lee H. Whittlesey, *Myth and History in the Creation of Yellowstone National Park,* 83–84.

CHAPTER 9

1. Yellowstone is home to various species of evergreen and deciduous trees, including the lodgepole pine, limber pine, whitebark pine, Engelmann spruce, alpine fir, Douglas fir, Rocky Mountain red cedar, dwarf juniper, quaking aspen, and smaller amounts of poplar, cottonwood, willow, birch, and mountain alder.
2. Replogle, *Mile-by-Mile,* 92–93.
3. Lystrup, *Ninety-Day Wonder,* 58.
4. Ibid., 59.
5. Ibid., 62.
6. R. Biddulph, *Remembering Lowell G. Biddulph,* 42.
7. Frank Kowski was the senior ranger at West Thumb in 1939.
8. Replogle, *Mile-by-Mile,* tape 14, side 2.
9. "Monthly Report of the Superintendent for July 1943," YNP Archives, General Stacks.
10. R. Biddulph, *Remembering Lowell G. Biddulph,* 41.
11. Beal history, chap. 7.
12. Lystrup, *Ninety-Day Wonder,* 50.
13. Replogle, *Mile-by-Mile* transcript, page and tape unknown. Dot Island is located in the center of the entrance to the west arm of Yellowstone Lake, called West Thumb. It is the smallest of three major islands in the lake, the others being Stevenson and Frank (the largest). Smaller, less significant islands include Molly and Peale at the farthest extremes of the southeastern and southern arms, respectively.
14. Lin Yutang was born in Taiwan and educated at Harvard University and the University of Leipzig. A writer, educator, and inventor, Lin was one of the most influential Chinese writers of his time.

CHAPTER 10

1. Beal history, chap. 4, "The Madison Junction Saga, Phase One."
2. *American Magazine* did a feature article on George Marler's winter spent at Old Faithful during the winter of 1951–52. Marler studied Old Faithful, as well as other geysers in the Firehole region, relative to temperature effects upon thermal features. He wrote *The Story of Old Faithful Geyser,* which was published in 1961 as the fourth in a series of interpretive works.
3. First completed in 1762, Fontana di Trevi is the largest baroque fountain in Rome, Italy, and one of the most famous. Local legend holds that visitors to Rome who throw a coin into the fountain are ensured to return to Rome. The 1954 Academy Award–winning film and theme song "Three Coins in the Fountain," starring Clifton Webb, Dorothy McGuire, and Jean Peters, was filmed around this fountain.
4. George Marler, "Misuse and Vandalism of Yellowstone's Geysers and Hot Springs," Brigham Young University, L. Tom Perry Special Collections Library, MS 2171, box 3.

5. Lystrup, *Ninety-Day Wonder,* 64.
6. Will Burdett, *Livingston Enterprise,* July 28, 1888. Eugene T. Allen and Arthur L. Day note in their *Hot Springs of the Yellowstone National Park* that Dr. Arnold Hague, who studied Yellowstone's thermal features, also told of this event and how Chinaman Springs got its name (200).
7. Allen and Day, *Hot Springs,* 207.
8. Whittlesey, *Death in Yellowstone.*
9. Replogle, *Mile-by-Mile,* tape and page number unmarked. Replogle's quote on the death of the employee: "One night two young men who worked at the hotel decided that they'd come down for a midnight swim, and they undressed and one of them ran and jumped in but the misfortune was that the two men didn't know Opal Pool from... Turquoise Pool, and when he jumped in Opal Pool he let out a scream of agony because the temperature of that pool is almost at the boiling point. The other boy started in and he was able to reach out and grab his partner and drag him out, but the boy died and the other boy was badly scalded. It's a tragedy which we dislike in the history of Yellowstone, but again, it's too bad that those who violated the law often are punished by nature."
10. Paper by George Marler, "Restoration of Handkerchief Pool," Marler Collection, Brigham Young University, L. Tom Perry Special Collections Library, MS 2171, box 5.
11. Haynes, *Haynes Guide,* 90.
12. Lystrup, *Ninety-Day Wonder,* 65.
13. Herbert T. Lystrup, "Keep Yellowstone Clean," *Yellowstone Nature Notes* 37, no. 1 (1953).
14. Ibid.
15. Marler, "Misuse and Vandalism."
16. Beal history, chap. 1.

CHAPTER 11

1. John Burroughs, "President Theodore Roosevelt as a Nature Lover," 551.
2. Ruth H. Biddulph, *Windows of My World,* 103.
3. David Beal, former assistant chief park naturalist in Yellowstone, letter to the author, July 2008.
4. Riley McClelland, "Report on the Swan Family at Swan Lake Flats," letter to the author, March 2, 2012, compiled from three sources: the July 1964 monthly report by Wayne Replogle (who was assistant North District naturalist, working for McClelland at the time), the July 1964 monthly report by Chief Naturalist John Good, and entries from Riley McClelland's 1964 personal journal.
5. Edwin Way Teale, ed., *The Wilderness World of John Muir,* 318.
6. *Yellowstone Nature Notes* 21, no. 6 (1947): 61–62.
7. Teale, *Wilderness World of Muir,* 311.
8. *Yellowstone Nature Notes* 20, no. 6 (1946): 3.

9. Ibid.
10. *Yellowstone Nature Notes* 27, no. 1 (1953).
11. Paul Schullery, ed., *Yellowstone Bear Tales,* 148.
12. *Yellowstone Nature Notes* 21, no. 6 (1947): 61–62.
13. January 20, 1960, minutes of the annual meeting of the Yellowstone Library and Museum Association Board of Directors.
14. 1959–60 Special issue, *Yellowstone Nature Notes* 33 (June 1960).
15. Paul Schullery and Lee Whittlesey, Yellowstone Nature Notes.

CHAPTER 12

1. Henry David Thoreau, *Walden,* 143.
2. *Yellowstone Nature Notes* 27, no. 1 (1953).
3. Beal history, chap. 10, 7.
4. Ibid., chap. 8, 2.
5. Marler history, 47.
6. Ibid., 46–47.
7. Lystrup, *Shavings Off the Stick,* 31–32.
8. John Yancey, also known as Uncle John Yancey, was a Kentucky-born man who owned and operated a way-station and hotel near the confluence of the Lamar and Yellowstone Rivers from 1882 until his death in 1903. Yancey's way-station served the tourists traveling from Cooke City (Northeast Entrance) to Mammoth Hot Springs by stagecoach.
9. William R. Keefer, *The Geologic Story of Yellowstone National Park,* 53. The canyon wall provides a geological picture window of the most prominent natural forces to shape Yellowstone: fire, water, and ice. Basalt is a fine-grained igneous rock deposited by lava flows that covered Yellowstone. Interspersed between these periods of volcanic activity, Yellowstone was covered by shallow inland seas that laid down, over time, deep layers of sediment. Much later, as glacial ice melted and rivers flowed across Yellowstone, they cut deep gorges that opened up this geological diary of creation. The basalt layers were cleaved in such a manner as to appear in vertical columns, similar in appearance to a picket fence.
10. S. Biddulph, *The Yellowstone Years,* 53.
11. Beal history, 4.
12. Ibid., 5.
13. Marler history, 27–28.
14. Ibid., 36.
15. Ibid., 60–61.
16. Replogle, *Mile-by-Mile,* tape 16.
17. Ibid., 27–28.
18. Ibid.
19. Biddulph history.
20. Turbid Lake lies about one mile northeast of Mary Bay on Yellowstone Lake at the eastern edge of Pelican Valley. Turbid Lake is relatively shallow and fed

by Sedge and Bear Creeks. Springs under the lake bubble and keep the water murky. The water is acidic and void of aquatic life and any green vegetation. It was named by the Hayden Party in 1878.

21. Lystrup, *Shavings Off the Stick,* 40.
22. Roger Contor's story in *Yellowstone Bear Tales,* edited by Schullery, 179.
23. Personal journal of Merrill Beal, August 26, 1960, Beal Special Collection, Idaho State University.
24. Lystrup, *Shavings Off the Stick,* 46–47.
25. *Yellowstone Nature Notes* 21, no. 6 (1947): 61–62.
26. *Yellowstone Nature Notes* 20, no. 6 (1946): 3.
27. George Marler, "Snowbound in Yellowstone."

CHAPTER 13

1. The Northern Pacific Railroad financed the original hotel at the lake. Robert Reamer, the architect famous for many of the rustic buildings of the park, redesigned and expanded the hotel in 1903. Further expansion was done in the 1920s and major renovations completed between 1984 and 1990.
2. The *Zillah* was brought from the Great Lakes to Yellowstone Lake in 1889 and was owned and operated by E. C. Waters, who was president of the Yellowstone Boat Company. The *Zillah* ferried tourists from West Thumb to Lake Hotel, offering them a reprieve from the dusty, bumpy stagecoach rides.
3. Dot Island lies at the mouth of Thumb Bay on Yellowstone Lake. According to Lee Whittlesey (*Yellowstone Place Names,* 47), the tiny island was named by the Hayden Party in 1871 because it appeared only as a dot on the map.
4. E. C. Waters obtained permission to bring animals onto Dot Island provided that they came from outside the park. He obtained two bulls and two cows from the Goodnight herd in Texas and had them shipped to Yellowstone and taken to Dot Island on a barge towed by the *Zillah.* They were kept there for tourists' pleasure until the park closed it down because the animals were not being properly cared for.
5. Haines, *The Yellowstone Story,* 2:228. The 360-foot bridge spanned the river diagonally upstream at a slightly different angle than today's structure. Its center was elevated in camel-back fashion to allow the passage of rowboats beneath. In 1919 the bridge was rebuilt to its current specifications. Walkways for foot traffic were added in 1937.
6. Lystrup, *Shavings Off the Stick,* 3.
7. Ibid., 4.
8. Ibid.
9. Ibid., 5.
10. Ibid.
11. Ibid.
12. Words and music by Carrie Jacobs-Bond (1862–1946).
13. Lystrup, *Shavings Off the Stick,* 5.
14. Lystrup, "Personal Reflections," *Yellowstone Nature Notes* 31, no. 3 (1957): 27.

15. S. Biddulph, *The Yellowstone Years,* 22–23.

CHAPTER 14

1.   http://en.wikipedia.org/wiki/International_Council_of_Museums.
2.   Henry David Thoreau wrote *Civil Disobedience* in 1849 on the subject of the relationship between government and society. He wrote *Walden* in 1854 as a spiritual-discovery, self-reliance, and social experiment. He used immersion into nature to help him gain a more objective understanding of society and the individual.
3.   National Park Service, *Park Structures and Facilities,* 3.
4.   Replogle, *Mile-by-Mile,* tape and page unmarked.
5.   Beal history, chap. 4, 1.
6.   Lystrup, *Shavings Off the Stick,* 15.
7.   *Report of Naturalist Division* 6 (1948–49): 2–3.
8.   Lystrup, "Old Faithful Junior," in *Shavings Off the Stick,* 33.
9.   Ibid.
10. Ibid., 35.
11. Replogle, Grant Village talk.
12. S. Biddulph, *The Yellowstone Years,* 71–72.
13. Ibid.
14. Lystrup, *Shavings Off the Stick,* 35.

CHAPTER 15

1.   "Tribute to Herbert T. Lystrup," used with the permission of Liz Lystrup.
2.   Carl E. Hayden, "Park Rangers Well Versed in, Well, Most Everything," *Salt Lake Tribune,* October 20, 1957.
3.   *Yellowstone Nature Notes* 31, no. 3 (1957): 27.
4.   Division of Interpretation, *Manual of General Information,* compiled by the Division of Interpretation for the use of ranger naturalists and other park personnel. The preface was written by Lemuel A. Garrison, park superintendent, and articles were written by Aubrey L. Haines (park historian), J. A. Martinek (assistant superintendent), Lawrence Hadley, George D. Marler, and John Good.
5.   *Yellowstone Nature Notes* 31, no. 3 (1957): 27.
6.   Beal history, "Nature Trails and Geyser Hill Walks."
7.   John M. Good and Kenneth L. Pierce, *Interpreting the Landscape: Recent and Ongoing Geology of Grand Teton and Yellowstone National Parks,* 33. "On a stormy day in December, I undertook to meander the Grand Canyon from the falls to the base of Mount Washburn, and during a storm of rain and sleet took shelter under the overhanging edge of a great rock in dense timber. Considerably to my surprise I discovered it to be very compact, coarsely crystalline feldspathic granite" (W. H. Holmes-Hayden Party, 1883).
8.   Keefer, *Geologic Story of Yellowstone,* 54.
9.   Biddulph history.

10. Replogle, *Mile-by-Mile;* Bob Jonas, letter to the author, 2004.
11. Replogle, *Mile-by-Mile,* transcript, 17.
12. Haines, *The Yellowstone Story,* 2:308; Replogle, Grant Village talk.
13. Beal history, "Campfire Programs."
14. Replogle, Grant Village talk, 8.
15. Lystrup, "The Curious Moose," in *Shavings Off the Stick,* 22–23.
16. Old gravestone in Cumberland, England.
17. *Yellowstone Nature Notes* 27, no. 1 (1953).

CHAPTER 16

1. Langford, Discovery of Yellowstone Park, 43–44.
2. Clyde Max Bauer, Yellowstone: Its Underworld, 45–47. Allen and Day drilled a 265-foot hole at Norris Geyser Basin in 1930 and found the temperature to be 401 degrees Fahrenheit with steam pressure at three hundred pounds per square inch. If the temperature continued at that rate, it would have been sufficient to melt rock at three thousand feet.
3. Yellowstone Nature Notes 20, no. 6 (1946): 3.
4. Ibid.
5. Reports of Naturalist Division 6 (June 1948): 6.
6. Naturalist report for 1961, personal file, Lowell Biddulph.
7. Good and Pierce, Interpreting the Landscape, 15–20.
8. Biddulph history.
9. Good and Pierce, Interpreting the Landscape, 6.
10. Yellowstone Nature Notes 31 (November–December 1947): 61–62.
11. Francis R. Boyd, "Welded Tuffs and Flows in the Rhyolite Plateau of Yellowstone Park, Wyoming."
12. Good and Pierce, Interpreting the Landscape, 6–7; map from US Geological Survey, http://vulcan.wr.usgs.gov/Volcanoes/Yellowstone/Maps/map_yellowstone_caldera.html.
13. Good and Pierce, Interpreting the Landscape, 8.
14. Chittenden, Yellowstone National Park, 123–24. See also Mark Herbert Brown, The Flight of the Nez Perce, 241.
15. Chittenden, Yellowstone National Park, 124.
16. Hiram M. Chittenden and Mark Herbert Brown corroborate that at Lewiston, Idaho, General Howard hired fifty-two frontiersmen, all skilled in useful work, and organized them into a company of "skilled laborers." This long name was quickly condensed by the troops into "skillets."
17. Yellowstone Nature Notes 14, nos. 5–6 (1937).
18. Replogle, Mile-by-Mile, 8, tape number unmarked.
19. William E. Kearns, "A Nez Perce Chief Revisits Yellowstone," Yellowstone Nature Notes 12 (June–July 1935): 41. See also Merrill D. Beal, The Story of Man in Yellowstone, 90.
20. R. Biddulph, Remembering Lowell G. Biddulph, 46.

21. Cornelius Hedges was a young lawyer in 1870, a graduate of Yale University, a frail and cultured man with a flair for journalism. In 1875 Hedges served as a probate judge in Helena, the superintendent of public instruction for the Territory of Montana, a state senator, and member of the state historical society. It was Hedges who Langford claimed spoke the words that inspired the "National Park Idea."

CHAPTER 17

1. Beal, *Man in Yellowstone,* 132.
2. Chittenden, *Yellowstone National Park,* 69.
3. Langford, *Discovery of Yellowstone Park,* 179–80.
4. Merrill D. Beal, *Sixty Years of Educational Endeavors in Idaho: Memoirs of Merrill D. Beal,* 148.
5. Replogle, *Mile-by-Mile,* tape 13, side 2.
6. Aubrey Haines served as a park ranger in Yellowstone prior to World War II. He returned to Yellowstone after the war and was appointed assistant park engineer. In 1959 he was appointed to fill the newly created position of park historian, remaining in that position until his retirement in 1969.
7. Haines, *The Yellowstone Story,* 1:172.
8. Beal history, chap. 9.
9. Ibid., chap. 6, 2.
10. Ibid., chap. 7.
11. Beal, *Sixty Years of Educational Endeavors,* 146–48.
12. Dave Condon was transferred to Great Smoky Mountains National Park in June 1959, and Dave Beal was transferred a year later to Grand Canyon National Park as chief park naturalist.
13. Beal history, chap. 9, 2.
14. Ibid., chap. 6, 3.
15. Beal, preface to *Sixty Years of Educational Endeavors.* Beal notes that he lost visual acuity at age sixty-four and could not read the printed page without exceptional magnification or audiobooks.
16. Beal history, chap. 6, 5.
17. Beal, *Sixty Years of Educational Endeavors,* 108.
18. Chittenden, *Yellowstone National Park,* 20.
19. Beal, *Man in Yellowstone,* appx. 2, 285.
20. Manuel Lisa was born September 8, 1772, in New Orleans, Louisiana, and died August 12, 1820, in St. Louis, Missouri. Lisa was a Spanish fur trader, explorer, and US Indian agent. He was among the founders of the Missouri Fur Company, an early fur-trading company.
21. Chittenden, *Yellowstone National Park,* 23.
22. Merrill J. Mattes, "Behind the Legend of Colter's Hell: The Early Exploration of Yellowstone National Park," 257.
23. Three Forks, Montana, is named for the three rivers that join in that vicinity to form the headwaters of the Missouri River. Two of these three forks are named after presidents of the United States—Jefferson and Madison—and

the third is the Gallatin. The Gallatin arises from the Gallatin Mountains in northwestern Yellowstone Park, and the Madison also arises in Yellowstone, formed by the convergence of the Gibbon and Firehole Rivers.

24. Coulter Creek is located on the park's south-central boundary. It was named in 1885 by the US Geological Survey for John M. Coulter, botanist in the Hayden Expedition of 1872.

25. David Beal, letter to the author, August 16, 2003.

26. Beal, *Yellowstone Nature Notes* 18, nos. 7–8 (1941): 37–38.

27. David Beal, letter to the author, January 2004. Also, Colleen E. Curry, supervisory museum curator in Yellowstone, verified the current location of the Hunt Stone on July 6, 2009.

28. David Beal, letter to the author, August 16, 2003, and e-mail from Alice M. Hart, curator, Grand Teton National Park, Moose, Wyoming, July 7, 2009.

29. Beal history, chap. 9.

30. Jack Kenneth Anderson was influenced to join the Park Service in 1946 by Frank Oberhansley, a former Yellowstone Park naturalist and superintendent of Hawaii Volcanoes National Park. Anderson served as superintendent of Grand Teton National Park prior to his assignment to Yellowstone in the fall and winter of 1966. Beal met Park Superintendent Anderson at Madison Junction while serving in his last season in Yellowstone. Beal never directly served under Anderson.

31. For a more complete historical treatise of this issue, see Schullery and Whittlesey, *Myth and History*.

CHAPTER 18

1. The Algonquian Confederacy included a close alliance between the Si Ksi ka (Blackfeet proper), Kainah (Bloods), Piegan, Atsina, and Sarsi.

2. The map is the creative property of the author, Stephen G. Biddulph, adapted from a map found in *Yellowstone's Bannock Indian Trails*.

3. Wayne F. Replogle, *Yellowstone's Bannock Indian Trails*, vii. Fan Mountain was called "Sleeping God" and the valley "land of the Sleeping God."

4. Soda Butte is the dome or core of an extinct geyser or hot spring. A recognizable landmark in the old days, Soda Butte was the location of a soldier station in the late 1800s, which eventually became a ranger station. It no longer exists, but the old buffalo ranch, a few miles away on Rose Creek, is the headquarters of the Yellowstone Institute.

5. A cairn is a flat stone or area, normally on a high elevation easily seen, upon which signal fires were built to send messages of warning to the main body of immigrants.

6. Jacobus Franciscus "Jim" Thorpe (May 28, 1888–March 28, 1953) was an American athlete. Considered one of the most versatile athletes in modern sports, he won Olympic gold medals in the 1912 pentathlon and decathlon, played American football at the collegiate and professional levels, and also played professional baseball and basketball.

7. Ibid., 6–7.

8. By the 1890s, hotels were being erected in Yellowstone, and the army had several stations or camps. A herd of cattle was pastured at Swan Lake Flats south of Mammoth Hot Springs for purposes of providing beef to these outlets. In a day prior to refrigeration, it was essential to have the cattle close to these stations for quick delivery. Henry E. Klamer maintained the park's beef herd about 1890 and operated a slaughterhouse near Indian and Panther Creeks, not far from Swan Lake Flats. Cattle were driven from the Madison Valley over the Gallatin Mountains to this slaughterhouse.

9. Replogle, *Yellowstone's Bannock Indian Trails*, 15–16, 30–31.

10. Ibid., 17.

11. Ibid., viii–ix.

12. Ibid., 39.

13. Undated letter from Henry Old Coyote, Replogle Collection, box 1, Yellowstone National Park Research Library.

CHAPTER 19

1. Meek's experience was published by Frances Fuller Victor in *The River of the West* (Hartford, CT: Columbia Book, 1871), 75–77.

2. Allen and Day, *Hot Springs*.

3. Ibid., 514.

4. George D. Marler, "Does the Cold of Winter Affect the Thermal Intensity of the Hot Springs in Yellowstone Park?"

5. Marler history, 39, BYU, Marler Collection M2171, L. Tom Perry Special Collections Library.

6. "When Cold Meets Heat," *Yellowstone Nature Notes* 21, no. 3 (1948): 13.

7. Marler, "Does the Cold of Winter Affect the Thermal Intensity?"

8. C. Max Bauer, *Yellowstone Geysers*. Bauer was a trained geologist with the National Park Service and did extensive studies and interpretations on Yellowstone geology.

9. George D. Marler, "How Old Is Old Faithful Geyser?"

10. Duncan Foley, Department of Geosciences, Pacific Lutheran University, Tacoma, Washington, letter to the author.

11. Clyde Max Bauer and George D. Marler, "An Example of Geyser Development in Yellowstone Park." See also Marler, *The Story of Old Faithful Geyser*.

12. Marler, *Story of Old Faithful*.

13. Duncan Foley, "Dating Castle Geyser," paper presented at the "Rocky Mountain (56th Annual) and Cordilleran (100th Annual) Joint Meeting," Geological Society of America, Paper no. 11-11, May 3–5, 2004, 15, Department of Geosciences, Pacific Lutheran University, Tacoma, Washington.

14. T. Scott Bryan, *The Geysers of Yellowstone*, 7.

15. Haines, *The Yellowstone Story*, 2:123.

16. "An Eruption of Fountain Pool," *Yellowstone Nature Notes* 21, no. 4 (1947): 38–41.

17. Fountain Geyser, named in 1871 by F. V. Hayden, was the main feature of the Fountain Group at the time. Fountain Flats derived its name from Fountain Geyser. In 1891 its name was also bestowed upon the nearby Fountain Hotel and the mud pot in the area now called Fountain Paint Pot. Fountain Pool was positioned just north of Fountain Geyser. It has had several names over the years. In 1899 it was called New Fountain Geyser. Later, it was named Fountain Pool, which was its name until 1947. In that same year, it was renamed Morning Pool because of its proclivity to erupt in the morning hours.

18. "An Eruption Pool," *Yellowstone Natural Notes* 21, no 4 (1947): 38–41.

19. *Yellowstone Nature Notes* 25, no. 4 (1951). Marler references E. J. Stanley, "Hayden Report, 1872." Continued observations and studies over the years have revealed that the Giant Group of geysers (Giant, Mastiff, and Bijou Geysers) likely shares an exchange of energy with the nearby Grotto Group (Grotto Fountain, South Grotto Fountain, Indicator Springs, Spa Geyser, and Rocket Geyser). For instance, it is known that Giant Geyser erupts only when there is a "hot period," which means increased activity within the geyser(s). But typically it will not erupt if the hot period is only within the Giant Group. However, when Giant does erupt, it is typically immediately following the beginning of an eruption of Grotto Geyser.

20. George Marler, "Exchange of Function as a Cause of Geyser Irregularity."

21. Personal letter from Dr. Graton, BYU, Marler Collection M2171, L. Tom Perry Special Collections Library.

22. Daisy Geyser is a well-known geyser named in 1890 by the Hague group. Daisy erupts at a distinct angle to the ground and is one of the more predictable or regular geysers.

23. Memo to Oscar Dick, August 3, 1960, BYU, Marler Collection, M2171, box 3, L. Tom Perry Special Collections Library.

24. Memo from E. L. Robinson and B. R. McClelland, subdistrict rangers, August 8, 1960, ibid.

25. Sam Beal, memo dated August 10, 1960.

26. Beal history, chap. 5, 2.

27. Ibid.

28. Ibid.

CHAPTER 20

1. *Hebgen Lake-Madison River Earthquake Disaster,* pt. 1 (Missoula, MT: US Department of Agriculture, Forest Service, Region 1), I-1.

2. Ibid., part 3, "Earthquake Effects."

3. Ibid., III-4-5.

4. Replogle, *Mile-by-Mile,* n.p.

5. George Marler, "Effects of Hebgen Lake Earthquake on the Hot Springs of the Firehole Geyser Basin of Yellowstone National Park," BYU, Marler Collection M2171, box 3, L. Tom Perry Special Collections Library.

6. Marler, history (no chapter or page listed), BYU, Marler Collection M2171, L. Tom Perry Special Collections Library.
7. Billings Geological Society's Eleventh Annual Field Conference, BYU, Marler Collection, M2171, box 3, L. Tom Perry Special Collections Library.
8. R. Biddulph, *Remembering Lowell G. Biddulph,* 45–46.
9. *U.S. Geological Professional Paper #435,* 185–97, BYU, Marler Collection, M2171, box 4, L. Tom Perry Special Collections Library.
10. Albright letter, October 2, 1959, ibid., box 3.
11. *Professional Paper #435,* 185–97.
12. Samuel W. Matthews and J. Baylor Roberts, "The Night the Mountains Moved," *National Geographic,* March 1960, 329-59.

CHAPTER 21

1. Osborne Russell, *Journal of a Trapper,* 46.
2. Haines, *The Yellowstone Story,* 1:99.
3. Personal letter from Fred M. Hayes to Herbert Lystrup dated December 27, 1948, used with the permission of Elizabeth Lystrup. Fred Hayes appreciated reading *Yellowstone Nature Notes* and the accounts of natural Yellowstone.
4. Beal history, epilogue, 3.
5. Ibid.
6. In 1905 Hiram Chittenden completed the last part of his road, a winding track from Dunraven Pass up the south flank of Mount Washburn to the summit, then down the north flank to rejoin the upper loop road of the park a few miles north of Dunraven Pass. The Chittenden Road was closed beginning in 1942, and people could no longer drive to the top of Mount Washburn. In 1959 the park rebuilt the road on the north side of Washburn, and automobiles and buses resumed its use until about 1965. The road is used today only for official park purposes, and all visitors must walk to the summit.
7. Replogle, "Mount Washburn Dedication," YNP History and Special Events File, Vertical Files, YNP Research Library.
8. Replogle, *Mile-by-Mile,* 49.
9. Hert, "Luxury in the Wilderness."
10. Replogle, *Mile-by-Mile,* tape 4, side 2, transcription p. 13.
11. Beal history, chap. 5.
12. Ibid., chap. 6, "Yellowstone Ranger Esprit de Corps."
13. Rydell and Culpin, *Managing the Matchless Wonders.*
14. Beal history, chap. 6.
15. Ruth Biddulph, "Beloved Journey" (unpublished) 26.
16. Replogle, Grant Village talk.
17. Beal history, chap. 6.
18. Rydell and Culpin, *Managing the Matchless Wonders*, 152.
19. Herbert T. Lystrup, "Keep Yellowstone Clean," *Yellowstone Nature Notes* 27, no. 1 (1953).
20. Rydell and Culpin, *Managing the Matchless Wonders*, 155.

21. Secretary Udall's map of long-range goals for national park areas, August 3, 1964.
22. R. Biddulph, "Beloved Journey," 26.

CHAPTER 22

1. Beal history, chap. 8, 5–6.
2. Replogle, *Mile-by-Mile,* tape 1, side 2, box 3.
3. Ibid., tape 13, side 1.
4. Haines, *The Yellowstone Story,* 2:94.
5. Copy of a letter from personal files of Lowell G. Biddulph from the president of the Trail Riders of the Wilderness to the secretary of the Department of the Interior dated September 22, 1961.
6. Beal history, chap. 4. History introduces Joseph Meek to us as a nineteen-year-old novice trapper with the American Trappers in 1829. The group with which he was traveling was attacked by Piegan (Blackfoot) Indians along the Yellowstone River in what is now northern Yellowstone Park. Two trappers were killed, and Joe Meek escaped into the Yellowstone wilderness with only a mule, a blanket, and his gun, where he wandered about for days before being found by others.
7. Chittenden, *Yellowstone National Park,* 133.
8. Beal history, chap. 4. The *Zillah* was a steamboat, eighty-one feet long and fourteen feet in the beam, brought from the Great Lakes in 1889 and used to ferry stage passengers from West Thumb to the soldier station at Lake. The *E. C. Waters,* a larger steam vessel used on Yellowstone Lake at the turn of the century, was scuttled on Stevenson Island in Yellowstone Lake in the spring of 1930 and was eventually burned by rangers. As the story goes, some rangers burned the old boat, but Ted Ogston, the ranger in charge at Lake Station who was not present during the burning, was called on the carpet for it and required to pay for the damages. Loyal to his men and not wanting to get anyone else in trouble, he paid up. See Haines, *The Yellowstone Story,* 2:126, 261, 401–53.
9. C. Max Bauer, *Yellowstone Geysers,* 54. The source has a picture of Excelsior Geyser in full eruption taken by Frank Haynes in 1888. The geyser is located in Midway Geyser Basin and was named by the Hayden Party in 1871. It was doubtless the largest geyser in the park to be witnessed by the early explorers, putting forth an average of ninety thousand gallons of hot water per minute and playing to a height of three hundred feet. Lee Whittlesey establishes the last known eruption of Excelsior in 1890: "Monarch of All These Mighty Wonders."
10. Haines, *The Yellowstone Story,* 2:74. Charles J. "Buffalo" Jones was appointed game warden in Yellowstone in 1902. He helped establish a buffalo enclosure one mile south of Mammoth Hot Springs and built a log cabin there, the one noted by Lockhard. Jones was instrumental in obtaining bison bulls and cows from the Allard herd in Montana and the Goodnight herd in Texas to establish

the Yellowstone herd. He also helped establish a buffalo enclosure at Pelican Creek for holding buffalo calves in the spring. Buffalo Jones came into conflict with park administration, especially the scouts, and finally resigned on September 15, 1905.

11. Replogle, *Mile-by-Mile,* 8, tape number unmarked.
12. Orrin H. Bonney and Lorraine Bonney, *Battle Drums and Geysers,* 2:588.
13. Replogle, *Mile-by-Mile,* tape 14, box 1.
14. George Marler, "Is the Trumpeter Swan to Remain Only a Refuge Bird?," *National Park Magazine,* October–December 1948.
15. Beal history, chap. 7, p. 5.
16. Ibid., chap. 9.
17. R. Biddulph, *Remembering Lowell G. Biddulph,* 90–91.
18. Mackintosh, *Interpretation in the National Park Service;* Vick, "Yellowstone National Park and Education of Adults"; William B. Sanborn, "Education Program."
19. Beal history, chap. 9, p. 4.
20. Ibid.
21. Ibid.
22. R. Biddulph, *Remembering Lowell G. Biddulph,* 46.
23. Journal of Ruth Biddulph (unpublished).
24. Mary Anne O'Hara, "Forty-Four Summers in Yellowstone."

CHAPTER 23

1. Haines, *The Yellowstone Story,* 2:318.
2. The date next to the name indicates the last season of service for the man.
3. Beal history, chap. 6.
4. Ibid., chap. 9, p. 7.
5. Beal, *Sixty Years.*
6. Beal history, chap. 10.
7. Lystrup, *Shavings Off the Stick,* 48.
8. Elizabeth Lystrup Smith letter.
9. Biddulph history.
10. Lowell G. Biddulph, "An Address Given at Ricks College Devotional Assembly," November 4, 1969.
11. Isaiah 40:9: "O *Zion,* that bringest *good tidings,* get thee up into the high mountain; O Jerusalem, that bringest good tidings, lift up thy voice with strength; lift *it* up, be not afraid; say unto the cities of *Judah,* Behold your God!"
12. Interview with Laura Marler in 2002.
13. Ibid.
14. "Ranger's Wife Recalls Park Life," *Alumni News: Bulletin of Mississippi University* (Fall 1978), Replogle Collection, box 3, YNPRL Archives.
15. Kansas alumni journal, December 1974.
16. Replogle's annual log for 1977, Replogle Collection, box 2, YNPRL Archives.

Bibliography

Allen, Eugene T., and Arthur L. Day. *Hot Springs of the Yellowstone National Park.* Washington, DC: Carnegie Institution, 1935.

"Annual Report of the Superintendent of Yellowstone National Park for 1943." In *Report of the Director of The National Park Service to the Secretary of the Interior for the Fiscal Year Ended June, 1943.* Washington, D.C.: Government Printing Office, 1943.

Bailey, Vernon. *Animal Life of Yellowstone National Park.* Springfield, IL: Charles C. Thomas, 1930.

Ball, R. M. *A Report: Earthquake! August 17, 1959.* N.p.: Montana Power Company.

Bartlett, Richard A. *Yellowstone: A Wilderness Besieged.* Tucson: University of Arizona Press, 1985.

Bauer, Clyde Max. *Yellowstone: Its Underworld.* Published by permission of the director, National Park Service, 1948. Later editions (1953, 1962) were published by the University of New Mexico Press.

————. *Yellowstone Geysers.* Yellowstone National Park, WY: Haynes, 1937.

Bauer, Clyde Max, and George D. Marler. "An Example of Geyser Development in Yellowstone Park." *Northwest Science* 13 (1939): 50–55.

Beal, Merrill D. *I Will Fight No More Forever: Chief Joseph and the Nez Perce War.* Seattle: University of Washington Press, 1963.

————. "Personal History." Beal Special Collections, MC010. Pocatello: Idaho State University.

————. *Sixty Years of Educational Endeavors in Idaho: Memoirs of Merrill D. Beal.* Pocatello: Idaho State University Press, 1984.

————. *The Story of Man in Yellowstone.* Interpretive Series, no. 7. Yellowstone National Park, WY: Yellowstone Library and Museum Association, 1956.

Biddulph, Lowell G. "Personal History." Unpublished.

Biddulph, Ruth H. "Beloved Journey." Unpublished.

————. *Remembering Lowell G. Biddulph.* Self-published, 1999.

————. *Windows of My World.* Self-published, 1993.

Biddulph, Stephen G. *The Yellowstone Years*. Rexburg, ID: Ricks College Press, 1986.

Bonney, Orrin H., and Lorraine Bonney. *Battle Drums and Geysers*. 3 vols. Houston, TX: by the authors, 1970.

Boruff, Nan Weber. *Mattie: A Woman's Journey West*. Moose, WY: Homestead, 1997.

Boyd, Francis R. "Welded Tuffs and Flows in the Rhyolite Plateau of Yellowstone Park, Wyoming." *Geological Society of America Bulletin* 72 (March 1961): 387–426.

Brockman, Frank C. "Park Naturalists and the Evolution of National Park Service Interpretation through World War II." *Forest and Conservation History* 22, no. 1 (1978): 24–43.

Broderick, Harold J. *Wild Animals of Yellowstone National Park*. Yellowstone National Park, WY: Yellowstone Library and Museum Association, 1952.

Brown, Mark Herbert. *The Flight of the Nez Perce*. Lincoln: Bison Books, University of Nebraska Press, 1982.

Bryan, T. Scott. *The Geysers of Yellowstone*. 4th ed. Boulder: University Press of Colorado, 2008.

Burroughs, John. "President Theodore Roosevelt as a Nature Lover." *Outlook*, May–June 1907.

Chittenden, Hiram Martin. *Yellowstone National Park*. 5th ed. Palo Alto, CA: Stanford University Press, 1949.

Christopherson, Edmund. *The Night the Mountain Fell: The Story of the Montana-Yellowstone Earthquake*. Missoula, MT: Lawton, 1960.

Craighead, John J., Frank C. Craighead Jr., and Ray J. Davis. *The Peterson: Field Guide to Rocky Mountain Wildflowers*. Boston: Riverside Press, Houghton Mifflin, 1963.

Crampton, Louis C. *Early History of Yellowstone National Park and Its Relation to National Park Policies*. Washington, DC: US Department of the Interior, National Park Service, 1932.

Culpin, Mary Shivers. *The History of the Construction of The Road System in Yellowstone National Park, 1872–1966*. Historic Resource Study, vol. 1. Washington, DC: National Park Service, 1994. http://www.nps.gov/history/history/online_books.

Cundall, Alan W., and Herbert T. Lystrup. *Hamilton's Guide to Yellowstone National Park*. West Yellowstone, MT: Hamilton Stores, 2002.

Division of Interpretation. *A Manual of General Information on Yellowstone National Park*. Copy no. 48. Yellowstone, WY: Yellowstone National Park, 1963.

Everts, Truman C. *Thirty-Seven Days of Peril*. San Francisco, CA: E. R. Grabhorn and James McDonald, 1923.

Fischer, William A. *Yellowstone's Living Geology: Earthquakes and Mountains*. Yellowstone National Park, WY: Yellowstone Library and Museum Association, 1960.

Foley, Duncan. "Dating Castle Geyser: Preliminary Results and Broad Speculations on the Geologic Development of Geysers and Hydrothermal Systems in Yellowstone National Park, Wyoming, USA." In report of the Geothermal Resource Council 2006 annual meeting, vol. 301, 413–17.

Good, John M., and Kenneth L. Pierce. *Interpreting the Landscape: Recent and Ongoing Geology of Grand Teton and Yellowstone National Parks.* Moose, WY: Grand Teton Natural History Association in cooperation with the National Park Service, 1996.

Goss, Robert V. "Yellowstone's First General Store: A Legacy of Jennie Henderson and Her Family." *Yellowstone Science* 13, no. 2 (2005).

Haines, Aubrey L. *Bannock Indian Trail.* Yellowstone National Park, WY: Yellowstone Library and Museum Association, 1964.

———. *The Yellowstone Story.* Vols. 1–2. Boulder: Yellowstone Library and Museum Association in cooperation with the Colorado Associated University Press, 1977.

Haynes, Jack Ellis. *Haynes Guide: Handbook of Yellowstone National Park.* Bozeman, MT: Haynes Studios, 1953.

Heinl, Colonel Robert D., Jr., US Marine Corps (Ret.). *The Marine Officer's Guide.* Annapolis, MD: Naval Institute Press, 1977.

Hert, Tamsen E. "Luxury in the Wilderness: Yellowstone's Grand Canyon Hotel, 1911–1960." *Yellowstone Science* 13, no. 3 (2005).

Howard, Arthur D. *Yellowstone through the Ages.* New York: Columbia University Press, 1938.

Keefer, William R. *The Geologic Story of Yellowstone National Park.* Geologic Survey Bulletin 1347. Washington, DC: US Geological Survey, 1972.

Langford, Nathaniel Pitt. *The Discovery of Yellowstone Park, 1870.* 2nd ed. St. Paul, MN: J. E. Haynes, 1905.

Love, J. D., and John C. Reed Jr. *Creation of the Teton Landscape: The Geologic Story of Grand Teton National Park.* Moose, WY: Grand Teton Natural History Association, 1968.

Lystrup, Herbert T. *The Ninety-Day Wonder: A Diary of a Ranger Naturalist in Yellowstone National Park, Wyoming.* Casper, WY: Prairie, 1938.

———. *Shavings Off the Stick: True Stories of Yellowstone Park Told by a Veteran Ranger.* Wilson, WY: Fireside Press, 1969.

Mackintosh, Barry. *Interpretation in the National Park Service: A Historical Perspective.* Washington, DC: Historical Division, National Park Service, Department of the Interior, 1986.

Marler, George D. "Does the Cold of Winter Affect the Thermal Intensity of the Hot Springs in Yellowstone Park?" *American Journal of Science* 252 (January 1954): 38–54.

———. "Exchange of Function as a Cause of Geyser Irregularity." *American Journal of Science* 249 (May 1951): 329–42.

———. "How Old Is Old Faithful Geyser?" *American Journal of Science* 254 (October 1956): 615–22.

———. *Inventory of Thermal Features of the Firehole River Geyser Basins and Other Selected Areas of Yellowstone National Park.* Washington, DC: US Geological Survey and National Park Service, June 1973.

———. "Personal History." Unpublished. MS 2171, box 6. Brigham Young University, L. Tom Perry Special Collections Library, Provo, Utah.

———. "Restoration of Handkerchief Pool," MS 2171, box 5. Marler Collection, Brigham Young University, L. Tom Perry Special Collections Library, Provo, Utah.

———. "Snowbound in Yellowstone." *Natural History Magazine* (December 1953).

———. *The Story of Old Faithful Geyser.* Yellowstone Interpretive Series, no. 4. Yellowstone National Park, WY: Yellowstone Library and Museum Association, 1961.

Mattes, Merrill J., and J. Baylor Roberts. "Behind the Legend of Colter's Hell: The Early Exploration of Yellowstone National Park." *Mississippi Valley Historical Review* 36 (September 1949): 251–82.

———. *Colter's Hell and Jackson's Hole: The Fur Trappers' Exploration of the Yellowstone and Grand Teton Park Region.* Yellowstone National Park, WY: Yellowstone Library and Museum Association and Grand Teton Natural History Association in cooperation with the National Park Service and US Department of the Interior, 1962.

Matthews, Samuel W. "The Night the Mountains Moved." *National Geographic,* March 1960.

McDougall, W. B., and Herma A. Baggley. *Plants of Yellowstone National Park.* Washington, DC: US Department of the Interior, National Park Service, 1936.

"Monthly and Weekly Park Naturalist Reports, July 1929–July 1931." Yellowstone National Park Archives Collection, Box K-11, Gardiner, Mont.

"Monthly Reports of the Naturalist Division, 1944–1949." Yellowstone National Park Archives Collection, Box K-12, File 144, Gardiner, Mont.

National Park Service. *Park Structures and Facilities.* Washington, DC: Government Printing Office, 1935.

O'Hara, Mary Anne. "Forty-Four Summers in Yellowstone." *National Park Service Newsletter* 10, no. 3 (1975).

Pritchard, James A. *Preserving Yellowstone's Natural Conditions.* Lincoln: University of Nebraska Press, 1999.

Replogle, Wayne F. *Mile-by-Mile: An Auditory History of Yellowstone Park.* Tapes and Transcript. Yellowstone National Park, WY: Yellowstone National Park Archives.

———. Transcript of Talk to Ranger Naturalist Given at Grant Village on 11 August 1965. Yellowstone National Park, WY: Yellowstone National Park Archives.

———. *Yellowstone's Bannock Indian Trails.* Yellowstone Interpretive Series, no. 6. Yellowstone National Park, WY: Yellowstone Library and Museum Association, 1956.

Russell, Osborne. *Journal of a Trapper.* Edited by Aubrey L. Haines. Portland: Oregon Historical Society, 1955.

Rydell, Kiki Leigh, and Mary Shivers Culpin. *Managing the Matchless Wonders: A History of Administrative Development in Yellowstone National Park, 1872–1965.*

Historic Resource Study, vol. 3. Park Administrative History, pt. 1. YCR-2006-03. Yellowstone National Park, WY: National Park Service, Yellowstone Center for Resources, 2006.

Sanborn, William B. "The Education Program of Yellowstone National Park." Master's thesis, Claremont College, 1949.

Schullery, Paul, ed. *Yellowstone Bear Tales*. Niwot, CO: Roberts Rinehart, 1991.

Schullery, Paul, and Lee H. Whittlesey. *Myth and History in the Creation of Yellowstone National Park*. Lincoln: University of Nebraska Press, 1991.

———. "*Yellowstone Nature Notes:* A Neglected Documentary Source." *Yellowstone Science* 8, no. 1 (2000).

Simon, James R. *Yellowstone Fishes*. Yellowstone Interpretive Series, no. 3. Yellowstone National Park, WY: Yellowstone Library and Museum Association, 1939.

Teale, Edwin Way, ed. *The Wilderness World of John Muir*. Boston: Houghton Mifflin, 1954.

Tebbe, Chas. L. *Hebgen Lake–Madison River Earthquake Disaster*. Washington, DC: US Department of Agriculture, Forest Service, August 1959.

Thoreau, Henry David. *Walden*. Vol. 1. Cambridge, MA: Houghton Mifflin, Riverside Press, 1854.

Tilden, Freeman. *The National Parks: What They Mean to You and Me*. New York: Alfred A. Knopf, 1951.

Turner, Frederick B. *Reptiles and Amphibians of Yellowstone National Park*. Interpretive Series, no. 5. Yellowstone National Park, WY: Yellowstone Library and Museum Association, 1955.

Tweed, William G., Laura E. Soulliere, and Henry G. Law. *National Park Service Rustic Architecture, 1916–1942*. San Francisco: National Park Service, West Regional Office, 1977.

USGS/Cascades Volcano Observatory. Yellowstone National Park, Wyoming Map. 1997. http://volcanoes.usgs.gov/observatories/cvo/. Modified from D. Dzurisin, R.L. Christiansen, and K.L. Pierce. *Volcano Hazards Fact Sheet: Yellowstone: Restless Volcanic Giant*. U.S. Geological Survey Open-File Report 95-59, 1995.

Vick, Denise. "Yellowstone National Park and Education of Adults." PhD diss., University of Wyoming, 1986.

West, Elliott. *The Last Indian War: The Nez Perce Story*. Oxford: Oxford University Press, 2009.

Whittlesey, Lee H. *Death in Yellowstone: Accidents and Foolhardiness in the First National Park*. Niwot, CO: Roberts Rinehart, 1995.

———, ed. *Lost in the Yellowstone: Truman Evert's "Thirty-Seven Days of Peril."* Salt Lake City: University of Utah Press, 2002.

———. "Monarch of All These Mighty Wonders." *Montana Magazine of Western History* (Spring 1990): 2–15.

———. *Storytelling in Yellowstone: Horse and Buggy Tour Guides*. Albuquerque: University of New Mexico Press, 2007.

————. *Yellowstone Place Names.* Helena: Montana Historical Society, 1988.

Williams, Jack R. "National Park Service Insignia and How the Uniform Grew." March 1965. http://www.cr.nps.gov/history/online_books/workman1/vol1s.htm.

Wright, George M., and Ben H. Thompson. *Fauna of the National Parks of the United States.* Fauna Series, no. 2. Washington, DC: US Department of the Interior, National Park Service, 1934.

Yeager, Dorr G. *Scarface: The Story of a Grizzly.* Philadelphia: PENN, October 1935.

Yellowstone National Park. *Yellowstone Nature Notes.* Yellowstone National Park, WY: Yellowstone Library and Museum Association, 1924–58.

Index